PHILIP'S

INTERNATIONAL SCHOOL ATLAS

PHILIP'S

INTERNATIONAL SCHOOL ATLAS

IN ASSOCIATION WITH
THE ROYAL GEOGRAPHICAL SOCIETY
WITH THE INSTITUTE OF BRITISH GEOGRAPHERS

Published in Great Britain in 1999
by George Philip Limited,
a division of Octopus Publishing Group Limited,
2–4 Heron Quays, London E14 4JP

Copyright © 1999 George Philip Limited

Cartography by Philip's

ISBN 0–540–07860–3

A CIP catalogue record for this book is available from the British Library.

Printed in China

Details of other Philip's titles and services can be found on our website at: www.philips-maps.co.uk

Philip's is proud to announce that its World Atlases
are now published in association with The Royal
Geographical Society (with The Institute of British
Geographers).

The Society was founded in 1830 and given a
Royal Charter in 1859 for 'the advancement of
geographical science'. It holds historical collections
of national and international importance, many of
which relate to the Society's association with and
support for scientific exploration and research
from the 19th century onwards. It was pivotal

in establishing geography as a teaching and research
discipline in British universities close to the turn of
the century, and has played a key role in geographical
and environmental education ever since.

Today the Society is a leading world centre
for geographical learning – supporting education,
teaching, research and expeditions, and promoting
public understanding of the subject.

The Society welcomes those interested in
geography as members. For further information,
please visit the website at: www.rgs.org

CONTENTS

Note: Each section is colour-coded on this contents page and on the heading of each page for ease of reference.

WORLD STATISTICS: *countries*

This alphabetical list includes all the countries and territories of the world. If a territory is not completely independent, then the country it is associated with is named. The area figures give the total area of land, inland water and ice. Units for areas and populations are thousands. The population figures are 1998 estimates. The annual income is the Gross National Product per capita in US dollars. The figures are the latest available, usually 1997.

Country/Territory	Area km² *Thousands*	Area miles² *Thousands*	Population *Thousands*	Capital	Annual Income US $
Adélie Land (France)	432	167	0.03	–	–
Afghanistan	652	252	24,792	Kabul	600
Albania	28.8	11.1	3,331	Tirana	750
Algeria	2,382	920	30,481	Algiers	1,490
American Samoa (US)	0.20	0.08	62	Pago Pago	2,600
Andorra	0.45	0.17	75	Andorra La Vella	16,200
Angola	1,247	481	11,200	Luanda	340
Anguilla (UK)	0.1	0.04	11	The Valley	6,800
Antigua & Barbuda	0.44	0.17	64	St John's	7,330
Argentina	2,767	1,068	36,265	Buenos Aires	8,750
Armenia	29.8	11.5	3,422	Yerevan	530
Aruba (Netherlands)	0.19	0.07	69	Oranjestad	15,890
Ascension Is. (UK)	0.09	0.03	1.5	Georgetown	–
Australia	7,687	2,968	18,613	Canberra	20,540
Austria	83.9	32.4	8,134	Vienna	27,980
Azerbaijan	86.6	33.4	7,856	Baku	510
Azores (Portugal)	2.2	0.87	238	Ponta Delgada	–
Bahamas	13.9	5.4	280	Nassau	11,940
Bahrain	0.68	0.26	616	Manama	7,840
Bangladesh	144	56	125,000	Dhaka	270
Barbados	0.43	0.17	259	Bridgetown	6,560
Belarus	207.6	80.1	10,409	Minsk	2,150
Belgium	30.5	11.8	10,175	Brussels	26,420
Belize	23	8.9	230	Belmopan	2,700
Benin	113	43	6,101	Porto-Novo	380
Bermuda (UK)	0.05	0.02	62	Hamilton	31,870
Bhutan	47	18.1	1,908	Thimphu	390
Bolivia	1,099	424	7,826	La Paz/Sucre	950
Bosnia-Herzegovina	51	20	3,366	Sarajevo	300
Botswana	582	225	1,448	Gaborone	4,381
Brazil	8,512	3,286	170,000	Brasília	4,720
British Antarctic Terr. (UK)	1,709	660	0.3	–	–
Brunei	5.8	2.2	315	Bandar Seri Begawan	15,800
Bulgaria	111	43	8,240	Sofia	1,140
Burkina Faso	274	106	11,266	Ouagadougou	240
Burma (= Myanmar)	677	261	47,305	Rangoon	1,790
Burundi	27.8	10.7	5,531	Bujumbura	180
Cambodia	181	70	11,340	Phnom Penh	300
Cameroon	475	184	15,029	Yaoundé	650
Canada	9,976	3,852	30,675	Ottawa	19,290
Canary Is. (Spain)	7.3	2.8	1,494	Las Palmas/Santa Cruz	–
Cape Verde Is.	4	1.6	399	Praia	1,010
Cayman Is. (UK)	0.26	0.10	35	George Town	20,000
Central African Republic	623	241	3,376	Bangui	320
Chad	1,284	496	7,360	Ndjaména	240
Chatham Is. (NZ)	0.96	0.37	0.05	Waitangi	–
Chile	757	292	14,788	Santiago	5,020
China	9,597	3,705	1,236,915	Beijing	860
Christmas Is. (Australia)	0.14	0.05	2	The Settlement	–
Cocos (Keeling) Is. (Australia)	0.01	0.005	1	West Island	–
Colombia	1,139	440	38,581	Bogotá	2,280
Comoros	2.2	0.86	545	Moroni	450
Congo	342	132	2,658	Brazzaville	660
Congo (= Zaïre)	2,345	905	49,001	Kinshasa	110
Cook Is. (NZ)	0.24	0.09	20	Avarua	900
Costa Rica	51.1	19.7	3,605	San José	2,640
Croatia	56.5	21.8	4,672	Zagreb	4,610
Cuba	111	43	11,051	Havana	1,300
Cyprus	9.3	3.6	749	Nicosia	13,420
Czech Republic	78.9	30.4	10,286	Prague	5,200
Denmark	43.1	16.6	5,334	Copenhagen	32,500
Djibouti	23.2	9	650	Djibouti	850
Dominica	0.75	0.29	78	Roseau	3,090
Dominican Republic	48.7	18.8	7,999	Santo Domingo	1,670
Ecuador	284	109	12,337	Quito	1,590
Egypt	1,001	387	66,050	Cairo	1,180
El Salvador	21	8.1	5,752	San Salvador	1,810
Equatorial Guinea	28.1	10.8	454	Malabo	530
Eritrea	94	36	3,842	Asmara	570
Estonia	44.7	17.3	1,421	Tallinn	3,330
Ethiopia	1,128	436	58,390	Addis Ababa	110
Falkland Is. (UK)	12.2	4.7	2	Stanley	–
Faroe Is. (Denmark)	1.4	0.54	41	Tórshavn	23,660
Fiji	18.3	7.1	802	Suva	2,470
Finland	338	131	5,149	Helsinki	24,080
France	552	213	58,805	Paris	26,050
French Guiana (France)	90	34.7	162	Cayenne	10,580
French Polynesia (France)	4	1.5	237	Papeete	7,500
Gabon	268	103	1,208	Libreville	4,230
Gambia, The	11.3	4.4	1,292	Banjul	320
Georgia	69.7	26.9	5,109	Tbilisi	840
Germany	357	138	82,079	Berlin/Bonn	28,260
Ghana	239	92	18,497	Accra	370
Gibraltar (UK)	0.007	0.003	29	Gibraltar Town	5,000
Greece	132	51	10,662	Athens	12,010
Greenland (Denmark)	2,176	840	59	Nuuk (Godthåb)	15,500
Grenada	0.34	0.13	96	St George's	2,880
Guadeloupe (France)	1.7	0.66	416	Basse-Terre	9,200
Guam (US)	0.55	0.21	149	Agana	6,000
Guatemala	109	42	12,008	Guatemala City	1,500
Guinea	246	95	7,477	Conakry	570
Guinea-Bissau	36.1	13.9	1,206	Bissau	240
Guyana	215	83	820	Georgetown	690
Haiti	27.8	10.7	6,781	Port-au-Prince	330
Honduras	112	43	5,862	Tegucigalpa	700
Hong Kong (China)	1.1	0.40	6,707	–	22,990
Hungary	93	35.9	10,208	Budapest	4,430
Iceland	103	40	271	Reykjavik	26,580
India	3,288	1,269	984,000	New Delhi	390
Indonesia	1,905	735	212,942	Jakarta	1,110
Iran	1,648	636	64,411	Tehran	4,700
Iraq	438	169	21,722	Baghdad	2,000
Ireland	70.3	27.1	3,619	Dublin	18,280
Israel	27	10.3	5,644	Jerusalem	15,810
Italy	301	116	56,783	Rome	20,120
Ivory Coast (Côte d'Ivoire)	322	125	15,446	Yamoussoukro	690
Jamaica	11	4.2	2,635	Kingston	1,560
Japan	378	146	125,932	Tokyo	37,850
Jordan	89.2	34.4	4,435	Amman	1,570
Kazakstan	2,717	1,049	16,847	Astana	1,340
Kenya	580	224	28,337	Nairobi	330
Kerguelen Is. (France)	7.2	2.8	0.7	–	–
Kermadec Is. (NZ)	0.03	0.01	0.1	–	–
Kiribati	0.72	0.28	85	Tarawa	920
Korea, North	121	47	21,234	Pyŏngyang	1,000
Korea, South	99	38.2	46,417	Seoul	10,550
Kuwait	17.8	6.9	1,913	Kuwait City	17,390
Kyrgyzstan	198.5	76.6	4,522	Bishkek	440
Laos	237	91	5,261	Vientiane	400
Latvia	65	25	2,385	Riga	2,430
Lebanon	10.4	4	3,506	Beirut	3,350
Lesotho	30.4	11.7	2,090	Maseru	670

Country/Territory	Area km² *Thousands*	Area miles² *Thousands*	Population *Thousands*	Capital	Annual Income US $
Liberia	111	43	2,772	Monrovia	770
Libya	1,760	679	4,875	Tripoli	6,510
Liechtenstein	0.16	0.06	32	Vaduz	33,000
Lithuania	65.2	25.2	3,600	Vilnius	2,230
Luxembourg	2.6	1	425	Luxembourg	45,360
Macau (China)	0.02	0.006	429	Macau	7,500
Macedonia	25.7	9.9	2,009	Skopje	1,090
Madagascar	587	227	14,463	Antananarivo	250
Madeira (Portugal)	0.81	0.31	253	Funchal	–
Malawi	118	46	9,840	Lilongwe	220
Malaysia	330	127	20,993	Kuala Lumpur	4,680
Maldives	0.30	0.12	290	Malé	1,080
Mali	1,240	479	10,109	Bamako	260
Malta	0.32	0.12	379	Valletta	12,000
Marshall Is.	0.18	0.07	63	Dalap-Uliga-Darrit	1,890
Martinique (France)	1.1	0.42	407	Fort-de-France	10,000
Mauritania	1,030	412	2,511	Nouakchott	450
Mauritius	2.0	0.72	1,168	Port Louis	3,800
Mayotte (France)	0.37	0.14	141	Mamoundzou	1,430
Mexico	1,958	756	98,553	Mexico City	3,680
Micronesia, Fed. States of	0.70	0.27	127	Palikir	2,070
Midway Is. (US)	0.005	0.002	2	–	–
Moldova	33.7	13	4,458	Chişinău	540
Monaco	0.002	0.0001	32	Monaco	25,000
Mongolia	1,567	605	2,579	Ulan Bator	390
Montserrat (UK)	0.10	0.04	12	Plymouth	4,500
Morocco	447	172	29,114	Rabat	1,250
Mozambique	802	309	18,641	Maputo	90
Namibia	825	318	1,622	Windhoek	2,220
Nauru	0.02	0.008	12	Yaren District	10,000
Nepal	141	54	23,698	Katmandu	210
Netherlands	41.5	16	15,731	Amsterdam/The Hague	25,820
Netherlands Antilles (Neths)	0.99	0.38	210	Willemstad	10,400
New Caledonia (France)	18.6	7.2	192	Nouméa	8,000
New Zealand	269	104	3,625	Wellington	16,480
Nicaragua	130	50	4,583	Managua	410
Niger	1,267	489	9,672	Niamey	200
Nigeria	924	357	110,532	Abuja	260
Niue (NZ)	0.26	0.10	2	Alofi	–
Norfolk Is. (Australia)	0.03	0.01	2	Kingston	–
Northern Mariana Is. (US)	0.48	0.18	50	Saipan	11,500
Norway	324	125	4,420	Oslo	36,090
Oman	212	82	2,364	Muscat	4,950
Pakistan	796	307	135,135	Islamabad	490
Palau	0.46	0.18	18	Koror	5,000
Panama	77.1	29.8	2,736	Panama City	3,080
Papua New Guinea	463	179	4,600	Port Moresby	940
Paraguay	407	157	5,291	Asunción	2,010
Peru	1,285	496	26,111	Lima	2,460
Peter 1st Is. (Norway)	0.18	0.07	0	–	–
Philippines	300	116	77,736	Manila	1,220
Pitcairn Is. (UK)	0.03	0.01	0.05	Adamstown	–
Poland	313	121	38,607	Warsaw	3,590
Portugal	92.4	35.7	9,928	Lisbon	10,450
Puerto Rico (US)	9	3.5	3,860	San Juan	7,800
Qatar	11	4.2	697	Doha	11,600
Réunion (France)	2.5	0.97	705	Saint-Denis	4,500
Romania	238	92	22,396	Bucharest	1,420
Russia	17,075	6,592	146,861	Moscow	2,740
Rwanda	26.3	10.2	7,956	Kigali	210
St Helena (UK)	0.12	0.05	7	Jamestown	–
St Kitts & Nevis	0.36	0.14	42	Basseterre	5,870
St Lucia	0.62	0.24	150	Castries	3,500
St Pierre & Miquelon (France)	0.24	0.09	7	Saint Pierre	–
St Vincent & Grenadines	0.39	0.15	120	Kingstown	2,370
San Marino	0.06	0.02	25	San Marino	20,000
São Tomé & Príncipe	0.96	0.37	150	São Tomé	330
Saudi Arabia	2,150	830	20,786	Riyadh	6,790
Senegal	197	76	9,723	Dakar	550
Seychelles	0.46	0.18	79	Victoria	6,850
Sierra Leone	71.7	27.7	5,080	Freetown	200
Singapore	0.62	0.24	3,490	Singapore	32,940
Slovak Republic	49	18.9	5,393	Bratislava	3,700
Slovenia	20.3	7.8	1,972	Ljubljana	9,680
Solomon Is.	28.9	11.2	441	Honiara	900
Somalia	638	246	6,842	Mogadishu	500
South Africa	1,220	471	42,835	C. Town/Pretoria/Bloem.	3,400
South Georgia (UK)	3.8	1.4	0.05	–	–
Spain	505	195	39,134	Madrid	14,510
Sri Lanka	65.6	25.3	18,934	Colombo	800
Sudan	2,506	967	33,551	Khartoum	800
Surinam	163	63	427	Paramaribo	1,000
Svalbard (Norway)	62.9	24.3	4	Longyearbyen	–
Swaziland	17.4	6.7	966	Mbabane	1,210
Sweden	450	174	8,887	Stockholm	26,220
Switzerland	41.3	15.9	7,260	Bern	44,220
Syria	185	71	16,673	Damascus	1,150
Taiwan	36	13.9	21,908	Taipei	12,400
Tajikistan	143.1	55.2	6,020	Dushanbe	330
Tanzania	945	365	30,609	Dodoma	210
Thailand	513	198	60,037	Bangkok	2,800
Togo	56.8	21.9	4,906	Lomé	330
Tokelau (NZ)	0.01	0.005	2	Nukunonu	–
Tonga	0.75	0.29	107	Nuku'alofa	1,790
Trinidad & Tobago	5.1	2	1,117	Port of Spain	4,230
Tristan da Cunha (UK)	0.11	0.04	0.33	Edinburgh	–
Tunisia	164	63	9,380	Tunis	2,090
Turkey	779	301	64,568	Ankara	3,130
Turkmenistan	488.1	188.5	4,298	Ashkhabad	630
Turks & Caicos Is. (UK)	0.43	0.17	16	Cockburn Town	5,000
Tuvalu	0.03	0.01	10	Fongafale	600
Uganda	236	91	22,167	Kampala	320
Ukraine	603.7	233.1	50,125	Kiev	1,040
United Arab Emirates	83.6	32.3	2,303	Abu Dhabi	17,360
United Kingdom	243.3	94	58,970	London	20,710
United States of America	9,373	3,619	270,290	Washington, DC	28,740
Uruguay	177	68	3,285	Montevideo	6,020
Uzbekistan	447.4	172.7	23,784	Tashkent	1,010
Vanuatu	12.2	4.7	185	Port-Vila	1,290
Vatican City	0.0004	0.0002	1	–	–
Venezuela	912	352	22,803	Caracas	3,450
Vietnam	332	127	76,236	Hanoi	320
Virgin Is. (UK)	0.15	0.06	13	Road Town	–
Virgin Is. (US)	0.34	0.13	118	Charlotte Amalie	12,000
Wake Is.	0.008	0.003	0.3	–	–
Wallis & Futuna Is. (France)	0.20	0.08	15	Mata-Utu	–
Western Sahara	266	103	280	El Aaiún	300
Western Samoa	2.8	1.1	224	Apia	1,170
Yemen	528	204	16,388	Sana	270
Yugoslavia	102.3	39.5	10,500	Belgrade	2,000
Zambia	753	291	9,461	Lusaka	380
Zimbabwe	391	151	11,044	Harare	750

This list shows the principal cities with more than 500,000 inhabitants (only cities with more than 1 million inhabitants are included for Brazil, China and India). The figures are taken from the most recent census or estimate available, and as far as possible are the population of the metropolitan area, e.g. greater New York, Mexico or Paris. All the figures are in thousands. Local name forms have been used for the smaller cities (e.g. Kraków).

City	**Population** *thousands*
Afghanistan	
Kabul	1,565
Algeria	
Algiers	2,168
Oran	916
Angola	
Luanda	2,418
Argentina	
Buenos Aires	11,256
Córdoba	1,208
Rosario	1,118
Mendoza	773
La Plata	642
San Miguel de Tucumán	622
Mar del Plata	512
Armenia	
Yerevan	1,248
Australia	
Sydney	3,770
Melbourne	3,217
Brisbane	1,489
Perth	1,262
Adelaide	1,080
Austria	
Vienna	1,595
Azerbaijan	
Baku	1,720
Bangladesh	
Dhaka	6,105
Chittagong	2,041
Khulna	877
Rajshahi	517
Belarus	
Minsk	1,700
Homyel	512
Belgium	
Brussels	948
Benin	
Cotonou	537
Bolivia	
La Paz	1,126
Santa Cruz	767
Bosnia-Herzegovina	
Sarajevo	526
Brazil	
São Paulo	16,417
Rio de Janeiro	9,888
Salvador	2,211
Belo Horizonte	2,091
Fortaleza	1,965
Brasília	1,821
Curitiba	1,476
Recife	1,346
Pôrto Alegre	1,288
Manaus	1,157
Belém	1,144
Goiânia	1,004
Bulgaria	
Sofia	1,116
Burkina Faso	
Ouagadougou	690
Burma (Myanmar)	
Rangoon	2,513
Mandalay	533
Cambodia	
Phnom Penh	920
Cameroon	
Douala	1,200
Yaoundé	800
Canada	
Toronto	4,344
Montréal	3,337
Vancouver	1,831
Ottawa–Hull	1,022
Edmonton	885
Calgary	831
Québec	693
Winnipeg	677
Hamilton	643
Central African Rep.	
Bangui	553
Chad	
Ndjaména	530
Chile	
Santiago	5,067
China	
Shanghai	15,082
Beijing	12,362
Tianjin	10,687
Hong Kong (SAR)*	6,502
Chongqing	3,870
Shenyang	3,860
Wuhan	3,520
Guangzhou	3,114
Harbin	2,505
Nanjing	2,211
Xi'an	2,115
Chengdu	1,933
Dalian	1,855
Changchun	1,810
Jinan	1,660
Taiyuan	1,642
Qingdao	1,584
Fuzhou, Fujian	1,380
Zibo	1,346
Zhengzhou	1,324
Lanzhou	1,296
Anshan	1,252
Fushun	1,246
Kunming	1,242
Changsha	1,198
Hangzhou	1,185
Nanchang	1,169
Shijiazhuang	1,159
Guiyang	1,131
Ürümqi	1,130
Jilin	1,118
Tangshan	1,110
Qiqihar	1,104
Baotou	1,033
Hefei	1,000
Colombia	
Bogotá	6,004
Cali	1,985
Medellín	1,970
Barranquilla	1,157
Cartagena	812
Congo	
Brazzaville	937
Pointe-Noire	576
Congo (Zaïre)	
Kinshasa	1,655
Lubumbashi	851
Mbuji-Mayi	806
Costa Rica	
San José	1,220
Croatia	
Zagreb	931
Cuba	
Havana	2,241
Czech Republic	
Prague	1,209
Denmark	
Copenhagen	1,362
Dominican Republic	
Santo Domingo	2,135
Santiago	691
Ecuador	
Guayaquil	1,973
Quito	1,487
Egypt	
Cairo	9,900
Alexandria	3,431
El Gîza	2,144
Shubra el Kheima	834
El Salvador	
San Salvador	1,522
Ethiopia	
Addis Ababa	2,112
Finland	
Helsinki	532
France	
Paris	9,319
Lyon	1,262
Marseille	1,087
Lille	959
Bordeaux	696
Toulouse	650
Nice	516
Georgia	
Tbilisi	1,300
Germany	
Berlin	3,470
Hamburg	1,706
Munich	1,240
Cologne	964
Frankfurt	651
Essen	616
Dortmund	600
Stuttgart	587
Düsseldorf	571
Bremen	549
Duisburg	535
Hanover	524
Ghana	
Accra	949
Greece	
Athens	3,097
Guatemala	
Guatemala	1,167
Guinea	
Conakry	1,508
Haiti	
Port-au-Prince	1,255
Honduras	
Tegucigalpa	813
Hungary	
Budapest	1,885
India	
Bombay (Mumbai)	12,572
Calcutta (Kolkata)	10,916
Delhi	7,207
Madras (Chennai)	5,361
Hyderabad	4,280
Bangalore	4,087
Ahmadabad	3,298
Pune	2,485
Kanpur	2,111
Nagpur	1,661
Lucknow	1,642
Surat	1,517
Jaipur	1,514
Coimbatore	1,136
Vadodara	1,115
Indore	1,104
Patna	1,099
Madurai	1,094
Bhopal	1,064
Vishakhapatnam	1,052
Varanasi	1,026
Ludhiana	1,012
Indonesia	
Jakarta	11,500
Surabaya	2,701
Bandung	2,368
Medan	1,910
Semarang	1,366
Palembang	1,352
Tangerang	1,198
Ujung Pandang	1,092
Bandar Lampung	832
Malang	763
Padang	721
Pakanbaru	558
Samarinda	536
Banjarmasin	535
Surakarta	516
Iran	
Tehran	6,750
Mashhad	1,964
Esfahan	1,221
Tabriz	1,166
Shiraz	1,043
Ahvaz	828
Qom	780
Bakhtaran	666
Karaj	588
Iraq	
Baghdad	3,841
Diyala	961
As Sulaymaniyah	952
Arbil	770
Al Mawsil	664
Kadhimain	521
Ireland	
Dublin	952
Israel	
Tel Aviv-Yafo	1,502
Jerusalem	591
Italy	
Rome	2,775
Milan	1,369
Naples	1,067
Turin	962
Palermo	698
Genoa	678
Ivory Coast	
Abidjan	2,500
Jamaica	
Kingston	644
Japan	
Tokyo–Yokohama	26,836
Osaka	10,601
Nagoya	2,152
Sapporo	1,757
Kyoto	1,464
Kobe	1,424
Fukuoka	1,285
Kawasaki	1,203
Hiroshima	1,109
Kitakyushu	1,020
Sendai	971
Chiba	857
Sakai	803
Kumamoto	650
Okayama	616
Sagamihara	571
Hamamatsu	562
Kagoshima	546
Funabashi	541
Higashiosaka	517
Hachioji	503
Jordan	
Amman	1,300
Az-Zarqā	609
Kazakstan	
Almaty	1,150
Qaraghandy	573
Kenya	
Nairobi	2,000
Mombasa	600
Korea, North	
Pyŏngyang	2,639
Hamhung	775
Chŏngjin	754
Chinnampo	691
Sinŭiju	500
Korea, South	
Seoul	11,641
Pusan	3,814
Taegu	2,449
Inchon	2,308
Taejŏn	1,272
Kwangju	1,258
Ulsan	967
Sŏngnam	869
Puch'on	779
Suwŏn	756
Anyang	590
Chŏnju	563
Chŏngju	531
Ansan	510
P'ohang	509
Kyrgyzstan	
Bishkek	584
Latvia	
Riga	846
Lebanon	
Beirut	1,900
Tripoli	500
Libya	
Tripoli	1,083
Lithuania	
Vilnius	580
Macedonia	
Skopje	541
Madagascar	
Antananarivo	1,053
Malaysia	
Kuala Lumpur	1,145
Mali	
Bamako	800
Mauritania	
Nouakchott	735
Mexico	
Mexico City	15,048
Guadalajara	2,847
Monterrey	2,522
Puebla	1,055
León	872
Ciudad Juárez	798
Tijuana	743
Culiacán Rosales	602
Mexicali	602
Acapulco de Juárez	592
Mérida	557
Chihuahua	530
San Luis Potosí	526
Aguascalientés	506
Moldova	
Chişinău	700
Mongolia	
Ulan Bator	627
Morocco	
Casablanca	3,079
Rabat-Salé	1,344
Fès	735
Marrakesh	621
Mozambique	
Maputo	2,000
Nepal	
Katmandu	535
Netherlands	
Amsterdam	1,101
Rotterdam	1,076
The Hague	694
Utrecht	548
New Zealand	
Auckland	997
Nicaragua	
Managua	864
Nigeria	
Lagos	10,287
Ibadan	1,365
Ogbomosho	712
Kano	657
Norway	
Oslo	714
Pakistan	
Karachi	9,863
Lahore	5,085
Faisalabad	1,875
Peshawar	1,676
Gujranwala	1,663
Rawalpindi	1,290
Multan	1,257
Hyderabad	1,107
Paraguay	
Asunción	945
Peru	
Lima–Callao	6,601
Callao	638
Arequipa	620
Trujillo	509
Philippines	
Manila	9,280
Quezon City	1,989
Davao	1,191
Caloocan	1,023
Cebu	662
Zamboanga	511
Poland	
Warsaw	1,638
Lódz	825
Kraków	745
Wroclaw	642
Poznań	581
Portugal	
Lisbon	2,561
Oporto	1,174
Romania	
Bucharest	2,060
Russia	
Moscow	9,233
St Petersburg	4,883
Nizhniy Novgorod	1,425
Novosibirsk	1,400
Yekaterinburg	1,300
Samara	1,200
Omsk	1,200
Chelyabinsk	1,100
Kazan	1,100
Ufa	1,100
Volgograd	1,003
Perm	1,000
Rostov	1,000
Voronezh	908
Saratov	895
Krasnoyarsk	869
Togliatti	689
Simbirsk	678
Izhevsk	654
Krasnodar	645
Vladivostok	632
Yaroslavl	629
Khabarovsk	618
Barnaul	596
Irkutsk	585
Novokuznetsk	572
Ryazan	536
Penza	534
Orenburg	532
Tula	532
Naberezhnyye-Chelny	526
Kemerovo	503
Saudi Arabia	
Riyadh	1,800
Jedda	1,500
Mecca	630
Senegal	
Dakar	1,571
Sierra Leone	
Freetown	505
Singapore	
Singapore	3,104
Somalia	
Mogadishu	1,000
South Africa	
Cape Town	2,350
East Rand	1,379
Johannesburg	1,196
Durban	1,137
Pretoria	1,080
West Rand	870
Port Elizabeth	853
Vanderbijlpark–Vereeniging	774
Soweto	597
Sasolburg	540
Spain	
Madrid	3,029
Barcelona	1,614
Valencia	763
Sevilla	719
Zaragoza	607
Málaga	532
Sri Lanka	
Colombo	1,863
Sudan	
Nyala	1,267
Khartoum	925
Sharg el Nil	879
Sweden	
Stockholm	1,744
Göteburg	775
Switzerland	
Zürich	1,175
Bern	942
Syria	
Aleppo	1,591
Damascus	1,549
Homs	644
Taiwan	
Taipei	2,653
Kaohsiung	1,405
Taichung	817
Tainan	700
Panchiao	544
Tajikistan	
Dushanbe	524
Tanzania	
Dar-es-Salaam	1,361
Thailand	
Bangkok	5,572
Togo	
Lomé	590
Tunisia	
Tunis	1,827
Turkey	
Istanbul	7,490
Ankara	3,028
Izmir	2,333
Adana	1,472
Bursa	1,317
Konya	1,040
Gaziantep	930
Icel	908
Antalya	734
Diyarbakir	677
Kocaeli	661
Urfa	649
Kayseri	648
Manisa	641
Hatay	561
Samsun	557
Eskisehir	508
Balikesir	501
Turkmenistan	
Ashkhabad	536
Uganda	
Kampala	773
Ukraine	
Kiev	2,630
Kharkiv	1,555
Dnipropetrovsk	1,147
Donetsk	1,088
Odesa	1,046
Zaporizhzhya	887
Lviv	802
Kryvyy Rih	720
Mariupol	510
Mykolayiv	508
United Kingdom	
London	8,089
Birmingham	2,373
Manchester	2,353
Liverpool	852
Glasgow	832
Sheffield	661
Nottingham	649
Newcastle	617
Bristol	552
Leeds	529
United States	
New York	16,329
Los Angeles	12,410
Chicago	7,668
Philadelphia	4,949
Washington, DC	4,466
Detroit	4,307
Houston	3,653
Atlanta	3,331
Boston	3,240
Dallas	2,898
Minneapolis–St Paul	2,688
San Diego	2,632
St Louis	2,536
Phoenix	2,473
Baltimore	2,458
Pittsburgh	2,402
Cleveland	2,222
San Francisco	2,182
Seattle	2,180
Tampa	2,157
Miami	2,025
Newark	1,934
Denver	1,796
Portland (Or.)	1,676
Kansas City (Mo.)	1,647
Cincinnati	1,581
San Jose	1,557
Norfolk	1,529
Indianapolis	1,462
Milwaukee	1,456
Sacramento	1,441
San Antonio	1,437
Columbus (Oh.)	1,423
New Orleans	1,309
Charlotte	1,260
Buffalo	1,189
Salt Lake City	1,178
Hartford	1,151
Oklahoma	1,007
Jacksonville (Fl.)	665
Omaha	663
Memphis	614
El Paso	579
Austin	514
Nashville	505
Uruguay	
Montevideo	1,378
Uzbekistan	
Tashkent	2,107
Venezuela	
Caracas	2,784
Maracaibo	1,364
Valencia	1,032
Maracay	800
Barquisimeto	745
Ciudad Guayana	524
Vietnam	
Ho Chi Minh City	4,322
Hanoi	3,056
Haiphong	783
Yemen	
Sana	972
Aden	562
Yugoslavia	
Belgrade	1,137
Zambia	
Lusaka	982
Zimbabwe	
Harare	1,189
Bulawayo	622

* SAR = Special Administrative Region of China

WORLD STATISTICS: *physical dimensions*

Each topic list is divided into continents and within a continent the items are listed in order of size. The bottom part of many of the lists is selective in order to give examples from as many different countries as possible. The figures are rounded as appropriate.

World, Continents, Oceans

	km^2	$miles^2$	%
The World	509,450,000	196,672,000	–
Land	149,450,000	57,688,000	29.3
Water	360,000,000	138,984,000	70.7
Asia	44,500,000	17,177,000	29.8
Africa	30,302,000	11,697,000	20.3
North America	24,241,000	9,357,000	16.2
South America	17,793,000	6,868,000	11.9
Antarctica	14,100,000	5,443,000	9.4
Europe	9,957,000	3,843,000	6.7
Australia & Oceania	8,557,000	3,303,000	5.7
Pacific Ocean	179,679,000	69,356,000	49.9
Atlantic Ocean	92,373,000	35,657,000	25.7
Indian Ocean	73,917,000	28,532,000	20.5
Arctic Ocean	14,090,000	5,439,000	3.9

Ocean Depths

Atlantic Ocean

	m	ft
Puerto Rico (Milwaukee) Deep	9,220	30,249
Cayman Trench	7,680	25,197
Gulf of Mexico	5,203	17,070
Mediterranean Sea	5,121	16,801
Black Sea	2,211	7,254
North Sea	660	2,165

Indian Ocean

	m	ft
Java Trench	7,450	24,442
Red Sea	2,635	8,454

Pacific Ocean

	m	ft
Mariana Trench	11,022	36,161
Tonga Trench	10,882	35,702
Japan Trench	10,554	34,626
Kuril Trench	10,542	34,587

Arctic Ocean

	m	ft
Molloy Deep	5,608	18,399

Mountains

Europe

		m	ft
Elbrus	*Russia*	5,642	18,510
Mont Blanc	*France/Italy*	4,807	15,771
Monte Rosa	*Italy/Switzerland*	4,634	15,203
Dom	*Switzerland*	4,545	14,911
Liskamm	*Switzerland*	4,527	14,852
Weisshorn	*Switzerland*	4,505	14,780
Taschorn	*Switzerland*	4,490	14,730
Matterhorn/Cervino	*Italy/Switzerland*	4,478	14,691
Mont Maudit	*France/Italy*	4,465	14,649
Dent Blanche	*Switzerland*	4,356	14,291
Nadelhorn	*Switzerland*	4,327	14,196
Grandes Jorasses	*France/Italy*	4,208	13,806
Jungfrau	*Switzerland*	4,158	13,642
Grossglockner	*Austria*	3,797	12,457
Mulhacén	*Spain*	3,478	11,411
Zugspitze	*Germany*	2,962	9,718
Olympus	*Greece*	2,917	9,570
Triglav	*Slovenia*	2,863	9,393
Gerlachovka	*Slovak Republic*	2,655	8,711
Galdhöpiggen	*Norway*	2,468	8,100
Kebnekaise	*Sweden*	2,117	6,946
Ben Nevis	*UK*	1,343	4,406

Asia

		m	ft
Everest	*China/Nepal*	8,848	29,029
K2 (Godwin Austen)	*China/Kashmir*	8,611	28,251
Kanchenjunga	*India/Nepal*	8,598	28,208
Lhotse	*China/Nepal*	8,516	27,939
Makalu	*China/Nepal*	8,481	27,824
Cho Oyu	*China/Nepal*	8,201	26,906
Dhaulagiri	*Nepal*	8,172	26,811
Manaslu	*Nepal*	8,156	26,758
Nanga Parbat	*Kashmir*	8,126	26,660
Annapurna	*Nepal*	8,078	26,502
Gasherbrum	*China/Kashmir*	8,068	26,469
Broad Peak	*China/Kashmir*	8,051	26,414
Xixabangma	*China*	8,012	26,286
Kangbachen	*India/Nepal*	7,902	25,925
Trivor	*Pakistan*	7,720	25,328
Pik Kommunizma	*Tajikistan*	7,495	24,590
Demavend	*Iran*	5,604	18,386
Ararat	*Turkey*	5,165	16,945
Gunong Kinabalu	*Malaysia (Borneo)*	4,101	13,455
Fuji-San	*Japan*	3,776	12,388

Africa

		m	ft
Kilimanjaro	*Tanzania*	5,895	19,340
Mt Kenya	*Kenya*	5,199	17,057
Ruwenzori	*Uganda/Congo (Zaïre)*	5,109	16,762
Ras Dashan	*Ethiopia*	4,620	15,157
Meru	*Tanzania*	4,565	14,977
Karisimbi	*Rwanda/Congo (Zaïre)*	4,507	14,787
Mt Elgon	*Kenya/Uganda*	4,321	14,176
Batu	*Ethiopia*	4,307	14,130
Toubkal	*Morocco*	4,165	13,665
Mt Cameroon	*Cameroon*	4,070	13,353

Oceania

		m	ft
Puncak Jaya	*Indonesia*	5,029	16,499
Puncak Trikora	*Indonesia*	4,750	15,584
Puncak Mandala	*Indonesia*	4,702	15,427
Mt Wilhelm	*Papua New Guinea*	4,508	14,790
Mauna Kea	*USA (Hawaii)*	4,205	13,796
Mauna Loa	*USA (Hawaii)*	4,170	13,681
Mt Cook (Aoraki)	*New Zealand*	3,753	12,313
Mt Kosciuszko	*Australia*	2,237	7,339

North America

		m	ft
Mt McKinley (Denali)	*USA (Alaska)*	6,194	20,321
Mt Logan	*Canada*	5,959	19,551
Citlaltepetl	*Mexico*	5,700	18,701
Mt St Elias	*USA/Canada*	5,489	18,008
Popocatepetl	*Mexico*	5,452	17,887
Mt Foraker	*USA (Alaska)*	5,304	17,401
Ixtaccihuatl	*Mexico*	5,286	17,342
Lucania	*Canada*	5,227	17,149
Mt Steele	*Canada*	5,073	16,644
Mt Bona	*USA (Alaska)*	5,005	16,420
Mt Whitney	*USA*	4,418	14,495
Tajumulco	*Guatemala*	4,220	13,845
Chirripó Grande	*Costa Rica*	3,837	12,589
Pico Duarte	*Dominican Rep.*	3,175	10,417

South America

		m	ft
Aconcagua	*Argentina*	6,960	22,834
Bonete	*Argentina*	6,872	22,546
Ojos del Salado	*Argentina/Chile*	6,863	22,516
Pissis	*Argentina*	6,779	22,241
Mercedario	*Argentina/Chile*	6,770	22,211
Huascaran	*Peru*	6,768	22,204
Llullaillaco	*Argentina/Chile*	6,723	22,057
Nudo de Cachi	*Argentina*	6,720	22,047
Yerupaja	*Peru*	6,632	21,758
Sajama	*Bolivia*	6,542	21,463
Chimborazo	*Ecuador*	6,267	20,561
Pico Colon	*Colombia*	5,800	19,029
Pico Bolivar	*Venezuela*	5,007	16,427

Antarctica

	m	ft
Vinson Massif	4,897	16,066
Mt Kirkpatrick	4,528	14,855

Rivers

Europe

		km	miles
Volga	*Caspian Sea*	3,700	2,300
Danube	*Black Sea*	2,850	1,770
Ural	*Caspian Sea*	2,535	1,575
Dnepr (Dnipro)	*Black Sea*	2,285	1,420
Kama	*Volga*	2,030	1,260
Don	*Volga*	1,990	1,240
Petchora	*Arctic Ocean*	1,790	1,110
Oka	*Volga*	1,480	920
Dnister (Dniester)	*Black Sea*	1,400	870
Vyatka	*Kama*	1,370	850
Rhine	*North Sea*	1,320	820
N. Dvina	*Arctic Ocean*	1,290	800
Elbe	*North Sea*	1,145	710

Asia

		km	miles
Yangtze	*Pacific Ocean*	6,380	3,960
Yenisey–Angara	*Arctic Ocean*	5,550	3,445
Huang He	*Pacific Ocean*	5,464	3,395
Ob–Irtysh	*Arctic Ocean*	5,410	3,360
Mekong	*Pacific Ocean*	4,500	2,795
Amur	*Pacific Ocean*	4,400	2,730
Lena	*Arctic Ocean*	4,400	2,730
Irtysh	*Ob*	4,250	2,640
Yenisey	*Arctic Ocean*	4,090	2,540
Ob	*Arctic Ocean*	3,680	2,285
Indus	*Indian Ocean*	3,100	1,925
Brahmaputra	*Indian Ocean*	2,900	1,800
Syrdarya	*Aral Sea*	2,860	1,775
Salween	*Indian Ocean*	2,800	1,740
Euphrates	*Indian Ocean*	2,700	1,675
Amudarya	*Aral Sea*	2,540	1,575

Africa

		km	miles
Nile	*Mediterranean*	6,670	4,140
Congo	*Atlantic Ocean*	4,670	2,900
Niger	*Atlantic Ocean*	4,180	2,595
Zambezi	*Indian Ocean*	3,540	2,200
Oubangi/Uele	*Congo (Zaïre)*	2,250	1,400
Kasai	*Congo (Zaïre)*	1,950	1,210
Shaballe	*Indian Ocean*	1,930	1,200
Orange	*Atlantic Ocean*	1,860	1,155
Cubango	*Okavango Swamps*	1,800	1,120
Limpopo	*Indian Ocean*	1,600	995
Senegal	*Atlantic Ocean*	1,600	995

Australia

		km	miles
Murray–Darling	*Indian Ocean*	3,750	2,330
Darling	*Murray*	3,070	1,905
Murray	*Indian Ocean*	2,575	1,600
Murrumbidgee	*Murray*	1,690	1,050

North America

		km	miles
Mississippi–Missouri	*Gulf of Mexico*	6,020	3,740
Mackenzie	*Arctic Ocean*	4,240	2,630
Mississippi	*Gulf of Mexico*	3,780	2,350
Missouri	*Mississippi*	3,780	2,350
Yukon	*Pacific Ocean*	3,185	1,980
Rio Grande	*Gulf of Mexico*	3,030	1,880
Arkansas	*Mississippi*	2,340	1,450
Colorado	*Pacific Ocean*	2,330	1,445
Red	*Mississippi*	2,040	1,270
Columbia	*Pacific Ocean*	1,950	1,210
Saskatchewan	*Lake Winnipeg*	1,940	1,205

South America

		km	miles
Amazon	*Atlantic Ocean*	6,450	4,010
Paraná–Plate	*Atlantic Ocean*	4,500	2,800
Purus	*Amazon*	3,350	2,080
Madeira	*Amazon*	3,200	1,990
São Francisco	*Atlantic Ocean*	2,900	1,800
Paraná	*Plate*	2,800	1,740
Tocantins	*Atlantic Ocean*	2,750	1,710
Paraguay	*Paraná*	2,550	1,580
Orinoco	*Atlantic Ocean*	2,500	1,550
Pilcomayo	*Paraná*	2,500	1,550
Araguaia	*Tocantins*	2,250	1,400

Lakes

Europe

		km^2	$miles^2$
Lake Ladoga	*Russia*	17,700	6,800
Lake Onega	*Russia*	9,700	3,700
Saimaa system	*Finland*	8,000	3,100
Vänern	*Sweden*	5,500	2,100

Asia

		km^2	$miles^2$
Caspian Sea	*Asia*	371,800	143,550
Lake Baykal	*Russia*	30,500	11,780
Aral Sea	*Kazakstan/Uzbekistan*	28,687	11,086
Tonlé Sap	*Cambodia*	20,000	7,700
Lake Balqash	*Kazakstan*	18,500	7,100

Africa

		km^2	$miles^2$
Lake Victoria	*East Africa*	68,000	26,000
Lake Tanganyika	*Central Africa*	33,000	13,000
Lake Malawi/Nyasa	*East Africa*	29,600	11,430
Lake Chad	*Central Africa*	25,000	9,700
Lake Turkana	*Ethiopia/Kenya*	8,500	3,300
Lake Volta	*Ghana*	8,500	3,300

Australia

		km^2	$miles^2$
Lake Eyre	*Australia*	8,900	3,400
Lake Torrens	*Australia*	5,800	2,200
Lake Gairdner	*Australia*	4,800	1,900

North America

		km^2	$miles^2$
Lake Superior	*Canada/USA*	82,350	31,800
Lake Huron	*Canada/USA*	59,600	23,010
Lake Michigan	*USA*	58,000	22,400
Great Bear Lake	*Canada*	31,800	12,280
Great Slave Lake	*Canada*	28,500	11,000
Lake Erie	*Canada/USA*	25,700	9,900
Lake Winnipeg	*Canada*	24,400	9,400
Lake Ontario	*Canada/USA*	19,500	7,500
Lake Nicaragua	*Nicaragua*	8,200	3,200

South America

		km^2	$miles^2$
Lake Titicaca	*Bolivia/Peru*	8,300	3,200
Lake Poopo	*Peru*	2,800	1,100

Islands

Europe

		km^2	$miles^2$
Great Britain	*UK*	229,880	88,700
Iceland	*Atlantic Ocean*	103,000	39,800
Ireland	*Ireland/UK*	84,400	32,600
Novaya Zemlya (N.)	*Russia*	48,200	18,600
Sicily	*Italy*	25,500	9,800
Corsica	*France*	8,700	3,400

Asia

		km^2	$miles^2$
Borneo	*South-east Asia*	744,360	287,400
Sumatra	*Indonesia*	473,600	182,860
Honshu	*Japan*	230,500	88,980
Celebes	*Indonesia*	189,000	73,000
Java	*Indonesia*	126,700	48,900
Luzon	*Philippines*	104,700	40,400
Hokkaido	*Japan*	78,400	30,300

Africa

		km^2	$miles^2$
Madagascar	*Indian Ocean*	587,040	226,660
Socotra	*Indian Ocean*	3,600	1,400
Réunion	*Indian Ocean*	2,500	965

Oceania

		km^2	$miles^2$
New Guinea	*Indonesia/Papua NG*	821,030	317,000
New Zealand (S.)	*Pacific Ocean*	150,500	58,100
New Zealand (N.)	*Pacific Ocean*	114,700	44,300
Tasmania	*Australia*	67,800	26,200
Hawaii	*Pacific Ocean*	10,450	4,000

North America

		km^2	$miles^2$
Greenland	*Atlantic Ocean*	2,175,600	839,800
Baffin Is.	*Canada*	508,000	196,100
Victoria Is.	*Canada*	212,200	81,900
Ellesmere Is.	*Canada*	212,000	81,800
Cuba	*Caribbean Sea*	110,860	42,800
Hispaniola	*Dominican Rep./Haiti*	76,200	29,400
Jamaica	*Caribbean Sea*	11,400	4,400
Puerto Rico	*Atlantic Ocean*	8,900	3,400

South America

		km^2	$miles^2$
Tierra del Fuego	*Argentina/Chile*	47,000	18,100
Falkland Is. (E.)	*Atlantic Ocean*	6,800	2,600

WORLD MAPS

SETTLEMENTS

⬡ **PARIS**   ▣ **Berne**   ◉ **Livorno**   ◉ **Brugge**   ◎ *Algeciras*   ◦ *Frejus*   ○ *Oberammergau*   ○ *Thira*

Settlement symbols and type styles vary according to the scale of each map and indicate the importance
of towns on the map rather than specific population figures

∴   Ruins or Archæological Sites   ᴗ   Wells in Desert

ADMINISTRATION

_____ International Boundaries

_ _ _ International Boundaries
(Undefined or Disputed)

········· Internal Boundaries

⬠ National Parks

Country Names

NICARAGUA

Administrative
Area Names

K E N T

CALABRIA

International boundaries show the *de facto* situation where there are rival claims to territory

COMMUNICATIONS

_____ Principal Roads

⌒ Other Roads

-·-·- Trails and Seasonal Roads

≍ Passes

✿ Airfields

⌒ Principal Railways

--·-- Railways
Under Construction

⌒ Other Railways

⌐---⌐ Railway Tunnels

············ Principal Canals

PHYSICAL FEATURES

⌇ Perennial Streams

·-·-· Intermittent Streams

⬭ Perennial Lakes

⬭ Intermittent Lakes

Swamps and Marshes

Permanent Ice
and Glaciers

▲ 8848   Elevations in metres

▾ 8050   Sea Depths in metres

1134   Height of Lake Surface
Above Sea Level
in metres

ELEVATION AND DEPTH TINTS

Height of Land Above Sea Level

Land Below Sea Level

Depth of Sea

in metres   6000   4000   3000   2000   1500   1000   400   200   0

in feet   18 000   12 000   9000   6000   4500   3000   1200   600

6000   12 000   15 000   18 000   24 000   in feet

0   200   2000   4000   5000   6000   8000   in metres

Some of the maps have different contours to highlight and clarify the principal relief features

Projection: Hammer Equal Area

Hanoi ● Capital Cities

CARTOGRAPHY BY PHILIP'S.

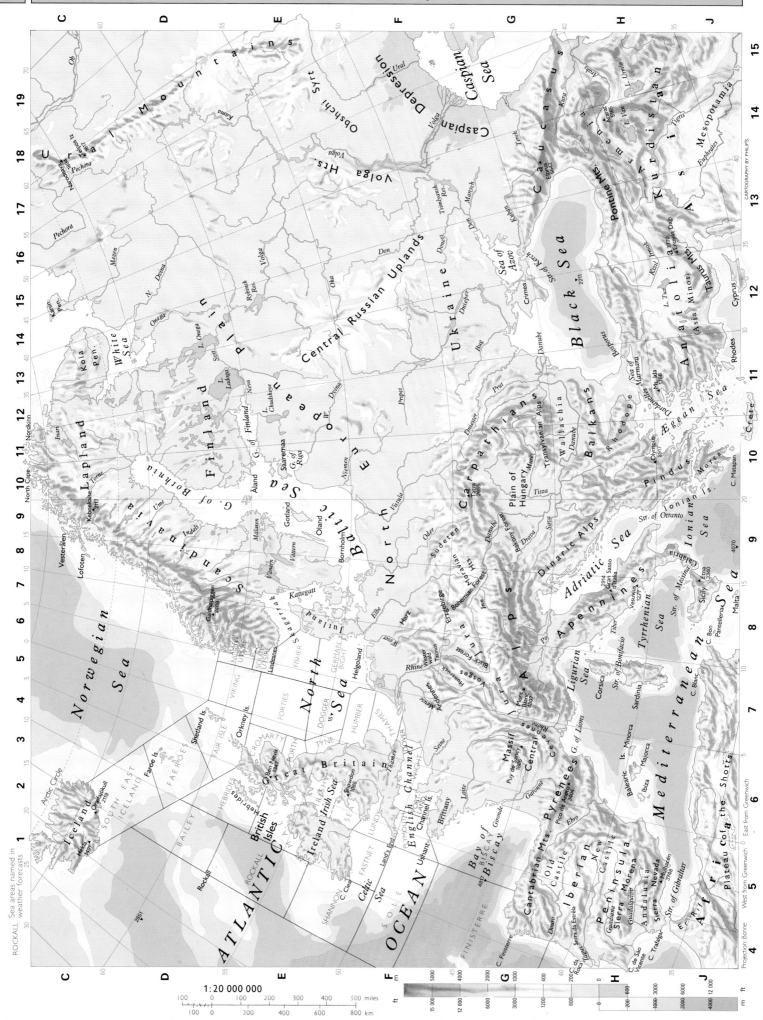

ROCKALL Sea areas named in weather forecasts

Projection: Bonne

1 : 20 000 000

| 100 | 0 | 100 | 200 | 300 | 400 | 500 miles |

| 100 | 0 | 200 | 400 | 600 | 800 km |

West from Greenwich 0 East from Greenwich

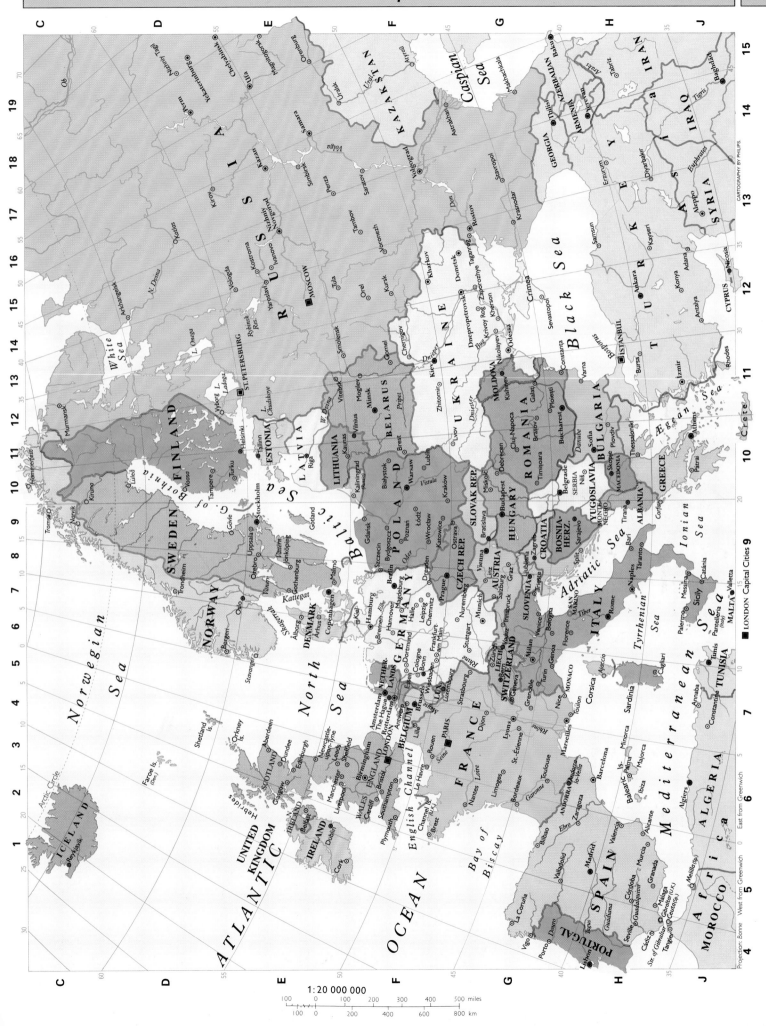

CARTOGRAPHY BY PHILIPS

■ LONDON Capital Cities 9

Projection: Bonne

1:20 000 000

100 0 100 200 300 400 500 miles

100 0 200 400 600 800 km

ICELAND
On the same scale
West from Greenwich

Projection: Conical with two standard parallels

East from Greenwich

COPYRIGHT. GEORGE PHILIP & SON. LTD.

1:10 000 000

50   0   50   100   150   200   250 miles

50   0   50   100   150   200   250   300   350   400 km

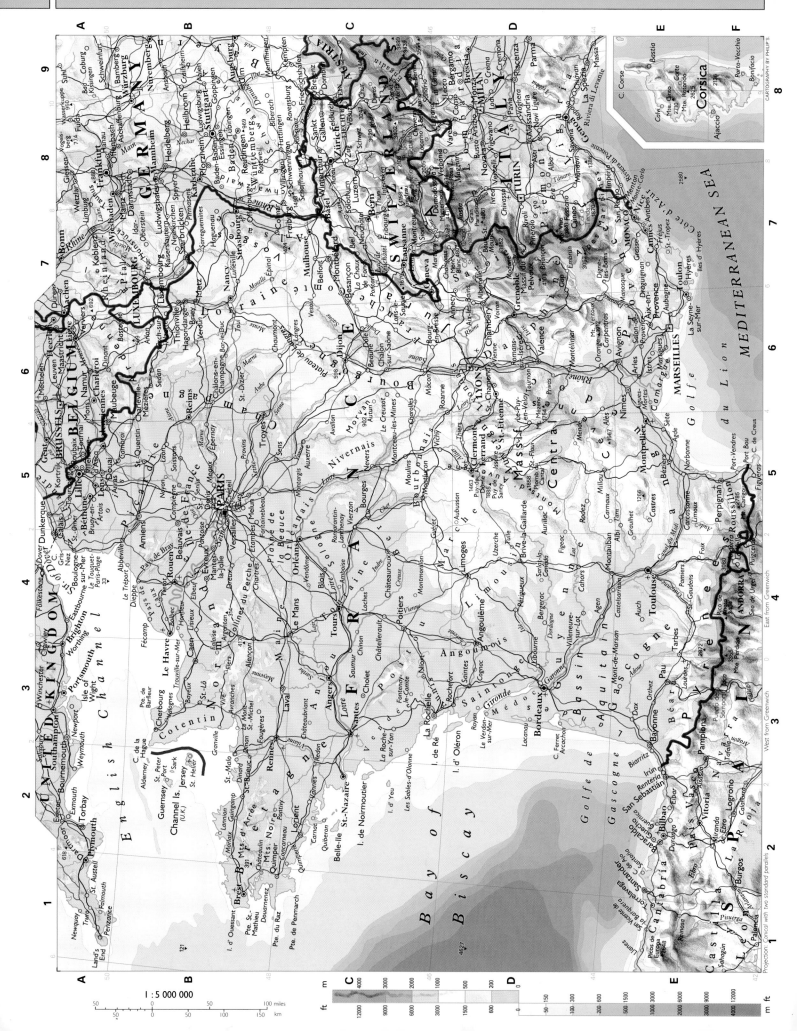

Projection: Conical with two standard parallels

CARTOGRAPHY BY PHILIP'S

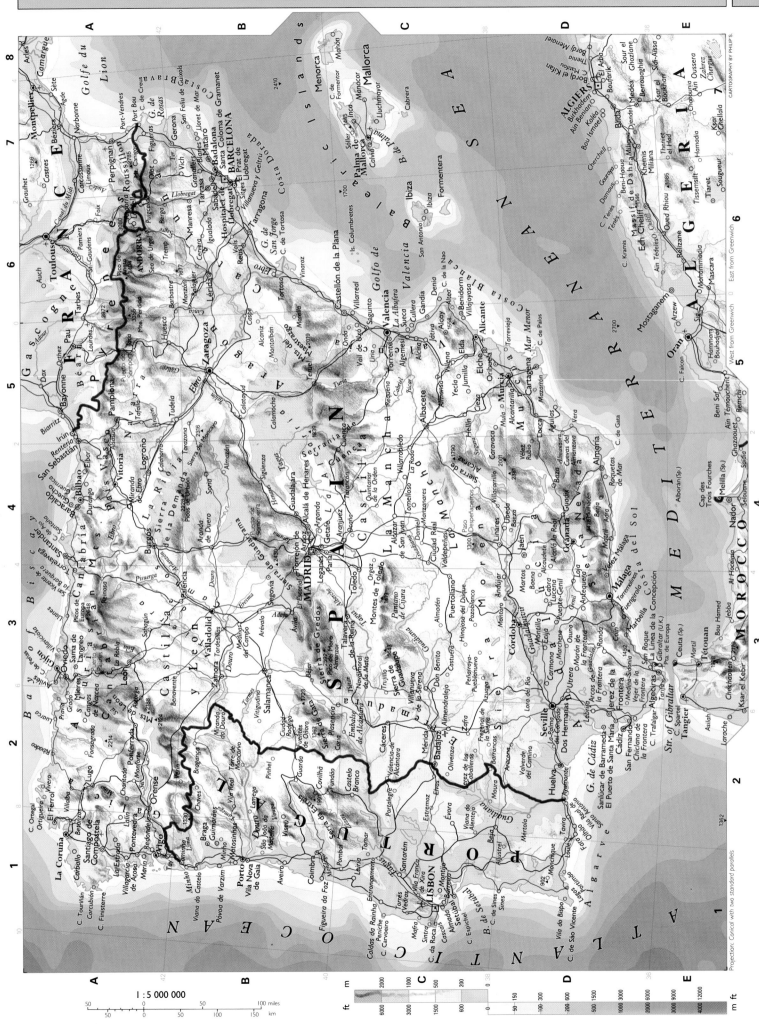

1 : 5 000 000

Projection: Conical with two standard parallels

CARTOGRAPHY BY PHILIP'S

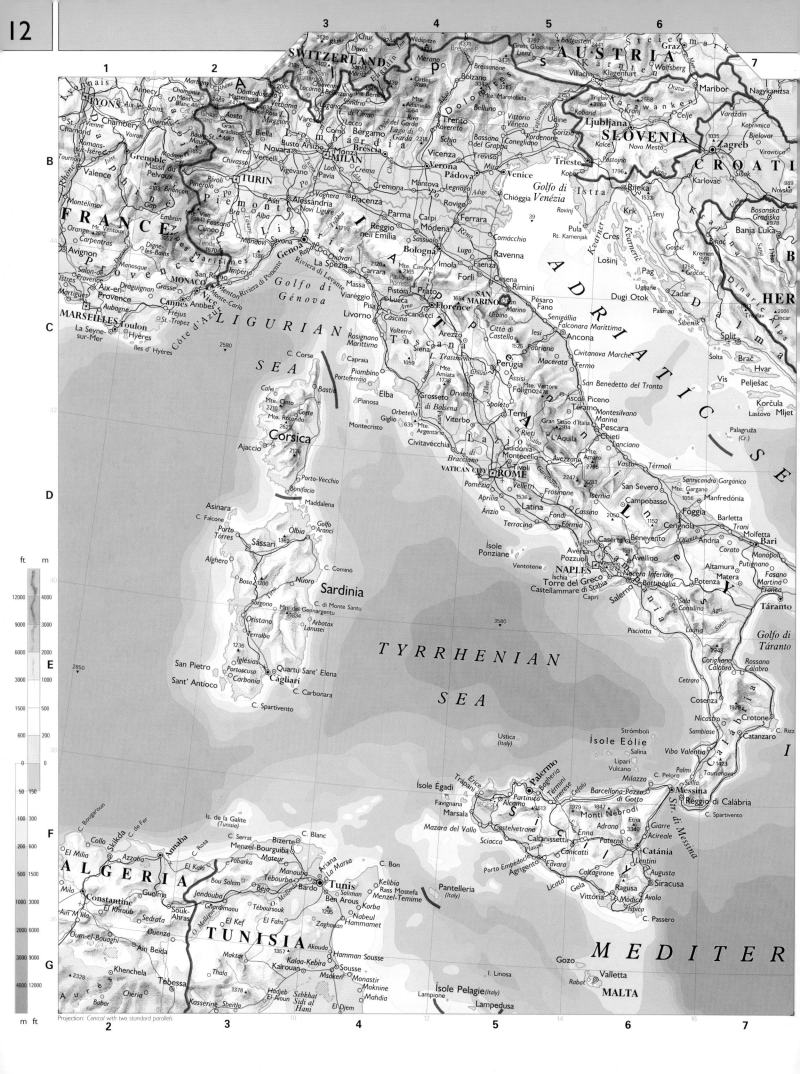

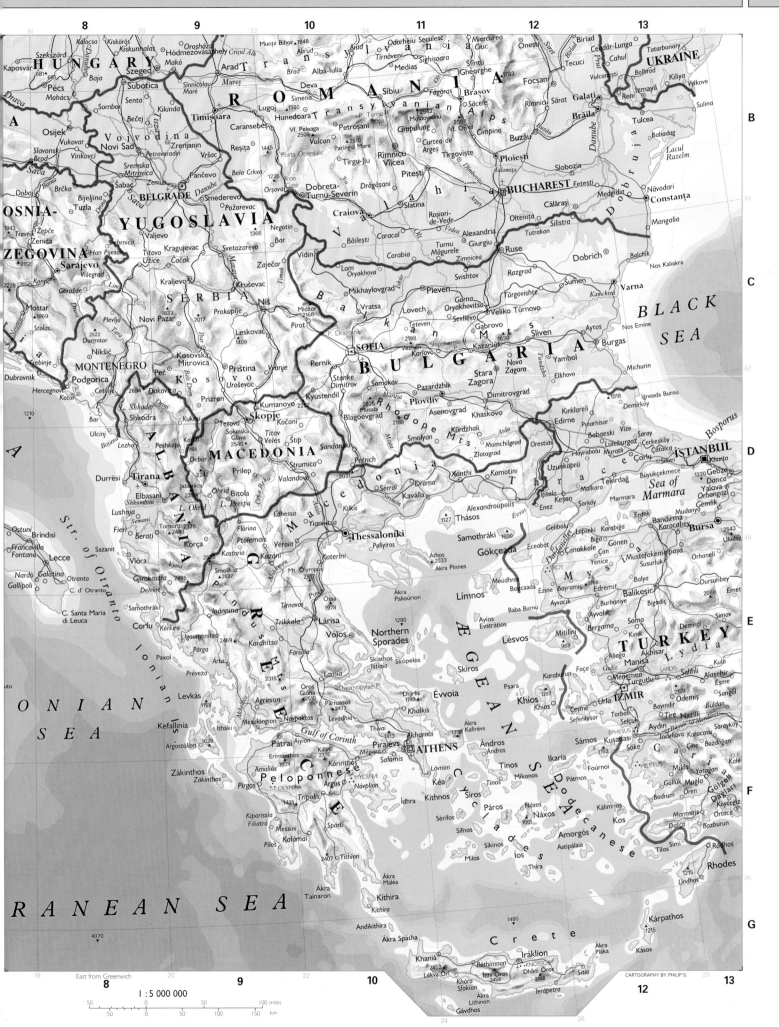

East from Greenwich

1 : 5 000 000

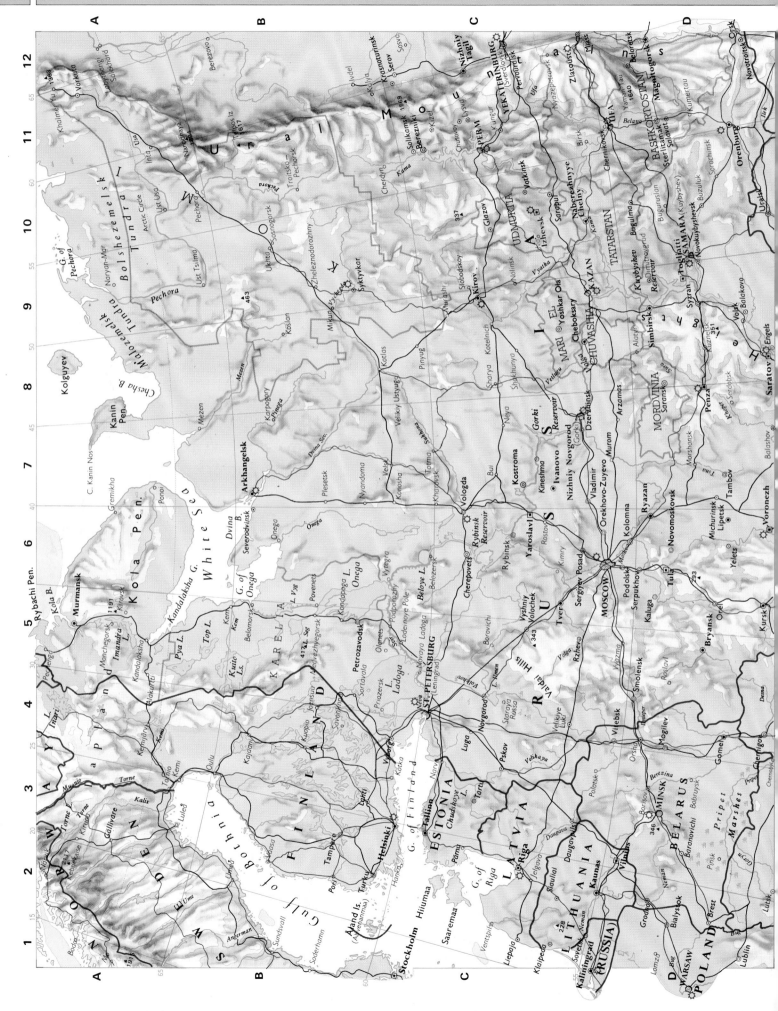

Inset legend:
1. Crimea (Ukr.)
2. Adygea (Russ.)
3. Karachey-Cherkessia (Russ.)
4. Kabardino-Balkana (Russ.)
5. North Ossetia (Russ.)
6. Ingushetia (Russ.)
7. Chechenia (Russ.)
8. Nakhichevan (Azer.)

Karagiye Depression
-132
-28m below sea-level

1:10 000 000

Projection: Conical with two standard parallels

Division Between Greeks and Turks
in Cyprus, Turks to the North

East from Greenwich

ft   m
12,000   4000
6000   2000
3000   1000
1200   400
600   200
0   0
600   200
3000   1000
6000   2000
12,000   4000

50   0   50   100   150   200   250 miles
50   0   50   100   150   200   250   300   350   400 km

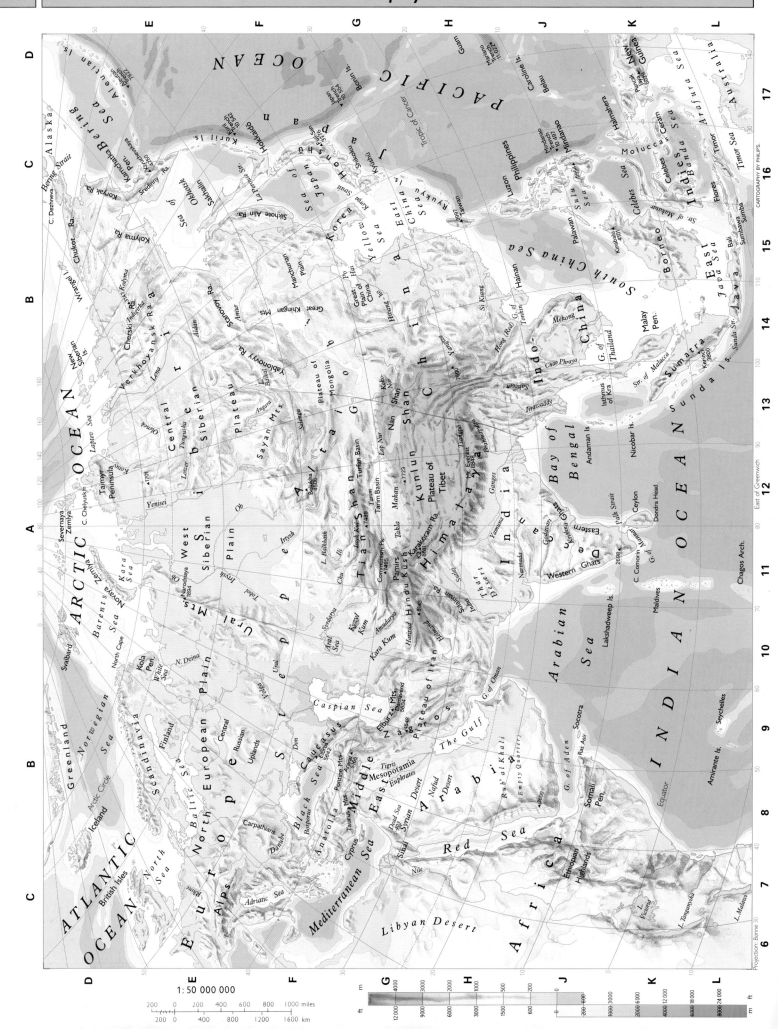

CARTOGRAPHY BY PHILIPS

1 : 50 000 000

200	0	200	400	600	800	1000 miles
200	0	400	800	1200	1600 km

Projection: Bonne 30

East of Greenwich

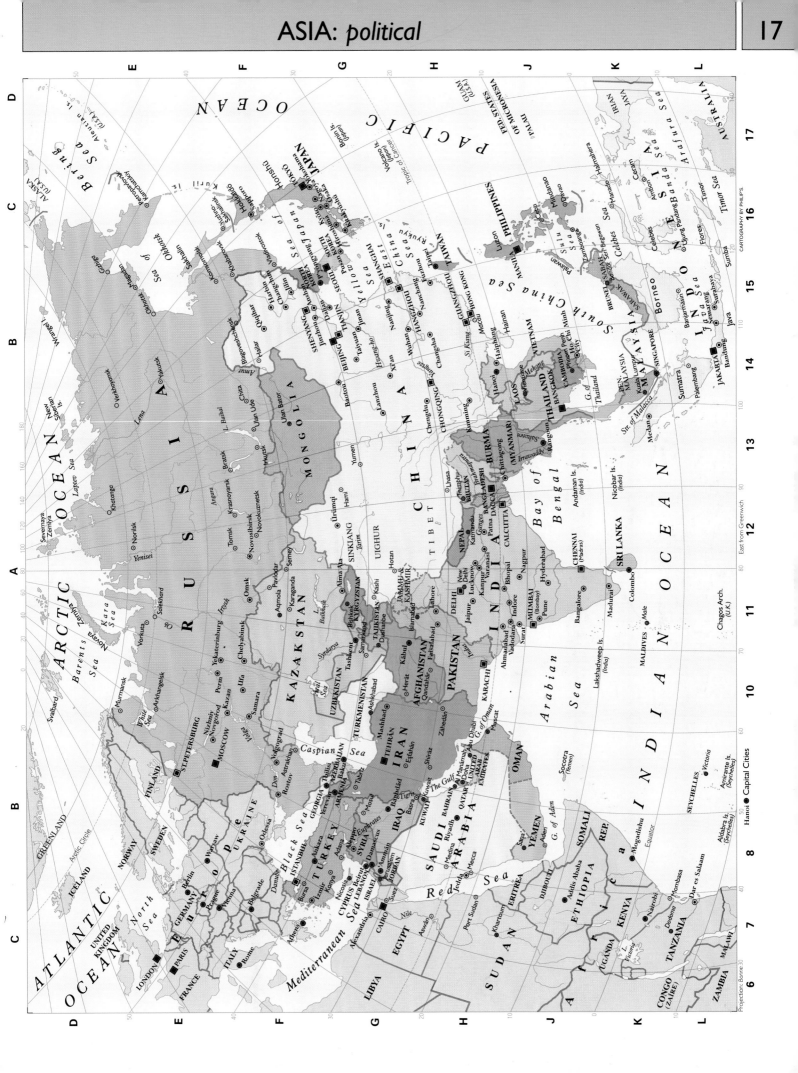

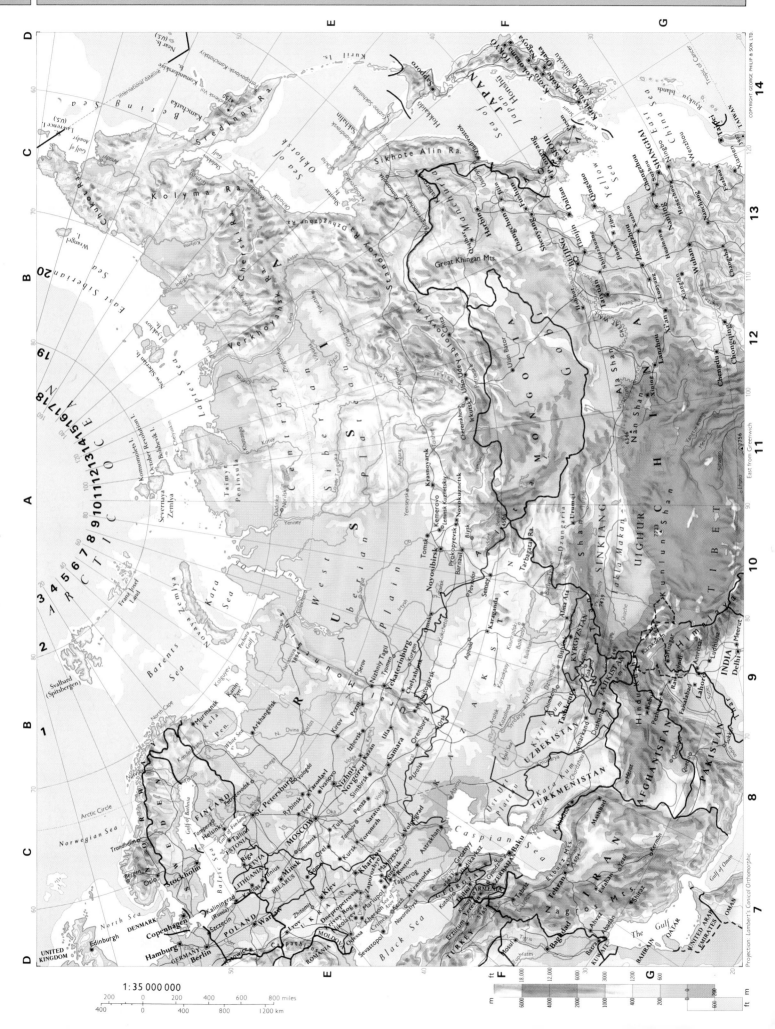

1:35 000 000

Projection: Lambert's Conical Orthomorphic

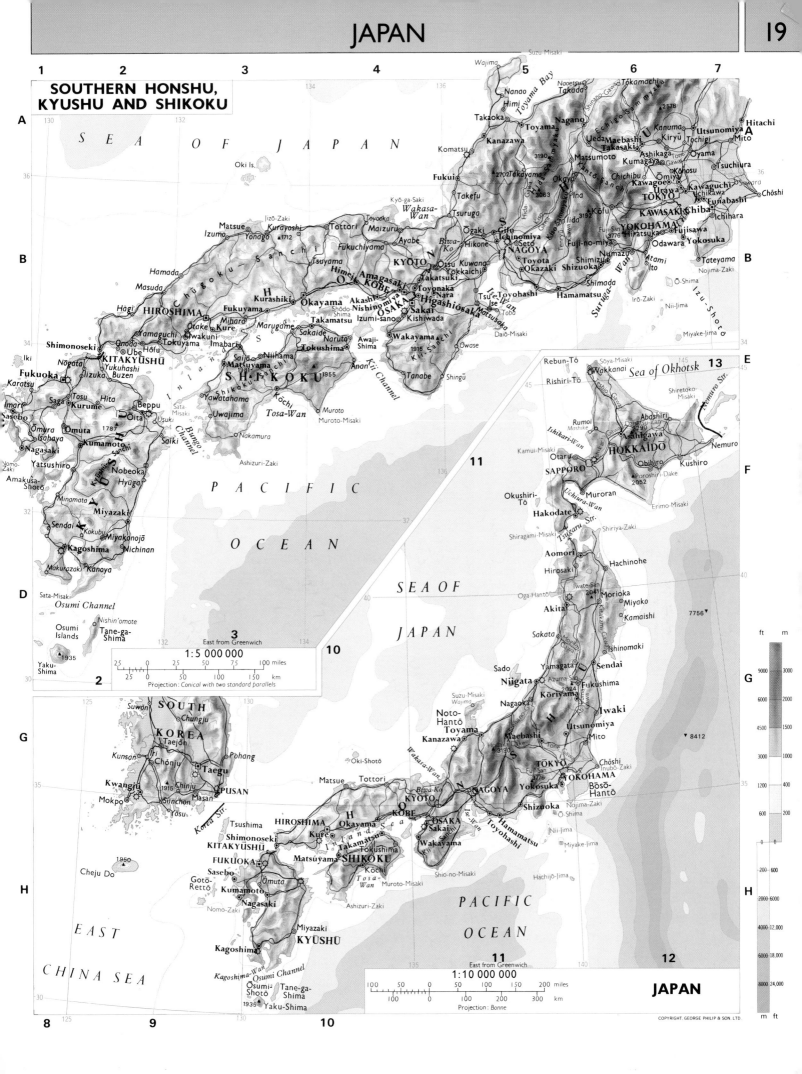

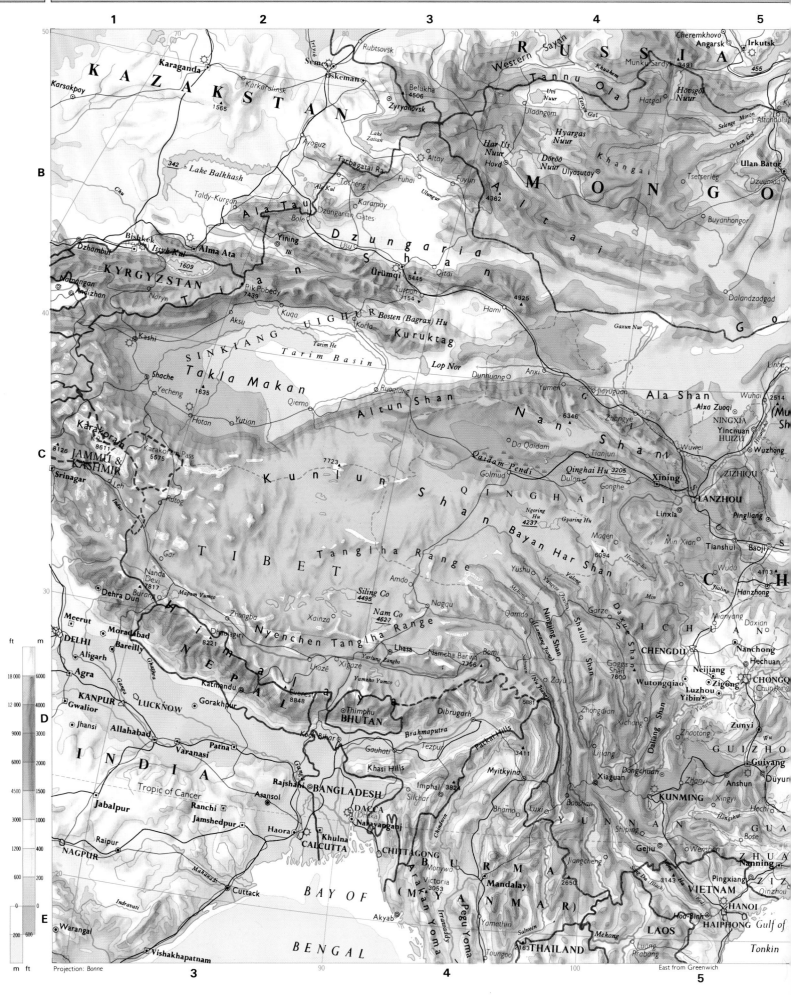

1:15 000 000

COPYRIGHT GEORGE PHILIP & SON LTD

100 0 100 200 300 400 miles

100 0 100 200 300 400 500 600 km

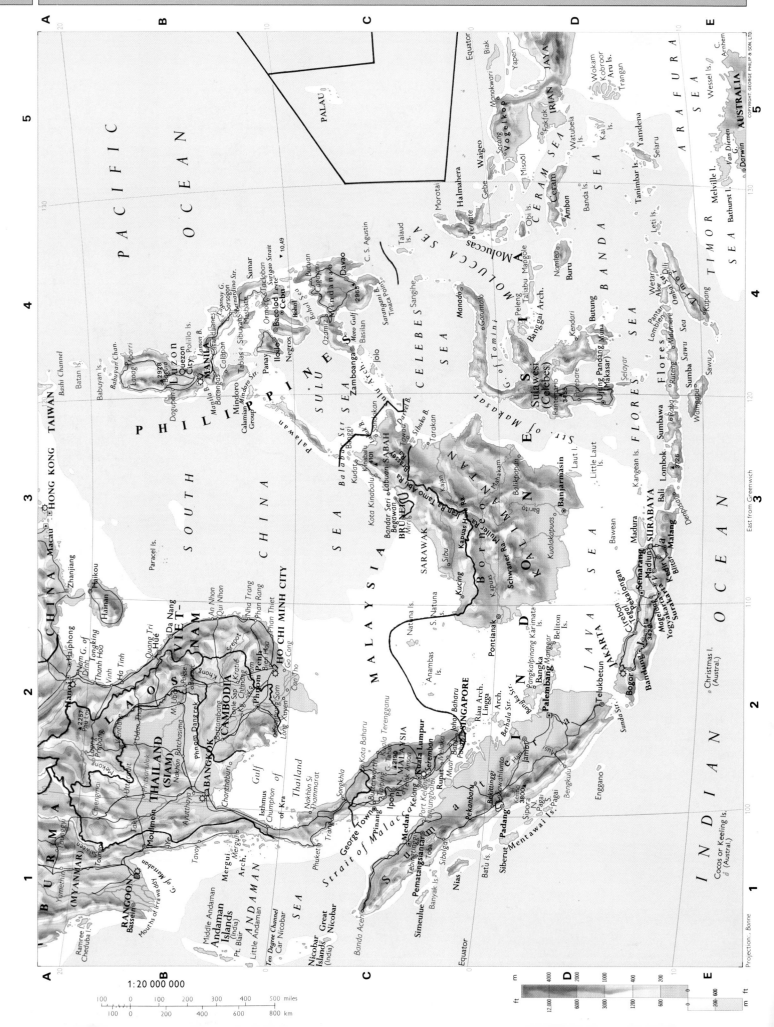

1 : 20 000 000

100   0   100   200   300   400   500 miles
100 0   200   400   600   800 km

Projection : Bonne

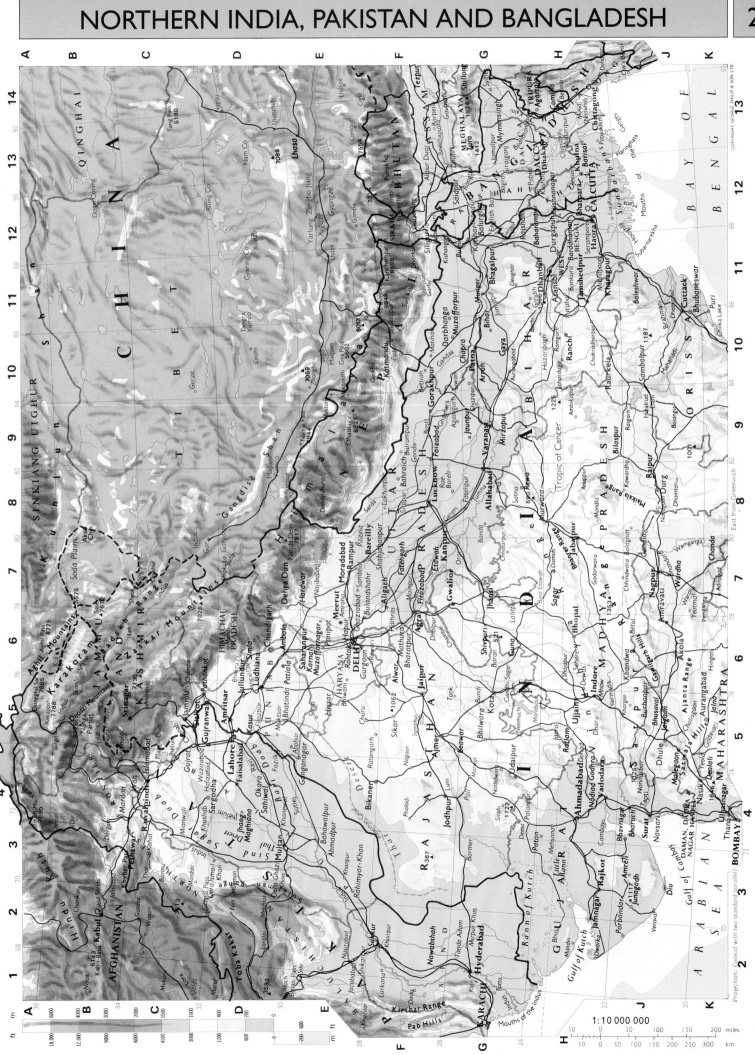

ft m
18,000 6000
12,000 4000
9000 3000
6000 2000
3000 1000
1200 400
600 200
0 0
200 600
m ft

Projection : Alber's Equal Area with two standard parallels

East from Greenwich

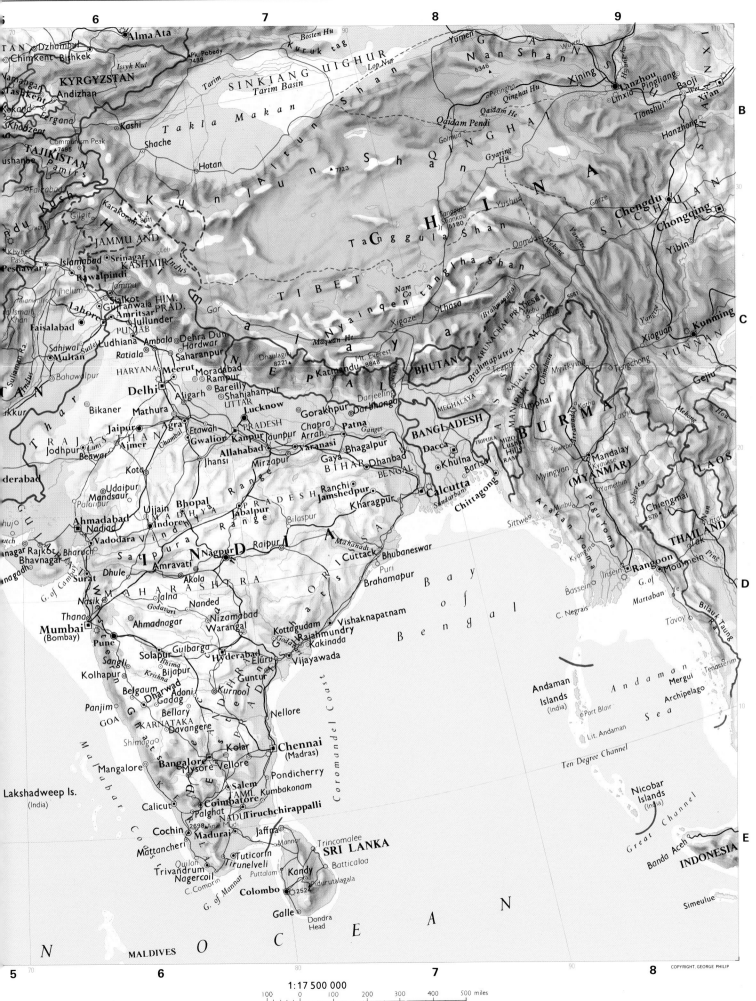

1:17 500 000

100   0   100   200   300   400   500 miles

100   0   100   200   300   400   500   600   700   800 km

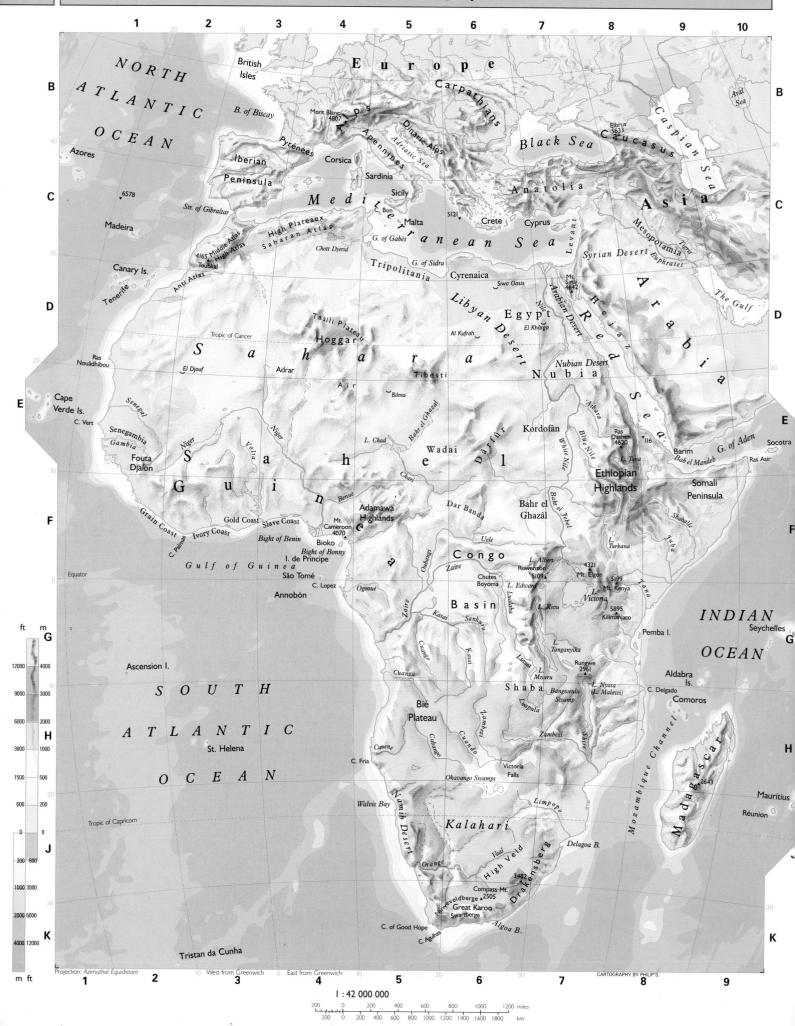

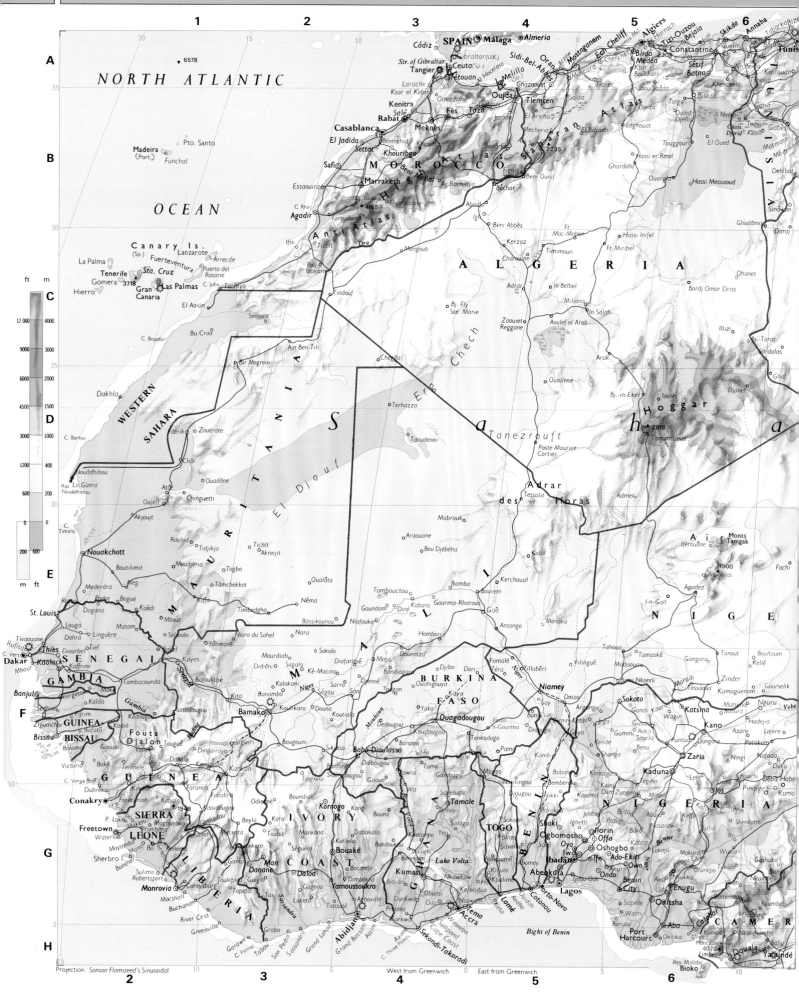

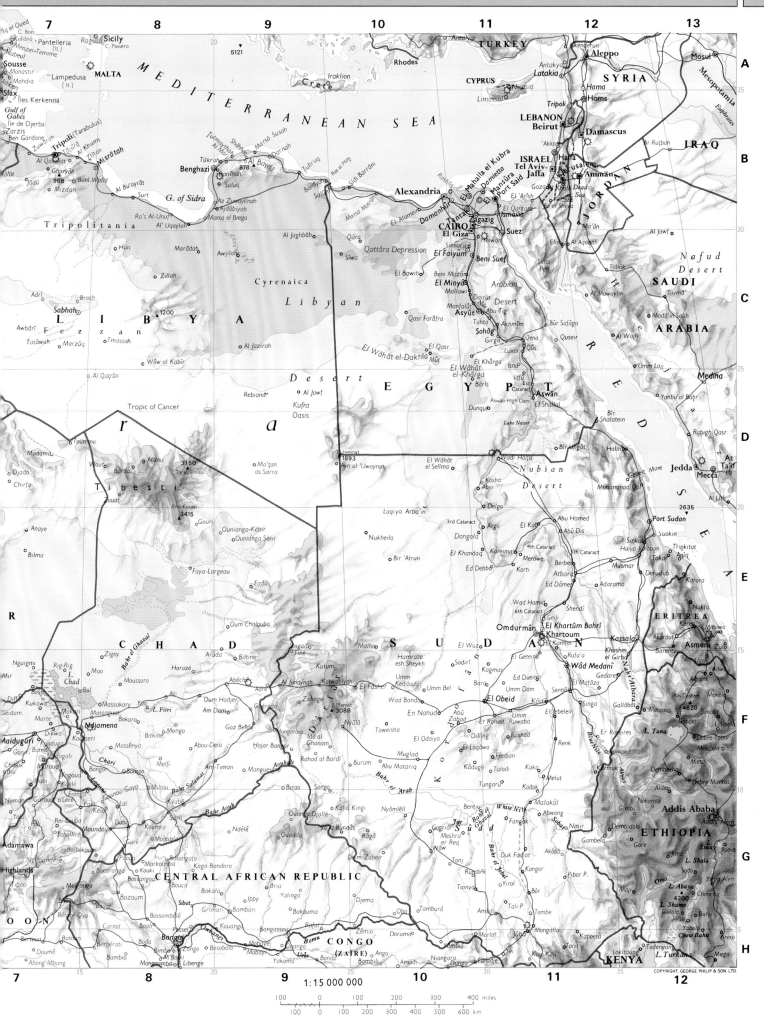

1:15 000 000

COPYRIGHT. GEORGE PHILIP & SON. LTD

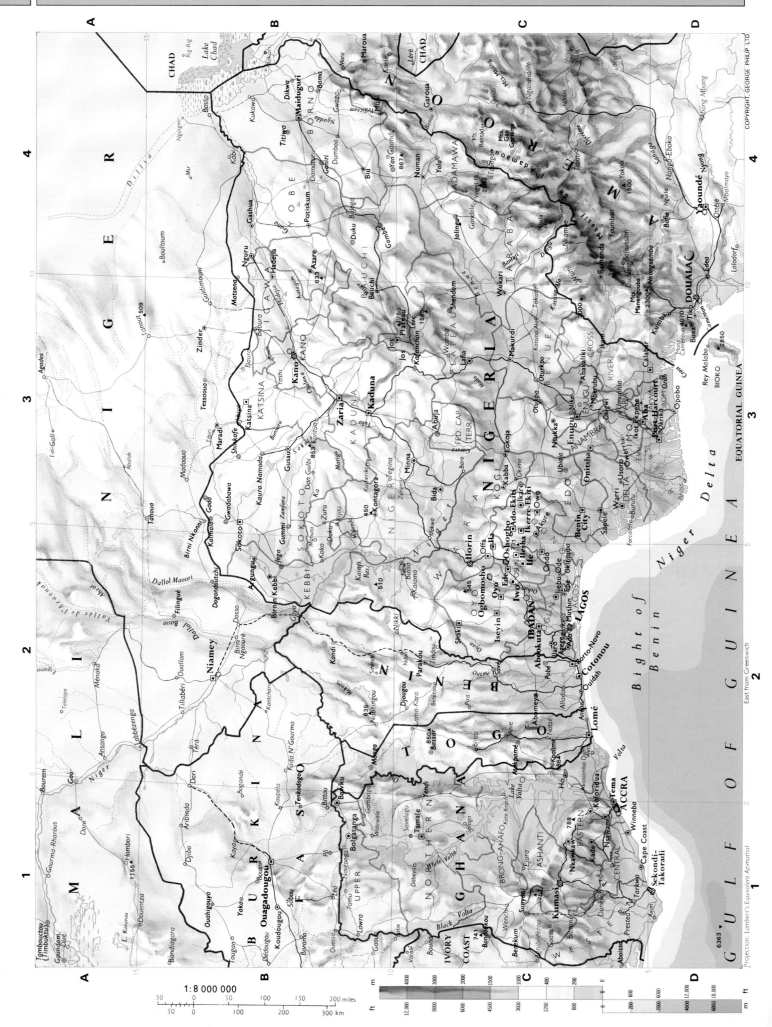

1:8 000 000

COPYRIGHT: GEORGE PHILIP LTD

Projection: Lambert's Equivalent Azimuthal

East from Greenwich

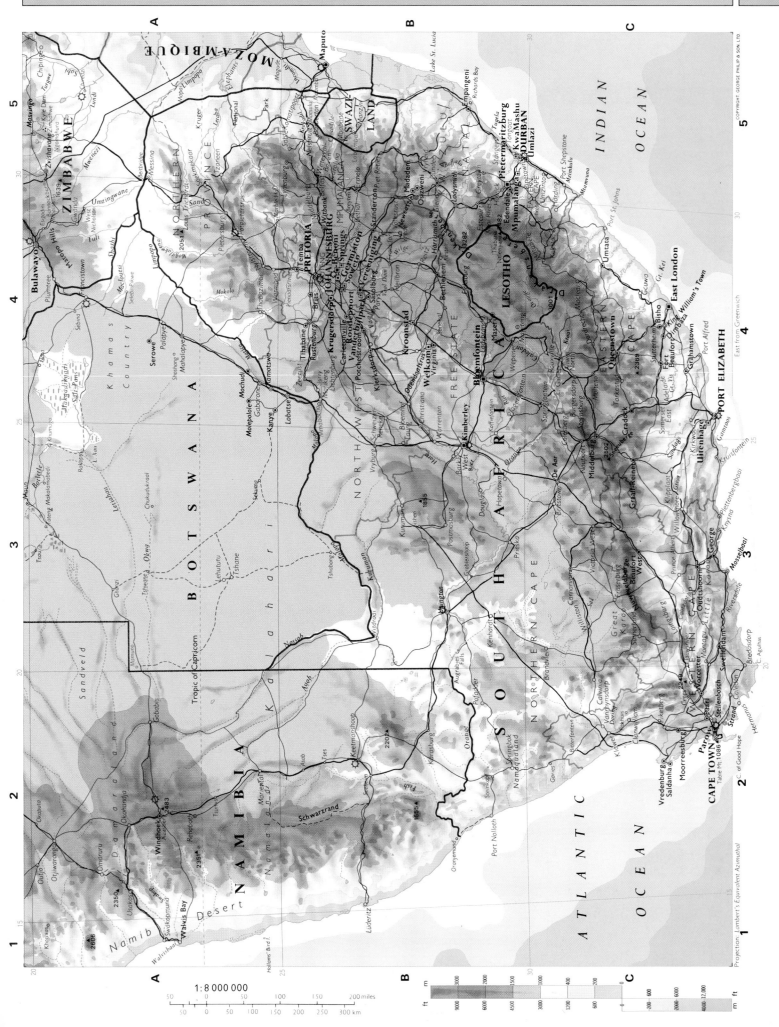

1:8 000 000

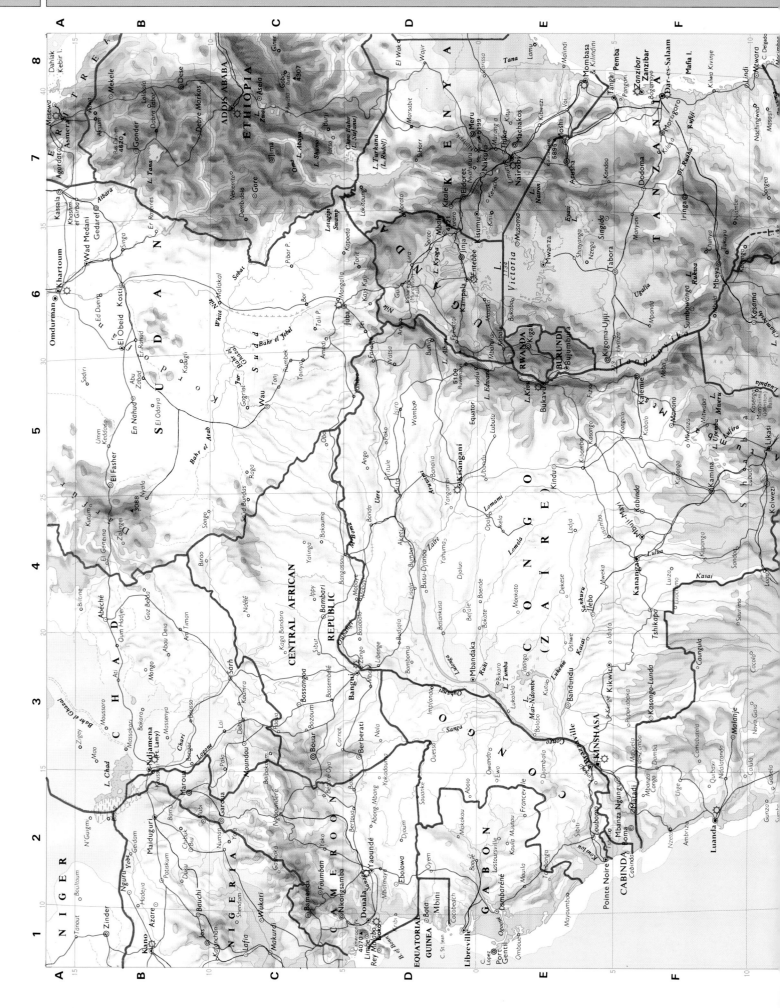

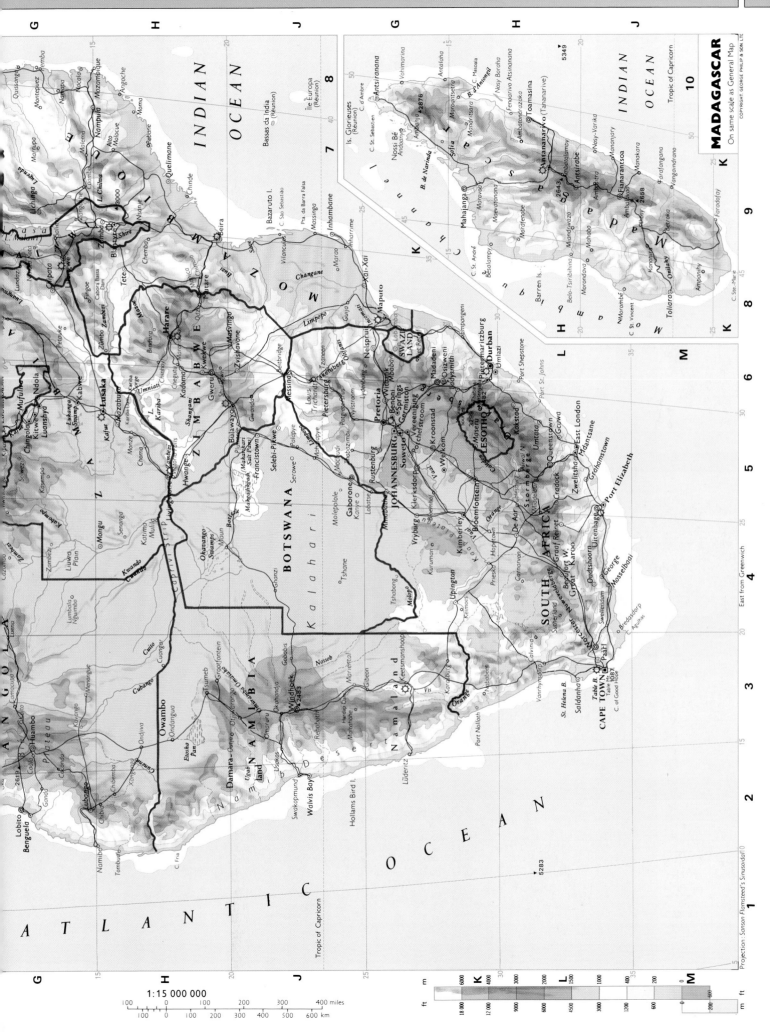

MADAGASCAR
On same scale as General Map

1:15 000 000

Projection: Sanson Flamsteed's Sinusoidal

INDIAN OCEAN

ATLANTIC OCEAN

INDONESIA

Sulawesi
(Celebes)

Kendari

Butung
5300

Banda Sea

7260

Kai Is.
3350

Aru Is.

Ujung Pandang
(Makasar)

Wetar

Alor

Dili

Leti

Babar

Tanimbar
Is.

Pulau Yos Sudarso

Misool

Fakfak

Sorong

Vogelkop

Biak

Irian Jaya

Pegunungan Maoke
Puncak Jaya
5029

Jayapura

New
Guinea

Wewak

Mount Hagen

Madang

4508

Mt.
Wilhelm

Lae

Owen Stanley Range

Fly

Gulf of
Papua

Port
Moresby

PAPUA NEW GUINEA

Bismarck
Archipelago

Kavieng

New
Ireland

Rabaul

New
Britain

9140

Solomon
Sea

D'Entrecasteaux

Louisiade
Archipelago

Sumbawa

Flores

Raba

Ende

Kupang

Timor

6204

3310

Sumba

Flores Sea

Arafura Sea

Timor Sea

Torres Strait

C. York

C. Croker

C. Arnhem

Melville I.

Darwin

Arnhem
Land

Weipa

Cape
York

Gulf of
Carpentaria

Wellesley
I.

Coral

C. Londonderry

Cambridge G.

Wyndham

Kimberley

Plateau

Derby

Broome

NORTHERN

Daly Waters

Larrimah

Tennant Creek

Tanami
Desert

Barkly Tableland

Mitchell

Normanton

Forsayth

Cooktown

Cairns

1611
Bartle Frere

Townsville

Charters Towers

Mackay

Coral

Sea

Islands

Territory

Great Sandy Desert

TERRITORY

Kajabbi

Mount Isa

Flinders

Hughenden

Winton

Longreach

Yaraka

QUEENSLAND

Rockhampton

Gladstone

Bundaberg

AUSTRALIA

L. Mackay

Macdonnell Ranges
1510 Mt.
Ziel

Alice Springs

Simpson
Desert

Diamantina

Maryborough

Gympie

N.W.
Cape

Dampier

Port
Hedland

Lake
Disappointment

Gibson Desert

Ayers
Rock

Mt.
Woodroffe
1440

SOUTH

Cooper Creek

Charleville

Roma

Grey Range

Quilpie

Cunnamulla

BRISBANE

Toowoomba

Ipswich

Mt. Bruce
1226

Hamersley
Range

Newman

WESTERN

Musgrave Ranges

Thargomindah

Warrego

Dirranbandi

Gold
Coast

Lismore

Carnarvon

L. Carnegie

Great Victoria Desert

AUSTRALIA

Lake Eyre

Marree

Bourke

Walgett

1615
Round
Mt.

Meekatharra

AUSTRALIA

Leonora

Tarcoola

Flinders Range

Broken Hill

Darling

Cobar

Tamworth

NEW SOUTH

Dubbo

Taree

Geraldton

Murchison

Lake
Barlee

Kalgoorlie-
Boulder

Deakin

Penong

Port Augusta

Whyalla

Port Pirie

WALES

Orange

Newcastle

Bathurst

SYDNEY

Perth

Northam

Norseman

Nullarbor Plain

Port Lincoln

Spencer Gulf

Adelaide

Murray

Mildura

Wagga Wagga

Albury

Murray

Mt.
Kosciuszko
2237

CAPITAL TERRITORY

Canberra

Wollongong
Shellharbour

Bunbury

Esperance

Great Australian Bight

Kangaroo I.

Encounter B.

5632

Horsham

Shepparton

Australian

Alps

Bombala

C. Howe

C. Leeuwin
Augusta

Albany

Bendigo

VICTORIA

Ballarat

MELBOURNE

Geelong

Mount Gambier

Warrnambool

King I.

Bass Strait

Furneaux Group

INDIAN OCEAN

Burnie

Launceston

1617
Mt. Ossa

TASMANIA

Hobart

S.E. Cape

Darling Range

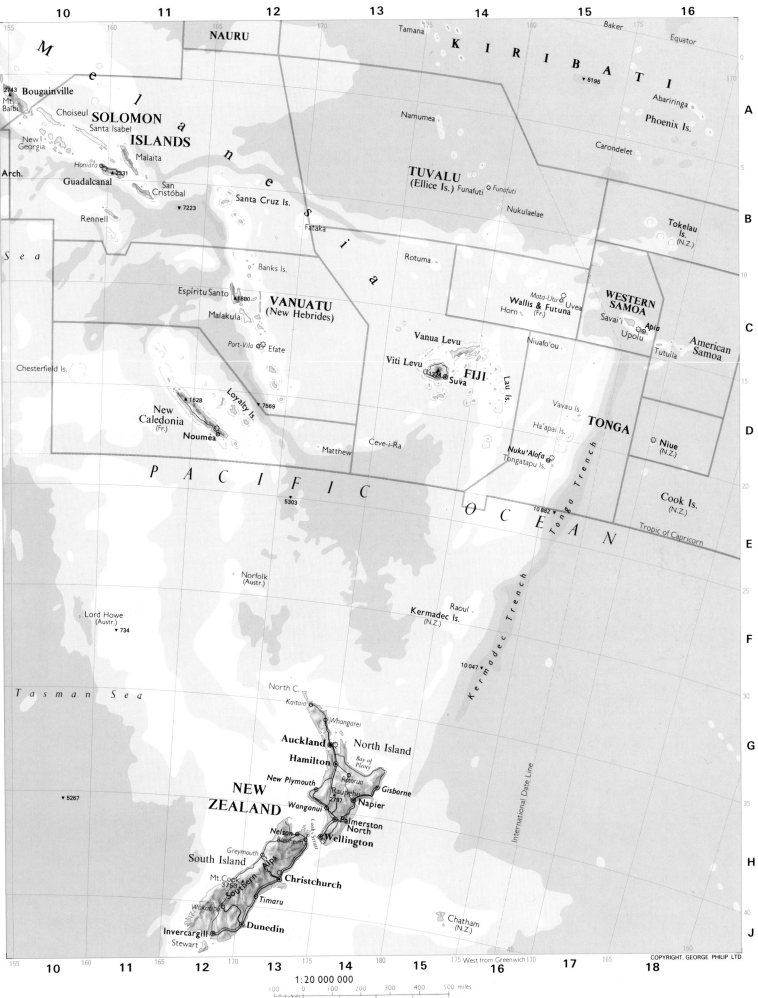

M e l a n e s i a

NAURU

Tamana

K I R I B A T I

Baker

Equator

2743 Mt. Balbi
Bougainville

Choiseul

Santa Isabel

SOLOMON
ISLANDS

New Georgia

Malaita

Honiara ⊙ ▲2331
Guadalcanal

San Cristóbal

Rennell

Arch.

Sea

Santa Cruz Is.

▼ 7223

Fataka

▼ 6195

Namumea

Abariringa

Phoenix Is.

Carondelet

TUVALU
(Ellice Is.) Funafuti ⊙ Funafuti

Nukulaelae

Tokelau Is.
(N.Z.)

Rotuma.

Banks Is.

Espíritu Santo ▲1880
VANUATU
(New Hebrides)

Malakula

Port-Vila ⊙ Efate

Vanua Levu

Mata-Utu ⊙ Uvea
Wallis & Futuna
Horn (Fr.)

WESTERN
SAMOA

Savai'i ⊙ Apia
Upolu

American
Samoa

Niuafo'ou

Tutuila

Chesterfield Is.

Loyalty Is.
▲1628 ▼ 7569

New Caledonia
(Fr.)

Nouméa

Matthew

Ceve-i-Ra

Viti Levu
▲1324
Suva

Vanua Levu

FIJI

Lau Is.

Vavau Is.

Ha'apai Is.

TONGA

Niue
(N.Z.)

P A C I F I C

▼ 5303

Nuku'Alofa
Tongatapu Is.

Tonga Trench

O C E A N

▼ 10 882

Cook Is.
(N.Z.)

Tropic of Capricorn

Norfolk
(Austr.)

Raoul

Kermadec Is.
(N.Z.)

Kermadec Trench

Lord Howe
(Austr.)
▼ 734

▼ 10 047

International Date Line

Tasman Sea

North C.

Kaitaia

Whangarei

Auckland

North Island

Bay of Plenty

Hamilton

New Plymouth

Rotorua

Gisborne

▼ 5267

NEW
ZEALAND

Wanganui

Ruapehu
2797
Napier

Palmerston
North

Nelson
Blenheim

Wellington

Cook Strait

Greymouth

Southern Alps

South Island

Mt.Cook
3753

Christchurch

Wakatipu

Timaru

Chatham
(N.Z.)

Invercargill
Stewart

Dunedin

COPYRIGHT. GEORGE PHILIP LTD.

1:20 000 000

100   0   100   200   300   400   500 miles

100   0   200   400   600   800 km

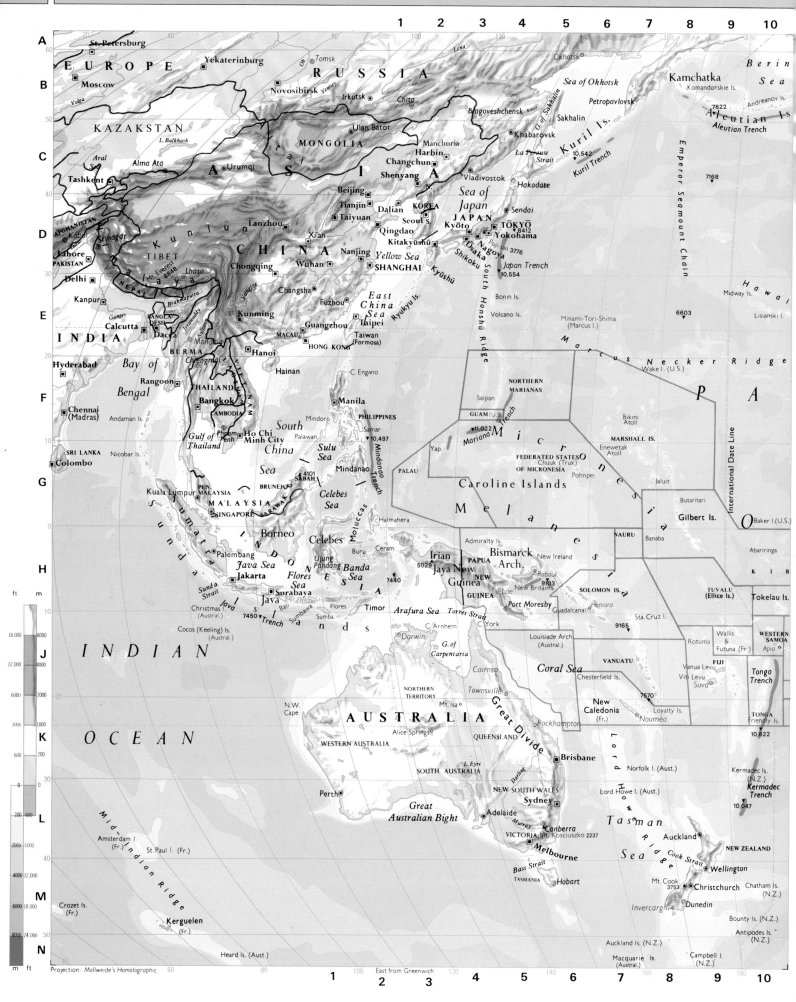

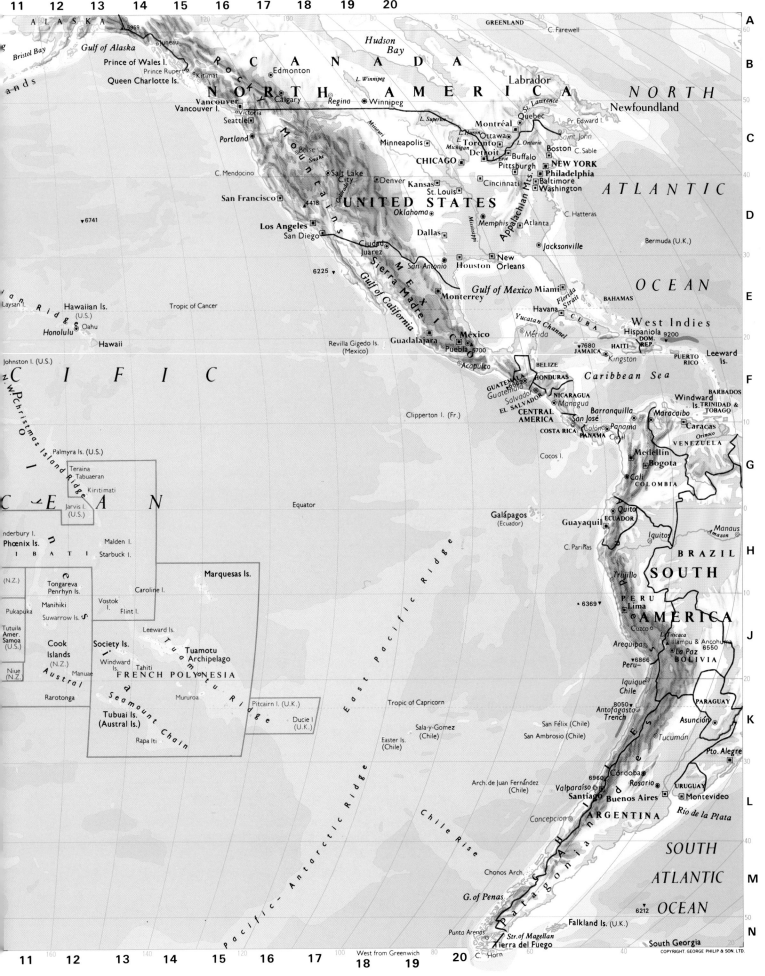

1:54 000 000

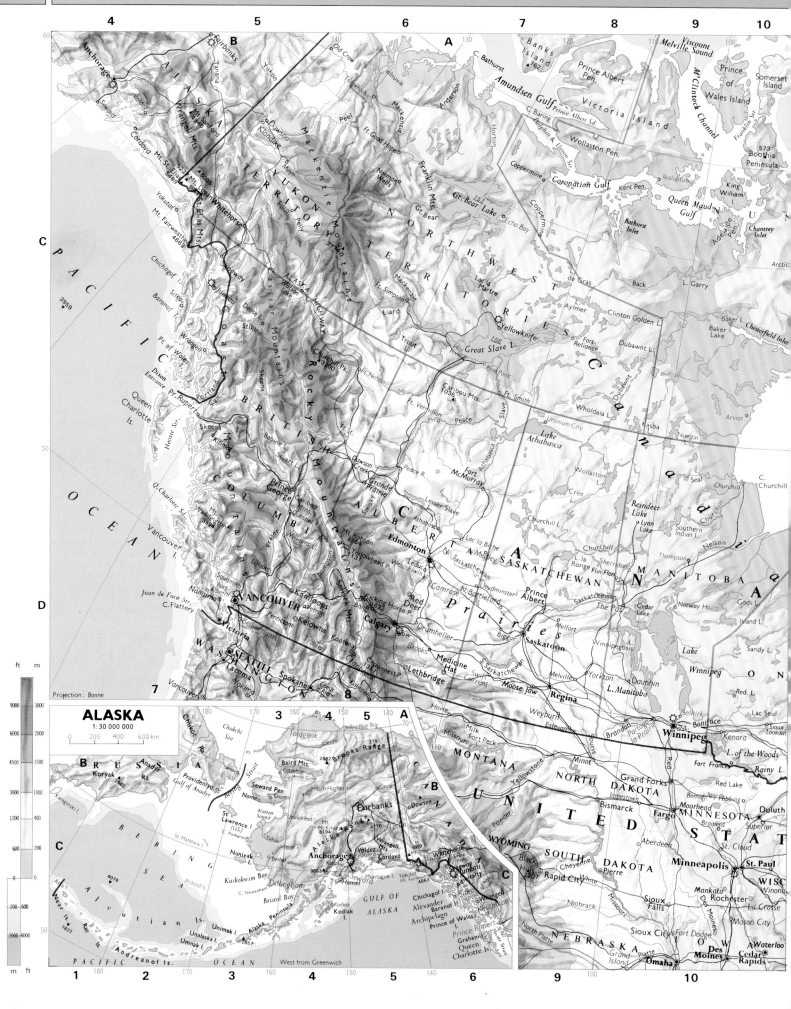

ALASKA
1:30 000 000
0 200 400 600 km

Projection: Bonne

11   12   13   14   15   16

A

B

C

D

E

Devon Island
Lancaster Sound

2134
Bylot I.
Pond Inlet

*Brodeur
Peninsula*

*Gulf
of
Boothia*

Baffin Bay

2136

*Svartenhuk
Peninsula*

Angmagssalik

**G R E E N L A N D
(KALAALLIT NUNAAT)**

King Frederick VI Coast

*Sondre
Stromfjord*

C. Hewett

Disko I.

Davis Strait

C. Dyer

*Godthaab
(Nuuk)*

Frederikshaab

Sydproven

Julianehaab

Sydproven

C. Farewell

Fury & Hecla Str.

Melville
Peninsula

V
U   T   Prince
Charles
I.

Foxe
Basin

Nettilling
L.

Committee B.

C. Dorchester

Foxe
Penin.

*Amadjuak
L.*

iqaluit

269

Cumberland
Peninsula

C. Mercy

Cumberland Sd.

Circle

Foxe
Channel

*Wager
B.*

Roes Welcome Sd.

Southampton
I.

glugligaarjuk

Coats
I.

Mansel
I.

Ivujivik

Kangiqsujuaq

Amaud

Kangirsuk

Akpatok
I.

Frobisher Bay

Resolution I.

H u d s o n   S t r a i t

C. Chidley

Quaqtaq

C. Dorchester

H u d s o n

Ottawa
Is.

258

B a y

Inukjuak

King George Is.

Belcher
Is.

C. Henrietta
Maria

James Bay

Akimiski
I.

Chisasibi

*Ungava
Peninsula*

Ungava Bay

1676

Kangiqsualujjuaq

Feuilles

George

Koksoak

L. Minto

Kaniapiskau

Lac Bienville

L. Bienville

Scheffervile
Petitsikapau
L.

Kaniapiskau

Nain

Hopedale

C. Harrison

Indian Harbour

Rigolet
L. Melville
Cartwright

Michikamau
L.

*Happy Valley-
Goose Bay*

Churchill

Battle Harb.

3809

A T L A N T I C

N E W

L a b r a d o r

F

O

U

N

D

L

A

N

D

Str. of Belle Isle

Gander

Grand
Falls

Bonavista

Carbonear

St. John's

C. Race

Newfoundland

Corner
Brook

Channel-Port
aux Basques

Q   U   E   B   E   C

A   S   h   i   e   l   d

1128
Gagnon

Severn

Winisk

Big
Trout L.

Attawapiskat

Albany

Moosonee

Missinaibi

Waskaganish

Rupert
L.

Mistassini
L.

Eastmain

Harricanaw

Chibougamau

Gouin
Reservoir

L.
St. John

Saguenay

Manicouagan

Baie Comeau

Sept Iles

Port-Cartier

St. Lawrence

R. St. Lawrence

Matane

Rimouski

Campbellton

Bathurst

Chatham

Mingan

Anticosti
I.

Natashquan

Corner
Brook

814

Z

Ray

Cabot Str.

**PR. EDWARD
I.**

Summerside

Charlottetown

D

O

N

*Gulf of
St. Lawrence*

Cape Breton I.

Glace Bay

Sydney

**ST. PIERRE
& MIQUELON**
(Fr.)

**N E W
BRUNSWICK**

Moncton

Amherst

Truro

New Glasgow

N O V A

Dartmouth

Halifax

Bridgewater

6309

O

C

E

A

N

Hearst

Geraldton

Oba

Timmins

Kirkland Lake

Rouyn

Val d'Or

La Tuque

Shawinigan

Trois Rivieres

1190

Quebec

Thetford Mines

St-Hyacinthe

Montreal

Sherbrooke

MAINE

Bangor

Fredericton

**Saint
John**

Kentville

B. of Fundy

C. Sable

Yarmouth

*Sable I.
(Nova Scotia)*

Thunder Bay

Lake Superior

Marquette

Sault Ste.
Marie

Sault Ste. Marie

Sudbury

North
Bay

Georgian
Bay

Lake
Huron

Peterboro.

Orillia

Owen Sound

Cornwall

Kingston

L. Champlain

Burlington

1917

VERMONT

**NEW
HAMPSHIRE**

Concord

Manchester

Portland

Lewiston

Cabonga
Reservoir

Hull

Ottawa R.

Ottawa

L. Ontario

Oshawa

TORONTO

Hamilton

Niagara
Falls

Rochester

Syracuse

Springfield

Albany

NEW YORK

Binghamton

Scranton

New Haven

**NEW
YORK**

MASS.

BOSTON

C. Cod

Providence

CONN.

R.I.

MILWAUKEE

Madison

Rockford

CHICAGO

ILLINOIS

Gary

INDIANA

Wausau

Green
Bay

Appleton

ONSIN

Saginaw

**Grand
Rapids**

London

Sarnia

DETROIT

Windsor

Toledo

Erie

CLEVELAND

Akron

OHIO

PENNSYLVANIA

Allentown

NEW JERSEY

Newark

Kitchener

Traverse
City

Lake Michigan

WIS

ES

MICH

TARIO

L. St. Joseph

L.
Nipigon

Nipigon

West from Greenwich

COPYRIGHT. GEORGE PHILIP & SON. LTD.

1:15 000 000

100   0   100   200   300   400 miles

100   0   100   200   300   400   500   600 km

11   12   13   14

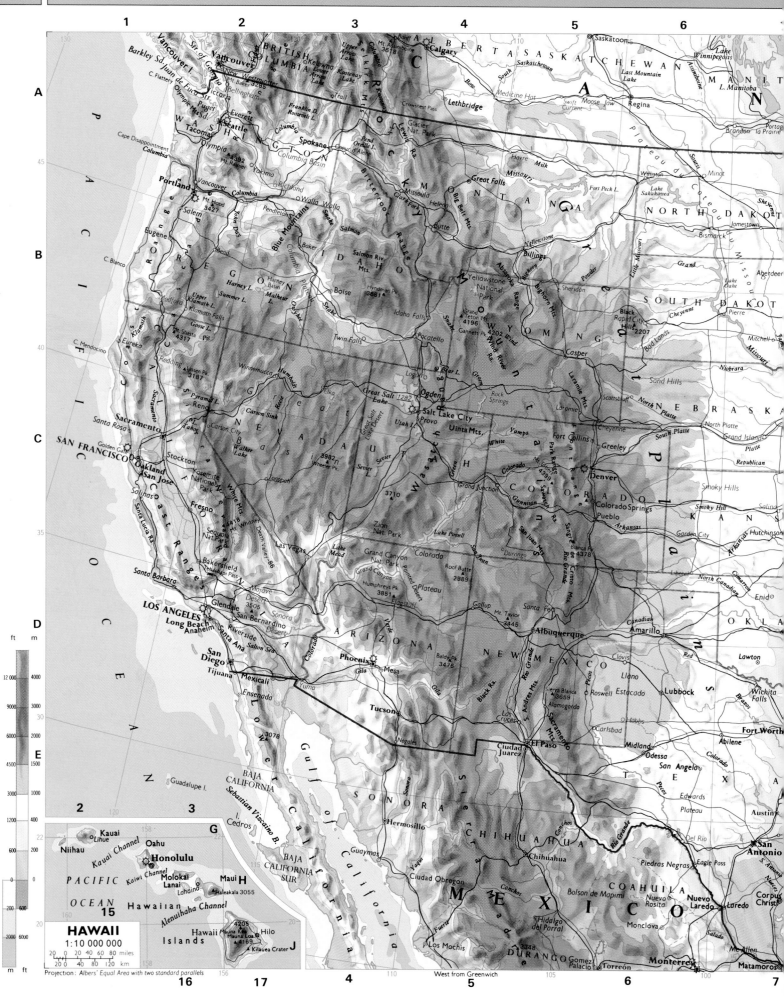

HAWAII
1:10 000 000

Projection: Albers' Equal Area with two standard parallels

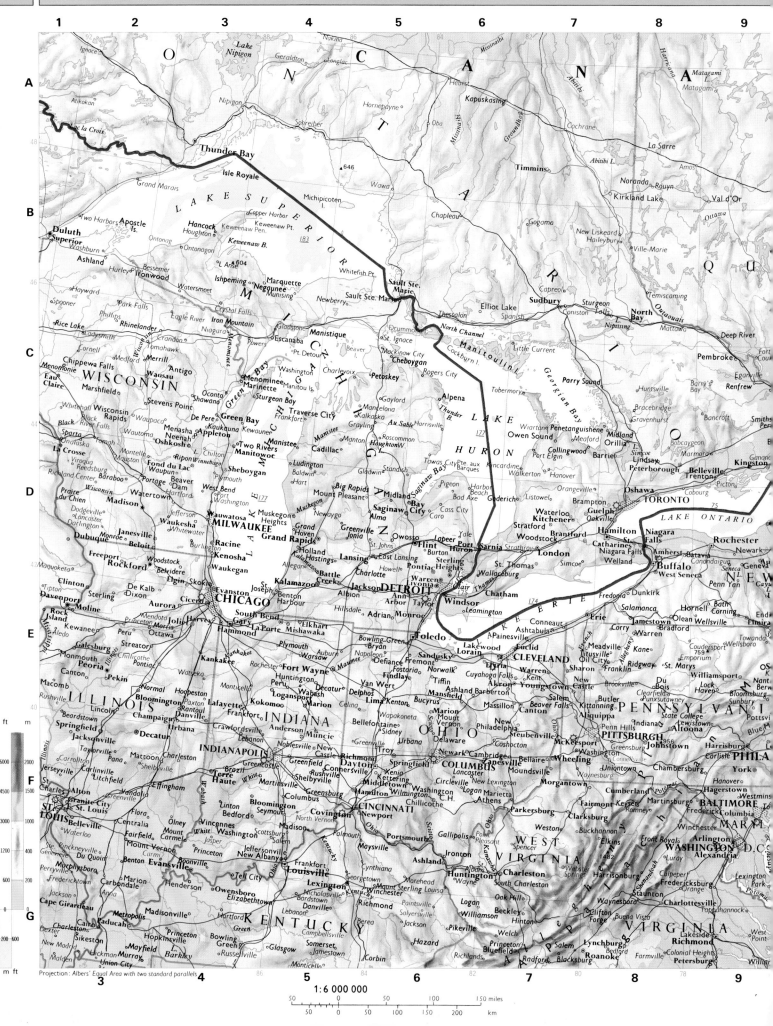

D A

556 Chibougamau
Chibougamau L.

Gouin
Res.

Pipmuacan L.

Port-Cartier

Anticosti I.

Jupiter

West Pt.

Heath Pt.

A

Peribonca

Dolbeau

St-Félicien
Roberval

Lac
St. Jean

Chicoutimi
Saguenay

Jonquière

St. Lawrence

Cap Chat

Matane

1310

Shickshock Mts.

Gaspé Peninsula

Gaspé
C. Gaspé

GULF OF

ST. LAWRENCE

▼572

48

Rimouski

Dalhousie

Chaleur Bay

Campbellton

Bathurst

Magdalen
Is.
(Quebec)

C. North

La Tuque

Rivière du Loup

Edmundston

819

NEW

Newcastle
Chatham

Miramichi B.

North Pt.
Tignish

PRINCE EDWARD
ISLAND

C. North

Cape Breton
Island

532

B

Grand-Mère
Shawinigan
Cap-de-la-Madeleine
Trois-Rivières
Louiseville

Quebec
Lévis

Île d'Orléans
Montmagny

Fort
Kent Van
Eagle Buren
Lake Caribou

Grand
Falls

BRUNSWICK

Chipman

Summerside

Northumberland Str.

Charlottetown

East Pt.

Glace Bay

Sydney

Bras d'Or
L.

Chedabucto B.

B

L'Annonciation

Res.
Baskatong

968

Plessisville

St-George

Ste-Marie

Presque Isle

St. John Allagash

Eagle L.
Chamberlain
L.

Chesuncook
L.

1605

St. John

Houlton

Grand L.

Moncton

Sackville

Springhill
Stellarton

New Glasgow

Truro

Canso

NOVA SCOTIA

C

Joliette

Sorel

Victoriaville

Thetford
Mines

Drummondville
Asbestos

Lac
Mégantic

Mt. Katahdin

Patten

Chipurneticook
Lakes

Fredericton

Sussex

Kentville

Dartmouth

St-Jérôme

St-
Hyacinthe

Mooshead
L.

Millinocket

Saint
John

C

Hawkesbury

Ottawa

MONTREAL
Lachine

Granby

Sherbrooke

Magog

Greenville

Mattawamkeag
Lincoln

St. Stephen

Bay of Fundy

Digby

Bridgewater

Halifax

Ottawa

St-Jean
Beauharnois

Coaticook
Colebrook

Richardson
Lakes

Dover
Foxcroft

Calais

East-port

Rossignol Res.

Cornwall

Cowansville

MAINE

Old Town
Brewer

Machias

Grand
Manan I.

Shelburne

Malone
Plattsburg

Newport
St. Albans

Island Pond

Rangeley

Bangor
Skowhegan

Ellsworth

C. Sable

D

Massena
Ogdensburg
Potsdam
Canton

Champlain
L.

Winooski

Farmington

Waterville
Augusta

Belfast

Bar
Harbor

Mt. Desert
I.

Yarmouth

Saranac Lakes
Gouverneur

Burlington

Montpelier

Johnsbury

Berlin

Mt.
Washington
1917

Rumford

Gardiner

Rockland

Penobscot B.

Watertown

Lowell

Adirondack Mts.
1629

Barre

VERMONT

Lancaster

Conway

Lewiston
Auburn
Brunswick

Bath

44

Lake Pleasant

Middlebury

White
Mts.

NEW HAMPSHIRE

Portland

38

Rome
Utica

Gloversville

Rutland

Glens
Falls

Granville
Springfield

Hudson
Falls

Claremont

Concord

Westbrook

Saco
Biddeford

Oneida
Syracuse

Amsterdam

Saratoga Springs

Keene

Manchester

Laconia
Franklin

Rochester

York

Schenectady

Albany
Troy

Greenfield

Fitchburg
Leominster

Nashua

Haverhill
Lawrence
Lowell

Dover

Portsmouth

42

Norwich

Pittsfield

Northampton
Chicopee
Springfield

MASS.

Salem

C. Ann

Cortland
Johnson City
Binghamton

Oneonta

Catskill

Catskill
Mts.

1281

Worcester

Cambridge
Quincy

BOSTON

Brockton

Cape Cod

Kingston

Hudson

Hartford
New Britain

Woonsocket
Pawtucket
Providence
Warwick

Taunton
Fall River
New
Bedford

Martha's
Vineyard

Nantucket

Carbondale
Dunmore

Poughkeepsie
Newburgh
Beacon

Waterbury
Danbury

CONN.

Meriden
New
Haven

Newport

Block I.

E

Wilkes-
Barre

Middletown

New London

YORK

Delaware

Stamford

Hazelton

Paterson

Yonkers

Mount
Vernon

Long Island

Riverhead

Easton
Bethlehem

Jersey City
Newark
Elizabeth

NEW YORK

Reading

Pottstown

New Brunswick

Long Branch

Asbury Park

40

PHIA

Trenton

Norristown

NEW
JERSEY

Camden
Chester
Wilmington

Hammonton
Vineland

Millville
Bridgeton

Atlantic City
Ocean City

ATLANTIC

F

Dover

Cape May
Henlopen

DELAWARE

38

Cambridge
Salisbury

OCEAN

Snow Hill

G

Accomac

Cape Charles
C. Charles

76 74 West from Greenwich 72 70

Inset map

14 15 16 17

D

GREENLAND
(Denmark)

ICELAND

ALASKA
(USA)

Arctic Circle

Godthåb

60

Anchorage

CANADA

E

Vancouver

Seattle

Edmonton

Winnipeg

Ottawa
Montréal

Toronto

Boston

50

San Francisco

CHICAGO

Detroit

NEW YORK
PHILADELPHIA

Washington D.C.

40

LOS ANGELES

Denver

St. Louis

UNITED STATES

Atlanta

Bermuda
(U.K.)

30

Houston

New
Orleans

Tropic of Cancer

MEXICO

Monterrey

Miami

BAHAMAS

Havana CUBA

DOMINICAN
REP.

PUERTO
RICO

Guadalajara

JAMAICA
Kingston

HAITI

MEXICO

BELIZE

GUATEMALA
Guatemala
EL SALVADOR

HONDURAS

NICARAGUA

COSTA RICA

PANAMÁ
Panamá

NORTH AMERICA
Political 1 : 70 000 000

PANAMA CANAL
1:1 000 000
0   10   20 km

JAMAICA
1:5 000 000
0   50 km

TRINIDAD AND TOBAGO
1:5 000 000
0   50 km

LEEWARD ISLANDS
1:5 000 000
0   50 km

WINDWARD ISLANDS
1:5 000 000
0   50 km

Projection: Bonne

8 9 10 11 12 13

A

Columbus C. Fear

Atlanta *Augusta*
Macon *Charleston*
umbus
hany **Savannah**

30

B

ATLANTIC OCEAN

Jacksonville

Daytona Beach

Orlando C. Canaveral

Tampa *West Palm Beach*
ersburg **Grand Bahama I.** 25

L. Okeechobee *Freeport* Gt. Abaco I.
Miami *Fort Lauderdale* New Providence I.

C. Sable *Nassau* Cat I. C
Key West **BAHAMAS** S. Salvador Tropic of Cancer

Florida Andros I. Long I.

Havana *Matanzas* Mayaguana
io *Cárdenas* Acklins Turks & Caicos Is.
C U *Sta. Clara* I. (U.K.) 20
Cienfuegos B **Camagüey** Gt. Inagua I.
I. de Juventud *Sancti Spíritus* *Morón* PUERTO RICO (U.S.A.)
G R *Ciego de Ávila* Holguín Santiago San Francisco St. Thomas (U.S.A.)
Manzanillo de Macorís Charlotte Amalie
Santiago 2000 Cap Haitien **San Juan** Virgin Is.(U.K.) D
Grand Cayman E *Bayamo* de Cuba *Gonaïves* 1338 Anguilla St. Martin (Fr. & Neth.)
(U.K.) A T DOMINICAN La Romana **Ponce** St. Croix ST. KITTS-NEVIS
Montego Bay R **Santiago** 175 REP. Mayagüez (U.S.A.) ANTIGUA &
JAMAICA **Kingston** Les Cayes 2280 Santo Domingo St. John's BARBUDA
A **Port au Prince** Barahona Hispaniola Montserrat (U.K.) Guadeloupe (Fr.)
N T I L L E S Pointe à Pitre
LESSER Leeward Islands DOMINICA 15

Caratasca Lagoon C A R I B B E A N   S E A ANTILLES Martinique (Fr.)
C. Gracias á Dios Windward Fort de France E
Providencia Pta. Gallinas Gulf of Venezuela ST. VINCENT ST. LUCIA
(Col.) Aruba (Neth.) Curaçao & BARBADOS
San Andrés Pen. de la Willemstad THE GRENADINES Bridgetown
(Col.) Guajira Bonaire Islands GRENADA
Bluefields **Barranquilla** Pen. de NETH. La Blanquilla Tobago
Santa Marta Paraguaná ANTILLES (Ven.) Margarita Port of Spain
Punto Coro Carúpano TRINIDAD & TOBAGO
Limón Fijo La Tortuga **Cumaná** G. of San Fernando
Cartagena 5800 (Ven.) Barcelona Paria Delta of the
Colón Sierra Nevada **Maracaibo** **Caracas** Maturín Orinoco
Vol. Barú de Santa Marta L. de **Maracay** El Tigre
3837 **Panama** Cabimas **Valencia** **Barquisimeto** Ciudad
David G. of Maracaibo Guayana
Azuero Darién **Mérida** Barinas Ciudad **Georgetown**
Coiba Pen. 5007 Bolívar New
G. of Sincelejo **Cúcuta** Apure Orinoco Amsterdam
Panama Atrato 4100 San Fernando Caura
Barrancabermeja **San Cristóbal** de Apure Angel
Rica 3980 Arauca Arauca Falls
Cauca **Bucaramanga** VENEZUELA 2560 Roraima
Quibdó Meta Pto. Ayacucho 2810
Medellín 2285
Manizales Tunja Caroní
COLOMBIA Sierra Pacaraima
Pereira **Bogotá** Caura
Armenia Tolima 5215 Sa. Parima
Girardot Guaviare
Buenaventura Casiquiare
Cali 2750 G
Popayán
4646 BRAZIL

West from Greenwich COPYRIGHT. GEORGE PHILIP & SON. LTD.

1:15 000 000

100   0   100   200   300   400 miles
100   0 100 200 300 400 500 600 km

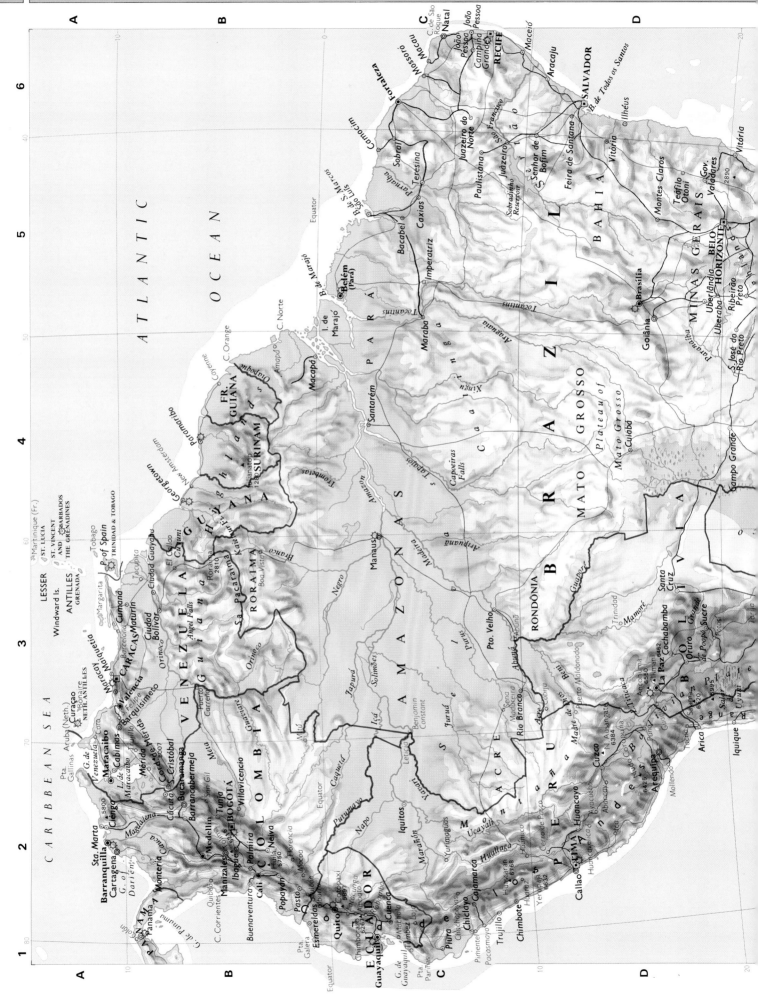

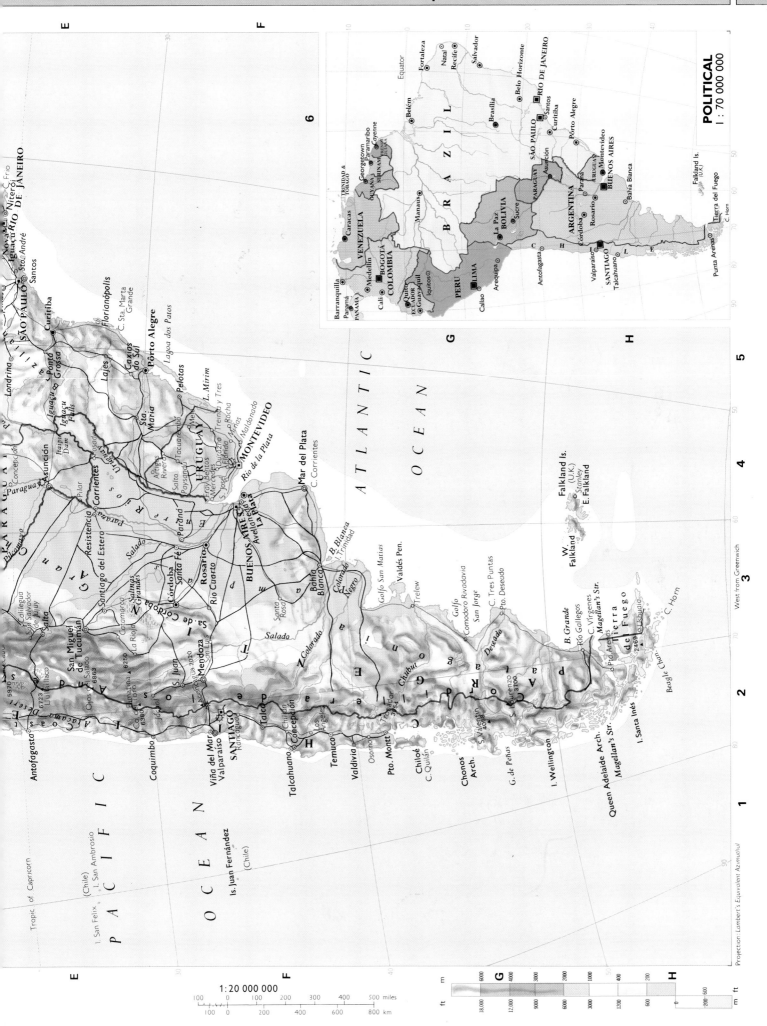

POLITICAL
1 : 70 000 000

1:20 000 000

1:20 000 000

100   0   100   200   300   400   500 miles
100   0   200   400   600   800 km

Projection: Lambert's Equivalent Azimuthal

West from Greenwich

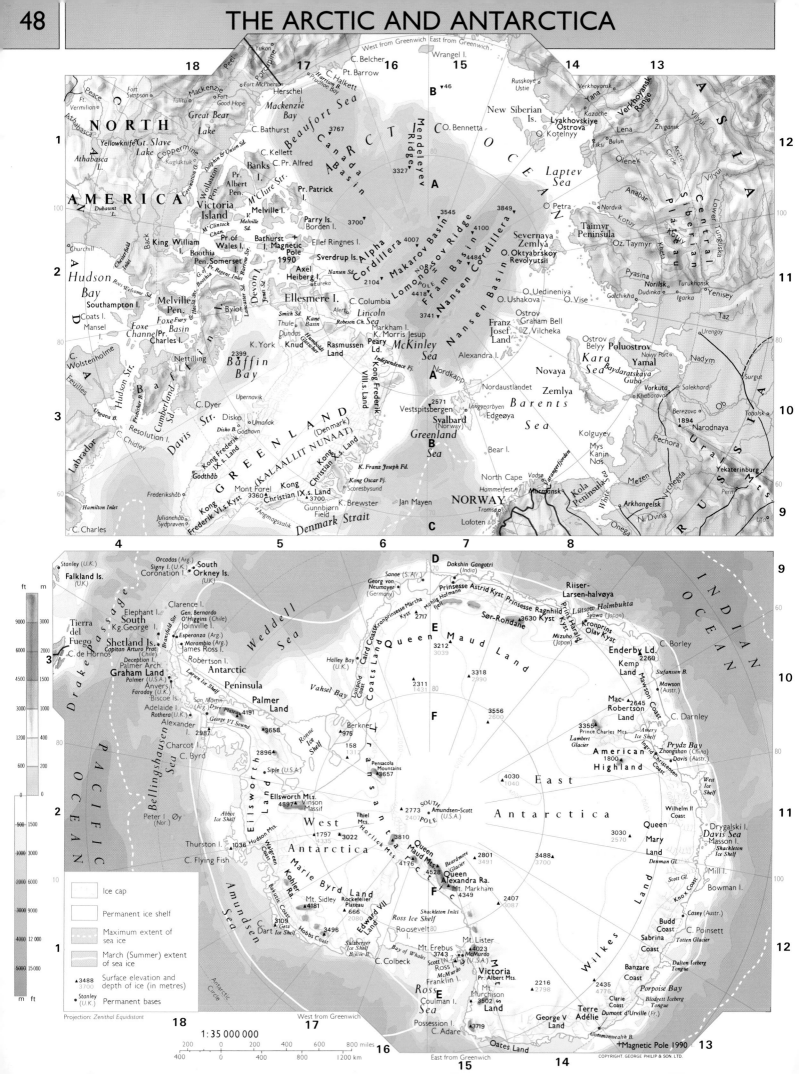

WORLD THEMATIC MAPS

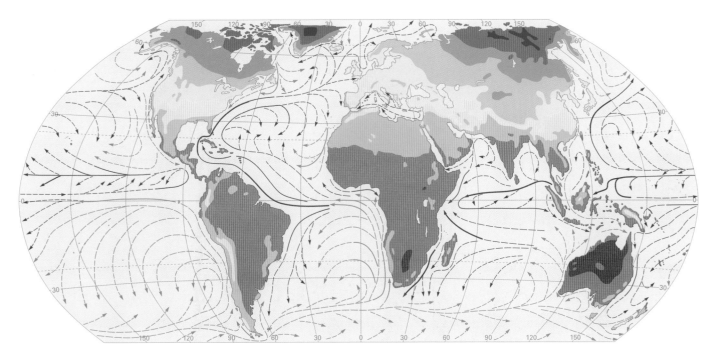

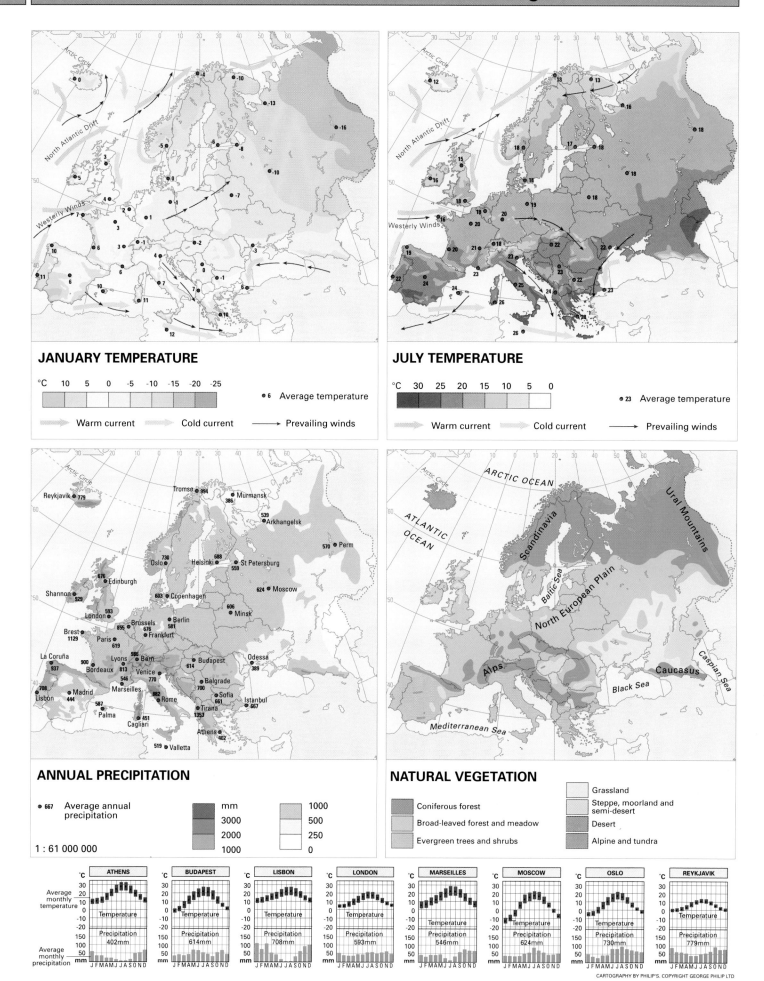

JANUARY TEMPERATURE

°C 10 5 0 -5 -10 -15 -20 -25

● 6 Average temperature

Warm current   Cold current   → Prevailing winds

JULY TEMPERATURE

°C 30 25 20 15 10 5 0

● 23 Average temperature

Warm current   Cold current   → Prevailing winds

ANNUAL PRECIPITATION

● 667 Average annual precipitation

1 : 61 000 000

mm	
3000	1000
2000	500
1000	250
	0

NATURAL VEGETATION

Coniferous forest

Broad-leaved forest and meadow

Evergreen trees and shrubs

Grassland

Steppe, moorland and semi-desert

Desert

Alpine and tundra

CARTOGRAPHY BY PHILIP'S. COPYRIGHT GEORGE PHILIP LTD

Climate graphs: ATHENS (Precipitation 402mm), BUDAPEST (Precipitation 614mm), LISBON (Precipitation 708mm), LONDON (Precipitation 593mm), MARSEILLES (Precipitation 546mm), MOSCOW (Precipitation 624mm), OSLO (Precipitation 730mm), REYKJAVIK (Precipitation 779mm)

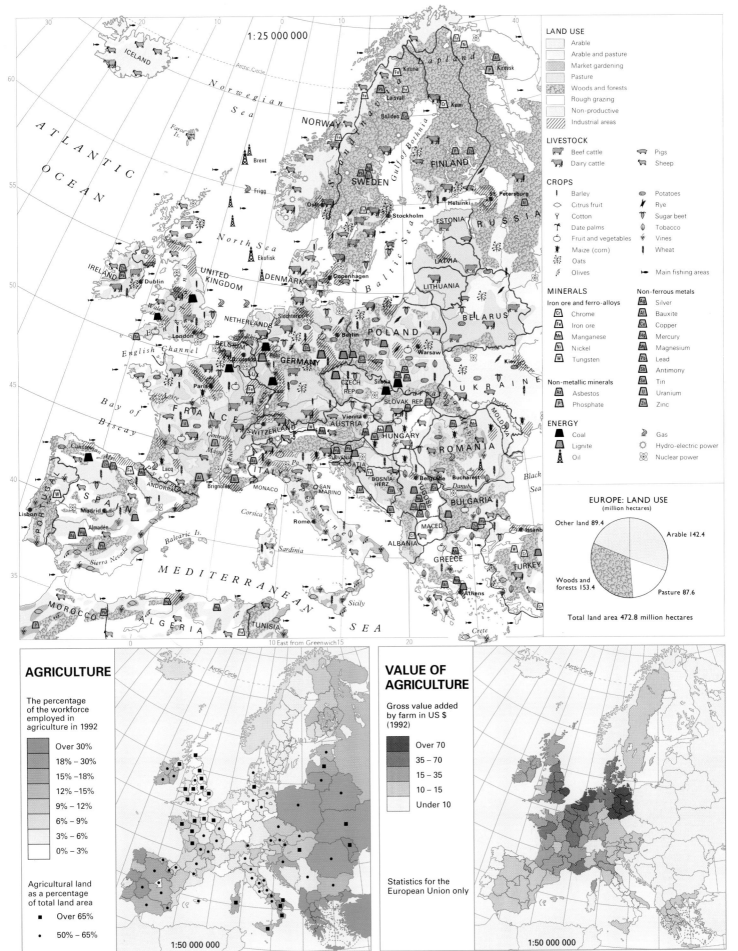

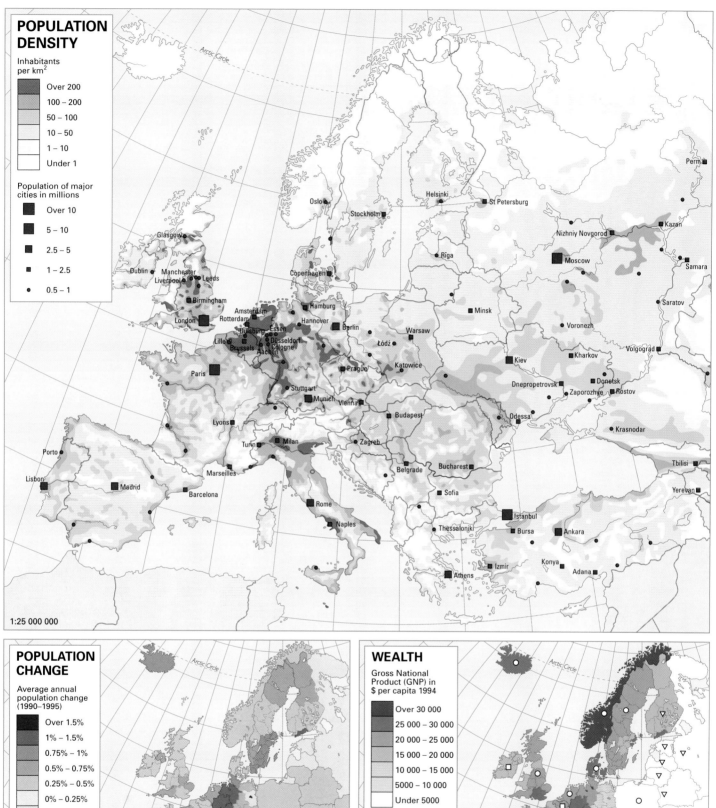

POPULATION DENSITY

Inhabitants per km²

- Over 200
- 100 – 200
- 50 – 100
- 10 – 50
- 1 – 10
- Under 1

Population of major cities in millions

- Over 10
- 5 – 10
- 2.5 – 5
- 1 – 2.5
- 0.5 – 1

1:25 000 000

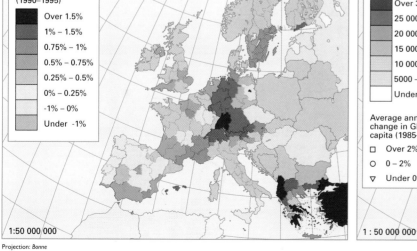

POPULATION CHANGE

Average annual population change (1990–1995)

- Over 1.5%
- 1% – 1.5%
- 0.75% – 1%
- 0.5% – 0.75%
- 0.25% – 0.5%
- 0% – 0.25%
- -1% – 0%
- Under -1%

1:50 000 000

WEALTH

Gross National Product (GNP) in $ per capita 1994

- Over 30 000
- 25 000 – 30 000
- 20 000 – 25 000
- 15 000 – 20 000
- 10 000 – 15 000
- 5000 – 10 000
- Under 5000

Average annual change in GNP per capita (1985–1994)

- ☐ Over 2%
- ○ 0 – 2%
- ▽ Under 0%

1 : 50 000 000

Projection: *Bonne*

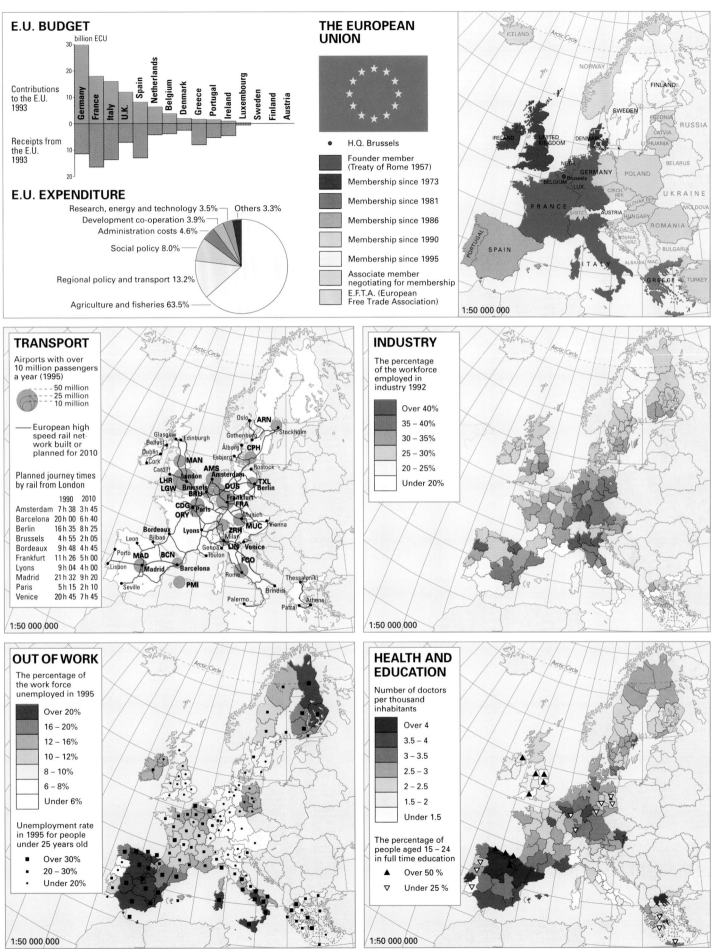

E.U. BUDGET

billion ECU

Contributions to the E.U. 1993

Receipts from the E.U. 1993

Germany France Italy U.K. Spain Netherlands Belgium Denmark Greece Portugal Ireland Luxembourg Sweden Finland Austria

E.U. EXPENDITURE

Research, energy and technology 3.5%
Others 3.3%
Development co-operation 3.9%
Administration costs 4.6%
Social policy 8.0%
Regional policy and transport 13.2%
Agriculture and fisheries 63.5%

THE EUROPEAN UNION

● H.Q. Brussels

Founder member (Treaty of Rome 1957)
Membership since 1973
Membership since 1981
Membership since 1986
Membership since 1990
Membership since 1995
Associate member negotiating for membership
E.F.T.A. (European Free Trade Association)

1:50 000 000

TRANSPORT

Airports with over 10 million passengers a year (1995)
- 50 million
- 25 million
- 10 million

European high speed rail network built or planned for 2010

Planned journey times by rail from London

	1990	2010
Amsterdam	7 h 38	3 h 45
Barcelona	20 h 00	6 h 40
Berlin	16 h 35	8 h 25
Brussels	4 h 55	2 h 05
Bordeaux	9 h 48	4 h 45
Frankfurt	11 h 26	5 h 00
Lyons	9 h 04	4 h 00
Madrid	21 h 32	9 h 20
Paris	5 h 15	2 h 10
Venice	20 h 45	7 h 45

1:50 000 000

INDUSTRY

The percentage of the workforce employed in industry 1992

Over 40%
35 – 40%
30 – 35%
25 – 30%
20 – 25%
Under 20%

1:50 000 000

OUT OF WORK

The percentage of the work force unemployed in 1995

Over 20%
16 – 20%
12 – 16%
10 – 12%
8 – 10%
6 – 8%
Under 6%

Unemployment rate in 1995 for people under 25 years old
■ Over 30%
■ 20 – 30%
● Under 20%

1:50 000 000

Projection: Bonne

HEALTH AND EDUCATION

Number of doctors per thousand inhabitants

Over 4
3.5 – 4
3 – 3.5
2.5 – 3
2 – 2.5
1.5 – 2
Under 1.5

The percentage of people aged 15 – 24 in full time education
▲ Over 50 %
▽ Under 25 %

1:50 000 000

CARTOGRAPHY BY PHILIP'S. COPYRIGHT GEORGE PHILIP LTD

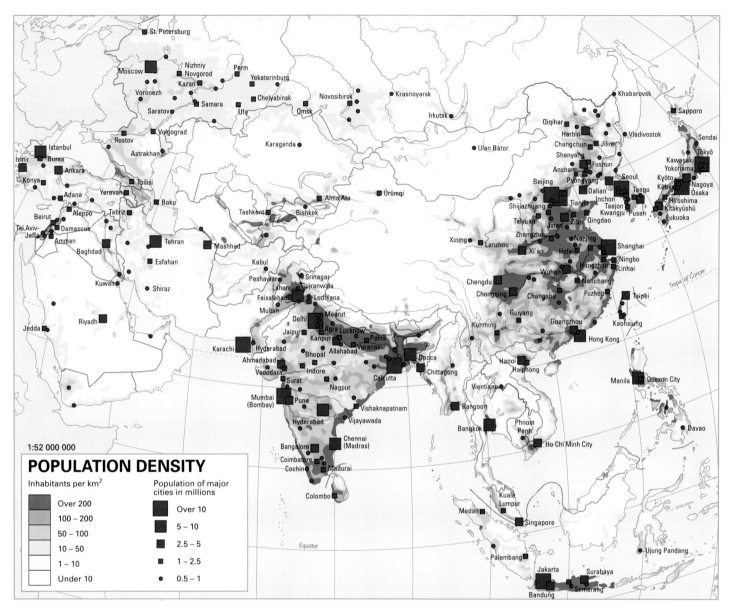

1:52 000 000

POPULATION DENSITY

Inhabitants per km²

- Over 200
- 100 – 200
- 50 – 100
- 10 – 50
- 1 – 10
- Under 10

Population of major cities in millions

- Over 10
- 5 – 10
- 2.5 – 5
- 1 – 2.5
- 0.5 – 1

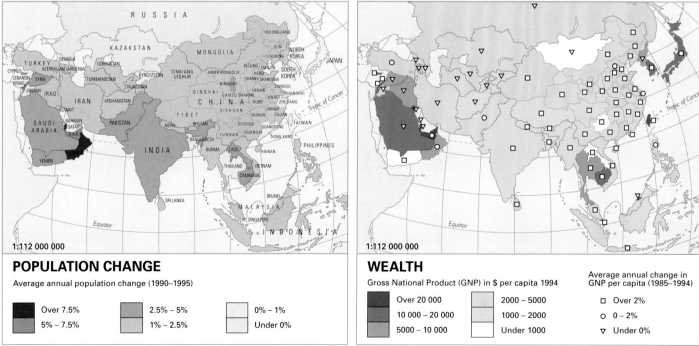

1:112 000 000

POPULATION CHANGE

Average annual population change (1990–1995)

- Over 7.5%
- 5% – 7.5%
- 2.5% – 5%
- 1% – 2.5%
- 0% – 1%
- Under 0%

1:112 000 000

WEALTH

Gross National Product (GNP) in $ per capita 1994

- Over 20 000
- 10 000 – 20 000
- 5000 – 10 000
- 2000 – 5000
- 1000 – 2000
- Under 1000

Average annual change in GNP per capita (1985–1994)

- □ Over 2%
- ○ 0 – 2%
- ▽ Under 0%

Projection: *Bonne*

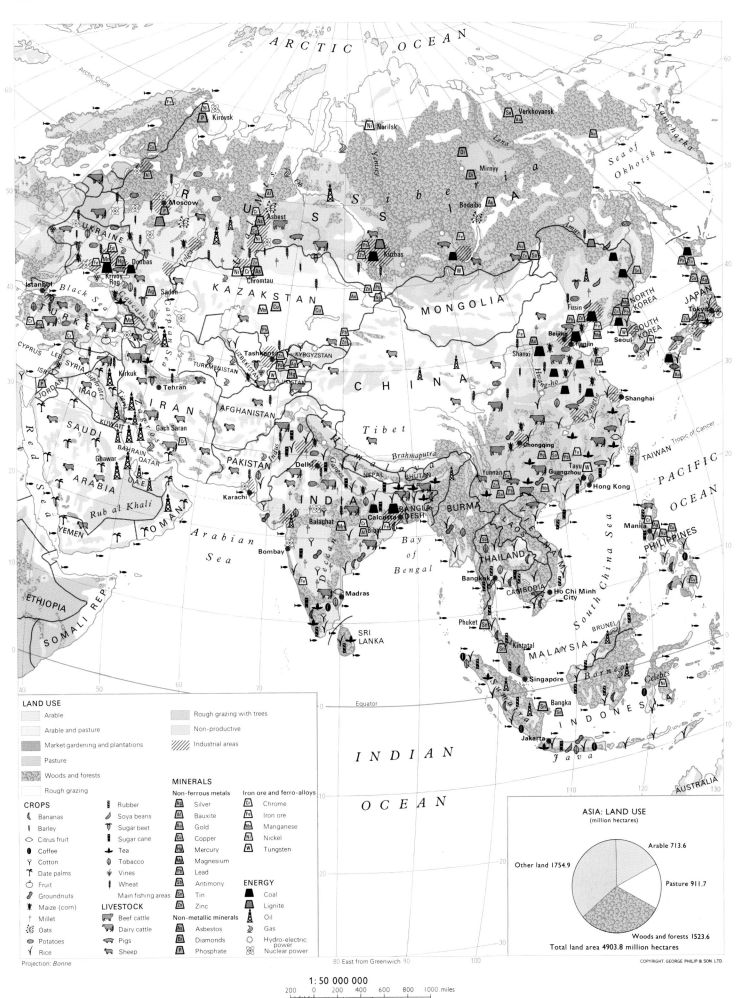

LAND USE

- Arable
- Arable and pasture
- Market gardening and plantations
- Pasture
- Woods and forests
- Rough grazing
- Rough grazing with trees
- Non-productive
- Industrial areas

CROPS

- Bananas
- Barley
- Citrus fruit
- Coffee
- Cotton
- Date palms
- Fruit
- Groundnuts
- Maize (corn)
- Millet
- Oats
- Potatoes
- Rice
- Rubber
- Soya beans
- Sugar beet
- Sugar cane
- Tea
- Tobacco
- Vines
- Wheat
- Main fishing areas

LIVESTOCK

- Beef cattle
- Dairy cattle
- Pigs
- Sheep

MINERALS

Non-ferrous metals

- Ag Silver
- Ba Bauxite
- Au Gold
- Cu Copper
- Hg Mercury
- Mg Magnesium
- Pb Lead
- Sb Antimony
- Sn Tin
- Zn Zinc

Non-metallic minerals

- As Asbestos
- Di Diamonds
- P Phosphate

Iron ore and ferro-alloys

- Cr Chrome
- Fe Iron ore
- Mn Manganese
- Ni Nickel
- W Tungsten

ENERGY

- Coal
- Lignite
- Oil
- Gas
- Hydro-electric power
- Nuclear power

ASIA: LAND USE
(million hectares)

Arable 713.6

Pasture 911.7

Other land 1754.9

Woods and forests 1523.6

Total land area 4903.8 million hectares

Projection: *Bonne*

80 East from Greenwich 90   100

COPYRIGHT. GEORGE PHILIP & SON. LTD

1: 50 000 000

200   0   200   400   600   800   1000 miles

200   0   400   800   1200   1600 km

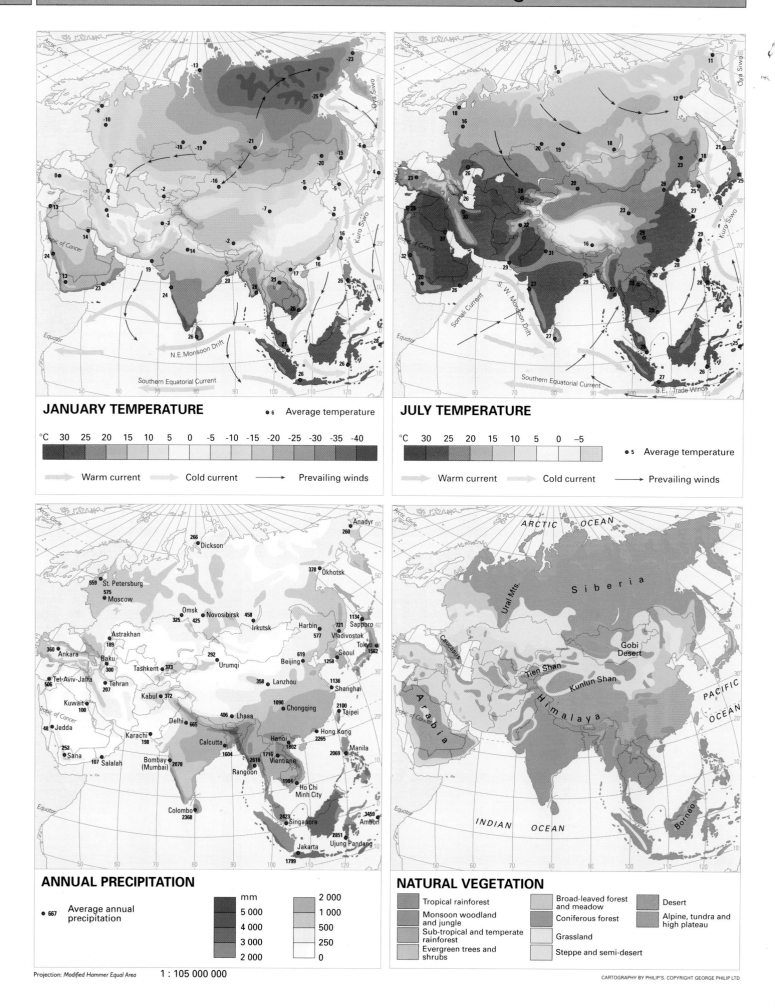

JANUARY TEMPERATURE

● 6 Average temperature

°C 30 25 20 15 10 5 0 -5 -10 -15 -20 -25 -30 -35 -40

➡ Warm current   ➡ Cold current   → Prevailing winds

JULY TEMPERATURE

°C 30 25 20 15 10 5 0 -5

● 5 Average temperature

➡ Warm current   ➡ Cold current   → Prevailing winds

ANNUAL PRECIPITATION

● 667 Average annual precipitation

mm	
5 000	2 000
4 000	1 000
3 000	500
2 000	250
	0

Projection: *Modified Hammer Equal Area*   1 : 105 000 000

NATURAL VEGETATION

- Tropical rainforest
- Monsoon woodland and jungle
- Sub-tropical and temperate rainforest
- Evergreen trees and shrubs
- Broad-leaved forest and meadow
- Coniferous forest
- Grassland
- Steppe and semi-desert
- Desert
- Alpine, tundra and high plateau

CARTOGRAPHY BY PHILIP'S. COPYRIGHT GEORGE PHILIP LTD

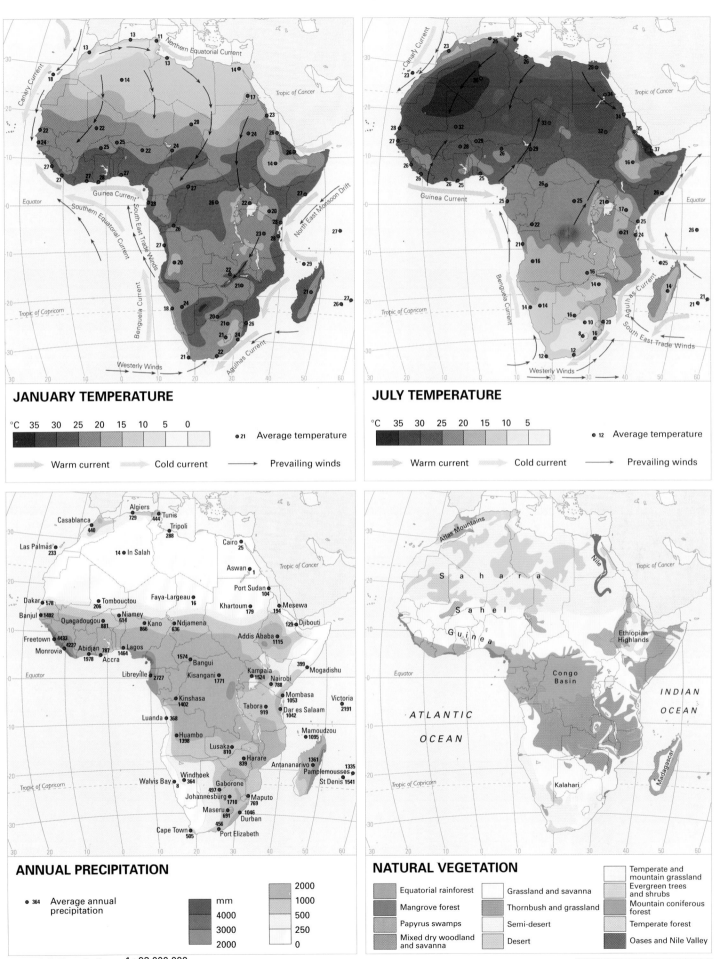

JANUARY TEMPERATURE

°C 35 30 25 20 15 10 5 0

● 21 Average temperature

Warm current Cold current → Prevailing winds

JULY TEMPERATURE

°C 35 30 25 20 15 10 5

● 12 Average temperature

Warm current Cold current → Prevailing winds

ANNUAL PRECIPITATION

● 364 Average annual precipitation

mm
2000
1000
500
250
0

4000
3000
2000

NATURAL VEGETATION

Equatorial rainforest
Mangrove forest
Papyrus swamps
Mixed dry woodland and savanna

Grassland and savanna
Thornbush and grassland
Semi-desert
Desert

Temperate and mountain grassland
Evergreen trees and shrubs
Mountain coniferous forest
Temperate forest
Oases and Nile Valley

Projection: *Modified Hammer Equal Area* 1 : 93 000 000

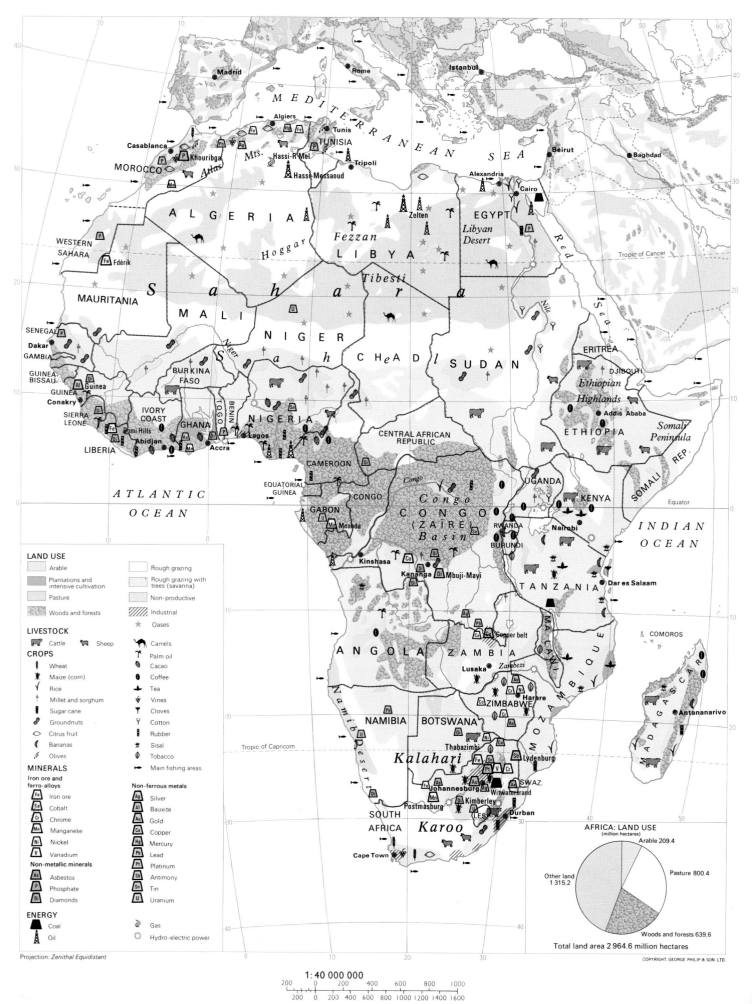

LAND USE
Arable
Plantations and intensive cultivation
Pasture
Woods and forests
Rough grazing
Rough grazing with trees (savanna)
Non-productive
Industrial
Oases

LIVESTOCK
Cattle
Sheep
Camels

CROPS
Wheat
Maize (corn)
Rice
Millet and sorghum
Sugar cane
Groundnuts
Citrus fruit
Bananas
Olives
Palm oil
Cacao
Coffee
Tea
Vines
Cloves
Cotton
Rubber
Sisal
Tobacco
Main fishing areas

MINERALS
Iron ore and ferro-alloys
Fe Iron ore
Co Cobalt
Cr Chrome
Mn Manganese
Ni Nickel
V Vanadium
Non-metallic minerals
As Asbestos
P Phosphate
Di Diamonds

Non-ferrous metals
Ag Silver
Al Bauxite
Au Gold
Cu Copper
Hg Mercury
Pb Lead
Pt Platinum
Sb Antimony
Sn Tin
U Uranium

ENERGY
Coal
Oil
Gas
Hydro-electric power

AFRICA: LAND USE
(million hectares)
Arable 209.4
Pasture 800.4
Woods and forests 639.6
Other land 1 315.2
Total land area 2 964.6 million hectares

Projection: _Zenithal Equidistant_

COPYRIGHT. GEORGE PHILIP & SON. LTD.

1:40 000 000
200 0 200 400 600 800 1000
200 0 200 400 600 800 1000 1200 1400 1600

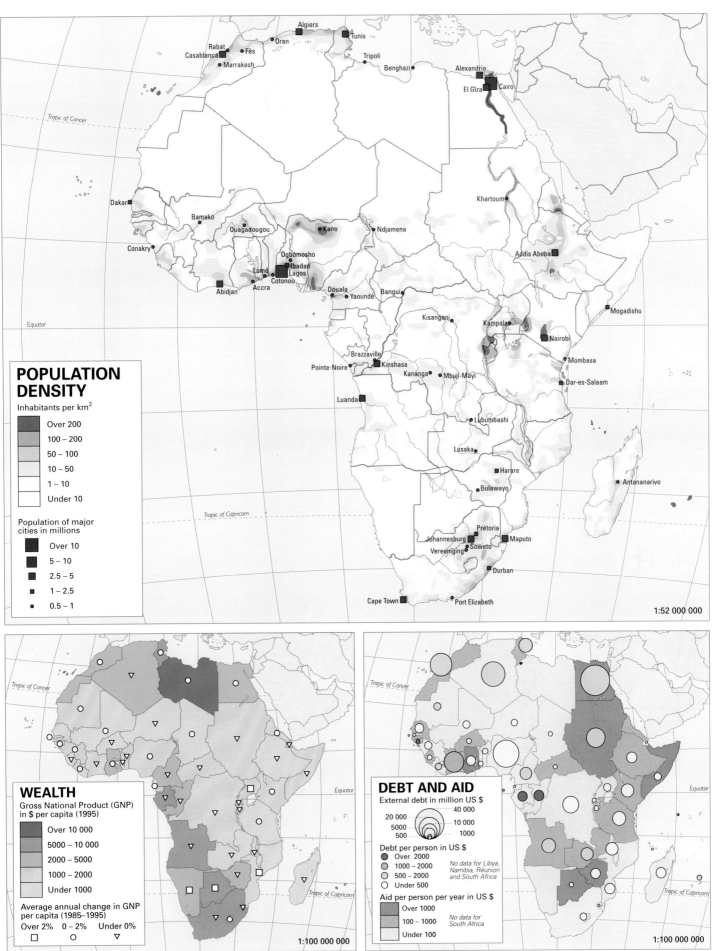

POPULATION DENSITY

Inhabitants per km²

- Over 200
- 100 – 200
- 50 – 100
- 10 – 50
- 1 – 10
- Under 10

Population of major cities in millions

- Over 10
- 5 – 10
- 2.5 – 5
- 1 – 2.5
- 0.5 – 1

1:52 000 000

Algiers
Rabat
Fès
Casablanca
Marrakesh
Oran
Tunis
Tripoli
Benghazi
Alexandria
El Gîza
Cairo
Tropic of Cancer
Dakar
Bamako
Khartoum
Ouagadougou
Kano
Ndjamena
Conakry
Ogbomosho
Addis Abeba
Lomé
Ibadan
Lagos
Cotonou
Abidjan
Accra
Douala
Yaoundé
Bangui
Mogadishu
Equator
Kisangani
Kampala
Nairobi
Brazzaville
Mombasa
Pointe-Noire
Kinshasa
Kananga
Mbuji-Mayi
Dar-es-Salaam
Luanda
Lubumbashi
Lusaka
Harare
Antananarivo
Bulawayo
Tropic of Capricorn
Pretoria
Johannesburg
Maputo
Vereeniging
Soweto
Durban
Cape Town
Port Elizabeth

WEALTH

Gross National Product (GNP) in $ per capita (1995)

- Over 10 000
- 5000 – 10 000
- 2000 – 5000
- 1000 – 2000
- Under 1000

Average annual change in GNP per capita (1985–1995)

Over 2%	0 – 2%	Under 0%
□	○	▽

1:100 000 000

Tropic of Cancer
Equator
Tropic of Capricorn

DEBT AND AID

External debt in million US $

- 40 000
- 20 000
- 10 000
- 5000
- 1000
- 500

Debt per person in US $

- Over 2000
- 1000 – 2000
- 500 – 2000
- Under 500

No data for Libya, Namibia, Réunion and South Africa

Aid per person per year in US $

- Over 1000
- 100 – 1000
- Under 100

No data for South Africa

1:100 000 000

Tropic of Cancer
Equator
Tropic of Capricorn

Projection: *Zenithal Equidistant*

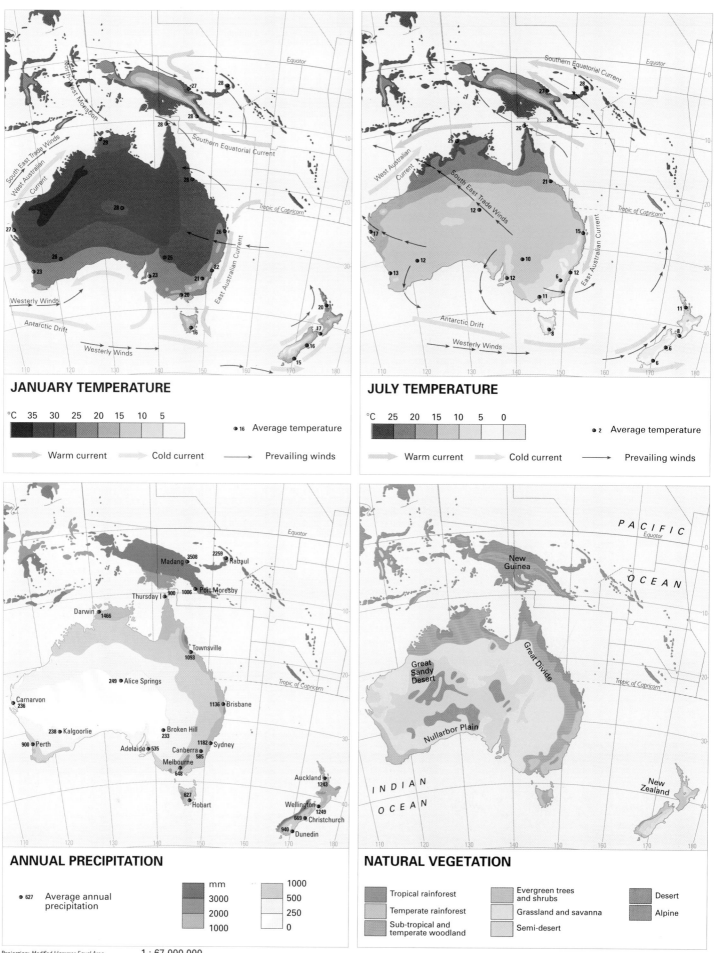

JANUARY TEMPERATURE

°C   35   30   25   20   15   10   5

● 16   Average temperature

➜ Warm current   ➜ Cold current   → Prevailing winds

JULY TEMPERATURE

°C   25   20   15   10   5   0

● 2   Average temperature

➜ Warm current   ➜ Cold current   → Prevailing winds

ANNUAL PRECIPITATION

● 627   Average annual precipitation

mm	
3000	1000
2000	500
1000	250
	0

NATURAL VEGETATION

- Tropical rainforest
- Temperate rainforest
- Sub-tropical and temperate woodland
- Evergreen trees and shrubs
- Grassland and savanna
- Semi-desert
- Desert
- Alpine

Projection: *Modified Hammer Equal Area*   1 : 67 000 000

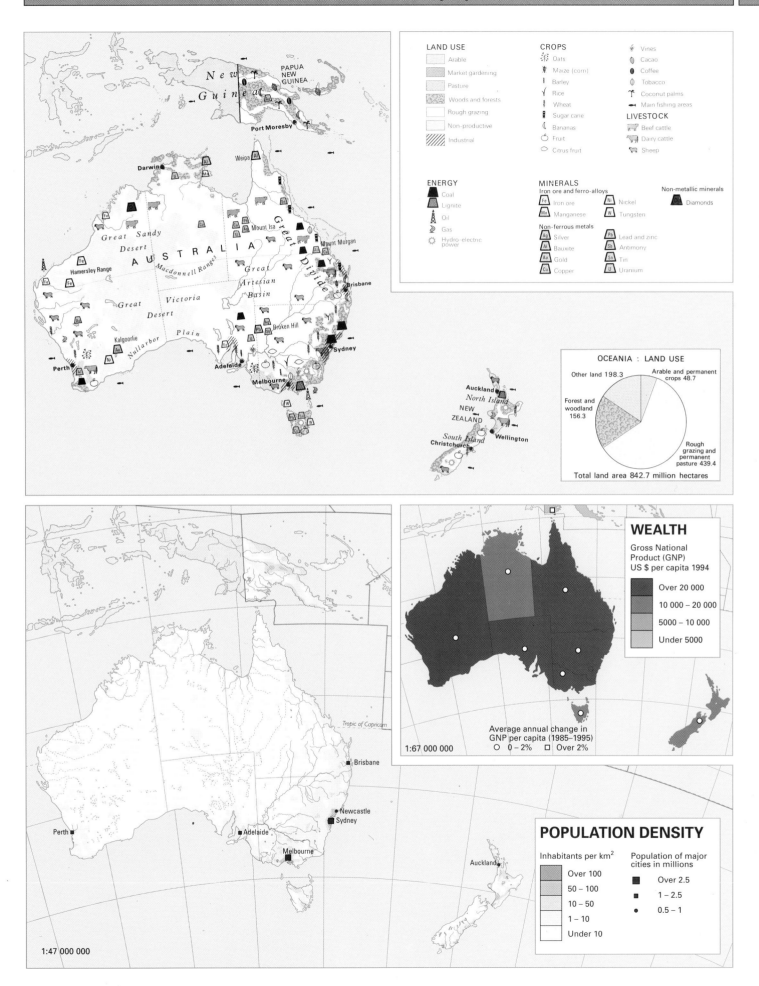

LAND USE
- Arable
- Market gardening
- Pasture
- Woods and forests
- Rough grazing
- Non-productive
- Industrial

CROPS
- Oats
- Maize (corn)
- Barley
- Rice
- Wheat
- Sugar cane
- Bananas
- Fruit
- Citrus fruit
- Vines
- Cacao
- Coffee
- Tobacco
- Coconut palms
- Main fishing areas

LIVESTOCK
- Beef cattle
- Dairy cattle
- Sheep

ENERGY
- Coal
- Lignite
- Oil
- Gas
- Hydro-electric power

MINERALS
Iron ore and ferro-alloys
- Fe Iron ore
- Mn Manganese
- Ni Nickel
- W Tungsten

Non-ferrous metals
- Ag Silver
- Al Bauxite
- Au Gold
- Cu Copper
- Pb Lead and zinc
- Sb Antimony
- Sn Tin
- U Uranium

Non-metallic minerals
- Di Diamonds

OCEANIA : LAND USE

Other land 198.3

Arable and permanent crops 48.7

Forest and woodland 156.3

Rough grazing and permanent pasture 439.4

Total land area 842.7 million hectares

WEALTH

Gross National Product (GNP) US $ per capita 1994
- Over 20 000
- 10 000 – 20 000
- 5000 – 10 000
- Under 5000

1:67 000 000

Average annual change in GNP per capita (1985–1995)
- ○ 0 – 2%
- ◻ Over 2%

POPULATION DENSITY

Inhabitants per km²
- Over 100
- 50 – 100
- 10 – 50
- 1 – 10
- Under 10

Population of major cities in millions
- Over 2.5
- 1 – 2.5
- 0.5 – 1

1:47 000 000

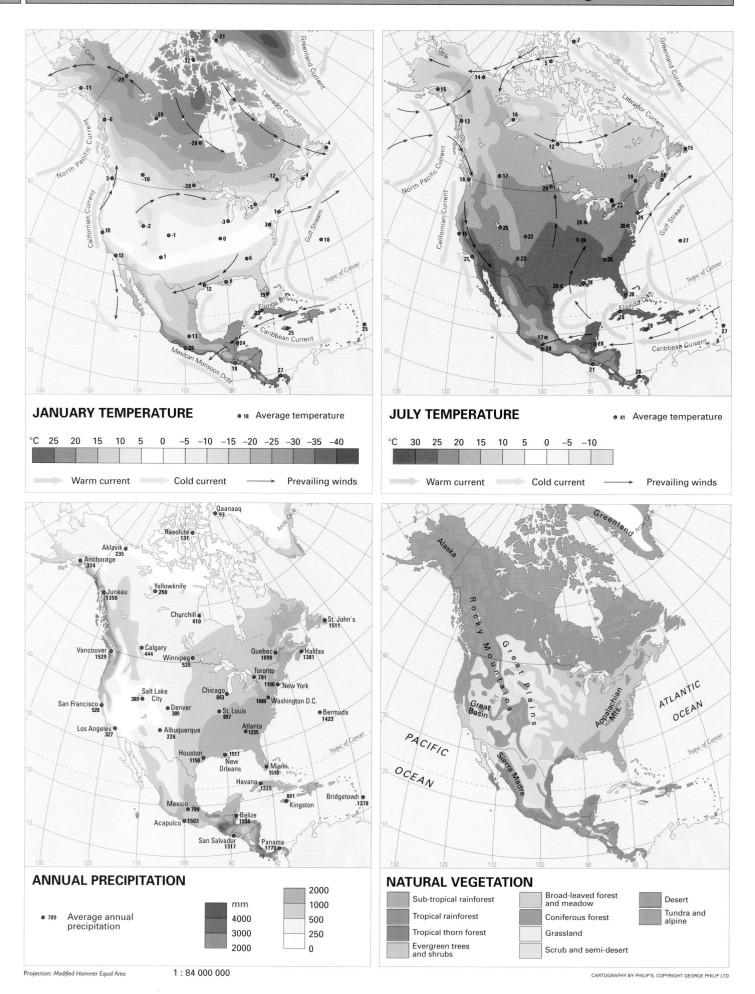

JANUARY TEMPERATURE

• 18   Average temperature

°C 25 20 15 10 5 0 −5 −10 −15 −20 −25 −30 −35 −40

Warm current   Cold current   → Prevailing winds

JULY TEMPERATURE

• 41   Average temperature

°C 30 25 20 15 10 5 0 −5 −10

Warm current   Cold current   → Prevailing winds

ANNUAL PRECIPITATION

• 709   Average annual precipitation

mm
2000
1000
500
250
0

4000
3000
2000

NATURAL VEGETATION

- Sub-tropical rainforest
- Tropical rainforest
- Tropical thorn forest
- Evergreen trees and shrubs
- Broad-leaved forest and meadow
- Coniferous forest
- Grassland
- Scrub and semi-desert
- Desert
- Tundra and alpine

Projection: *Modified Hammer Equal Area*   1 : 84 000 000

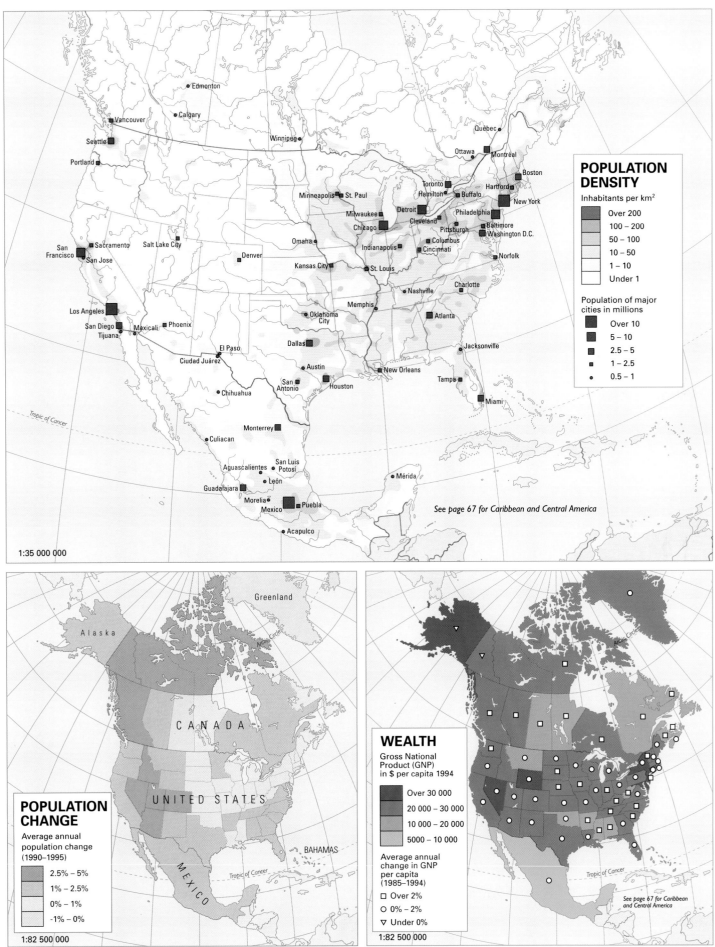

POPULATION DENSITY

Inhabitants per km²

- Over 200
- 100 – 200
- 50 – 100
- 10 – 50
- 1 – 10
- Under 1

Population of major cities in millions

- Over 10
- 5 – 10
- 2.5 – 5
- 1 – 2.5
- 0.5 – 1

Edmonton · Calgary · Vancouver · Seattle · Portland · Winnipeg · Québec · Ottawa · Montréal · Boston · Hartford · Toronto · Hamilton · Buffalo · New York · Minneapolis · St. Paul · Milwaukee · Detroit · Philadelphia · Chicago · Cleveland · Baltimore · Pittsburgh · Washington D.C. · San Francisco · Sacramento · Salt Lake City · Denver · Omaha · Columbus · Indianapolis · Cincinnati · San Jose · Kansas City · St. Louis · Norfolk · Los Angeles · Nashville · Charlotte · San Diego · Mexicali · Phoenix · Memphis · Tijuana · Oklahoma City · Atlanta · El Paso · Dallas · Jacksonville · Ciudad Juárez · Austin · New Orleans · Tampa · Chihuahua · San Antonio · Houston · Monterrey · Miami · Culiacan · Aguascalientes · San Luis Potosí · Mérida · León · Guadalajara · Morelia · Mexico · Puebla · Acapulco

1:35 000 000

See page 67 for Caribbean and Central America

POPULATION CHANGE

Average annual population change (1990–1995)

- 2.5% – 5%
- 1% – 2.5%
- 0% – 1%
- -1% – 0%

Greenland · Alaska · CANADA · UNITED STATES · MEXICO · BAHAMAS

1:82 500 000

WEALTH

Gross National Product (GNP) in $ per capita 1994

- Over 30 000
- 20 000 – 30 000
- 10 000 – 20 000
- 5000 – 10 000

Average annual change in GNP per capita (1985–1994)

- □ Over 2%
- ○ 0% – 2%
- ▽ Under 0%

1:82 500 000

See page 67 for Caribbean and Central America

Projection: *Polyconic*

CARTOGRAPHY BY PHILIP'S. COPYRIGHT GEORGE PHILIP LTD

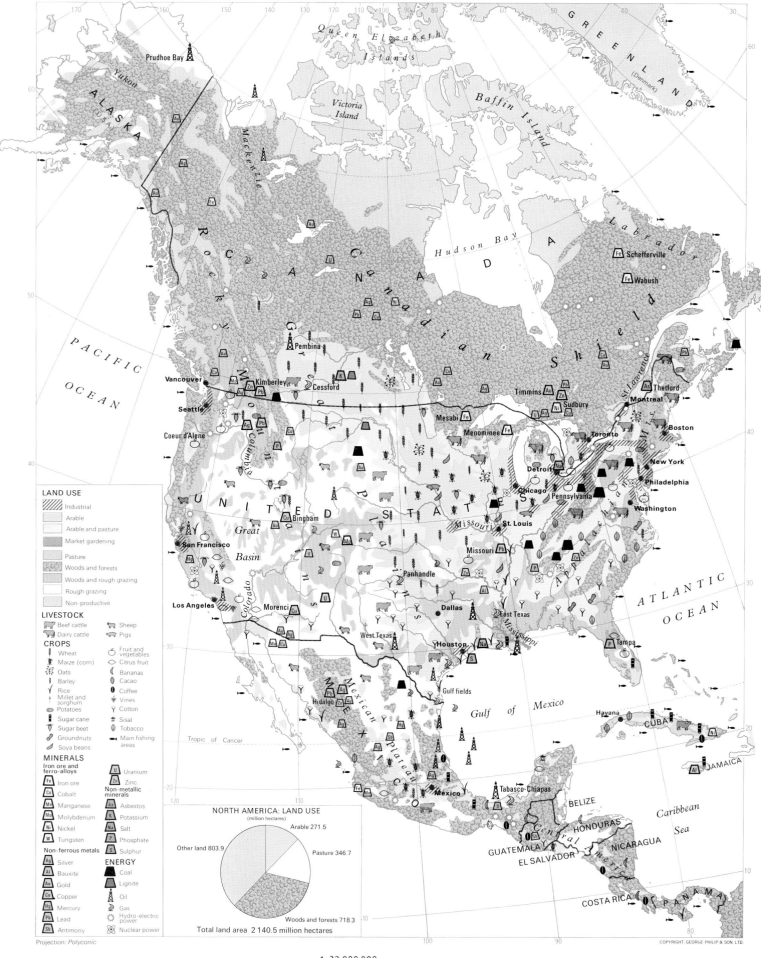

LAND USE

- Industrial
- Arable
- Arable and pasture
- Market gardening
- Pasture
- Woods and forests
- Woods and rough grazing
- Rough grazing
- Non-productive

LIVESTOCK

- Beef cattle
- Dairy cattle
- Sheep
- Pigs

CROPS

- Wheat
- Maize (corn)
- Oats
- Barley
- Rice
- Millet and sorghum
- Potatoes
- Sugar cane
- Sugar beet
- Groundnuts
- Soya beans
- Fruit and vegetables
- Citrus fruit
- Bananas
- Cacao
- Coffee
- Vines
- Cotton
- Sisal
- Tobacco
- Main fishing areas

MINERALS

Iron ore and ferro-alloys

- Fe Iron ore
- Co Cobalt
- Mn Manganese
- Mo Molybdenum
- Ni Nickel
- W Tungsten

Non-ferrous metals

- Ag Silver
- Al Bauxite
- Au Gold
- Cu Copper
- Hg Mercury
- Pb Lead
- Sb Antimony

- U Uranium
- Zn Zinc

Non-metallic minerals

- As Asbestos
- K Potassium
- Na Salt
- P Phosphate
- S Sulphur

ENERGY

- Coal
- Lignite
- Oil
- Gas
- Hydro-electric power
- Nuclear power

NORTH AMERICA: LAND USE
(million hectares)

- Arable 271.5
- Pasture 346.7
- Woods and forests 718.3
- Other land 803.9

Total land area 2 140.5 million hectares

Projection: *Polyconic*

COPYRIGHT. GEORGE PHILIP & SON. LTD.

1:32 000 000

200   0   200   400   600 miles
400   0   400   800 km

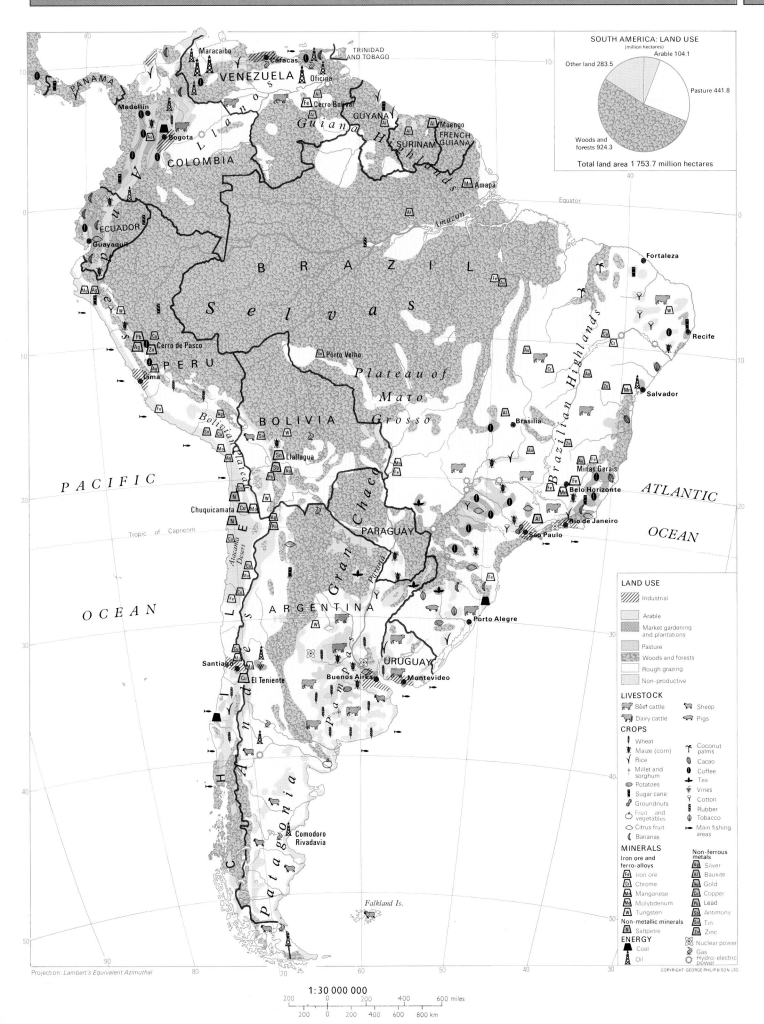

SOUTH AMERICA: LAND USE
(million hectares)

Other land 283.5
Arable 104.1
Pasture 441.8
Woods and forests 924.3

Total land area 1 753.7 million hectares

LAND USE

- Industrial
- Arable
- Market gardening and plantations
- Pasture
- Woods and forests
- Rough grazing
- Non-productive

LIVESTOCK

- Beef cattle
- Sheep
- Dairy cattle
- Pigs

CROPS

- Wheat
- Maize (corn)
- Rice
- Millet and sorghum
- Potatoes
- Sugar cane
- Groundnuts
- Fruit and vegetables
- Citrus fruit
- Bananas
- Coconut palms
- Cacao
- Coffee
- Tea
- Vines
- Cotton
- Rubber
- Tobacco
- Main fishing areas

MINERALS

Iron ore and ferro-alloys
- Fe Iron ore
- Cr Chrome
- Mn Manganese
- Mo Molybdenum
- W Tungsten

Non-metallic minerals
- N Saltpetre

Non-ferrous metals
- Ag Silver
- Al Bauxite
- Au Gold
- Cu Copper
- Pb Lead
- Sb Antimony
- Sn Tin
- Zn Zinc

ENERGY

- Coal
- Oil
- Nuclear power
- Gas
- Hydro-electric power

Projection: *Lambert's Equivalent Azimuthal*

COPYRIGHT GEORGE PHILIP & SON LTD

1:30 000 000

200   0   200   400   600 miles
200 0 200 400 600 800 km

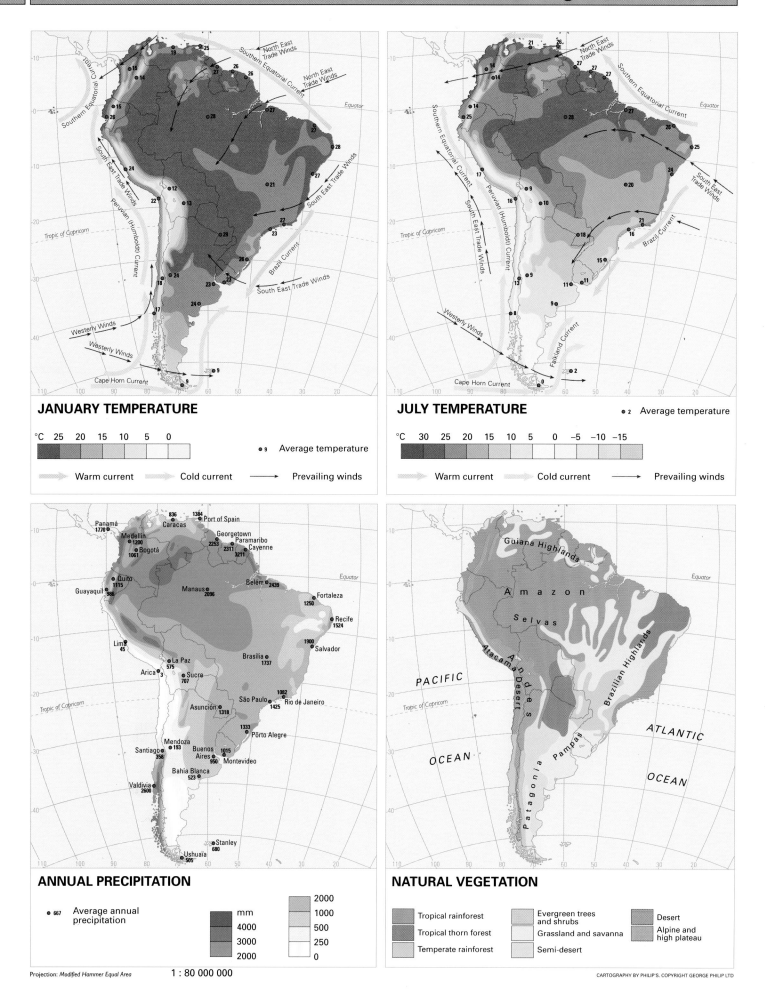

JANUARY TEMPERATURE

°C 25 20 15 10 5 0

• 9 Average temperature

Warm current   Cold current   Prevailing winds

JULY TEMPERATURE

• 2 Average temperature

°C 30 25 20 15 10 5 0 −5 −10 −15

Warm current   Cold current   Prevailing winds

ANNUAL PRECIPITATION

• 667 Average annual precipitation

mm
2000
1000
500
250
0

4000
3000
2000

NATURAL VEGETATION

Tropical rainforest

Tropical thorn forest

Temperate rainforest

Evergreen trees and shrubs

Grassland and savanna

Semi-desert

Desert

Alpine and high plateau

Panamá 1770
Caracas 836 1384 Port of Spain
Medellín 1200
Bogotá 1061
Georgetown 2253 Paramaribo 2311 Cayenne 3211
Quito 1115
Guayaquil 386
Manaus 2096
Belém 2439
Fortaleza 1250
Recife 1524
Lima 45
La Paz 575
Brasília 1737
1900 Salvador
Arica 3
Sucre 707
São Paulo 1082
1425 Rio de Janeiro
Asunción 1318
Mendoza 193
Santiago 358
Buenos Aires 1015
950 Montevideo
1333 Pôrto Alegre
Bahía Blanca 523
Valdivia 2600
Stanley 680
Ushuaïa 505

Guiana Highlands
A m a z o n
S e l v a s
Andes
Atacama Desert
Brazilian Highlands
Patagonia Pampas
PACIFIC OCEAN
ATLANTIC OCEAN

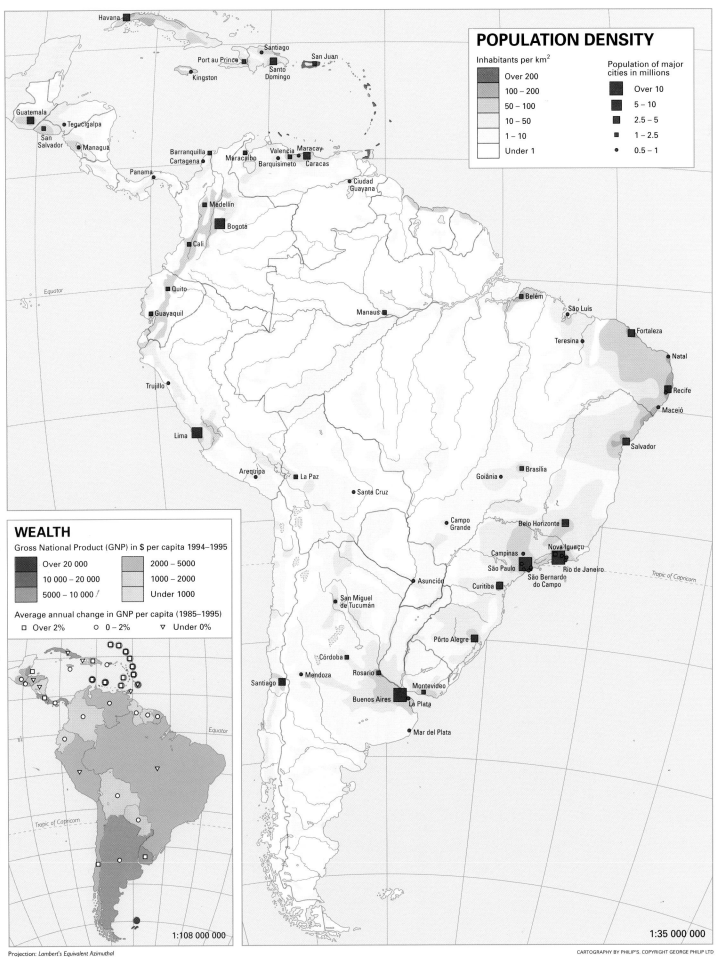

POPULATION DENSITY

Inhabitants per km²

Over 200
100 – 200
50 – 100
10 – 50
1 – 10
Under 1

Population of major cities in millions

Over 10
5 – 10
2.5 – 5
1 – 2.5
0.5 – 1

WEALTH

Gross National Product (GNP) in $ per capita 1994–1995

Over 20 000   2000 – 5000
10 000 – 20 000   1000 – 2000
5000 – 10 000   Under 1000

Average annual change in GNP per capita (1985–1995)

☐ Over 2%   ○ 0 – 2%   ▽ Under 0%

1:108 000 000

1:35 000 000

Projection: *Lambert's Equivalent Azimuthal*

CARTOGRAPHY BY PHILIP'S. COPYRIGHT GEORGE PHILIP LTD

Projection: Hammer Equal Area

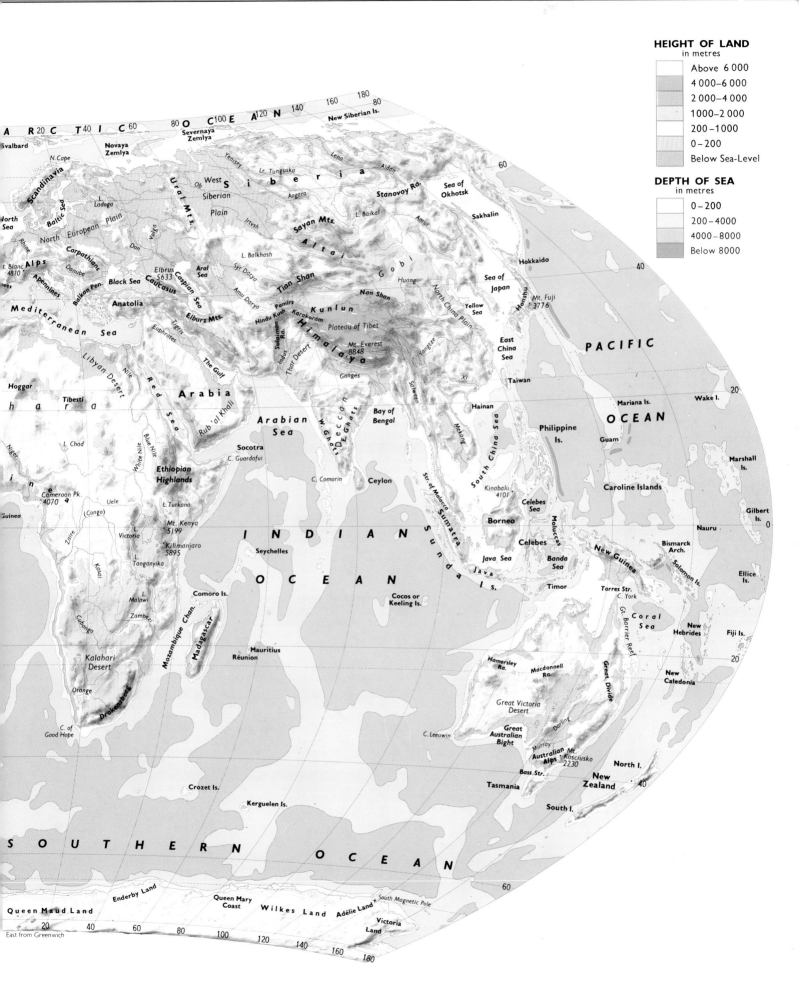

HEIGHT OF LAND
in metres
Above 6 000
4 000–6 000
2 000–4 000
1 000–2 000
200–1 000
0–200
Below Sea-Level

DEPTH OF SEA
in metres
0–200
200–4 000
4 000–8 000
Below 8 000

ARCTIC OCEAN

Svalbard
N. Cape
Novaya Zemlya
Severnaya Zemlya
New Siberian Is.
Scandinavia
North Sea
Baltic Sea
L. Ladoga
Ural Mts.
Ob
West Siberian Plain
Yenisey
Lr. Tunguska
Lena
Aldan
Siberia
Stanovoy Ra.
Sea of Okhotsk
North European Plain
Rhine
Volga
Angara
Irtysh
Sayan Mts.
L. Baikal
Amur
Sakhalin
Carpathians
Danube
Don
Altai
Sea of Japan
Hokkaido
Mt. Blanc 4810
Alps
Apennines
Balkan Pen.
Black Sea
Caucasus
Caspian Sea
Aral Sea
Syr Darya
L. Balkhash
Tian Shan
Gobi
Huang
North China Plain
Mt. Fuji 3776
Honshu
Elbrus 5633
Anatolia
Elburz Mts.
Amu Darya
Pamirs
Hindu Kush
Karakoram
Kunlun
Nan Shan
Yellow Sea
East China Sea
Mediterranean Sea
Tigris
Euphrates
Sulaiman Ra.
Thar Desert
Indus
Plateau of Tibet
Himalaya
Mt. Everest 8848
Yangtze
Salween
Xi
Taiwan
PACIFIC OCEAN
Libyan Desert
Nile
Red Sea
Arabia
The Gulf
Ganges
Hainan
Mariana Is.
Wake I.
Hoggar
Tibesti
Rub al Khali
Arabian Sea
W. Ghats
Deccan
E. Ghats
Bay of Bengal
Philippine Is.
Guam
OCEAN
Sahara
L. Chad
Niger
White Nile
Blue Nile
Socotra
C. Guardafui
C. Comorin
Ceylon
Str. of Malacca
Sumatra
South China Sea
Kinabalu 4101
Celebes Sea
Caroline Islands
Marshall Is.
Cameroon Pk. 4070
Guinea
Uele
(Congo)
Zaire
Ethiopian Highlands
L. Turkana
Mt. Kenya 5199
Kilimanjaro 5895
L. Victoria
Borneo
Celebes
Moluccas
Nauru
Gilbert Is.
Seychelles
INDIAN
New Guinea
Bismarck Arch.
Solomon Is.
Ellice Is.
L. Tanganyika
Comoro Is.
OCEAN
Java Sea
Banda Sea
Java
Sunda Is.
Timor
Coral Sea
New Hebrides
Fiji Is.
Kasai
L. Malawi
Zambezi
Mozambique Chan.
Madagascar
Cocos or Keeling Is.
Torres Str.
C. York
Gt. Barrier Reef
Cubango
Mauritius
Réunion
Hamersley Ra.
Macdonnell Ra.
Great Divide
New Caledonia
Kalahari Desert
Great Victoria Desert
Orange
Drakensberg
C. of Good Hope
C. Leeuwin
Great Australian Bight
Darling
Murray
Australian Alps
Mt. Kosciusko 2230
North I.
New Zealand
Crozet Is.
Bass Str.
Tasmania
South I.
Kerguelen Is.
SOUTHERN OCEAN
Queen Maud Land
Enderby Land
Queen Mary Coast
Wilkes Land
Adélie Land
South Magnetic Pole
Victoria Land
East from Greenwich

1 : 80 000 000

Copyright, George Philip & Son, Ltd.

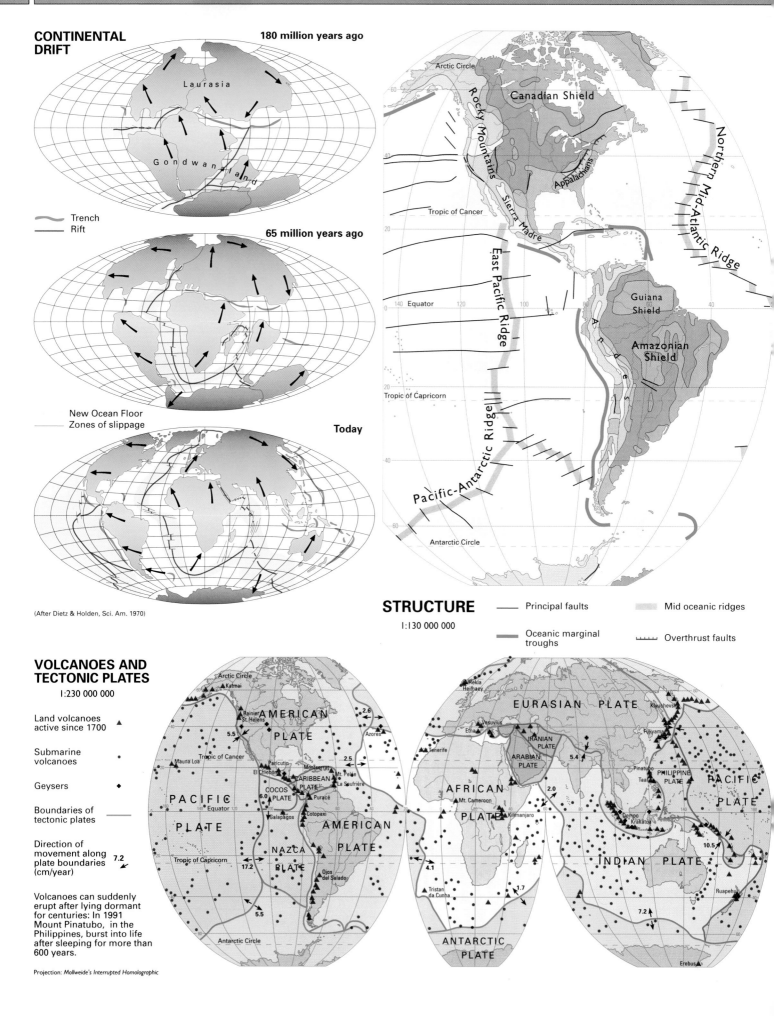

CONTINENTAL DRIFT

180 million years ago

Laurasia

Gondwanaland

～～ Trench
── Rift

65 million years ago

── New Ocean Floor
Zones of slippage

Today

(After Dietz & Holden, Sci. Am. 1970)

Arctic Circle
Canadian Shield
Rocky Mountains
Appalachians
Northern Mid-Atlantic Ridge
Tropic of Cancer
Sierra Madre
East Pacific Ridge
Equator
Guiana Shield
Amazonian Shield
Andes
Tropic of Capricorn
Pacific-Antarctic Ridge
Antarctic Circle

STRUCTURE
1:130 000 000

── Principal faults
━━ Oceanic marginal troughs
▨ Mid oceanic ridges
⊥⊥⊥ Overthrust faults

VOLCANOES AND TECTONIC PLATES
1:230 000 000

▲ Land volcanoes active since 1700

• Submarine volcanoes

✦ Geysers

── Boundaries of tectonic plates

Direction of movement along plate boundaries (cm/year) **7.2**

Volcanoes can suddenly erupt after lying dormant for centuries: In 1991 Mount Pinatubo, in the Philippines, burst into life after sleeping for more than 600 years.

Projection: Mollweide's Interrupted Homolographic

Arctic Circle
Katmai
Rainier
St. Helens
AMERICAN PLATE
2.6
Azores
5.5
Mauna Loa
Tropic of Cancer
Paricutin
El Chichón
Montserrat
CARIBBEAN PLATE
Mt. Pelée
La Soufrière
2.5
COCOS PLATE
6.0
Puracé
PACIFIC PLATE
Equator
Galapagos
Cotopaxi
AMERICAN PLATE
NAZCA PLATE
17.2
Tropic of Capricorn
7.2
Ojos del Salado
5.5
Antarctic Circle

Hekla
Heimaey
EURASIAN PLATE
Klyuchevsk
Vesuvius
Etna
IRANIAN PLATE
ARABIAN PLATE
5.4
Fujiyama
Tenerife
2.0
Pinatubo
Taal
PHILIPPINE PLATE
PACIFIC PLATE
AFRICAN PLATE
Mt. Cameroon
Kilimanjaro
Dempo
Krakatoa
4.1
10.5
INDIAN PLATE
Tristan da Cunha
1.7
Ruapehu
7.2
ANTARCTIC PLATE
Erebus

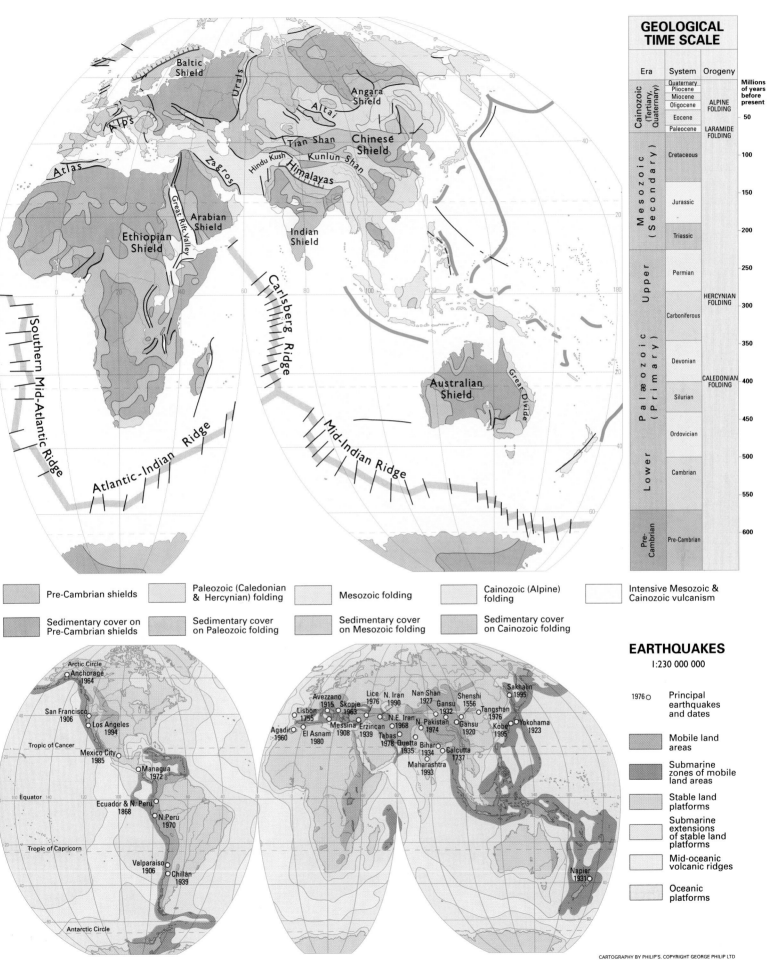

GEOLOGICAL TIME SCALE

Era	System	Orogeny	Millions of years before present
Cainozoic (Tertiary, Quaternary)	Quaternary		
	Pliocene	ALPINE FOLDING	
	Miocene		
	Oligocene		50
	Eocene		
	Paleocene	LARAMIDE FOLDING	
Mesozoic (Secondary)	Cretaceous		100
	Jurassic		150
	Triassic		200
Upper Paleozoic (Primary)	Permian		250
	Carboniferous	HERCYNIAN FOLDING	300
Lower Paleozoic (Primary)	Devonian	CALEDONIAN FOLDING	350
	Silurian		400
	Ordovician		450
	Cambrian		500
			550
Pre-Cambrian	Pre-Cambrian		600

Legend

- Pre-Cambrian shields
- Paleozoic (Caledonian & Hercynian) folding
- Mesozoic folding
- Cainozoic (Alpine) folding
- Intensive Mesozoic & Cainozoic vulcanism
- Sedimentary cover on Pre-Cambrian shields
- Sedimentary cover on Paleozoic folding
- Sedimentary cover on Mesozoic folding
- Sedimentary cover on Cainozoic folding

EARTHQUAKES

1:230 000 000

- 1976 ○ Principal earthquakes and dates
- Mobile land areas
- Submarine zones of mobile land areas
- Stable land platforms
- Submarine extensions of stable land platforms
- Mid-oceanic volcanic ridges
- Oceanic platforms

CARTOGRAPHY BY PHILIP'S. COPYRIGHT GEORGE PHILIP LTD

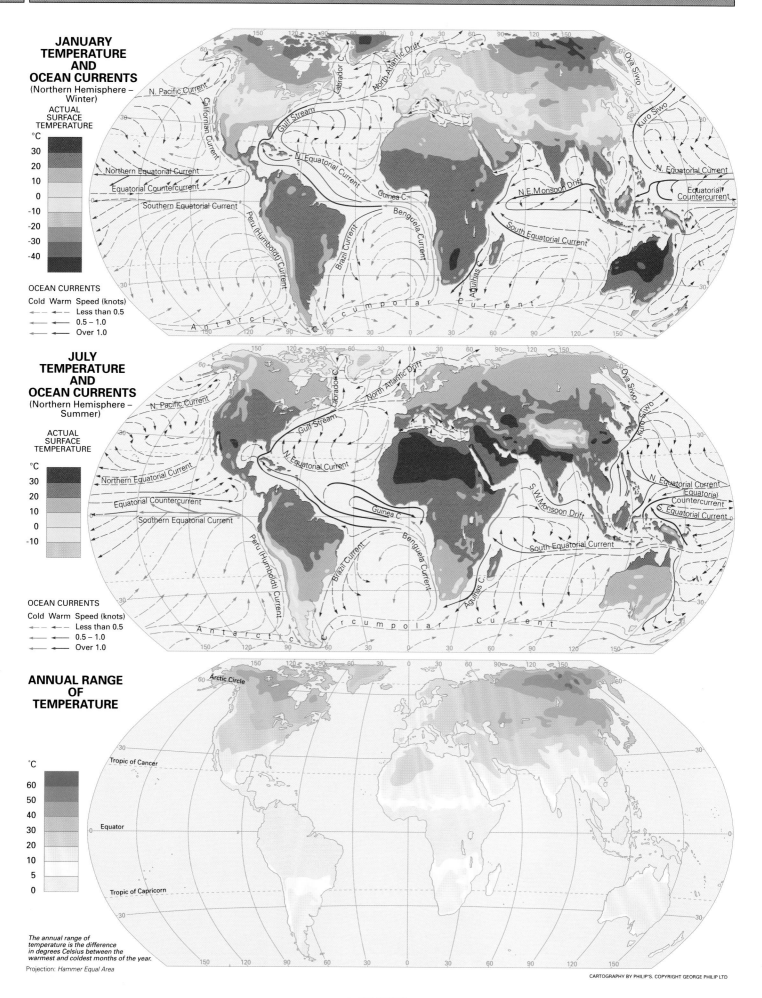

JANUARY TEMPERATURE AND OCEAN CURRENTS
(Northern Hemisphere – Winter)

ACTUAL SURFACE TEMPERATURE

°C
30
20
10
0
-10
-20
-30
-40

OCEAN CURRENTS

Cold Warm Speed (knots)
Less than 0.5
0.5 – 1.0
Over 1.0

JULY TEMPERATURE AND OCEAN CURRENTS
(Northern Hemisphere – Summer)

ACTUAL SURFACE TEMPERATURE

°C
30
20
10
0
-10

OCEAN CURRENTS

Cold Warm Speed (knots)
Less than 0.5
0.5 – 1.0
Over 1.0

ANNUAL RANGE OF TEMPERATURE

°C
60
50
40
30
20
10
5
0

The annual range of temperature is the difference in degrees Celsius between the warmest and coldest months of the year.

Projection: *Hammer Equal Area*

CARTOGRAPHY BY PHILIP'S. COPYRIGHT GEORGE PHILIP LTD

1 : 190 000 000

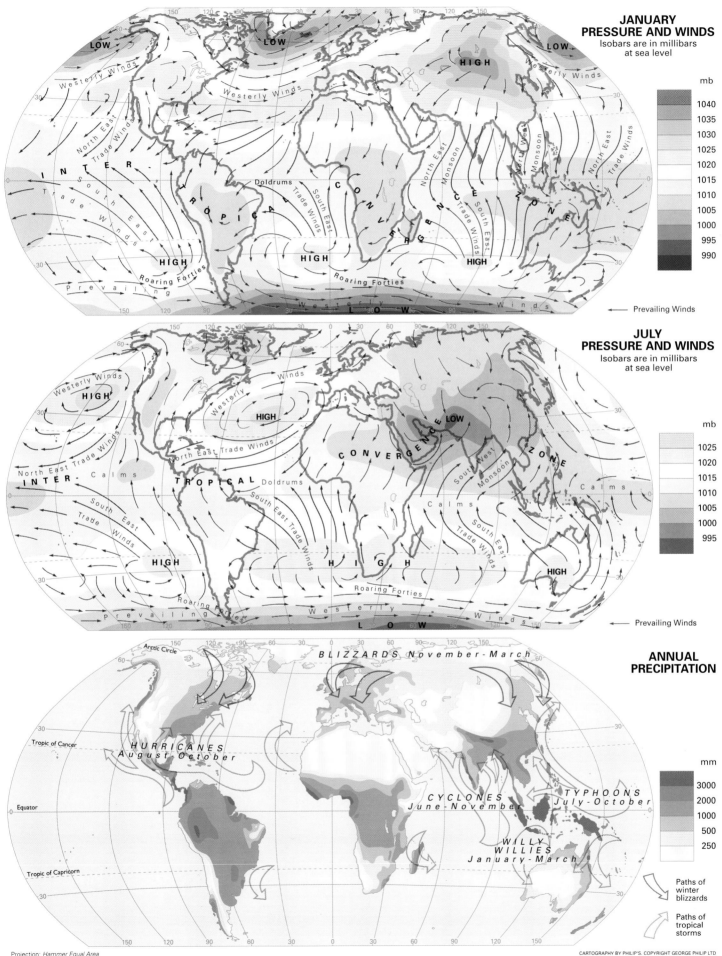

JANUARY PRESSURE AND WINDS
Isobars are in millibars at sea level

mb

	1040
	1035
	1030
	1025
	1020
	1015
	1010
	1005
	1000
	995
	990

⟶ Prevailing Winds

JULY PRESSURE AND WINDS
Isobars are in millibars at sea level

mb

	1025
	1020
	1015
	1010
	1005
	1000
	995

⟶ Prevailing Winds

ANNUAL PRECIPITATION

mm

	3000
	2000
	1000
	500
	250

⟱ Paths of winter blizzards

⟰ Paths of tropical storms

Projection: *Hammer Equal Area*

CARTOGRAPHY BY PHILIP'S. COPYRIGHT GEORGE PHILIP LTD

1 : 190 000 000

CLIMATIC REGIONS after Köppen

Köppen's classification recognises five major climatic regions corresponding broadly to the five principal vegetation types and these are designated by the letters A, B, C, D and E. Each one of these are subdivided on the basis of temperature and rainfall. This map shows a climate graph for a selected place within each of the 12 sub-regions.

TROPICAL RAINY CLIMATES A

Af	Rain Forest Climate	All mean monthly temperatures above 18°C and an annual variation in temperature of less than 6°C
Am	Monsoon Climate	
Aw	Savanna Climate	All monthly temperatures above 18°C but with an annual variation in temperature of less than 12°C

DRY CLIMATES B

| BS | Steppe Climate | The principal difference between this grouping and groups A, C, D and E is the combination of a wide range of temperatures with low rainfall |
| BW | Desert Climate | |

WARM TEMPERATE RAINY CLIMATES C

The climatic group is separated from group A by having the mean temperature of the coolest month below 18°C but above -3°C. The mean temperature of the warmest month is over 10°C.

Cw	Dry Winter Climate	The wettest month of summer has at least ten times as much rain as the driest winter month
Cs	Dry Summer Climate (Mediterranean)	The wettest month of winter has at least three times as much rain as the driest month of summer. The driest summer month itself has less than 30mm rainfall.
Cf	Climate with no Dry Season	Even rainfall throughout the year.

COLD TEMPERATE RAINY CLIMATES D

| Dw | Dry Winter Climate | The mean temperature of the coldest month is below -3°C but the mean temperature of the warmest month is still over 10°C. |
| Df | Climate with no Dry Season | |

POLAR CLIMATES E

| ET | Tundra Climate | The mean temperature of the warmest month is below 10°C giving permanently frozen subsoil. |
| EF | Polar Climate | The mean temperature of the warmest month is below 0°C giving permanently ice and snow. |

The classification is in some cases subdivided by the addition of the following letters after the major types :-

Used with groups C and D
- **a** Hot summer – mean temperature of the hottest month above 22°C and with more than four months of over 10°C.
- **b** Warm summer – mean temperature of the hottest month below 22°C but still with more than four months of over 10°C.
- **c** Cool short summer – mean temperature of the hottest month below 22°C but with less than four months of over 10°C.

Used with group D
- **d** Cool short summer and cold winter – mean temperature of the hottest month below 22°C and of the coolest month below -38°C

Used with group B
- **h** Hot dry climate – mean annual temperature above 18°C.
- **k** Cool dry climate – mean annual temperature below 18°C.

Used with group E
- **H** Polar climate due to elevation being over 1500m.

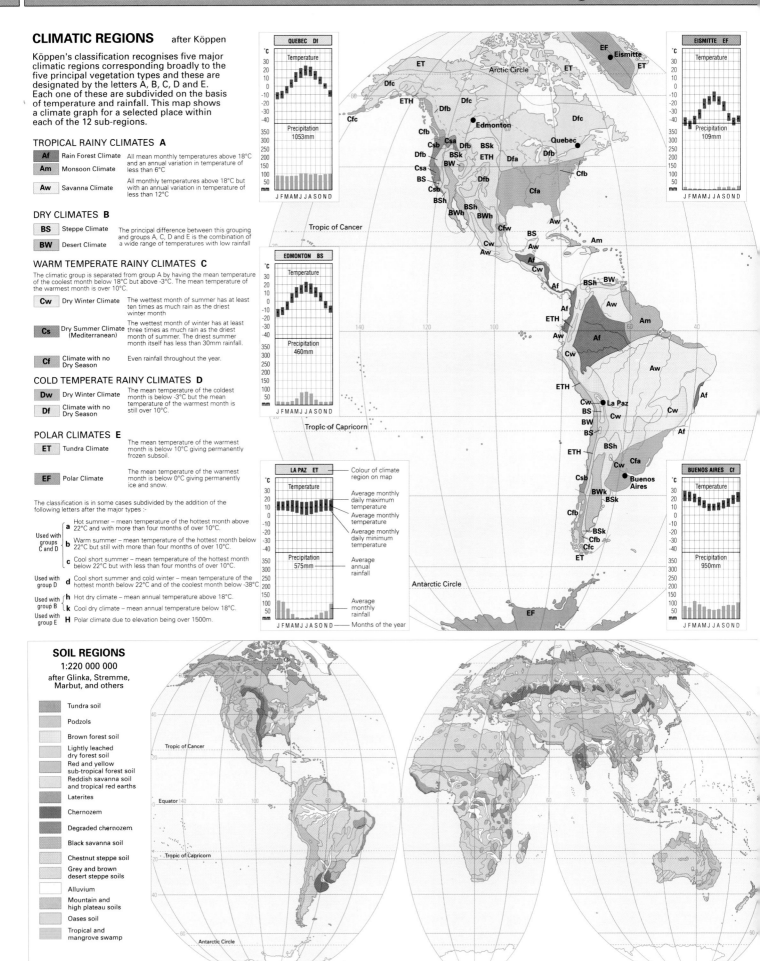

SOIL REGIONS

1:220 000 000

after Glinka, Stremme, Marbut, and others

- Tundra soil
- Podzols
- Brown forest soil
- Lightly leached dry forest soil
- Red and yellow sub-tropical forest soil
- Reddish savanna soil and tropical red earths
- Laterites
- Chernozem
- Degraded chernozem
- Black savanna soil
- Chestnut steppe soil
- Grey and brown desert steppe soils
- Alluvium
- Mountain and high plateau soils
- Oases soil
- Tropical and mangrove swamp

Projection: *Interrupted Mollweide's Homolographic*

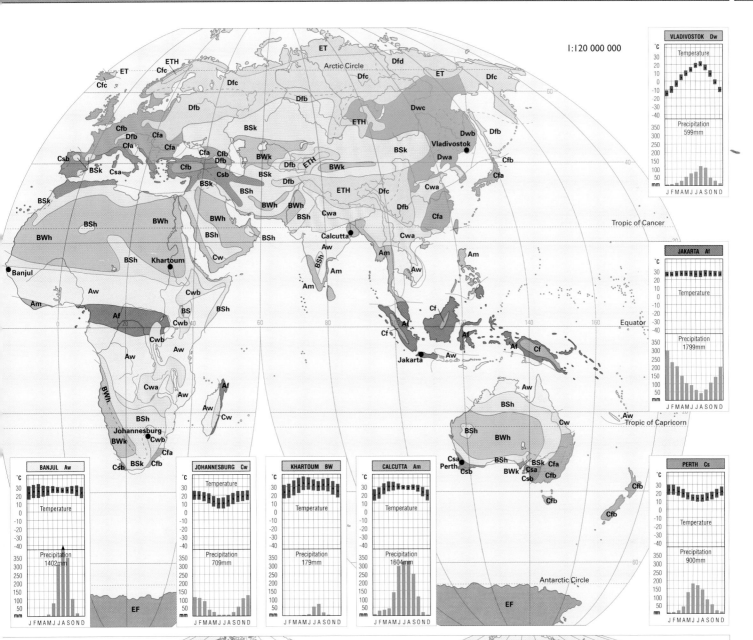

1:120 000 000

VLADIVOSTOK Dw
Temperature
Precipitation
599mm
J F M A M J J A S O N D

JAKARTA Af
Temperature
Precipitation
1799mm
J F M A M J J A S O N D

BANJUL Aw
Temperature
Precipitation
1402mm
J F M A M J J A S O N D

JOHANNESBURG Cw
Temperature
Precipitation
709mm
J F M A M J J A S O N D

KHARTOUM BW
Temperature
Precipitation
179mm
J F M A M J J A S O N D

CALCUTTA Am
Temperature
Precipitation
1604mm
J F M A M J J A S O N D

PERTH Cs
Temperature
Precipitation
900mm
J F M A M J J A S O N D

NATURAL VEGETATION

1:220 000 000
after Austin Miller

- Tropical rainforest
- Subtropical and temperate rainforest
- Monsoon woodland and open jungle
- Subtropical and temperate woodland, scrub and bush
- Tropical savanna, with low trees and bush
- Tropical savanna and grasslands
- Dry semi-desert, with shrub and grass
- Desert shrub
- Desert
- Dry steppe and shrub
- Temperate grasslands, prairie and steppe
- Mediterranean hardwood forest and scrub
- Temperate deciduous forest and meadow
- Temperate deciduous and coniferous forest
- Northern coniferous forest (taiga)
- Mountainous forest, mainly coniferous
- High plateau steppe and tundra
- Arctic tundra
- Polar and mountainous ice desert

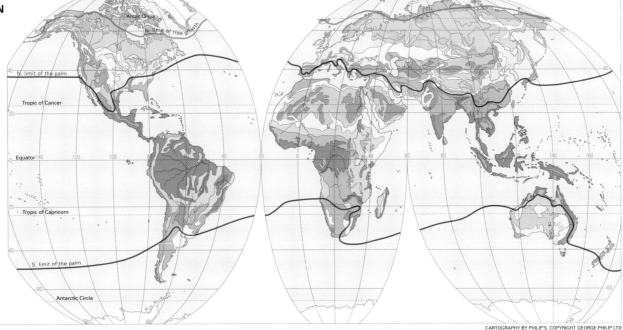

CARTOGRAPHY BY PHILIP'S. COPYRIGHT GEORGE PHILIP LTD

Key (example)	Jan	Feb	Explanation
Addis Ababa Ethiopia 2410m			Height of meteorological station above sea level in metres
Temperature Daily Max.°C	23	24	Average monthly maximum temperature in degrees Celsius
Daily Min.°C	6	7	Average monthly minimum temperature in degrees Celsius
Average Monthly °C	14	15	Average monthly temperature in degrees Celsius
Rainfall Monthly Total mm	13	35	Average monthly precipitation in millimetres
Sunshine Hours per Day	8.7	8.2	Average daily duration of bright sunshine per month in hours

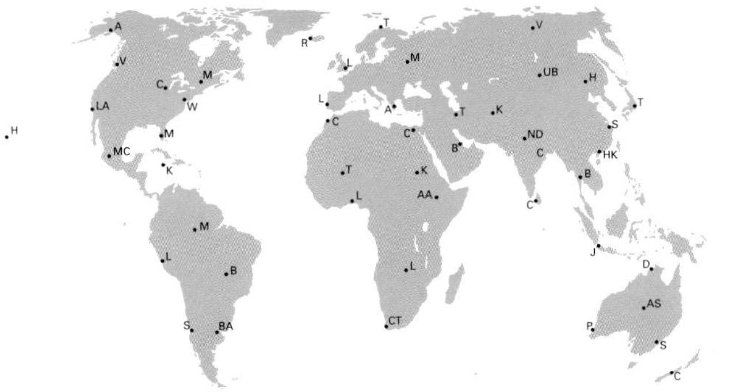

	Jan	Feb	Mar	Apr	May	June	July	Aug	Sep	Oct	Nov	Dec	Year
Addis Ababa Ethiopia 2410m													
Temperature Daily Max.°C	23	24	25	24	25	23	20	20	21	22	23	22	23
Daily Min.°C	6	7	9	10	9	10	11	11	10	7	5	5	8
Average Monthly °C	14	15	17	17	17	16	16	15	15	15	14	14	15
Rainfall Monthly Total mm	13	35	67	91	81	117	247	255	167	29	8	5	1115
Sunshine Hours per Day	8.7	8.2	7.6	8.1	6.5	4.8	2.8	3.2	5.2	7.6	6.7	7	6.4
Alice Springs Australia 580m													
Temperature Daily Max.°C	35	35	32	27	23	19	19	23	27	31	33	35	28
Daily Min.°C	21	20	17	12	8	5	4	6	10	15	18	20	13
Average Monthly °C	28	27	25	20	15	12	12	14	18	23	25	27	21
Rainfall Monthly Total mm	44	33	27	10	15	13	7	8	7	18	29	38	249
Sunshine Hours per Day	10.3	10.4	9.3	9.2	8	8	8.9	9.8	10	9.7	10.1	10	9.5
Anchorage USA 183m													
Temperature Daily Max.°C	-7	-3	0	7	13	18	19	17	13	6	-2	-6	-6
Daily Min.°C	-15	-12	-9	-2	4	8	10	9	5	-2	-9	-14	-2
Average Monthly °C	-11	-7	-4	3	9	13	15	13	9	2	-5	-10	-4
Rainfall Monthly Total mm	20	18	13	11	13	25	47	64	64	47	28	24	374
Sunshine Hours per Day	2.4	4.1	6.6	8.3	8.3	9.2	8.5	6	4.4	3.1	2.6	1.6	5.4
Athens Greece 107m													
Temperature Daily Max.°C	13	14	16	20	25	30	33	33	29	24	19	15	23
Daily Min.°C	6	7	8	11	16	20	23	23	19	15	12	8	14
Average Monthly °C	10	10	12	16	20	25	28	28	24	20	15	11	18
Rainfall Monthly Total mm	62	37	37	23	23	14	6	7	15	51	56	71	402
Sunshine Hours per Day	3.9	5.2	5.8	7.7	8.9	10.7	11.9	11.5	9.4	6.8	4.8	3.8	7.3
Bahrain City Bahrain 2m													
Temperature Daily Max.°C	20	21	25	29	33	36	37	38	36	32	27	22	30
Daily Min.°C	14	15	18	22	25	29	31	32	29	25	22	16	23
Average Monthly °C	17	18	21	25	29	32	34	35	32	29	25	19	26
Rainfall Monthly Total mm	18	12	10	9	2	0	0	0	0	0.4	3	16	70
Sunshine Hours per Day	5.9	6.9	7.9	8.8	10.6	13.2	12.1	12	12	10.3	7.7	6.4	9.5
Bangkok Thailand 10m													
Temperature Daily Max.°C	32	33	34	35	34	33	32	32	32	31	31	31	33
Daily Min.°C	20	23	24	26	25	25	25	24	24	24	23	20	24
Average Monthly °C	26	28	29	30	30	29	28	28	28	28	27	26	28
Rainfall Monthly Total mm	9	30	36	82	165	153	168	183	310	239	55	8	1438
Sunshine Hours per Day	8.2	8	8	10	7.5	6.1	4.7	5.2	5.2	6.1	7.3	7.8	7
Brasilia Brazil 910m													
Temperature Daily Max.°C	28	28	28	28	27	27	27	29	30	29	28	27	28
Daily Min.°C	18	18	18	17	15	13	13	14	16	18	18	18	16
Average Monthly °C	23	23	23	22	21	20	20	21	23	24	23	22	22
Rainfall Monthly Total mm	252	204	227	93	17	3	6	3	30	127	255	343	1560
Sunshine Av. Monthly Dur.	5.8	5.7	6	7.4	8.7	9.3	9.6	9.8	7.9	6.5	4.8	4.4	7.2
Buenos Aires Argentina 25m													
Temperature Daily Max.°C	30	29	26	22	18	14	14	16	18	21	25	28	22
Daily Min.°C	17	17	16	12	9	5	6	6	8	10	14	16	11
Average Monthly °C	23	23	21	17	13	10	10	11	13	15	19	22	16
Rainfall Monthly Total mm	79	71	109	89	76	61	56	61	79	86	84	99	950
Sunshine Hours per Day	9.2	8.5	7.5	6.8	4.9	3.5	3.8	5.2	6	6.8	8.1	8.5	6.6
Cairo Egypt 75m													
Temperature Daily Max.°C	19	21	24	28	32	35	35	35	33	30	26	21	28
Daily Min.°C	9	9	12	14	18	20	22	22	20	18	14	10	16
Average Monthly °C	14	15	18	21	25	28	29	28	26	24	20	15	22
Rainfall Monthly Total mm	4	4	3	1	2	1	0	0	1	1	3	7	27
Sunshine Hours per Day	6.9	8.4	8.7	9.7	10.5	11.9	11.7	11.3	10.4	9.4	8.3	6.4	9.5
Calcutta India 5m													
Temperature Daily Max.°C	27	29	34	36	35	34	32	32	32	32	29	26	31
Daily Min.°C	13	15	21	24	25	26	26	26	26	23	18	13	21
Average Monthly °C	20	22	27	30	30	30	29	29	29	28	23	20	26
Rainfall Monthly Total mm	10	30	34	44	140	297	325	332	253	114	20	5	1604
Sunshine Hours per Day	8.6	8.7	8.9	9	8.7	5.4	4.1	4.1	5.1	6.5	8.3	8.4	7.1
Cape Town South Africa 44m													
Temperature Daily Max.°C	26	26	25	23	20	18	17	18	19	21	24	25	22
Daily Min.°C	15	15	14	11	9	7	7	7	8	10	13	15	11
Average Monthly °C	21	20	20	17	14	13	12	12	14	16	18	20	16
Rainfall Monthly Total mm	12	19	17	42	67	98	68	76	36	45	12	13	505
Sunshine Hours per Day	11.4	10.2	9.4	7.7	6.1	5.7	6.4	6.6	7.6	8.6	10.2	10.9	8.4

	Jan	Feb	Mar	Apr	May	June	July	Aug	Sep	Oct	Nov	Dec	Yea[illegible]
Casablanca Morocco 59m													
Temperature Daily Max.°C	17	18	20	21	22	24	26	26	26	24	21	18	2[illegible]
Daily Min.°C	8	9	11	12	15	18	19	20	18	15	12	10	1[illegible]
Average Monthly °C	13	13	15	16	18	21	23	23	22	20	17	14	1[illegible]
Rainfall Monthly Total mm	78	61	54	37	20	3	0	1	6	28	58	94	44[illegible]
Sunshine Hours per Day	5.2	6.3	7.3	9	9.4	9.7	10.2	9.7	9.1	7.4	5.9	5.3	7.[illegible]
Chicago USA 186m													
Temperature Daily Max.°C	0.6	1.5	6.4	14.1	20.6	26.4	28.9	28	23.8	17.4	8.4	2.1	14.[illegible]
Daily Min.°C	-7	-6	-2	5	11	16	20	19	14	8	0	-5	-[illegible]
Average Monthly °C	-3	-2	2	9	16	21	24	23	19	13	4	-2	[illegible]
Rainfall Monthly Total mm	47	41	70	77	96	103	86	80	69	71	56	48	84[illegible]
Sunshine Hours per Day	4	5	6.6	6.9	8.9	10.2	10	9.2	8.2	6.9	4.5	3.7	[illegible]
Christchurch New Zealand 5m													
Temperature Daily Max.°C	21	21	19	17	13	11	10	11	14	17	19	21	1[illegible]
Daily Min.°C	12	12	10	7	4	2	1	3	5	7	8	11	[illegible]
Average Monthly °C	16	16	15	12	9	6	6	7	9	12	13	16	1[illegible]
Rainfall Monthly Total mm	56	46	43	46	76	69	61	58	51	51	51	61	66[illegible]
Sunshine Hours per Day	7	6.5	5.6	4.7	4.3	3.9	4.1	4.7	5.6	6.1	6.9	6.3	5.[illegible]
Colombo Sri Lanka 10m													
Temperature Daily Max.°C	30	31	31	31	30	30	29	29	30	29	29	30	3[illegible]
Daily Min.°C	22	22	23	24	25	25	25	25	25	24	23	22	2[illegible]
Average Monthly °C	26	26	27	28	28	27	27	27	27	27	26	26	2[illegible]
Rainfall Monthly Total mm	101	66	118	230	394	220	140	102	174	348	333	142	236[illegible]
Sunshine Hours per Day	7.9	9	8.1	7.2	6.4	5.4	6.1	6.3	6.2	6.5	6.4	7.8	6.[illegible]
Darwin Australia 30m													
Temperature Daily Max.°C	32	32	33	33	33	31	31	32	33	34	34	33	3[illegible]
Daily Min.°C	25	25	25	24	23	21	19	21	23	25	26	26	24
Average Monthly °C	29	29	29	29	28	26	25	26	28	29	30	29	28
Rainfall Monthly Total mm	405	309	279	77	8	2	0	1	15	48	108	214	1466
Sunshine Hours per Day	5.8	5.8	6.6	9.8	9.3	10	9.9	10.4	10.1	9.4	9.6	6.8	8.6
Harbin China 175m													
Temperature Daily Max.°C	-14	-9	0	12	21	26	29	27	20	12	-1	-11	[illegible]
Daily Min.°C	-26	-23	-12	-1	7	14	18	16	8	0	-12	-22	-[illegible]
Average Monthly °C	-20	-16	-6	6	14	20	23	22	14	6	-7	-17	[illegible]
Rainfall Monthly Total mm	4	6	17	23	44	92	167	119	52	36	12	5	57[illegible]
Sunshine Hours per Day	6.4	7.8	8	7.8	8.3	8.6	8.6	8.2	7.2	6.9	6.1	5.7	7.[illegible]
Hong Kong China 35m													
Temperature Daily Max.°C	18	18	20	24	28	30	31	31	30	27	24	20	2[illegible]
Daily Min.°C	13	13	16	19	23	26	26	26	25	23	19	15	2[illegible]
Average Monthly °C	16	15	18	22	25	28	28	28	27	25	21	17	2[illegible]
Rainfall Monthly Total mm	30	60	70	133	332	479	286	415	364	33	46	17	226[illegible]
Sunshine Hours per Day	4.7	3.5	3.1	3.8	5	5.4	6.8	6.5	6.6	7	6.2	5.5	5.[illegible]
Honolulu Hawaii 5m													
Temperature Daily Max.°C	26	26	26	27	28	29	29	29	30	29	28	26	28
Daily Min.°C	19	19	19	20	21	22	23	23	23	22	21	20	21
Average Monthly °C	23	22	23	23	24	26	26	26	26	26	24	23	24
Rainfall Monthly Total mm	96	84	73	33	25	8	11	23	25	47	55	76	556
Sunshine Hours per Day	7.3	7.7	8.3	8.6	8.8	9.1	9.4	9.3	9.2	8.3	7.5	6.2	8.3
Jakarta Indonesia 10m													
Temperature Daily Max.°C	29	29	30	31	31	31	31	31	31	31	30	29	30
Daily Min.°C	23	23	23	24	24	23	23	23	23	23	23	23	23
Average Monthly °C	26	26	27	27	27	27	27	27	27	27	27	26	27
Rainfall Monthly Total mm	300	300	211	147	114	97	64	43	66	112	142	203	1799
Sunshine Av. Monthly Dur.	6.1	6.5	7.7	8.5	8.4	8.5	9.1	9.5	9.6	9	7.7	7.1	8.1
Kabul Afghanistan 1791 m													
Temperature Daily Max.°C	2	4	12	19	26	31	33	33	30	22	17	8	20
Daily Min.°C	-8	-6	1	6	11	13	16	15	11	6	1	-3	5
Average Monthly °C	-3	-1	6	13	18	22	25	24	20	14	9	3	12
Rainfall Monthly Total mm	28	61	72	117	33	1	7	1	0	1	37	14	372
Sunshine Av. Monthly Dur.	5.9	6	5.7	6.8	10.1	11.5	11.4	11.2	9.8	9.4	7.8	6.1	8.5
Khartoum Sudan 380m													
Temperature Daily Max.°C	32	33	37	40	42	41	38	36	38	39	35	32	37
Daily Min.°C	16	17	20	23	26	27	26	25	25	25	21	17	22
Average Monthly °C	24	25	28	32	34	34	32	30	32	32	28	25	30
Rainfall Monthly Total mm	0	0	0	1	7	5	56	80	28	2	0	0	179
Sunshine Av. Monthly Dur.	10.6	11.2	10.4	10.8	10.4	10.1	8.6	8.6	9.6	10.3	10.8	10.6	10.2

	Jan	Feb	Mar	Apr	May	June	July	Aug	Sep	Oct	Nov	Dec	Year
gston Jamaica 35m													
nperature Daily Max.°C	30	30	30	31	31	32	32	32	32	31	31	31	31
Daily Min.°C	20	20	20	21	22	24	23	23	23	23	22	21	22
Average Monthly °C	25	25	25	26	26	28	28	28	27	27	26	26	26
nfall Monthly Total mm	23	15	23	31	102	89	38	91	99	180	74	36	801
shine Av. Monthly Dur.	8.3	8.8	8.7	8.7	8.3	7.8	8.5	8.5	7.6	7.3	8.3	7.7	8.2
gos Nigeria 40m													
nperature Daily Max.°C	32	33	33	32	31	29	28	28	29	30	31	32	31
Daily Min.°C	22	23	23	23	23	22	22	21	22	22	23	22	22
Average Monthly °C	27	28	28	28	27	26	25	24	25	26	27	27	26
nfall Monthly Total mm	28	41	99	99	203	300	180	56	180	190	63	25	1464
shine Av. Monthly Dur.	5.9	6.8	6.3	6.1	5.6	3.8	2.8	3.3	3	5.1	6.6	6.5	5.2
na Peru 120m													
nperature Daily Max.°C	28	29	29	27	24	20	20	19	20	22	24	26	24
Daily Min.°C	19	20	19	17	16	15	14	14	14	15	16	17	16
Average Monthly °C	24	24	24	22	20	17	17	16	17	18	20	21	20
nfall Monthly Total mm	1	1	1	1	5	5	8	8	8	3	3	1	45
shine Av. Monthly Dur.	6.3	6.8	6.9	6.7	4	1.4	1.1	1	1.1	2.5	4.1	5	3.9
bon Portugal 77m													
nperature Daily Max.°C	14	15	17	20	21	25	27	28	26	22	17	15	21
Daily Min.°C	8	8	10	12	13	15	17	17	17	14	11	9	13
Average Monthly °C	11	12	14	16	17	20	22	23	21	18	14	12	17
nfall Monthly Total mm	111	76	109	54	44	16	3	4	33	62	93	103	708
shine Av. Monthly Dur.	4.7	5.9	6	8.3	9.1	10.6	11.4	10.7	8.4	6.7	5.2	4.6	7.7
ndon (Kew) United Kingdom 5m													
nperature Daily Max.°C	6	7	10	13	17	20	22	21	19	14	10	7	14
Daily Min.°C	2	2	3	6	8	12	14	13	11	8	5	4	7
Average Monthly °C	4	5	7	9	12	16	18	17	15	11	8	5	11
nfall Monthly Total mm	54	40	37	37	46	45	57	59	49	57	64	48	593
shine Av. Monthly Dur.	1.7	2.3	3.5	5.7	6.7	7	6.6	6	5	3.3	1.9	1.4	4.3
s Angeles USA 30m													
nperature Daily Max.°C	18	18	18	19	20	22	24	24	24	23	22	19	21
Daily Min.°C	7	8	9	11	13	15	17	17	16	14	11	9	12
Average Monthly °C	12	13	14	15	17	18	21	21	20	18	16	14	17
nfall Monthly Total mm	69	74	46	28	3	3	0	0	5	10	28	61	327
shine Av. Monthly Dur.	6.9	8.2	8.9	8.8	9.5	10.3	11.7	11	10.1	8.6	8.2	7.6	9.2
saka Zambia 1154m													
nperature Daily Max.°C	26	26	26	27	25	23	23	26	29	31	29	27	27
Daily Min.°C	17	17	16	15	12	10	9	11	15	18	18	17	15
Average Monthly °C	22	22	21	21	18	17	16	19	22	25	23	22	21
nfall Monthly Total mm	224	173	90	19	3	1	0	1	1	17	85	196	810
shine Av. Monthly Dur.	5.1	5.4	6.9	8.9	9	9	9.1	9.6	9.5	9	7	5.5	7.8
naus Brazil 45m													
nperature Daily Max.°C	31	31	31	31	31	31	32	33	34	34	33	32	32
Daily Min.°C	24	24	24	24	24	24	24	24	24	25	25	24	24
Average Monthly °C	28	28	28	27	28	28	28	29	29	29	29	28	28
nfall Monthly Total mm	278	278	300	287	193	99	61	41	62	112	165	220	2096
shine Av. Monthly Dur.	3.9	4	3.6	3.9	5.4	6.9	7.9	8.2	7.5	6.6	5.9	4.9	5.7
xico City Mexico 2309m													
nperature Daily Max.°C	21	23	26	27	26	25	23	24	23	22	21	21	24
Daily Min.°C	5	6	7	9	10	11	11	11	11	9	6	5	8
Average Monthly °C	13	15	16	18	18	18	17	17	17	16	14	13	16
nfall Monthly Total mm	8	4	9	23	57	111	160	149	119	46	16	7	709
shine Av. Monthly Dur.	7.3	8.1	8.5	8.1	7.8	7	6.2	6.4	5.6	6.3	7	7.3	7.1
ami USA 2m													
nperature Daily Max.°C	24	25	27	28	30	31	32	32	31	29	27	25	28
Daily Min.°C	14	15	16	19	21	23	24	24	24	22	18	15	20
Average Monthly °C	19	20	21	23	25	27	28	28	27	25	22	20	24
nfall Monthly Total mm	51	48	58	99	163	188	170	178	241	208	71	43	1518
shine Av. Monthly Dur.	7.7	8.3	8.7	9.4	8.9	8.5	8.7	8.4	7.1	6.5	7.5	7.1	8.1
ntreal Canada 57m													
nperature Daily Max.°C	-6	-4	2	11	18	23	26	25	20	14	5	-3	11
Daily Min.°C	-13	-11	-5	2	9	14	17	16	11	6	0	-9	3
Average Monthly °C	-9	-8	-2	6	13	19	22	20	16	10	3	-6	7
nfall Monthly Total mm	87	76	86	83	81	91	98	87	96	84	89	89	1047
shine Av. Monthly Dur.	2.8	3.4	4.5	5.2	6.7	7.7	8.2	7.7	5.6	4.3	2.4	2.2	5.1
scow Russia 156m													
nperature Daily Max.°C	-6	-4	1	9	18	22	24	22	17	10	1	-5	9
Daily Min.°C	-14	-16	-11	-1	5	9	12	9	4	-2	-6	-12	-2
Average Monthly °C	-10	-10	-5	4	12	15	18	16	10	4	-2	-8	4
nfall Monthly Total mm	31	28	33	35	52	67	74	74	58	51	36	36	575
shine Av. Monthly Dur.	1	1.9	3.7	5.2	7.8	8.3	8.4	7.1	4.4	2.4	1	0.6	4.4
w Delhi India 220m													
nperature Daily Max.°C	21	24	29	36	41	39	35	34	34	34	28	23	32
Daily Min.°C	6	10	14	20	26	28	27	26	24	17	11	7	18
Average Monthly °C	14	17	22	28	33	34	31	30	29	26	20	15	25
nfall Monthly Total mm	25	21	13	8	13	77	178	184	123	10	2	11	665
shine Av. Monthly Dur.	7.7	8.2	8.2	8.7	9.2	7.9	6	6.3	6.9	9.4	8.7	8.3	8

	Jan	Feb	Mar	Apr	May	June	July	Aug	Sep	Oct	Nov	Dec	Year
Perth Australia 60m													
Temperature Daily Max.°C	29	30	27	25	21	18	17	18	19	21	25	27	23
Daily Min.°C	17	18	16	14	12	10	9	9	10	11	14	16	13
Average Monthly °C	23	24	22	19	16	14	13	13	15	16	19	22	18
Rainfall Monthly Total mm	8	13	22	44	128	189	177	145	84	58	19	13	900
Sunshine Av. Monthly Dur.	10.4	9.8	8.8	7.5	5.7	4.8	5.4	6	7.2	8.1	9.6	10.4	7.8
Reykjavik Iceland 18m													
Temperature Daily Max.°C	2	3	5	6	10	13	15	14	12	8	5	4	8
Daily Min.°C	-3	-3	-1	1	4	7	9	8	6	3	0	-2	3
Average Monthly °C	0	0	2	4	7	10	12	11	9	5	3	1	5
Rainfall Monthly Total mm	89	64	62	56	42	42	50	56	67	94	78	79	779
Sunshine Av. Monthly Dur.	0.8	2	3.6	4.5	5.9	6.1	5.8	5.4	3.5	2.3	1.1	0.3	3.7
Santiago Chile 520m													
Temperature Daily Max.°C	30	29	27	24	19	15	15	17	19	22	26	29	23
Daily Min.°C	12	11	10	7	5	3	3	4	6	7	9	11	7
Average Monthly °C	21	20	18	15	12	9	9	10	12	15	17	20	15
Rainfall Monthly Total mm	3	3	5	13	64	84	76	56	31	15	8	5	363
Sunshine Av. Monthly Dur.	10.8	8.9	8.5	5.5	3.6	3.3	3.3	3.6	4.8	6.1	8.7	10.1	6.4
Shanghai China 5m													
Temperature Daily Max.°C	8	8	13	19	24	28	32	32	27	23	17	10	20
Daily Min.°C	-1	0	4	9	14	19	23	23	19	13	7	2	11
Average Monthly °C	3	4	8	14	19	23	27	27	23	18	12	6	15
Rainfall Monthly Total mm	48	59	84	94	94	180	147	142	130	71	51	36	1136
Sunshine Av. Monthly Dur.	4	3.7	4.4	4.8	5.4	4.7	6.9	7.5	5.3	5.6	4.7	4.5	5.1
Sydney Australia 40m													
Temperature Daily Max.°C	26	26	25	22	19	17	17	18	20	22	24	25	22
Daily Min.°C	18	19	17	14	11	9	8	9	11	13	16	17	14
Average Monthly °C	22	22	21	18	15	13	12	13	16	18	20	21	18
Rainfall Monthly Total mm	89	101	127	135	127	117	117	76	74	71	74	74	1182
Sunshine Av. Monthly Dur.	7.5	7	6.4	6.1	5.7	5.3	6.1	7	7.3	7.5	7.5	7.5	6.8
Tehran Iran 1191m													
Temperature Daily Max.°C	9	11	16	21	29	30	37	36	29	24	16	11	22
Daily Min.°C	-1	1	4	10	16	20	23	23	18	12	6	1	11
Average Monthly °C	4	6	10	15	22	25	30	29	23	18	11	6	17
Rainfall Monthly Total mm	37	23	36	31	14	2	1	1	1	5	29	27	207
Sunshine Av. Monthly Dur.	5.9	6.7	7.5	7.4	8.6	11.6	11.2	11	10.1	7.6	6.9	6.3	8.4
Timbuktu Mali 269m													
Temperature Daily Max.°C	31	35	38	41	43	42	38	35	38	40	37	31	37
Daily Min.°C	13	16	18	22	26	27	25	24	24	23	18	14	21
Average Monthly °C	22	25	28	31	34	34	32	30	31	31	28	23	29
Rainfall Monthly Total mm	0	0	0	1	4	20	54	93	31	3	0	0	206
Sunshine Av. Monthly Dur.	9.1	9.6	9.6	9.7	9.8	9.4	9.6	9	9.3	9.5	9.5	8.9	9.4
Tokyo Japan 5m													
Temperature Daily Max.°C	9	9	12	18	22	25	29	30	27	20	16	11	19
Daily Min.°C	-1	-1	3	4	13	17	22	23	19	13	7	1	10
Average Monthly °C	4	4	8	11	18	21	25	26	23	17	11	6	14
Rainfall Monthly Total mm	48	73	101	135	131	182	146	147	217	220	101	61	1562
Sunshine Av. Monthly Dur.	6	5.9	5.7	6	6.2	5	5.8	6.6	4.5	4.4	4.8	5.4	5.5
Tromsø Norway 100m													
Temperature Daily Max.°C	-2	-2	0	3	7	12	16	14	10	5	2	0	5
Daily Min.°C	-6	-6	-5	-2	1	6	9	8	5	1	-2	-4	0
Average Monthly °C	-4	-4	-3	0	4	9	13	11	7	3	0	-2	3
Rainfall Monthly Total mm	96	79	91	65	61	59	56	80	109	115	88	95	994
Sunshine Av. Monthly Dur.	0.1	1.6	2.9	6.1	5.7	6.9	7.9	4.8	3.5	1.7	0.3	0	3.52
Ulan Bator Mongolia 1305m													
Temperature Daily Max.°C	-19	-13	-4	7	13	21	22	21	14	6	-6	-16	4
Daily Min.°C	-32	-29	-22	-8	-2	7	11	8	2	-8	-20	-28	-11
Average Monthly °C	-26	-21	-13	-1	6	14	16	14	8	-1	-13	-22	-4
Rainfall Monthly Total mm	1	1	2	5	10	28	76	51	23	5	5	2	209
Sunshine Av. Monthly Dur.	6.4	7.8	8	7.8	8.3	8.6	8.6	8.2	7.2	6.9	6.1	5.7	7.5
Vancouver Canada 5m													
Temperature Daily Max.°C	6	7	10	14	17	20	23	22	19	14	9	7	14
Daily Min.°C	0	1	3	5	8	11	13	12	10	7	3	2	6
Average Monthly °C	3	4	6	9	13	16	18	17	14	10	6	4	10
Rainfall Monthly Total mm	214	161	151	90	69	65	39	44	83	172	198	243	1529
Sunshine Av. Monthly Dur.	1.6	3	3.8	5.9	7.5	7.4	9.5	8.2	6	3.7	2	1.4	5
Verkhoyansk Russia 137m													
Temperature Daily Max.°C	-47	-40	-20	-1	11	21	24	21	12	-8	-33	-42	-8
Daily Min.°C	-51	-48	-40	-25	-7	4	6	1	-6	-20	-39	-50	-23
Average Monthly °C	-49	-44	-30	-13	2	12	15	11	3	-14	-36	-46	-16
Rainfall Monthly Total mm	7	5	5	4	5	25	33	30	13	11	10	7	155
Sunshine Av. Monthly Dur.	0	2.6	6.9	9.6	9.7	10	9.7	7.5	4.1	2.4	0.6	0	5.4
Washington USA 22m													
Temperature Daily Max.°C	7	8	12	19	25	29	31	30	26	20	14	8	19
Daily Min.°C	-1	-1	2	8	13	18	21	20	16	10	4	-1	9
Average Monthly °C	3	3	7	13	19	24	26	25	21	15	9	4	14
Rainfall Monthly Total mm	84	68	96	85	103	88	108	120	100	78	75	75	1080
Sunshine Av. Monthly Dur.	4.4	5.7	6.7	7.4	8.2	8.8	8.6	8.2	7.5	6.5	5.3	4.5	6.8

AGRICULTURAL PRODUCTION

Staple Crops

Wheat

China 18.9% | India 12.2% | U.S.A. 11.0% | France 5.7% | Russia 5.5% | Canada 4.6%

World total (1996): 584,874,000 tonnes

Rice

China 34.0% | India 21.7% | Indonesia 9.0% | Bangladesh 4.8% | Vietnam 4.5% | Thailand 3.8% | Burma 3.6%

World total (1996): 562,259,000 tonnes

Millet

India 33.2% | Nigeria 18.3% | China 16.1% | Niger 6.4%

World total (1996): 29,563,000 tonnes

Rye

Poland 27.7% | Germany 20.0% | Russia 18.1% | Belarus 9.5% | Ukraine 5.3%

World total (1996): 23,156,000 tonnes

Maize

U.S.A. 36.4% | China 21.8% | Brazil 7.0%

World total (1996): 576,821,000 tonnes

Potatoes

China 16.0% | Russia 14.0% | Poland 8.7% | U.S.A. 7.1% | India 6.3% | Ukraine 5.2% | Germany 3.6%

World total (1996): 294,834,000 tonnes

Soya

U.S.A. 47.1% | Brazil 20.4% | China 10.7% | Argentina 9.6%

World total (1996): 130,302,000 tonnes

Cassava

Nigeria 19.2% | Brazil 15.6% | Thailand 11.1% | Congo (Zaire) 10.7% | Indonesia 9.4% | Ghana 4.2% | India 3.3% | Tanzania 3.6%

World total (1996): 162,942,000 tonnes

Animal Products

Milk

U.S.A. 15.2% | Russia 8.4% | Germany 6.0% | France 5.5% | India 3.7% | Ukraine 3.7%

World total (1996): 466,317,000 tonnes

Butter

India 19.0% | U.S.A. 8.9% | Germany 7.2% | France 6.7% | Russia 6.2% | Pakistan 5.5% | New Zealand 4.6%

World total (1996): 6,565,000 tonnes

Lamb and Mutton

China 15.1% | Australia 8.5% | N.Zealand 7.9% | U.K. 5.2% | Turkey 3.8% | Iran 3.6% | Russia 3.6% | Pakistan 3.6%

World total (1996): 7,289,000 tonnes

Beef and Veal

U.S.A. 21.7% | Brazil 8.6% | China 6.5% | Russia 5.9% | Argentina 4.6% | France 3.6%

World total (1996): 53,956,000 tonnes

Pork

China 45.1% | U.S.A. 9.7% | Germany 4.3%

World total (1996): 85,761,000 tonnes

Sugars

Sugarcane

Brazil 26.0% | India 22.2% | China 6.0% | Thailand 5.0% | Pakistan 4.0% | Mexico 3.6%

World total (1996): 1,192,555,000 tonnes

Sugar beet

France 11.5% | Ukraine 11.2% | Germany 9.8% | U.S.A. 9.6% | Russia 7.2% | Poland 5.3% | Italy 5.0% | Turkey 4.2%

World total (1996): 255,500,000 tonnes

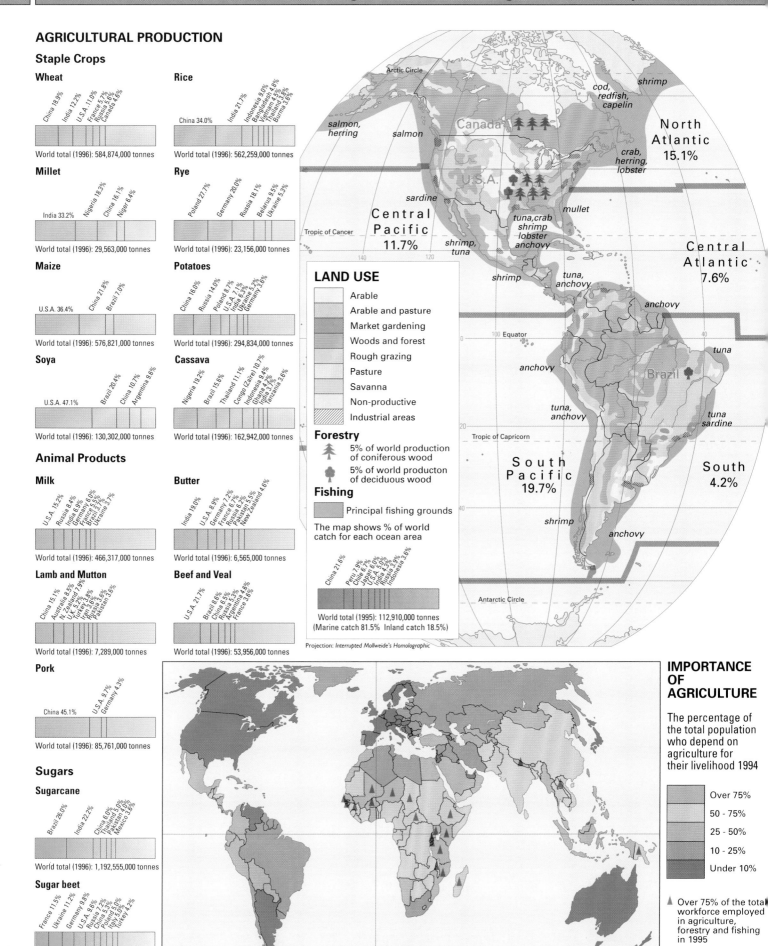

LAND USE

- Arable
- Arable and pasture
- Market gardening
- Woods and forest
- Rough grazing
- Pasture
- Savanna
- Non-productive
- Industrial areas

Forestry

🌲 5% of world production of coniferous wood

🌳 5% of world producton of deciduous wood

Fishing

Principal fishing grounds

The map shows % of world catch for each ocean area

China 21.6% | Peru 7.9% | Chile 6.7% | Japan 6.0% | U.S.A. 5.0% | India 4.3% | Russia 3.9% | Indonesia 3.6%

World total (1995): 112,910,000 tonnes
(Marine catch 81.5% Inland catch 18.5%)

Projection: *Interrupted Mollweide's Homolographic*

Ocean labels:
North Atlantic 15.1%
Central Pacific 11.7%
Central Atlantic 7.6%
South Pacific 19.7%
South 4.2%

Projection: *Modified Hammer Equal Area*

IMPORTANCE OF AGRICULTURE

The percentage of the total population who depend on agriculture for their livelihood 1994

- Over 75%
- 50 - 75%
- 25 - 50%
- 10 - 25%
- Under 10%

▲ Over 75% of the total workforce employed in agriculture, forestry and fishing in 1995

1:110 000 000

capelin, plaice, cod,
haddock   redfin
herring

Sweden

Russia

salmon

crab

herring

jack
mackerel,

salmon

tuna

mackerel

tuna

China

crab

sardine
mackerel

anchovy,
tuna

**North Pacific
33.0%**

sardine

India

mackerel

tuna
sardine

mackerel

anchovy

anchovy
mackerel,
tuna

**Central Pacific
11.7%**

tuna

shrimp,
sardine,
anchovy

shrimp

Nigeria

shrimp

ullet,
bster,
hrimp

Indonesia

mackerel

sardine

shrimp

tuna

tuna

tuna

mackerel

**Indian Ocean
8.7%**

tuna

mackerel

crab

Atlantic

sardine

jack
mackerel   lobster

mullet

mullet

tuna

sardine

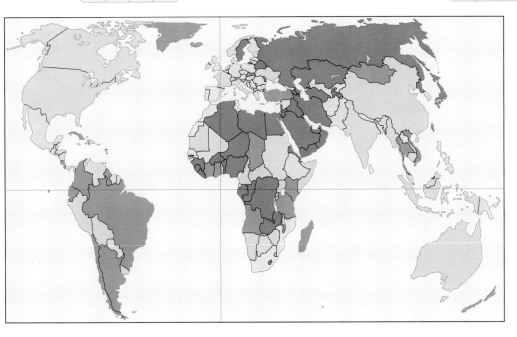

Food Production and Population by Continent

Comparison of food production and population by continent (latest available year). The left side of the pie indicates percentage shares of total world food production; the right shows population in proportion.

Africa	
North America	
South America	
Asia	
Europe	
Oceania	

Food — 6.7% — **Population**

6.5% 13.8%   12.6% 8%   5.6%

44.3%   60.4%

27.5%

1.2%   12.9%

0.5%

TRADE IN AGRICULTURAL PRODUCTS

Balance of trade in agricultural products (food and live animals) by value (latest available year)

	50% more exports than imports
	10% more exports than imports
	10% either side
	10% more imports than exports
	50% more imports than exports

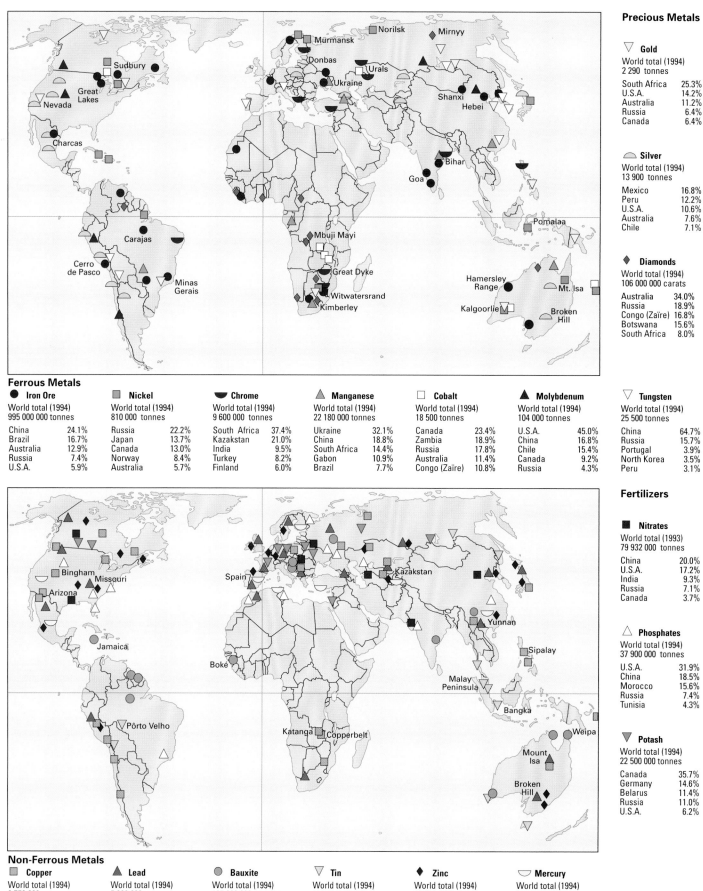

Precious Metals

▽ Gold
World total (1994)
2 290 tonnes

South Africa	25.3%
U.S.A.	14.2%
Australia	11.2%
Russia	6.4%
Canada	6.4%

◠ Silver
World total (1994)
13 900 tonnes

Mexico	16.8%
Peru	12.2%
U.S.A.	10.6%
Australia	7.6%
Chile	7.1%

◆ Diamonds
World total (1994)
106 000 000 carats

Australia	34.0%
Russia	18.9%
Congo (Zaïre)	16.8%
Botswana	15.6%
South Africa	8.0%

Ferrous Metals

● Iron Ore	■ Nickel	◗ Chrome	▲ Manganese	☐ Cobalt	▲ Molybdenum	▽ Tungsten
World total (1994) 995 000 000 tonnes	World total (1994) 810 000 tonnes	World total (1994) 9 600 000 tonnes	World total (1994) 22 180 000 tonnes	World total (1994) 18 500 tonnes	World total (1994) 104 000 tonnes	World total (1994) 25 500 tonnes
China 24.1%	Russia 22.2%	South Africa 37.4%	Ukraine 32.1%	Canada 23.4%	U.S.A. 45.0%	China 64.7%
Brazil 16.7%	Japan 13.7%	Kazakstan 21.0%	China 18.8%	Zambia 18.9%	China 16.8%	Russia 15.7%
Australia 12.9%	Canada 13.0%	India 9.5%	South Africa 14.4%	Russia 17.8%	Chile 15.4%	Portugal 3.9%
Russia 7.4%	Norway 8.4%	Turkey 8.2%	Gabon 10.9%	Australia 11.4%	Canada 9.2%	North Korea 3.5%
U.S.A. 5.9%	Australia 5.7%	Finland 6.0%	Brazil 7.7%	Congo (Zaïre) 10.8%	Russia 4.3%	Peru 3.1%

Fertilizers

■ Nitrates
World total (1993)
79 932 000 tonnes

China	20.0%
U.S.A.	17.2%
India	9.3%
Russia	7.1%
Canada	3.7%

△ Phosphates
World total (1994)
37 900 000 tonnes

U.S.A.	31.9%
China	18.5%
Morocco	15.6%
Russia	7.4%
Tunisia	4.3%

▽ Potash
World total (1994)
22 500 000 tonnes

Canada	35.7%
Germany	14.6%
Belarus	11.4%
Russia	11.0%
U.S.A.	6.2%

Non-Ferrous Metals

■ Copper	▲ Lead	● Bauxite	▽ Tin	◆ Zinc	◠ Mercury
World total (1994) 9 750 000 tonnes	World total (1994) 5 380 000 tonnes	World total (1994) 107 000 000 tonnes	World total (1994) 199 000 tonnes	World total (1994) 7 360 000 tonnes	World total (1994) 1 760 tonnes
U.S.A. 17.5%	U.S.A. 23.4%	Australia 39.0%	China 26.6%	China 13.2%	China 28.4%
Chile 13.1%	France 8.3%	Guinea 13.5%	Malaysia 21.1%	Japan 9.7%	Algeria 27.0%
Japan 11.5%	China 7.6%	Brazil 7.6%	Indonesia 15.6%	Canada 9.4%	Spain 17.0%
Russia 6.0%	U.K. 6.4%	India 5.0%	Brazil 15.2%	Germany 4.9%	Kyrgyzstan 11.4%
Canada 5.7%	Germany 6.2%	China 3.5%	Bolivia 7.7%	U.S.A. 4.8%	Finland 5.7%

Projection: *Modified Hammer Equal Area*

ENERGY PRODUCTION

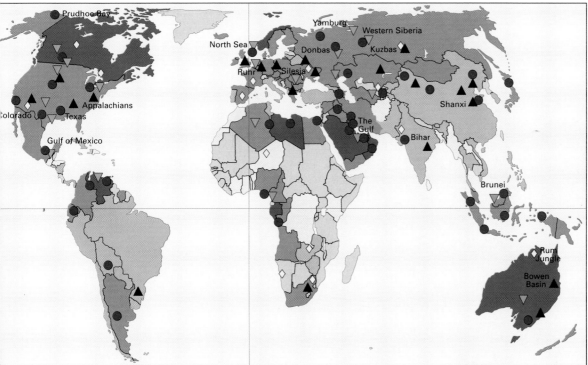

Primary energy production expressed in kilograms of coal equivalent per person 1994

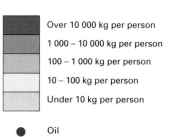

Over 10 000 kg per person

1 000 – 10 000 kg per person

100 – 1 000 kg per person

10 – 100 kg per person

Under 10 kg per person

● Oil

▽ Natural gas

▲ Coal and lignite

◇ Uranium *(the fuel used to generate nuclear power)*

In developing countries traditional fuels are still very important. Sometimes called biomass fuels, they include wood, charcoal and dried dung. The pie graph for Nigeria at the foot of the page shows their importance.

Oil		**Natural Gas**		**Coal (bituminous)**		**Coal (lignite)**		**Uranium**		**Nuclear Power**		**Hydro-Electric Power**	
World total (1994) 3 183 500 000 tonnes		World total (1993) 2 658 000 000 tonnes of coal equivalent		World total (1993) 3 160 000 000 tonnes		World total (1993) 1 265 000 000 tonnes		World total (1993) 32 532 tonnes (metal content)		World total (1994) 820 000 000 tonnes of coal equivalent		World total (1994) 922 000 000 tonnes of coal equivalent	
Saudi Arabia	13.2%	Canada	28.2%	China	36.0%	U.S.A.	23.7%	Canada	28.2%	U.S.A.	31.0%	Canada	12.8%
U.S.A.	12.6%	Nigeria	9.0%	U.S.A.	17.6%	Germany	17.5%	Niger	9.0%	France	16.3%	U.S.A.	12.2%
Russia	9.9%	Kazakstan	8.3%	India	7.9%	Russia	9.1%	Kazakstan	8.3%	Japan	11.8%	Former U.S.S.R.	10.4%
Iran	5.7%	Uzbekistan	8.0%	Russia	6.3%	China	7.4%	Uzbekistan	8.0%	Former U.S.S.R.	7.9%	Brazil	10.3%
Mexico	4.9%	Russia	7.4%	Australia South Africa }	5.8%	Poland	5.4%	Russia	7.4%	Germany	6.9%	China	6.9%

ENERGY CONSUMPTION

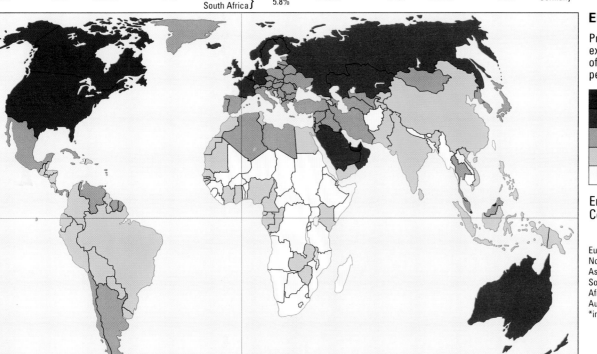

Primary energy consumption expressed in kilograms of coal equivalent per person 1994

Over 10 000 kg per person

5 000 – 10 000 kg per person

1 000 – 5 000 kg per person

100 – 1 000 kg per person

Under 100 kg per person

Energy consumption by Continent 1991

		Change 1990-91
Europe*	38.3%	*(-0.2%)*
North America	30.0%	*(+2.4%)*
Asia	25.0%	*(+1.9%)*
South America	3.0%	*(-2.9%)*
Africa	2.4%	*(-0.4%)*
Australasia	1.3%	*(no change)*
*includes former U.S.S.R.		

Projection: *Modified Hammer Equal Area*

TYPE OF ENERGY CONSUMED BY SELECTED COUNTRIES 1993

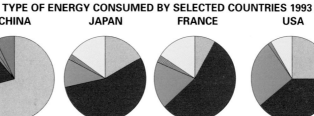

NIGERIA   CHINA   JAPAN   FRANCE   USA   NORWAY

Coal & Lignite

Oil

Natural gas

Hydro-electricity

Nuclear electricity

Traditional Fuels

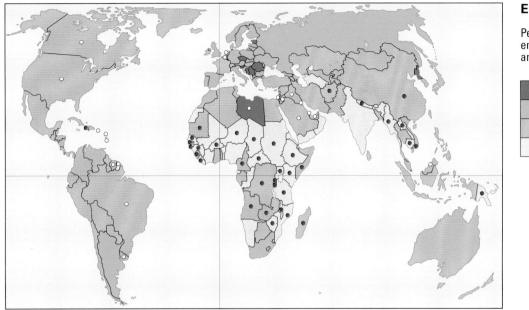

EMPLOYMENT IN INDUSTRY

Percentage of total workforce employed in manufacturing and mining 1995

	Over 30%
	20 – 30%
	10 – 20%
	Under 10%

● Over two thirds of total workforce employed in agriculture

○ Over a third of total workforce employed in service industries (work in offices, shops, tourism, transport, construction and government)

INDUSTRIAL PRODUCTION

Industrial output (mining, manufacturing, construction, energy and water production), top 40 nations, US $ billion (1991)

1.	U.S.A.	1,627	21. Saudi Arabia	56
2.	Japan	1,412	22. Indonesia	48
3.	Germany	614	23. Spain	47
4.	Italy	380	24. Argentina	46
5.	France	348	25. Poland	39
6.	U.K.	324	26. Norway	38
7.	Former U.S.S.R.	250	27. Finland	37
8.	Brazil	161	28. Thailand	36
9.	China	155	29. Turkey	33
10.	South Korea	127	30. Denmark	31
11.	Canada	117	31. Israel	23
12.	Australia	93	32. Iran	20
	Netherlands	93	33. Ex- Czechoslovakia	19
14.	Taiwan	86	34. Hong Kong	17
15.	Mexico	85	Portugal (1989)	17
16.	Sweden	70	36. Algeria	16
17.	Switzerland (1989)	61	Greece	16
18.	India	60	38. Iraq	15
19.	Austria	59	Philippines	15
	Belgium	59	Singapore	15

Graphs show the top ten producing countries for selected industrial goods.

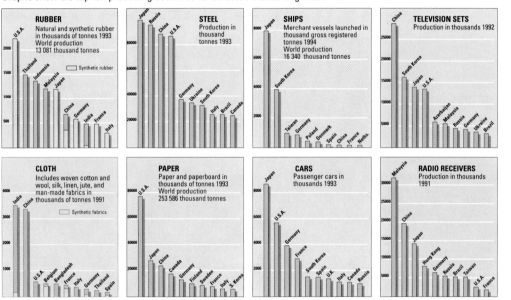

INDUSTRY AND TRADE

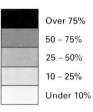

Manufactured goods (inc. machinery & transport) as a percentage of total exports (latest available year)

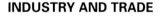

	Over 75%
	50 – 75%
	25 – 50%
	10 – 25%
	Under 10%

The Far East and South-East Asia (Japan 98.3%, Macau 97.8%, Taiwan 92.7%, Hong Kong 93.0%, South Korea 93.4%) are most dominant, but many countries in Europe (e.g. Slovenia 92.4%) are also heavily dependent on manufactured goods.

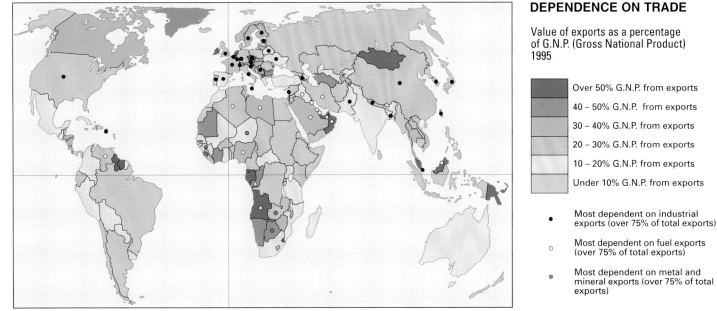

DEPENDENCE ON TRADE

Value of exports as a percentage of G.N.P. (Gross National Product) 1995

Over 50% G.N.P. from exports

40 – 50% G.N.P. from exports

30 – 40% G.N.P. from exports

20 – 30% G.N.P. from exports

10 – 20% G.N.P. from exports

Under 10% G.N.P. from exports

● Most dependent on industrial exports (over 75% of total exports)

○ Most dependent on fuel exports (over 75% of total exports)

◉ Most dependent on metal and mineral exports (over 75% of total exports)

BALANCE OF TRADE

Value of exports in proportion to the value of imports 1995

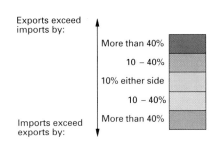

Exports exceed imports by:

More than 40%

10 – 40%

10% either side

10 – 40%

Imports exceed exports by:

More than 40%

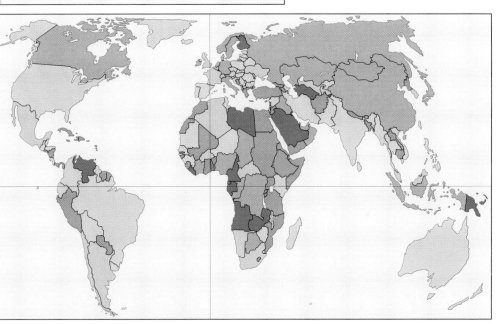

SHARE OF WORLD TRADE

Percentage share of total world exports by value 1995

Over 10% of world trade

5 – 10% of world trade

1 – 5% of world trade

0.5 – 1% of world trade

0.1 – 0.5% of world trade

Under 0.1% of world trade

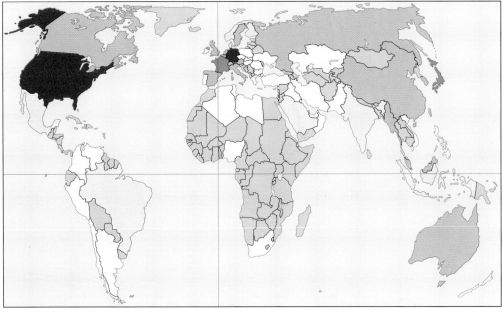

Projection: *Modified Hammer Equal Area*

AIR TRAVEL

Passenger kilometres flown 1994

Passenger kilometres are the number of passengers (international and domestic) multiplied by the distance flown by each passenger from airport of origin.

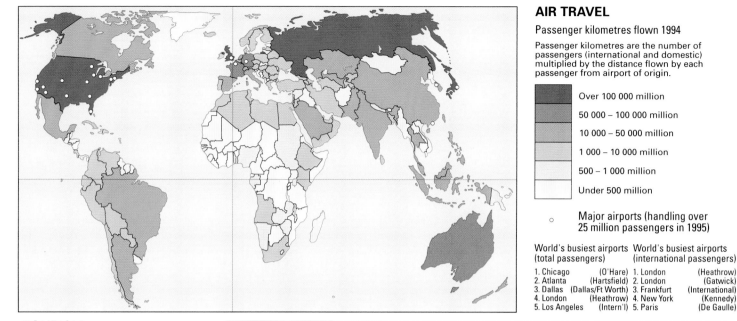

- Over 100 000 million
- 50 000 – 100 000 million
- 10 000 – 50 000 million
- 1 000 – 10 000 million
- 500 – 1 000 million
- Under 500 million

○ Major airports (handling over 25 million passengers in 1995)

World's busiest airports (total passengers)		World's busiest airports (international passengers)	
1. Chicago	(O'Hare)	1. London	(Heathrow)
2. Atlanta	(Hartsfield)	2. London	(Gatwick)
3. Dallas	(Dallas/Ft Worth)	3. Frankfurt	(International)
4. London	(Heathrow)	4. New York	(Kennedy)
5. Los Angeles	(Intern'l)	5. Paris	(De Gaulle)

TOURISM

Tourism receipts as a percentage of G.N.P. (Gross National Product) 1994

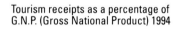

- Over 10% of G.N.P from tourism
- 5 – 10% of G.N.P. from tourism
- 2.5 – 5% of G.N.P. from tourism
- 1 – 2.5% of G.N.P. from tourism
- 0.5 – 1% of G.N.P. from tourism
- Under 0.5% of G.N.P. from tourism

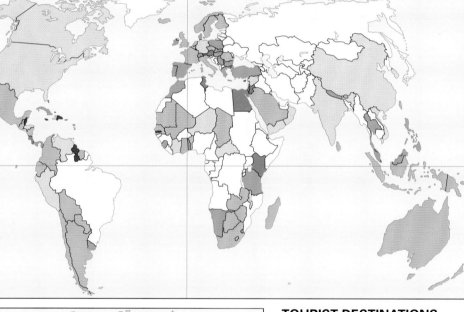

Countries spending the most on promoting tourism, millions of US $ (1996)		Fastest growing tourist destinations, % change in receipts (1994–5)	
Australia	88	South Korea	49%
Spain	79	Czech Republic	27%
U.K.	79	India	21%
France	73	Russia	19%
Singapore	54	Philippines	18%

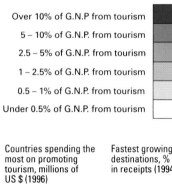
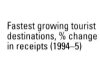

TOURIST DESTINATIONS

- ■ Cultural & historical centres
- □ Coastal resorts
- □ Ski resorts
- ▨ Centres of entertainment
- ▨ Places of pilgrimage
- ▨ Places of great natural beauty

~~~~~~ Popular holiday cruise routes

Projection: *Modified Hammer Equal Area*

CARTOGRAPHY BY PHILIP'S. COPYRIGHT GEORGE PHILIP LTD

TIME ZONES

Note: Certain of the time zones are affected by the incidence of "Summer Time" in countries where it is adopted.

Zones using Greenwich Mean Time	Half hour zones	International boundaries
Zones slow of Greenwich Mean Time	Zones fast of Greenwich Mean Time	Time zone boundaries
		International date line
		Selected air routes

10PM — Actual Solar Time when noon at Greenwich is shown along the top of the map.

10 — Hours slow or fast of Greenwich Mean Time

Equatorial scale: 1:220 000 000

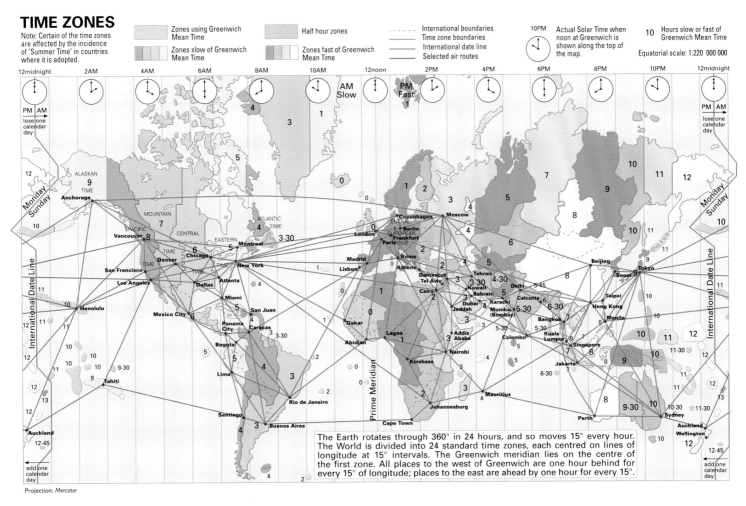

The Earth rotates through 360° in 24 hours, and so moves 15° every hour. The World is divided into 24 standard time zones, each centred on lines of longitude at 15° intervals. The Greenwich meridian lies on the centre of the first zone. All places to the west of Greenwich are one hour behind for every 15° of longitude; places to the east are ahead by one hour for every 15°.

Projection: Mercator

DISTANCE TABLE

The table shows air distances in miles and kilometres between twenty-four major cities. Known as 'Great Circle' distances, these measure the shortest routes between cities, which aircraft use where possible.

Kms (lower-left of diagonal) — Miles (upper-right of diagonal)

City	Beijing	Bogota	Buenos Aires	Cairo	Calcutta	Caracas	Chicago	Hong Kong	Honolulu	Johannesburg	Lagos	London	Los Angeles	Mexico City	Moscow	Nairobi	New York	Paris	Rio de Janeiro	Rome	Singapore	Sydney	Tokyo	Wellington
Beijing	Beijing	9263	11972	4688	2031	8947	6588	1220	5070	7276	7119	5057	6251	7742	3600	5727	6828	5106	10773	5049	2783	5561	1304	6700
Bogota	14908	Bogota	2911	6971	10223	637	2710	10480	5697	7125	5319	5262	3478	1961	6758	7672	2481	5358	2820	5831	11990	8903	8851	7527
Buenos Aires	19268	4685	Buenos Aires	7341	10268	3167	5599	11481	7558	5025	4919	6917	6122	4591	8374	6463	5298	6867	1214	6929	9867	7332	11410	6202
Cairo	7544	11218	11814	Cairo	3541	6340	6127	5064	8838	3894	2432	2180	7580	7687	1803	2197	5605	1994	6149	1325	5137	8959	5947	10268
Calcutta	3269	16453	16524	5699	Calcutta	9609	7978	1653	7048	5256	5727	4946	8152	9494	3438	3839	7921	4883	9366	4486	1800	5678	3195	7055
Caracas	14399	1026	5096	10203	15464	Caracas	2502	10166	6009	6847	4810	4664	3612	2228	6175	7173	2131	4738	2825	5196	11407	9534	8801	8154
Chicago	10603	4361	9011	9860	12839	4027	Chicago	7783	4247	8689	5973	3949	1742	1694	4971	8005	711	4132	5311	4809	9369	9243	6299	8358
Hong Kong	1963	16865	18478	8150	2659	16360	12526	Hong Kong	5543	6669	7360	5980	7232	8775	4439	5453	8047	5984	11001	5769	1615	4582	1786	5857
Honolulu	8160	9169	12164	14223	11343	9670	6836	8921	Honolulu	11934	10133	7228	2558	3781	7036	10739	4958	7437	8290	8026	6721	5075	3854	4669
Johannesburg	11710	11467	8088	6267	8459	11019	13984	10732	19206	Johannesburg	2799	5637	10362	9063	5692	1818	7979	5426	4420	4811	5381	6860	8418	7308
Lagos	11457	8561	7916	3915	9216	7741	9612	11845	16308	4505	Lagos	3118	7713	6879	3886	2366	5268	2929	3750	2510	6925	9643	8376	9973
London	8138	8468	11131	3508	7961	7507	6356	9623	11632	9071	5017	London	5442	5552	1552	4237	3463	212	5778	889	6743	10558	5942	11691
Los Angeles	10060	5596	9852	12200	13120	5812	2804	11639	4117	16676	12414	8758	Los Angeles	1549	6070	9659	2446	5645	6310	6331	8776	7502	5475	6719
Mexico City	12460	3156	7389	12372	15280	3586	2726	14122	6085	14585	11071	8936	2493	Mexico City	6664	9207	2090	5717	4780	6365	10321	8058	7024	6897
Moscow	5794	10877	13477	2902	5534	9938	8000	7144	11323	9161	6254	2498	9769	10724	Moscow	3942	4666	1545	7184	1477	5237	9008	4651	10283
Nairobi	9216	12347	10402	3536	6179	11544	12883	8776	17282	2927	3807	6819	15544	14818	6344	Nairobi	7358	4029	5548	3350	4635	7552	6996	8490
New York	10988	3993	8526	9020	12747	3430	1145	12950	7980	12841	8477	5572	3936	3264	7510	11842	New York	3626	4832	4280	9531	9935	6741	8951
Paris	8217	8622	11051	3210	7858	7625	6650	9630	11968	8732	4714	342	9085	9200	2486	6485	5836	Paris	5708	687	6671	10539	6038	11798
Rio de Janeiro	17338	4539	1953	9896	15073	4546	8547	17704	13342	7113	6035	9299	10155	7693	11562	8928	7777	9187	Rio de Janeiro	5725	9763	8389	11551	7367
Rome	8126	9383	11151	2133	7219	8363	7739	9284	12916	7743	4039	1431	10188	10243	2376	5391	6888	1105	9214	Rome	6229	10143	6127	11523
Singapore	4478	19296	15879	8267	2897	18359	15078	2599	10816	8660	11145	10852	14123	16610	8428	7460	15339	10737	15712	10025	Singapore	3915	3306	5298
Sydney	8949	14327	11800	14418	9138	15343	14875	7374	8168	11040	15519	16992	12073	12969	14497	12153	15989	16962	13501	16324	6300	Sydney	4861	1383
Tokyo	2099	14245	18362	9571	5141	14164	10137	2874	6202	13547	13480	9562	8811	11304	7485	11260	10849	9718	18589	9861	5321	7823	Tokyo	5762
Wellington	10782	12113	9981	16524	11354	13122	13451	9427	7513	11761	16050	18814	10814	11100	16549	13664	14405	18987	11855	18545	8526	2226	9273	Wellington

CARTOGRAPHY BY PHILIP'S.

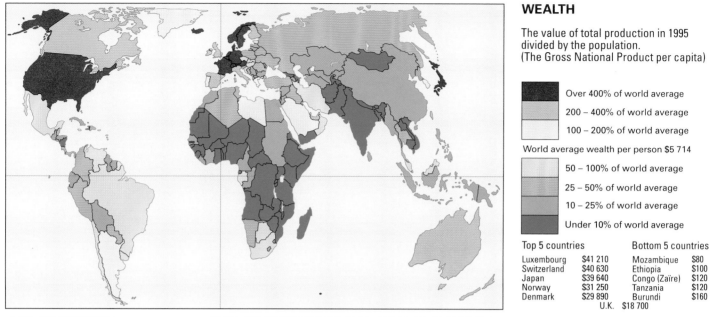

WEALTH

The value of total production in 1995 divided by the population.
(The Gross National Product per capita)

- Over 400% of world average
- 200 – 400% of world average
- 100 – 200% of world average

World average wealth per person $5 714

- 50 – 100% of world average
- 25 – 50% of world average
- 10 – 25% of world average
- Under 10% of world average

Top 5 countries		Bottom 5 countries	
Luxembourg	$41 210	Mozambique	$80
Switzerland	$40 630	Ethiopia	$100
Japan	$39 640	Congo (Zaïre)	$120
Norway	$31 250	Tanzania	$120
Denmark	$29 890	Burundi	$160
		U.K.	$18 700

CAR OWNERSHIP

Number of people per car
(latest available year)

- Over 1000 people per car
- 500 – 1000 people per car
- 100 – 500 people per car
- 25 – 100 people per car
- 5 – 25 people per car
- Under 5 people per car

Most people per car		Most cars (millions)	
Nepal	4247	U.S.A.	143.8
Bangladesh	2618	Germany	39.1
Cambodia	2328	Japan	39.0
Somalia	1790	Italy	29.6
Ethiopia	1423	France	24.0

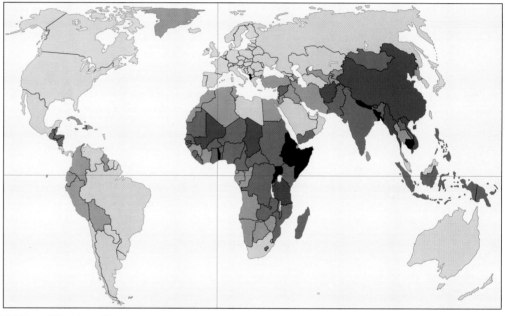

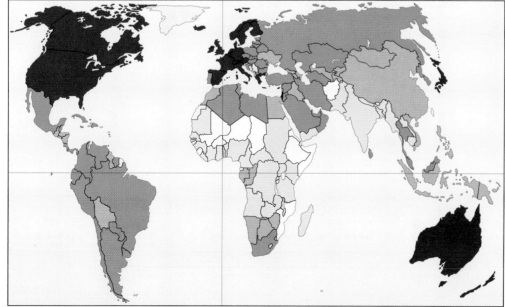

HUMAN DEVELOPMENT INDEX

The Human Development Index (H.D.I.) 1994 includes social and economic indicators and is calculated by the U.N. Development Programme as a measure of national human progress. Wealthy developed countries measure highest on the index.

- H.D.I. over 0.900
- H.D.I. 0.700 – 0.899
- H.D.I. 0.500 – 0.699
- H.D.I. 0.300 – 0.499
- H.D.I. under 0.299
- H.D.I. not available

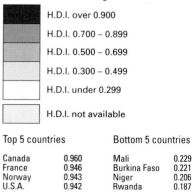

Top 5 countries		Bottom 5 countries	
Canada	0.960	Mali	0.229
France	0.946	Burkina Faso	0.221
Norway	0.943	Niger	0.206
U.S.A.	0.942	Rwanda	0.187
Iceland	0.942	Sierra Leone	0.176
		U.K.	0.931

Projection: *Modified Hammer Equal Area*

CARTOGRAPHY BY PHILIP'S. COPYRIGHT GEORGE PHILIP LTD

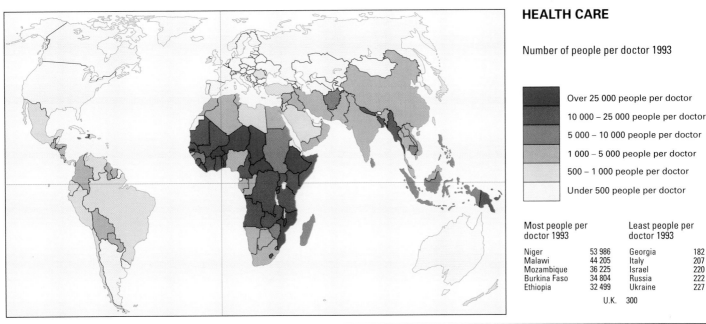

HEALTH CARE

Number of people per doctor 1993

- Over 25 000 people per doctor
- 10 000 – 25 000 people per doctor
- 5 000 – 10 000 people per doctor
- 1 000 – 5 000 people per doctor
- 500 – 1 000 people per doctor
- Under 500 people per doctor

Most people per doctor 1993		Least people per doctor 1993	
Niger	53 986	Georgia	182
Malawi	44 205	Italy	207
Mozambique	36 225	Israel	220
Burkina Faso	34 804	Russia	222
Ethiopia	32 499	Ukraine	227
		U.K.	300

ILLITERACY & EDUCATION

Percentage of total population unable to read or write 1995

- Over 75% of population illiterate
- 50 – 75% of population illiterate
- 25 – 50% of population illiterate
- 10 – 25% of population illiterate
- Under 10% of population illiterate

• Less than 6 years compulsory education per child

Educational expenditure per person (latest available year)

Top five countries		Bottom five countries	
Norway	$2,820	Congo (Zaïre)	$1
Denmark	$2,450	Somalia	$2
Switzerland	$2,256	Sierra Leone	$2
Japan	$1,853	Nigeria	$3
Finland	$1,706	Haiti	$3
		U.K.	$1,009

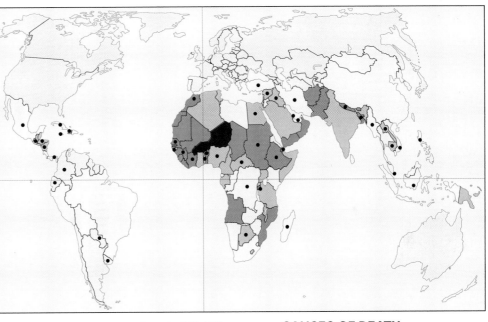

FERTILITY & EDUCATION

Fertility rates compared with female education, selected countries (1992–1995)

- Fertility rate: average number of children borne per woman
- Percentage of females aged 12 – 17 in secondary education

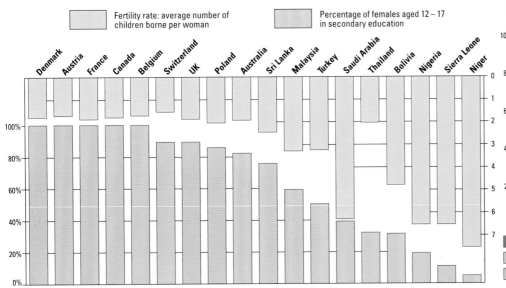

CAUSES OF DEATH

Causes of death for selected countries by percentage (1992–1994)

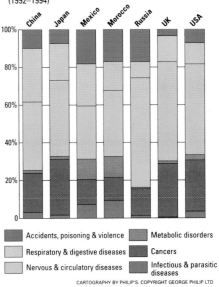

- Accidents, poisoning & violence
- Respiratory & digestive diseases
- Nervous & circulatory diseases
- Metabolic disorders
- Cancers
- Infectious & parasitic diseases

CARTOGRAPHY BY PHILIP'S. COPYRIGHT GEORGE PHILIP LTD

AGE DISTRIBUTION PYRAMIDS

The bars represent the percentage of the total population (males plus females) in the age group shown.

Developed countries such as the U.K. have populations evenly spread across age groups and usually a growing percentage of elderly people. Developing countries such as Kenya have the great majority of their people in the younger age groups, about to enter their most fertile years.

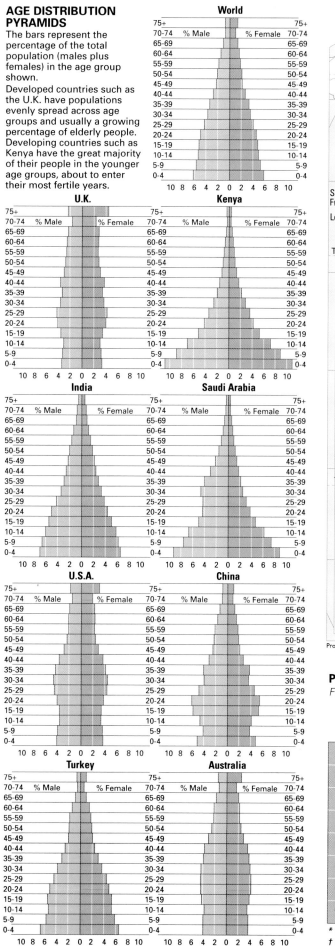

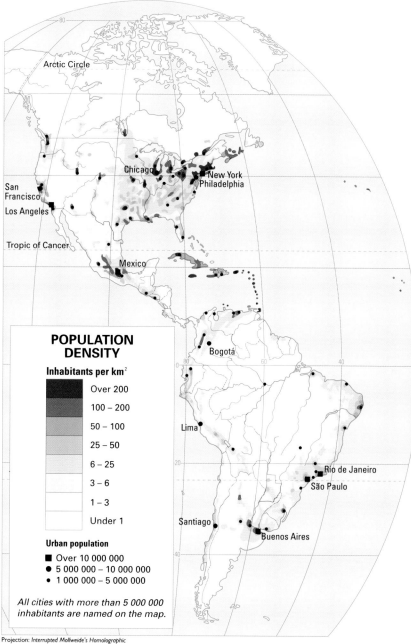

POPULATION DENSITY

Inhabitants per km²

- Over 200
- 100 – 200
- 50 – 100
- 25 – 50
- 6 – 25
- 3 – 6
- 1 – 3
- Under 1

Urban population

- ■ Over 10 000 000
- ● 5 000 000 – 10 000 000
- • 1 000 000 – 5 000 000

All cities with more than 5 000 000 inhabitants are named on the map.

Projection: Interrupted Mollweide's Homolographic

POPULATION CHANGE 1930-2020   Population totals are in millions

Figures in italics represent the percentage average annual increase for the period shown

	1930	1930-1960	1960	1960-1990	1990	1990-2020	2020
World	2013	*1.4%*	3019	*1.9%*	5292	*1.4%*	8062
Africa	155	*2.0%*	281	*2.85*	648	*2.7%*	1441
North America	135	*1.3%*	199	*1.1%*	276	*0.6%*	327
Latin America*	129	*1.8%*	218	*2.4%*	448	*1.6%*	719
Asia	1073	*1.5%*	1669	*2.1%*	3108	*1.4%*	4680
Europe	355	*0.6%*	425	*0.55*	498	*0.1%*	514
Oceania	10	*1.4%*	16	*1.75*	27	*1.1%*	37
C.I.S.†	176	*0.7%*	214	*1.0%*	288	*0.6%*	343

* South America plus Central America, Mexico, and the West Indies
† Commonwealth of Independent States, formerly the U.S.S.R.

1 : 105 000 000

Arctic Circle

Moscow

London
Paris

Istanbul

Tehran

Cairo

Karachi

Delhi

Mumbai
(Bombay)

Calcutta

Chennai
(Madras)

Dacca

Bangkok

Shenyang
Beijing
Tianjin
Seoul
Tokyo
Osaka

Shanghai

Hangzhou

Chongqing

Wenzhou

Guangzhou

Manila

Jakarta

Tropic of Cancer

Equator

Tropic of Capricorn

CARTOGRAPHY BY PHILIP'S.
COPYRIGHT GEORGE PHILIP LTD

POPULATION BY COUNTRY

NORTH
AMERICA

Can

G

United States

C

Mexico

G

E S

N

H

CR

DR

P R

H

J

T

Col

Ec

Peru

B

Brazil

Ch

Arg

Par

Ur

Ven

SOUTH
AMERICA

EUROPE

Ice

Ire

UK

N

B

France

P

Spain

Italy

M

F

N

S

La

Li

L

D

Germany

S A

C

Pol

C

S

H

Ser

M

Bel

Russia

Ukraine

Mol

G

Ar Az

Rom

B

A

G

Turkey

Iran

Cyp

Is

L

Syr

J

Iraq

S A

Yem

K

UAR

O

Kaz

Uzb

Kyr

T

Afgh

Pakistan

India

S L

M

Nep

B

China

Bangladesh

Thai

Mal

Burma

C

L

Br

Vietnam

M

HK

ASIA

N K

S K

Japan

Taiw

Philipp

Mor

Alg

N

T

W

S L

L

C

G

M

Mal

BF

B

C

Nigeria

T

Cam

G

An

Z

C

N

B

Zim

Egypt

Ch

Sud

Er

Ethiop

S

D

Sey

Congo
(Zaire)

Rw

Ug

Kenya

Tanz

Com

Moz

Mad

R

M

S Afr

AFRICA

Indonesia

PNG

S Is

Fiji

Australia

NZ

OCEANIA

Number of people

50 million

10 million

1 million

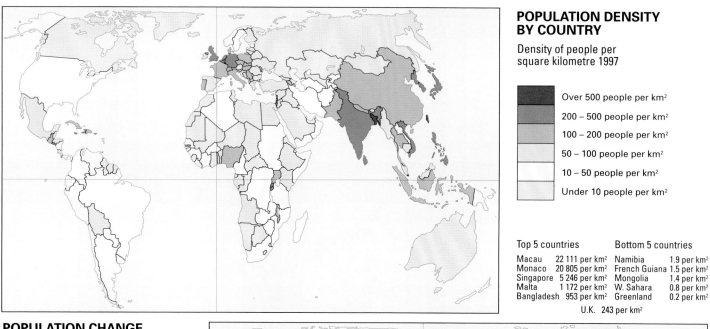

POPULATION DENSITY BY COUNTRY

Density of people per square kilometre 1997

	Over 500 people per km²
	200 – 500 people per km²
	100 – 200 people per km²
	50 – 100 people per km²
	10 – 50 people per km²
	Under 10 people per km²

Top 5 countries		Bottom 5 countries	
Macau	22 111 per km²	Namibia	1.9 per km²
Monaco	20 805 per km²	French Guiana	1.5 per km²
Singapore	5 246 per km²	Mongolia	1.4 per km²
Malta	1 172 per km²	W. Sahara	0.8 per km²
Bangladesh	953 per km²	Greenland	0.2 per km²
U.K.	243 per km²		

POPULATION CHANGE 1990-2000

The predicted population change for the years 1990-2000

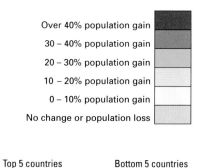

Over 40% population gain	
30 – 40% population gain	
20 – 30% population gain	
10 – 20% population gain	
0 – 10% population gain	
No change or population loss	

Top 5 countries		Bottom 5 countries	
Kuwait	+75.9%	Belgium	-0.1%
Namibia	+62.5%	Hungary	-0.2%
Afghanistan	+60.1%	Grenada	-2.4%
Mali	+55.5%	Germany	-3.2%
Tanzania	+54.6%	Tonga	-3.2%
	U.K.	+2.0%	

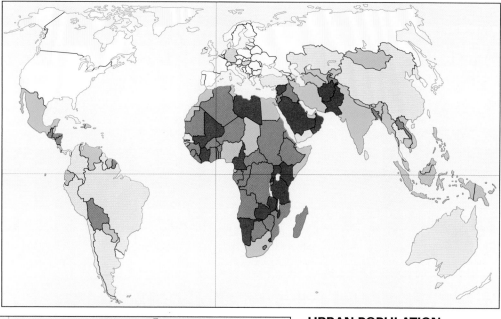

URBAN POPULATION

Percentage of total population living in towns and cities 1995

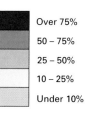

	Over 75%
	50 – 75%
	25 – 50%
	10 – 25%
	Under 10%

Most urbanized		Least urbanized	
Singapore	100%	Bhutan	6%
Belgium	97%	Rwanda	6%
Kuwait	97%	Burundi	7%
Iceland	92%	Uganda	12%
Venezuela	92%	Malawi	13%
	U.K.	89%	

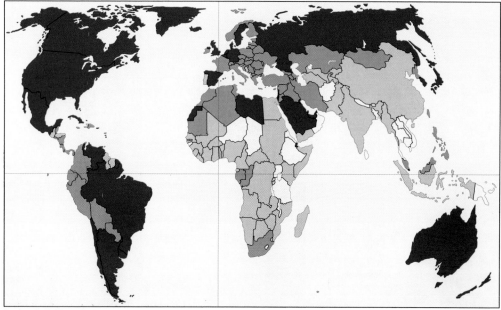

Projection: Modified Hammer Equal Area

CARTOGRAPHY BY PHILIP'S. COPYRIGHT GEORGE PHILIP LTD

CHILD MORTALITY

The number of babies who died
under the age of one
(average 1990–95)

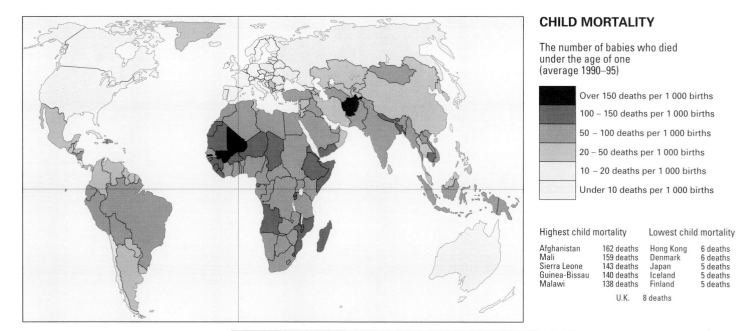

	Over 150 deaths per 1 000 births
	100 – 150 deaths per 1 000 births
	50 – 100 deaths per 1 000 births
	20 – 50 deaths per 1 000 births
	10 – 20 deaths per 1 000 births
	Under 10 deaths per 1 000 births

Highest child mortality		Lowest child mortality	
Afghanistan	162 deaths	Hong Kong	6 deaths
Mali	159 deaths	Denmark	6 deaths
Sierra Leone	143 deaths	Japan	5 deaths
Guinea-Bissau	140 deaths	Iceland	5 deaths
Malawi	138 deaths	Finland	5 deaths
	U.K.	8 deaths	

LIFE EXPECTANCY

Average expected lifespan
of babies born in 1997

Over 75 years	
70 – 75 years	
65 – 70 years	
60 – 65 years	
55 – 60 years	
50 – 55 years	
Under 50 years	

Highest life expectancy		Lowest life expectancy	
Iceland	81 years	Tanzania	42 years
Japan	80 years	Niger	41 years
Australia	80 years	Uganda	40 years
Canada	79 years	Rwanda	39 years
Luxembourg	79 years	Malawi	35 years
	U.K.	77 years	

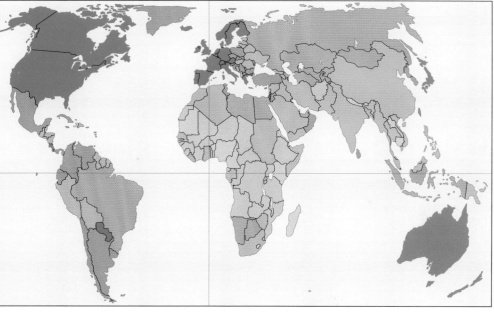

FAMILY SIZE

The average number of children a woman
can expect to bear during her lifetime 1995

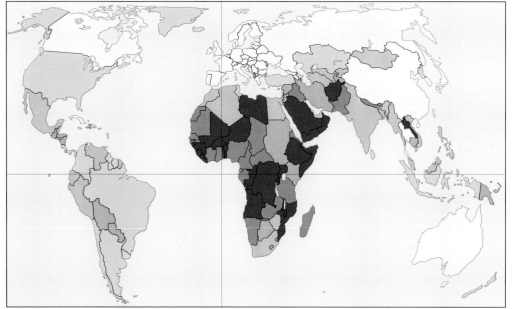

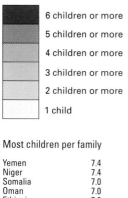

	6 children or more
	5 children or more
	4 children or more
	3 children or more
	2 children or more
	1 child

Most children per family

Yemen	7.4
Niger	7.4
Somalia	7.0
Oman	7.0
Ethiopia	7.0
U.K.	1.7

Projection: *Modified Hammer Equal Area*

CARTOGRAPHY BY PHILIP'S. COPYRIGHT GEORGE PHILIP LTD

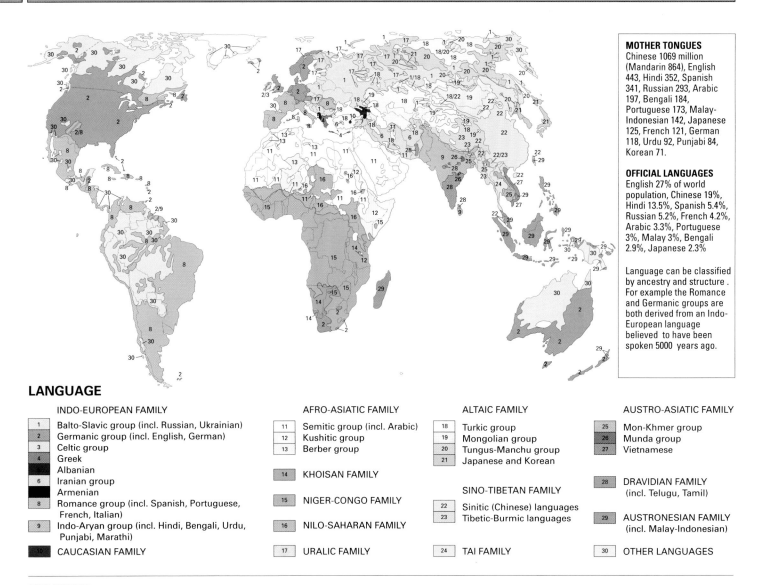

MOTHER TONGUES
Chinese 1069 million
(Mandarin 864), English
443, Hindi 352, Spanish
341, Russian 293, Arabic
197, Bengali 184,
Portuguese 173, Malay-
Indonesian 142, Japanese
125, French 121, German
118, Urdu 92, Punjabi 84,
Korean 71.

OFFICIAL LANGUAGES
English 27% of world
population, Chinese 19%,
Hindi 13.5%, Spanish 5.4%,
Russian 5.2%, French 4.2%,
Arabic 3.3%, Portuguese
3%, Malay 3%, Bengali
2.9%, Japanese 2.3%

Language can be classified
by ancestry and structure .
For example the Romance
and Germanic groups are
both derived from an Indo-
European language
believed to have been
spoken 5000 years ago.

LANGUAGE

INDO-EUROPEAN FAMILY

1	Balto-Slavic group (incl. Russian, Ukrainian)
2	Germanic group (incl. English, German)
3	Celtic group
4	Greek
5	Albanian
6	Iranian group
7	Armenian
8	Romance group (incl. Spanish, Portuguese, French, Italian)
9	Indo-Aryan group (incl. Hindi, Bengali, Urdu, Punjabi, Marathi)
10	CAUCASIAN FAMILY

AFRO-ASIATIC FAMILY

11	Semitic group (incl. Arabic)
12	Kushitic group
13	Berber group
14	KHOISAN FAMILY
15	NIGER-CONGO FAMILY
16	NILO-SAHARAN FAMILY
17	URALIC FAMILY

ALTAIC FAMILY

18	Turkic group
19	Mongolian group
20	Tungus-Manchu group
21	Japanese and Korean

SINO-TIBETAN FAMILY

22	Sinitic (Chinese) languages
23	Tibetic-Burmic languages
24	TAI FAMILY

AUSTRO-ASIATIC FAMILY

25	Mon-Khmer group
26	Munda group
27	Vietnamese
28	DRAVIDIAN FAMILY (incl. Telugu, Tamil)
29	AUSTRONESIAN FAMILY (incl. Malay-Indonesian)
30	OTHER LANGUAGES

RELIGION

- ▲ Roman Catholicism
- Orthodox and other Eastern Churches
- • Protestantism
- Sunni Islam
- Shia Islam
- Buddhism
- Hinduism
- Confucianism
- ✳ Judaism
- Shintoism
- Primitive Religions

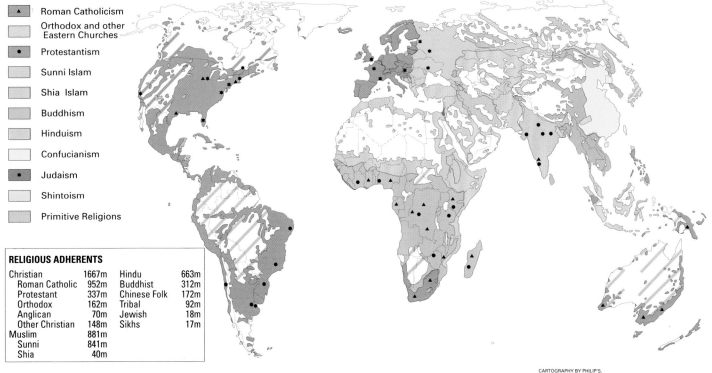

RELIGIOUS ADHERENTS

Christian	1667m	Hindu	663m
Roman Catholic	952m	Buddhist	312m
Protestant	337m	Chinese Folk	172m
Orthodox	162m	Tribal	92m
Anglican	70m	Jewish	18m
Other Christian	148m	Sikhs	17m
Muslim	881m		
Sunni	841m		
Shia	40m		

UNITED NATIONS

Created in 1945 to promote peace and co-operation and based in New York, the United Nations is the world's largest international organization, with 185 members and an annual budget of US $2.6 billion (1996–97). Each member of the General Assembly has one vote, while the permanent members of the 15-nation Security Council – USA, Russia, China, UK and France – hold a veto. The Secretariat is the UN's principal administrative arm. The 54 members of the Economic and Social Council are responsible for economic, social, cultural, educational, health and related matters. The UN has 16 specialized agencies – based in Canada, France, Switzerland and Italy, as well as the USA – which help members in fields such as education (UNESCO), agriculture (FAO), medicine (WHO) and finance (IFC). By the end of 1994, all the original 11 trust territories of The Trusteeship Council had become independent.

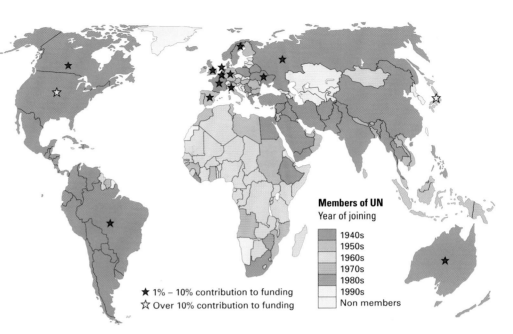

Members of UN
Year of joining

- 1940s
- 1950s
- 1960s
- 1970s
- 1980s
- 1990s
- Non members

★ 1% – 10% contribution to funding
☆ Over 10% contribution to funding

MEMBERSHIP OF THE UN In 1945 there were 51 members; by December 1994 membership had increased to 185 following the admission of Palau. There are 7 independent states which are not members of the UN – Kiribati, Nauru, Switzerland, Taiwan, Tonga, Tuvalu and the Vatican City. All the successor states of the former USSR had joined by the end of 1992. The official languages of the UN are Chinese, English, French, Russian, Spanish and Arabic.
FUNDING The UN budget for 1996–97 was US $2.6 billion. Contributions are assessed by the members' ability to pay, with the maximum 25% of the total, the minimum 0.01%. Contributions for 1996 were: USA 25.0%, Japan 15.4%, Germany 9.0%, France 6.4%, UK 5.3%, Italy 5.2%, Russia 4.5%, Canada 3.1%, Spain 2.4%, Brazil 1.6%, Netherlands 1.6%, Australia 1.5%, Sweden 1.2%, Ukraine 1.1%, Belgium 1.0%.

INTERNATIONAL ORGANIZATIONS

EU European Union (evolved from the European Community in 1993). The 15 members - Austria, Belgium, Denmark, Finland, France, Germany, Greece, Ireland, Italy, Luxembourg, Netherlands, Portugal, Spain, Sweden and the UK - aim to integrate economies, co-ordinate social developments and bring about political union. These members of what is now the world's biggest market share agricultural and industrial policies and tariffs on trade. The original body, the European Coal and Steel Community (ECSC), was created in 1951 following the signing of the Treaty of Paris.
EFTA European Free Trade Association (formed in 1960). Portugal left the original 'Seven' in 1989 to join what was then the EC, followed by Austria, Finland and Sweden in 1995. Only 4 members remain: Norway, Iceland, Switzerland and Liechtenstein.
ACP African-Caribbean-Pacific (formed in 1963). Members have economic ties with the EU.
NATO North Atlantic Treaty Organization (formed in 1949). It continues after 1991 despite the winding up of the Warsaw Pact. There are 16 member nations.
OAS Organization of American States (formed in 1948). It aims to promote social and economic co-operation between developed countries of North America and developing nations of Latin America.
ASEAN Association of South-east Asian Nations (formed in l967). Burma and Laos joined inJuly l997.
OAU Organization of African Unity (formed in 1963). Its 53 members represent over 94% of Africa's population. Arabic, French, Portuguese and English are recognized as working languages.
LAIA Latin American Integration Association (1980). Its aim is to promote freer regional trade.
OECD Organization for Economic Co-operation and Development (formed in 1961). It comprises the 29 major Western free-market economies. 'G7' is its' inner group' comprising the USA, Canada, Japan, UK, Germany, Italy and France. Russia attended the G7 summit in June 1997 ('Summit of the Eight').
COMMONWEALTH The Commonwealth of Nations evolved from the British Empire; it comprises 16 Oueen's realms, 32 republics and 5 indigenous monarchies, giving a total of 53.
OPEC Organization of Petroleum Exporting Countries (formed in 1960). It controls about three-quarters of the world's oil supply. Gabon left the organization in 1996.

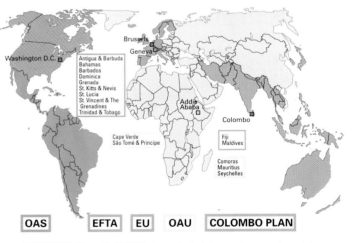

OAS   EFTA   EU   OAU   COLOMBO PLAN

ARAB LEAGUE (formed in 1945). The League's aim is to promote economic, social, political and military co-operation. There are 21 member nations.
COLOMBO PLAN (formed in 1951). Its 26 members aim to promote economic and social development in Asia and the Pacific.

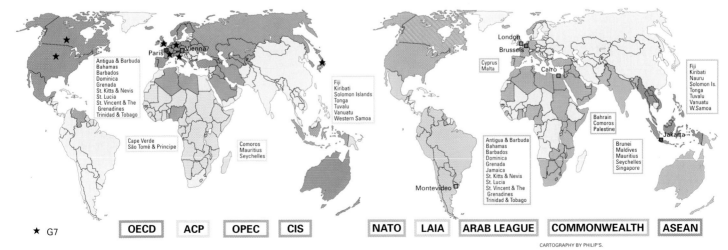

★ G7   OECD   ACP   OPEC   CIS   NATO   LAIA   ARAB LEAGUE   COMMONWEALTH   ASEAN

CARTOGRAPHY BY PHILIP'S.

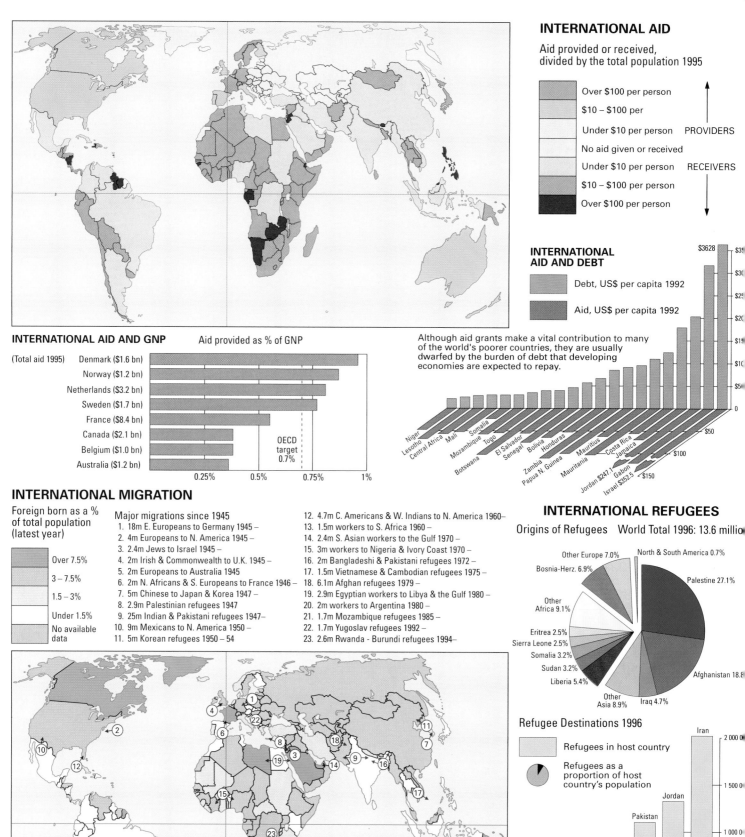

INTERNATIONAL AID

Aid provided or received,
divided by the total population 1995

Over $100 per person	
$10 – $100 per	
Under $10 per person	PROVIDERS
No aid given or received	
Under $10 per person	RECEIVERS
$10 – $100 per person	
Over $100 per person	

INTERNATIONAL AID AND DEBT

Debt, US$ per capita 1992

Aid, US$ per capita 1992

Although aid grants make a vital contribution to many
of the world's poorer countries, they are usually
dwarfed by the burden of debt that developing
economies are expected to repay.

$3628

Niger, Lesotho, Central Africa, Mali, Somalia, Mozambique, Togo, Botswana, El Salvador, Senegal, Bolivia, Honduras, Zambia, Papua N. Guinea, Mauritius, Mauritania, Costa Rica, Jamaica, Jordan $247.1, Gabon, Israel $352.5

INTERNATIONAL AID AND GNP

Aid provided as % of GNP

(Total aid 1995)

Denmark ($1.6 bn)	
Norway ($1.2 bn)	
Netherlands ($3.2 bn)	
Sweden ($1.7 bn)	
France ($8.4 bn)	
Canada ($2.1 bn)	
Belgium ($1.0 bn)	
Australia ($1.2 bn)	

OECD target 0.7%

0.25%   0.5%   0.75%   1%

INTERNATIONAL MIGRATION

Foreign born as a %
of total population
(latest year)

	Over 7.5%
	3 – 7.5%
	1.5 – 3%
	Under 1.5%
	No available data

Major migrations since 1945
1. 18m E. Europeans to Germany 1945 –
2. 4m Europeans to N. America 1945 –
3. 2.4m Jews to Israel 1945 –
4. 2m Irish & Commonwealth to U.K. 1945 –
5. 2m Europeans to Australia 1945
6. 2m N. Africans & S. Europeans to France 1946 –
7. 5m Chinese to Japan & Korea 1947 –
8. 2.9m Palestinian refugees 1947
9. 25m Indian & Pakistani refugees 1947–
10. 9m Mexicans to N. America 1950 –
11. 5m Korean refugees 1950 – 54

12. 4.7m C. Americans & W. Indians to N. America 1960–
13. 1.5m workers to S. Africa 1960 –
14. 2.4m S. Asian workers to the Gulf 1970 –
15. 3m workers to Nigeria & Ivory Coast 1970 –
16. 2m Bangladeshi & Pakistani refugees 1972 –
17. 1.5m Vietnamese & Cambodian refugees 1975 –
18. 6.1m Afghan refugees 1979 –
19. 2.9m Egyptian workers to Libya & the Gulf 1980 –
20. 2m workers to Argentina 1980 –
21. 1.7m Mozambique refugees 1985 –
22. 1.7m Yugoslav refugees 1992 –
23. 2.6m Rwanda - Burundi refugees 1994–

Projection: *Modified Hammer Equal Area*

INTERNATIONAL REFUGEES

Origins of Refugees   World Total 1996: 13.6 millio

- Other Europe 7.0%
- North & South America 0.7%
- Bosnia-Herz. 6.9%
- Palestine 27.1%
- Other Africa 9.1%
- Eritrea 2.5%
- Sierra Leone 2.5%
- Somalia 3.2%
- Sudan 3.2%
- Liberia 5.4%
- Other Asia 8.9%
- Iraq 4.7%
- Afghanistan 18.8

Refugee Destinations 1996

	Refugees in host country
	Refugees as a proportion of host country's population

Congo (Zaire), Yugo-slavia, Guinea, Gaza Strip, Pakistan, Jordan, Iran

2 000 0
1 500 0
1 000 0
500 000
0

HOUSING

**Number of people per household
(latest available year)**

- Over 6 people per household
- 5 – 6 people per household
- 4 – 5 people per household
- 3 – 4 people per household
- 2 – 3 people per household
- Under 2 people per household

**Expenditure on housing and energy as a
percentage of total consumer spending**

- ▲ Over 20% spent
- △ Under 5% spent

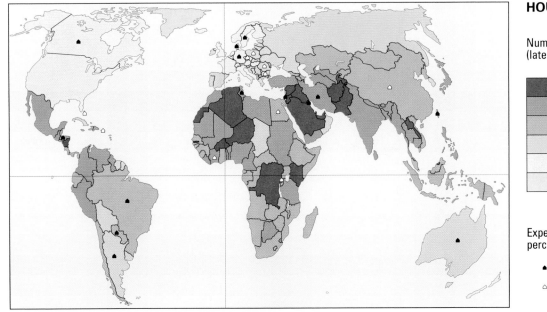

WATER SUPPLY

**Percentage of total population with
access to safe drinking water
(average 1990 – 1996)**

- Over 90% with safe water
- 75 – 90% with safe water
- 60 – 75% with safe water
- 45 – 60% with safe water
- 30 – 45% with safe water
- Under 30% with safe water

Least well provided countries

Afghanistan	23%	Papua New Guinea	28%
Chad	24%	Haiti	28%
Ethiopia	25%	Madagascar	29%

**Average daily domestic water
consumption per person**

△ Under 80 litres   ▲ Over 320 litres

*80 litres of water a day is considered
necessary for a reasonable quality of life*

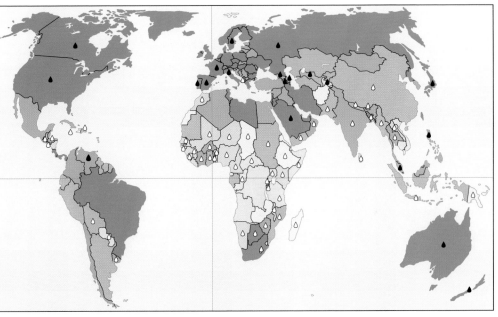

DAILY FOOD CONSUMPTION

**Average daily food intake
in calories per person 1992**

- Over 3 500 cals. per person
- 3 000 – 3 500 cals. per person
- 2 500 – 3 000 cals. per person
- 2 000 – 2 500 cals. per person
- Under 2 000 cals. per person
- No available data

Top 5 countries		Bottom 5 countries	
Ireland	3 847	Mozambique	1 680
Greece	3 815	Liberia	1 640
Cyprus	3 779	Ethiopia	1 610
U.S.A.	3 732	Afghanistan	1 523
Spain	3 708	Somalia	1 499

U.K.   3 317

Malnutrition in children under 5 years

- ■ Over 50% of children
- ■ 25 – 50% of children

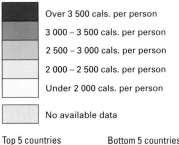

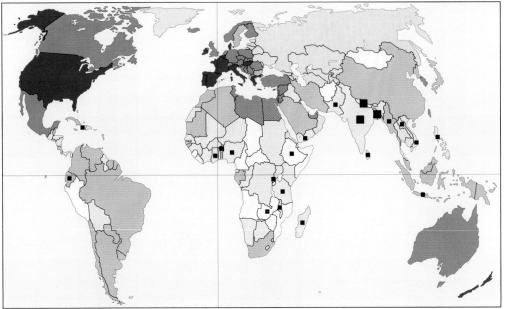

Projection: *Modified Hammer Equal Area*

CARTOGRAPHY BY PHILIP'S. COPYRIGHT GEORGE PHILIP LTD

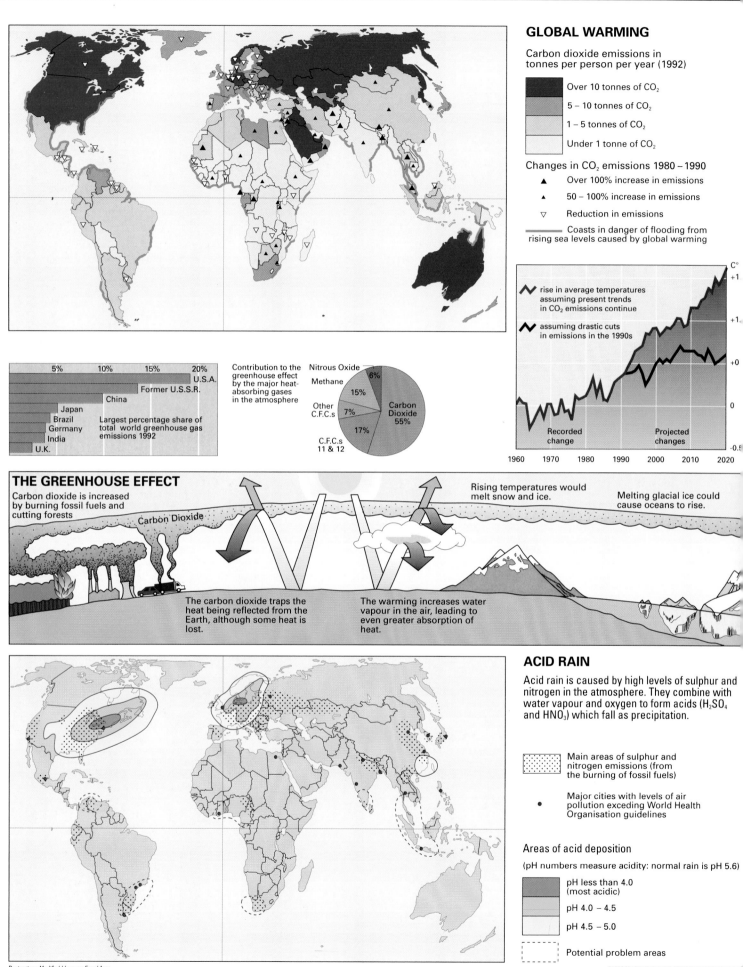

GLOBAL WARMING

Carbon dioxide emissions in tonnes per person per year (1992)

- Over 10 tonnes of CO_2
- 5 – 10 tonnes of CO_2
- 1 – 5 tonnes of CO_2
- Under 1 tonne of CO_2

Changes in CO_2 emissions 1980 – 1990

- ▲ Over 100% increase in emissions
- ▲ 50 – 100% increase in emissions
- ▽ Reduction in emissions
- ▬▬ Coasts in danger of flooding from rising sea levels caused by global warming

[Temperature graph]

- rise in average temperatures assuming present trends in CO_2 emissions continue
- assuming drastic cuts in emissions in the 1990s

Recorded change — Projected changes

1960 1970 1980 1990 2000 2010 2020

[Bar chart]

5% 10% 15% 20%

U.S.A.
Former U.S.S.R.
China
Japan
Brazil
Germany
India
U.K.

Largest percentage share of total world greenhouse gas emissions 1992

[Pie chart] Contribution to the greenhouse effect by the major heat-absorbing gases in the atmosphere

- Nitrous Oxide 6%
- Methane 15%
- Other C.F.C.s 7%
- C.F.C.s 11 & 12 17%
- Carbon Dioxide 55%

THE GREENHOUSE EFFECT

Carbon dioxide is increased by burning fossil fuels and cutting forests

Carbon Dioxide

Rising temperatures would melt snow and ice.

Melting glacial ice could cause oceans to rise.

The carbon dioxide traps the heat being reflected from the Earth, although some heat is lost.

The warming increases water vapour in the air, leading to even greater absorption of heat.

ACID RAIN

Acid rain is caused by high levels of sulphur and nitrogen in the atmosphere. They combine with water vapour and oxygen to form acids (H_2SO_4 and HNO_3) which fall as precipitation.

- Main areas of sulphur and nitrogen emissions (from the burning of fossil fuels)
- • Major cities with levels of air pollution exceeding World Health Organisation guidelines

Areas of acid deposition

(pH numbers measure acidity: normal rain is pH 5.6)

- pH less than 4.0 (most acidic)
- pH 4.0 – 4.5
- pH 4.5 – 5.0
- Potential problem areas

Projection: *Modified Hammer Equal Area*

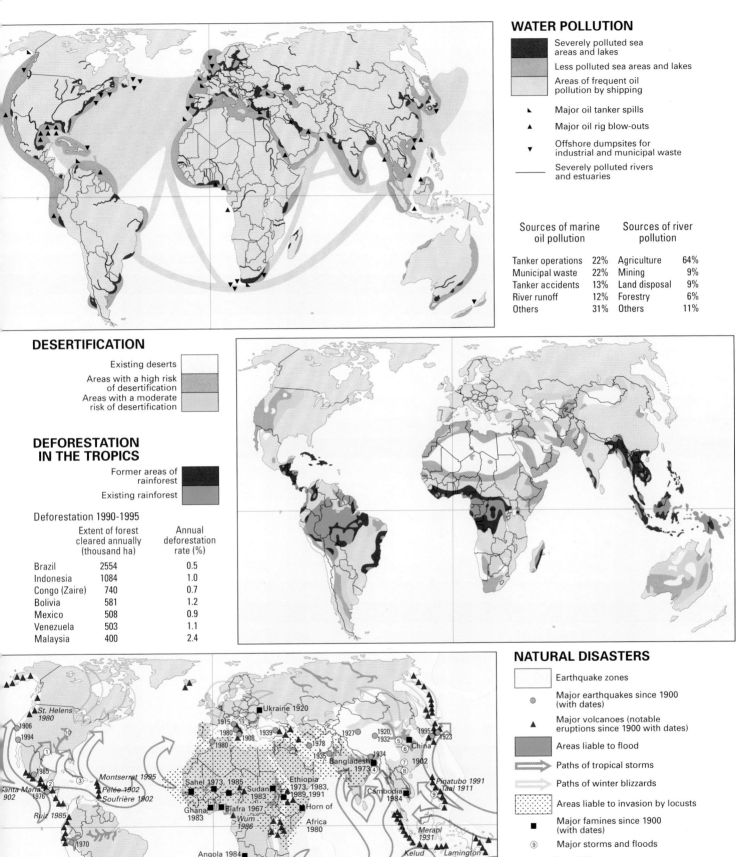

WATER POLLUTION

| Severely polluted sea areas and lakes |
| Less polluted sea areas and lakes |
| Areas of frequent oil pollution by shipping |

◤ Major oil tanker spills

▲ Major oil rig blow-outs

▼ Offshore dumpsites for industrial and municipal waste

—— Severely polluted rivers and estuaries

Sources of marine oil pollution		Sources of river pollution	
Tanker operations	22%	Agriculture	64%
Municipal waste	22%	Mining	9%
Tanker accidents	13%	Land disposal	9%
River runoff	12%	Forestry	6%
Others	31%	Others	11%

DESERTIFICATION

| Existing deserts |
| Areas with a high risk of desertification |
| Areas with a moderate risk of desertification |

DEFORESTATION IN THE TROPICS

| Former areas of rainforest |
| Existing rainforest |

Deforestation 1990-1995

	Extent of forest cleared annually (thousand ha)	Annual deforestation rate (%)
Brazil	2554	0.5
Indonesia	1084	1.0
Congo (Zaire)	740	0.7
Bolivia	581	1.2
Mexico	508	0.9
Venezuela	503	1.1
Malaysia	400	2.4

NATURAL DISASTERS

☐ Earthquake zones

● Major earthquakes since 1900 (with dates)

▲ Major volcanoes (notable eruptions since 1900 with dates)

▨ Areas liable to flood

⇨ Paths of tropical storms

⇨ Paths of winter blizzards

⋮ Areas liable to invasion by locusts

■ Major famines since 1900 (with dates)

⑨ Major storms and floods

1 Texas 1900
2 Central America 1966, 1974
3 West Indies 1928, 1963, 1979, 1988
4 Bangladesh 1960, 1963, 1965, 1970, 1985, 1988, 1989, 1991
5 Huang He 1887, 1931
6 Yangtze 1911, 1989, 1995
7 Hunan 1991
8 Haiphong 1881
9 Philippines 1970, 1991
10 Mississippi 1993

Projection: Modified Hammer Equal Area

CARTOGRAPHY BY PHILIP'S. COPYRIGHT GEORGE PHILIP LTD

	Population									Land and Agriculture					Energy	Trade	
	Population Total 1997	Population Density 1997	Average Annual Change 1970-80	Average Annual Change 1990-97	Birth Rate 1997	Death Rate 1997	Fertility Rate 1995	Life Expectancy Average 1997	Urban Population 1995	Land Area	Arable and Permanent Crops	Permanent grassland	Forest	Agriculture Population 1995	Consumption per capita 1994	Imports per capita 1995	Exports per capita 1995
	millions	persons per km²	%	%	births per thousand population	deaths per thousand population	children	years	%	thousand km²	% of land area	% of land area	% of land area	% of economically active pop.	tonnes of coal	US $	US $
Afghanistan	23	35	1.7	4.8	43	18	6.9	46	20	652	12	46	3	69	0.04	19	6
Albania	3.6	131	2.3	1.5	22	8	2.6	68	37	27.4	26	15	38	54	0.3	178	42
Algeria	29.3	12	3.1	2.3	28	6	3.5	69	56	2382	3	13	2	24	1.58	375	375
Angola	11.2	9	3.3	1.6	44	17	6.9	47	32	1247	3	43	18	74	0.08	198	309
Argentina	35.4	13	1.7	1.3	20	8	2.7	74	88	2737	10	52	19	11	2.15	579	603
Armenia	3.8	134	2	1.9	17	8	1.8	69	69	28.4	20	54	15	15	0.61	105	603
Australia	18.4	2	1.6	1.2	14	7	1.9	80	86	7644	6	54	19	5	7.61	3342	2942
Austria	8.2	99	0.1	1.1	11	10	1.5	77	65	82.7	18	24	39	7	4.16	8253	7166
Azerbaijan	7.7	89	1.8	1	22	9	2.3	65	56	86.1	23	52	11	30	2.6	105	86
Bahamas	0.3	28	2.1	1.5	18	6	2	73	85	10	1	0	32	5	2.97	4439	5418
Bangladesh	124	953	2.8	1	30	11	3.5	56	18	130	74	5	15	62	0.09	55	27
Barbados	0.3	616	0.4	0.6	15	8	1.8	75	46	0.43	37	5	12	6	1.58	2946	915
Belarus	10.5	51	0.7	0.3	11	13	1.4	69	69	208	31	14	34	18	3.38	297	243
Belgium	10.2	335	0.2	0.5	12	10	1.6	77	97	30.5	24	21	21	3	6.86	14702	16078
Benin	5.8	52	2.5	2.9	46	13	6	53	36	111	17	4	31	60	0.05	125	34
Bolivia	7.7	7	2.6	2.4	32	10	4.5	60	62	1084	2	24	53	45	0.49	192	149
Bosnia-Herzegovina	3.6	70	1	-2.7	6	7	1	60	41	51.2	16	24	39	10	0.36	204	12
Botswana	1.5	3	3.8	2.2	33	7	4.4	62	31	567	1	45	47	39	...	1153	1302
Brazil	159.5	19	2.4	1.4	20	9	2.4	62	78	8457	6	22	58	19	0.85	345	298
Bulgaria	8.6	77	0.4	-0.7	8	14	1.2	71	71	111	38	16	35	11	3.26	598	606
Burkina Faso	10.9	40	2.3	2.8	46	20	6.7	42	27	274	13	22	50	92	0.05	54	53
Burma	47.5	72	2.4	1.9	30	11	3.4	57	27	658	15	1	49	72	0.08	30	19
Burundi	6.3	243	1.6	0.5	42	15	6.5	49	7	25.7	46	39	13	91	0.02	39	18
Cambodia	10.5	59	-0.8	3.5	43	15	4.7	50	21	177	22	8	69	73	0.02	43	24
Cameroon	13.8	30	2.7	2.6	42	14	5.7	52	45	465	15	4	77	68	0.14	94	154
Canada	30.2	3	1.2	1.9	13	7	1.7	79	77	9221	5	3	54	3	11.21	5676	6491
Central African Rep.	3.4	5	2.3	1.8	40	18	5.1	45	39	623	3	5	75	79	0.04	54	52
Chad	6.8	5	2.1	2.5	44	17	5.9	48	22	1259	3	36	26	81	0.01	67	77
Chile	14.7	20	1.6	1.6	18	6	2.3	75	85	749	6	18	22	17	1.45	1121	1130
China	1210	130	1.8	1.2	17	7	1.9	70	29	9326	10	43	14	71	0.92	106	122
Colombia	35.9	35	2.3	1.2	21	5	2.8	73	73	1039	5	39	48	24	1	395	288
Congo	2.7	8	2.8	2.9	39	17	6	46	59	342	0	29	58	45	0.34	259	325
Congo (Zaïre)	47.2	21	2.9	4.1	48	17	6	47	29	2267	3	7	77	66	0.06	8	9
Costa Rica	3.5	69	2.8	2.2	23	4	2.8	76	50	51.1	10	46	31	22	0.87	977	811
Croatia	4.9	86	0.4	0.2	10	11	1.5	73	55	56.4	22	20	38	15	1.59	1586	969
Cuba	11.3	102	1.3	0.8	13	7	1.7	75	75	110	31	27	24	16	1.14	258	146
Cyprus	0.8	83	0.2	1.4	15	8	2.2	77	68	9.24	15	0	13	10	3.03	4986	1661
Czech Rep.	10.5	136	0.5	0.3	11	11	1.3	74	65	77	44	12	34	11	4.97	2450	2099
Denmark	5.4	126	0.4	0.3	12	10	1.8	78	86	42.4	56	7	10	4	5.15	8266	9378
Dominican Rep.	8.2	168	2.6	1.8	23	6	2.9	69	62	48.4	31	43	12	21	0.65	376	97
Ecuador	11.8	43	3	1.6	25	5	3.2	72	59	277	11	18	56	29	0.77	366	376
Egypt	63	63	2.1	2.6	28	9	3.4	62	45	995	4	0	0	33	0.66	199	58
El Salvador	6	287	2.3	1.8	27	6	3.7	69	52	20.7	35	29	5	32	0.5	504	176
Estonia	1.5	34	0.8	-1.1	12	14	1.3	68	73	43.2	27	7	48	14	4.9	1714	1240
Ethiopia	58.5	53	2.4	3.5	46	18	7	47	13	1101	11	20	13	86	0.03	19	7
Finland	5.2	17	0.4	0.6	11	11	1.8	76	63	305	9	0	76	7	7.4	5502	7744
France	58.8	107	0.6	0.7	13	9	1.7	79	74	550	35	19	27	4	5.15	4763	4941
Gabon	1.2	5	4.8	1.5	28	13	5.2	56	73	258	2	18	77	45	0.87	667	2055
Gambia, The	1.2	120	3.3	4.9	44	19	5.3	53	26	10	17	19	10	80	0.1	192	32
Georgia	5.5	78	0.8	0	14	9	1.9	68	58	69.7	16	24	33	25	0.85	39	22
Germany	82.3	236	0.1	0.5	9	11	1.2	76	87	349	34	15	31	3	5.48	5445	6227
Ghana	18.1	80	2.2	2.7	34	11	5.1	57	36	228	19	37	42	56	0.14	129	74
Greece	10.6	82	0.9	0.8	10	10	1.4	78	65	129	27	41	20	20	3.22	2056	899
Guatemala	11.3	104	2.8	2.9	33	7	4.7	66	42	108	18	24	54	51	0.29	310	203
Guinea	7.5	30	1.4	3.8	42	18	6.5	46	30	246	3	44	27	85	0.08	116	97
Guinea-Bissau	1.2	41	4.2	2.6	39	16	6	49	22	28.1	12	38	38	84	0.1	66	22
Guyana	0.8	4	0.7	-0.8	19	10	2.4	59	35	197	3	6	84	20	0.6	594	558
Haiti	7.4	269	1.7	1.8	33	15	4.4	50	32	27.6	33	18	5	66	0.04	91	16
Honduras	6.3	56	3.4	3	33	6	4.6	69	48	112	18	14	54	33	0.31	205	178
Hungary	10.2	110	0.4	-0.6	11	15	1.6	69	64	92.3	54	12	19	14	3.27	1472	1217
Iceland	0.3	3	1.1	1.2	17	6	2.1	81	92	100	0	23	1	10	6.7	6500	6678
India	980	330	2.2	2.5	25	9	3.2	60	27	2973	57	4	23	62	0.37	37	33
Indonesia	203.5	112	2.3	1.8	23	8	2.7	62	33	1812	17	7	62	53	0.47	211	234
Iran	69.5	42	3.2	3.5	33	6	4.5	68	58	1636	11	27	7	36	1.88	537	348
Iraq	22.5	51	3.6	2.5	43	6	5.4	67	73	437	12	9	4	12	1.76	278	383

Wealth							Social Indicators								Aid	
GNP 1995	GNP per capita 1995	Real GDP per capita 1995	Average Annual growth of Real GNP per capita 1985-95	GDP share Agriculture 1995	GDP share Industry 1995	GDP share services 1995	HDI Human Development Index 1994	Food Intake	Population per doctor 1993	% of GNP spent on health 1990-95	% of GNP spent on education 1993-94	%o GNP spent on military 1995	Adult Illiteracy		given (*) and received per capita 1994	
million US $	US $	US $	%	%	%	%		calories per day	persons	%	%	%	Female %	Male %	US $	
5000	300	800	-6	52	32	16	...	1523	7000	...	...	9.1	85	53	10	Afghanistan
2199	670	2750	-7	56	21	23	0.655	2605	735	2.7	3	2.8	0	0	21	Albania
44609	1600	5300	-2.6	13	47	40	0.737	2897	1062	4.6	5.6	2.5	51	26	11	Algeria
4422	410	1310	-6.1	12	59	29	0.335	1839	23725	4	...	4.8	71	44	40	Angola
278431	8030	8310	1.9	6	31	63	0.884	2880	330	10.6	3.8	1.7	4	4	7	Argentina
2752	730	2260	-15.1	44	35	21	0.651	...	261	7.8	7.3	4.4	2	1	27	Armenia
337909	18720	18940	1.4	3	28	69	0.931	3179	500	8.4	6	2.5	...	...	*62	Australia
216547	26890	21250	1.9	2	34	64	0.932	3497	231	9.7	5.5	1	0	0	*82	Austria
3601	480	1460	-16.3	27	32	41	0.636	...	257	7.5	5.5	5	4	1	3	Azerbaijan
3297	11940	14710	-1	3	9	88	0.894	2624	700	...	3.9	0.6	2	1	15	Bahamas
28599	240	1380	2.1	31	18	51	0.368	2019	12884	2.4	2.3	1.8	74	51	11	Bangladesh
1745	6560	10620	-0.2	5	17	78	0.907	3207	1000	5	7.5	0.7	3	2	...	Barbados
21356	2070	4220	-5.2	13	35	52	0.806	...	236	6.4	6.1	3.3	3	1	11	Belarus
250710	24710	21660	2.2	2	31	67	0.932	3681	274	8.2	5.6	1.7	0	0	*81	Belgium
2034	370	1760	-0.4	34	12	54	0.368	2532	14216	1.7	...	1.3	74	51	53	Benin
5905	800	2540	1.7	17	30	53	0.589	2094	2348	5	5.4	2.6	24	10	96	Bolivia
11650	2600	...	1.8	...	...	...	...	...	600	...	...	...	23	3	...	Bosnia-Herzegovina
4381	3020	5580	6	5	46	49	0.673	2266	5151	1.9	8.5	7.1	40	20	64	Botswana
579787	3640	5400	-0.7	14	37	49	0.783	2824	844	7.4	1.6	1.5	17	17	2	Brazil
11225	1330	4480	-2.2	13	34	53	0.78	2831	306	4	4.5	3.3	3	1	6	Bulgaria
2417	230	780	-0.1	34	27	39	0.221	2387	34804	5.5	3.6	2.4	91	71	48	Burkina Faso
45100	1000	1050	0.4	63	9	28	0.475	2598	12528	0.9	2.4	6.2	22	11	3	Burma
984	160	630	-1.3	56	18	26	0.247	1941	17153	0.9	3.8	5.3	78	51	46	Burundi
2718	270	1084	2	51	14	35	0.348	2021	9374	7.2	...	4.7	47	20	57	Cambodia
8615	650	2110	-7	39	23	38	0.468	1981	11996	1.4	3.1	1.8	48	25	35	Cameroon
573695	19380	21130	0.4	3	30	67	0.96	3094	464	9.8	7.6	1.6	2	2	*73	Canada
1123	340	1070	-2	44	13	43	0.355	1690	25920	1.7	2.8	1.8	48	32	50	Central African Rep.
1144	180	700	0.5	44	22	34	0.288	1989	30030	1.8	2.2	2.6	65	38	38	Chad
59151	4160	9520	6.1	8	34	58	0.891	2582	942	6.5	2.9	3.8	5	5	11	Chile
744890	620	2920	8	21	48	31	0.626	2727	1063	3.8	2.6	5.7	27	10	3	China
70263	1910	6130	2.8	14	32	54	0.848	2677	1105	7.4	3.7	2	9	9	6	Colombia
1784	680	2050	-3.2	10	38	52	0.5	2296	3713	6.8	8.3	1.7	33	17	50	Congo
5313	120	490	-8.5	51	16	33	0.381	2060	15150	2.4	1	2	32	13	4	Congo (Zaïre)
8884	2610	5850	2.9	17	24	59	0.889	2883	1133	8.5	4.7	0.3	5	5	8	Costa Rica
15508	3250	3960	-20	12	25	63	0.76	...	500	10.1	...	12.6	5	1	...	Croatia
13700	1250	3000	-10	...	...	...	0.723	2833	275	7.9	6.6	2.8	5	4	6	Cuba
8510	11500	13000	4.6	6	43	51	0.907	3779	450	3.9	4.3	4.5	7	2	30	Cyprus
39990	3870	9770	-1.8	6	39	55	0.882	...	273	9.9	5.9	2.8	0	0	5	Czech Rep.
156027	29890	21230	1.5	4	29	67	0.927	3664	360	6.6	8.5	1.8	0	0	*273	Denmark
11390	1460	3870	2.1	15	22	63	0.718	2286	949	5.3	1.9	1.3	18	18	16	Dominican Rep.
15997	1390	4220	0.8	12	36	52	0.775	2583	652	5.3	3	3.4	12	8	21	Ecuador
45507	790	3820	1.1	20	21	59	0.614	3335	1316	4.9	5	4.3	61	36	35	Egypt
9057	1610	2610	2.9	14	22	64	0.592	2663	1515	5	1.6	1.8	30	27	54	El Salvador
4252	2860	4220	-4.3	8	28	64	0.776	...	253	5.9	5.8	5.3	0	0	22	Estonia
5722	100	450	-0.5	57	10	33	0.244	1610	32499	1.1	6.4	2.1	75	55	16	Ethiopia
105174	20580	17760	-0.2	6	37	57	0.94	3018	406	8.3	8.4	2	0	0	*59	Finland
451051	24990	21030	1.5	2	27	71	0.946	3633	334	9.7	5.8	3.1	1	1	*137	France
3759	3490	3650	-1.6	9	59	32	0.562	2500	1987	0.5	3.2	1.7	47	26	138	Gabon
354	320	930	0.3	28	15	57	0.281	2360	14000	1.8	2.7	3.8	75	47	43	Gambia, The
2358	440	1470	-17	67	22	11	0.637	...	182	0.3	1.9	3.4	1	0	106	Georgia
2252343	27510	20070	1.9	1	30	69	0.924	3344	367	9.5	4.8	2	0	0	*81	Germany
6719	390	1990	1.5	46	16	38	0.468	2199	22970	3.5	3.1	1.2	47	24	38	Ghana
85885	8210	11710	1.2	21	36	43	0.923	3815	312	6.4	3	4.6	7	2	...	Greece
14255	1340	3340	0.3	25	19	56	0.572	2255	3999	2.7	1.6	1.4	51	38	21	Guatemala
3593	550	1100	1.4	24	31	45	0.271	2389	7445	0.9	2.2	1.4	78	50	62	Guinea
265	250	790	1.8	46	24	30	0.291	2556	3500	1.1	2.8	3	58	32	113	Guinea-Bissau
493	590	2420	0.8	50	35	15	0.649	2384	3000	10.4	5	1.1	2	1	...	Guyana
1777	250	910	-5.2	44	12	44	0.338	1706	10855	3.6	1.4	2.1	58	52	104	Haiti
3566	600	1900	0.2	21	33	46	0.575	2305	1266	5.6	4	1.3	27	27	75	Honduras
42129	4120	6410	-1	8	33	59	0.857	3503	306	7.3	6.7	1.4	1	1	7	Hungary
6686	24950	20460	0.3	13	29	58	0.942	3058	360	6.9	5.4	...	0	0	...	Iceland
319660	340	1400	3.1	29	29	42	0.446	2395	2459	3.5	3.8	2.5	62	35	2	India
190105	980	3800	6	17	42	41	0.668	2752	7028	1.5	1.3	1.6	22	10	7	Indonesia
328000	4800	5470	0.5	25	34	41	0.78	2860	3142	4.5	5.9	3.9	24	22	3	Iran
36200	1800	3150	...	28	20	52	0.531	2121	1659	...	5.1	14.8	55	29	16	Iraq

	Population									Land and Agriculture					Energy	Trade	
	Population Total 1997	Population Density 1997	Average Annual Change 1970-80	Average Annual Change 1990-97	Birth Rate 1997	Death Rate 1997	Fertility Rate 1995	Life Expectancy Average 1997	Urban Population 1995	Land Area	Arable and Permanent Crops	Permanent grassland	Forest	Agriculture Population 1995	Consumption per capita 1994	Imports per capita 1995	Exports per capita 1995
	millions	persons per km²	%	%	births per thousand population	deaths per thousand population	children	years	%	thousand km²	% of land area	% of land area	% of land area	% of economically active pop.	tonnes of coal	US $	US $
Ireland	3.6	53	1.4	0.5	13	9	1.9	76	58	68.9	19	45	5	13	4.31	9237	12469
Israel	5.9	286	2.7	3.6	20	6	2.4	78	91	20.6	21	7	6	3	3.26	5337	3436
Italy	57.8	196	0.5	0.2	10	10	1.2	78	67	294	38	15	23	7	3.95	3562	4038
Ivory Coast	15.1	47	4	3.4	42	17	5.3	45	46	318	12	41	34	57	0.26	231	301
Jamaica	2.6	240	1.3	0.8	22	6	2.4	75	53	10.8	20	24	17	24	1.66	1089	545
Japan	125.9	334	1.1	0.3	10	8	1.5	80	78	377	12	2	66	6	4.98	2684	3540
Jordan	5.6	63	2.4	4.9	36	4	4.8	73	72	88.9	5	9	1	15	1.01	680	325
Kazakstan	17	6	1.3	0.2	19	10	2.3	64	58	2670	13	70	4	21	5.93	40	70
Kenya	31.9	56	3.8	4.1	32	11	4.7	54	25	570	8	37	30	78	0.12	98	62
Korea, North	24.5	203	2.2	1.7	22	5	2.2	71	61	120	17	0	61	34	4.21	75	41
Korea, South	46.1	466	1.8	1.1	16	6	1.8	74	75	98.7	21	1	65	14	3.77	3013	2788
Kyrgyzstan	4.7	24	2	0.8	26	9	3.3	64	40	191	7	44	4	31	0.76	71	76
Laos	5.2	23	1.7	3.3	41	13	6.5	53	22	231	4	3	54	77	0.04	40	20
Latvia	2.5	38	0.7	-1.3	12	15	1.3	67	72	64.1	28	13	46	14	2.3	697	520
Lebanon	3.2	313	0.8	2.5	28	6	2.8	70	87	10.2	30	1	8	4	1.83	2058	197
Lesotho	2.1	69	2.3	2.7	32	14	4.6	52	23	30.4	11	66	0	39	...	520	58
Liberia	3	30	3.1	2.9	42	12	6.5	59	45	96.8	4	21	48	70	0.06	116	197
Libya	5.5	3	4.4	2.8	44	7	6.1	65	86	1760	1	8	0	6	3.34	1240	2596
Lithuania	3.7	57	0.9	-0.1	14	13	1.5	68	71	65.2	47	7	31	18	3.04	696	545
Luxembourg	0.4	163.5	0.7	1.9	13	8	1.7	79	88	2.6	...	...	...	...	12.82	20295	16090
Macedonia	2.2	86	1.6	0.9	13	9	2.2	72	60	24.9	26	25	39	17	1.9	600	500
Madagascar	15.5	27	2.7	4.8	42	14	5.8	53	27	582	5	41	40	76	0.04	36	25
Malawi	10.3	109	3.2	3.1	41	25	6.6	35	13	94.1	18	20	39	86	0.04	49	41
Malaysia	20.9	64	2.4	2.2	26	5	3.4	70	52	329	23	1	68	23	2.29	3751	3563
Mali	11	9	2.3	4.4	51	19	6.8	47	27	1220	2	25	10	84	0.02	70	42
Malta	0.4	1172	1.1	0.9	15	7	1.9	79	88	0.32	41	0	0	2	1.97	7951	5170
Mauritania	2.4	2	2.4	2.5	47	15	5.2	50	54	1025	0	38	4	49	0.61	284	223
Mauritius	1.2	569	1.6	1.1	19	7	2.2	71	44	2.03	52	3	22	12	0.7	1797	1410
Mexico	97.4	51	2.9	1.8	26	5	3	74	75	1909	13	39	26	24	2.03	508	520
Moldova	4.5	132	1.1	0.3	17	12	2	65	50	33.7	66	13	13	31	1.55	185	162
Mongolia	2.5	2	2.8	1.9	25	8	3.4	61	60	1567	1	75	9	29	1.55	158	208
Morocco	28.1	63	2.4	1.6	27	6	3.4	70	52	446	21	47	20	41	0.47	315	172
Mozambique	19.1	24	2.6	4.3	44	18	6.2	45	32	784	4	56	22	81	0.03	45	10
Namibia	1.7	2	2.5	2	37	8	5	65	34	823	1	46	15	45	...	916	881
Nepal	22.1	162	2.6	2.1	37	12	5.3	54	13	137	17	15	42	93	0.03	64	16
Netherlands	15.9	469	0.8	0.9	12	9	1.6	78	89	33.9	28	31	10	4	7.22	11419	12680
New Zealand	3.7	14	1	1.1	15	8	2.1	77	86	268	14	50	28	10	5.47	3951	3882
Nicaragua	4.6	39	3	2.5	33	6	4.1	66	63	119	10	45	26	23	0.36	212	115
Niger	9.7	8	3	3.3	54	24	7.4	41	16	1267	3	8	2	89	0.06	37	27
Nigeria	118	130	2.2	3.1	43	12	5.5	55	38	911	36	44	12	38	0.21	71	94
Norway	4.4	14	0.5	0.8	11	11	1.9	78	73	307	3	0	27	5	7.44	7563	9632
Oman	2.4	11	4.2	6.9	38	4	7	71	13	212	0	5	0	42	5.41	1994	2682
Pakistan	136	176	2.6	2.8	35	11	5.2	59	34	771	28	6	5	48	0.33	88	62
Panama	2.7	37	2.5	1.7	22	5	2.7	74	55	74.4	9	20	44	22	1.2	955	238
Papua New Guinea	4.4	10	2.5	1.8	33	10	4.8	58	16	453	1	0	93	78	0.29	357	651
Paraguay	5.2	13	3	2.8	30	4	4	74	52	397	6	55	32	35	0.38	669	196
Peru	24.5	19	2.7	1.3	24	6	3.1	70	72	1280	3	21	66	33	0.46	392	237
Philippines	73.5	247	2.6	2.4	29	7	3.7	66	52	298	31	4	46	42	0.43	403	249
Poland	38.8	127	0.9	0.1	12	10	1.6	72	64	304	48	13	29	26	3.51	753	593
Portugal	10.1	110	0.8	-0.3	11	10	1.4	76	36	92	32	11	36	14	2.13	3261	2280
Puerto Rico	3.8	432	1.7	1.4	18	8	2.1	75	77	8.86	9	26	16	3	3.07	4300	5900
Romania	22.6	98	0.9	-0.3	10	12	1.4	70	55	230	43	21	29	19	2.54	453	349
Russia	147.8	9	0.6	0	11	16	1.4	64	75	16996	8	5	45	12	6	261	427
Rwanda	7	284	3.3	-0.4	39	21	6.2	39	6	24.7	47	28	10	91	0.03	46	10
Saudi Arabia	19.1	9	5	4.4	38	5	6.2	70	79	2150	2	56	1	14	5.77	1539	2335
Senegal	8.9	46	2.9	2.8	45	11	5.7	57	42	193	12	30	39	74	0.16	156	103
Sierra Leone	4.6	64	2.1	1.5	47	18	6.5	48	35	71.6	8	31	28	67	0.05	30	6
Singapore	3.2	5246	1	2.5	16	5	1.7	79	100	0.61	2	0	5	1	9.67	41639	39553
Slovak Rep.	5.4	112	1.7	0.3	13	9	1.5	73	58	48.1	34	17	41	12	4.07	1250	1025
Slovenia	2	99	0.9	0.2	8	10	1.3	75	50	20.3	14	25	54	5	3.11	4793	4199
Somalia	9.9	16	3.8	1.9	44	13	7	56	27	627	2	69	26	74	0.05	26	5
South Africa	42.3	35	2.3	1.6	27	12	3.9	56	57	1221	11	67	7	11	2.73	718	653
Spain	39.3	79	1.1	0	10	9	1.2	79	77	499	40	21	32	9	3.01	2890	2334
Sri Lanka	18.7	289	1.7	1.2	18	6	2.3	73	22	64.6	29	7	32	47	0.16	290	212
Sudan	31	13	3	3	41	11	4.8	56	35	2376	5	46	18	68	0.06	44	21

Wealth							Social Indicators								Aid	
GNP 1995	GNP per capita 1995	Real GDP per capita 1995	Average Annual growth of Real GNP per capita 1985-95	GDP share Agriculture 1995	GDP share Industry 1995	GDP share services 1995	HDI Human Development Index 1994	Food Intake 1993	Population per doctor 1993	% of GNP spent on health 1990-95	% of GNP spent on education 1993-94	%o GNP spent on military 1995	Adult Illiteracy		given (*) and received per capita 1994	
million US $	US $	US $	%	%	%	%		calories per day	persons	%	%	%o	Female %	Male %	US $	
52765	14710	15680	5.2	9	37	54	0.929	3847	632	7.9	6.4	1.2	0	0	*35	Ireland
87875	15920	16490	2.5	3	32	65	0.913	3050	220	4.1	6	9.2	7	3	226	Israel
1088085	19020	19870	1.7	3	31	66	0.921	3561	207	8.3	5.2	1.8	4	2	*37	Italy
9548	660	1580	-4.3	31	20	49	0.368	2491	11739	3.4	...	1	70	50	87	Ivory Coast
3803	1510	3540	3.7	9	38	53	0.736	2607	6420	5.4	4.7	0.6	11	19	43	Jamaica
4963587	39640	22110	2.9	2	38	60	0.94	2903	608	7	4.7	1.1	0	0	*106	Japan
6354	1510	4060	-2.8	8	27	65	0.73	3022	554	7.9	3.8	6.7	21	7	127	Jordan
22143	1330	3010	-8.6	12	30	58	0.709	...	254	2.2	5.4	3	4	1	2	Kazakstan
7583	280	1380	0.1	29	17	54	0.463	2075	21970	1.9	6.8	2.3	30	14	42	Kenya
24000	1000	4000	-8	...	...	...	0.765	2833	370	...	...	25.2	5	5	1	Korea, North
435137	9700	11450	7.6	7	43	50	0.89	3285	951	5.4	4.5	3.4	2	2	1	Korea, South
3158	700	1800	-6.9	44	24	32	0.635	...	303	3.5	6.8	3.5	4	1	19	Kyrgyzstan
1694	350	2500	2.7	52	18	30	0.459	2259	4446	2.6	2.3	4.2	56	31	66	Laos
5708	2270	3370	-6.6	9	31	60	0.711	...	278	3.7	6.5	3.2	0	0	14	Latvia
10673	2660	4800	2.7	7	24	69	0.794	3317	537	5.3	2	5.3	10	5	48	Lebanon
1519	770	1780	1.5	10	56	34	0.457	2201	24095	3.5	4.8	5.5	38	19	57	Lesotho
2300	850	1000	1.5	...	...	...	...	1640	25000	8.2	...	4.8	78	46	23	Liberia
38000	7000	6000	1	8	48	44	0.801	3308	957	...	9.6	5.5	37	12	1	Libya
7070	1900	4120	-11.7	11	36	53	0.762	...	235	4.8	4.5	2.4	2	1	14	Lithuania
16876	41210	37930	1	1	33	66	0.899	...	460	6.3	3.1	0.9	0	0	*148	Luxembourg
1813	860	4000	-15	19	44	37	0.748	...	427	7.7	5.6	...	16	6	...	Macedonia
3178	230	640	-2	34	13	53	0.35	2135	8385	1	1.9	1.1	27	12	23	Madagascar
1623	170	750	-0.7	42	27	31	0.32	1825	44205	2.3	3.4	1.2	58	28	40	Malawi
78321	3890	9020	5.7	13	43	44	0.832	2888	2441	1.4	5.3	4.5	22	11	6	Malaysia
2410	250	550	0.6	46	17	37	0.229	2278	18376	1.3	2.1	2.4	77	61	57	Mali
4070	11000	13000	5.1	3	28	69	0.887	3486	410	12.1	5.1	1.1	4	4	...	Malta
1049	460	1540	0.5	27	30	43	0.355	2685	15772	1.5	...	1.9	74	50	99	Mauritania
3815	3380	13210	5.7	9	33	58	0.831	...	1165	2.2	3.7	0.5	21	13	21	Mauritius
304596	3320	6400	0.1	8	26	66	0.853	3146	615	5.3	5.8	0.9	13	8	4	Mexico
3996	920	1600	-8.2	50	28	22	0.612	...	250	5.1	5.5	3.7	6	1	5	Moldova
767	310	1950	-3.8	21	46	33	0.661	1899	371	4.7	5.2	2.4	23	11	88	Mongolia
29545	1110	3340	0.8	14	33	53	0.566	2984	4665	3.4	5.4	4.3	69	43	19	Morocco
1353	80	810	3.6	33	21	46	0.281	1680	36225	4.6	6.2	3.7	77	42	66	Mozambique
3098	2000	4150	2.8	14	29	57	0.57	2134	4328	7.6	8.7	2.7	26	22	125	Namibia
4391	200	1170	2.4	42	22	36	0.347	1957	13634	5	2.9	1	86	59	21	Nepal
371039	24000	19950	1.8	3	27	70	0.94	3222	399	8.8	5.5	2.2	0	0	*172	Netherlands
51655	14340	16360	0.6	7	25	68	0.937	3669	518	7.5	7.3	1.7	1	1	*31	New Zealand
1659	380	2000	-5.8	33	20	47	0.53	2293	2039	7.8	3.8	1.8	33	35	155	Nicaragua
1961	220	750	-2.1	39	18	43	0.206	2257	53986	2.2	3.1	0.9	93	79	30	Niger
28411	260	1220	1.2	43	27	30	0.393	2124	5208	2.7	1.3	2.9	53	33	2	Nigeria
136077	31250	21940	1.6	3	36	61	0.943	3244	308	7.3	9.2	2.6	0	0	*255	Norway
10578	4820	8140	0.3	3	48	49	0.718	...	1131	2.5	4.5	15.1	76	42	29	Oman
59991	460	2230	1.2	26	24	50	0.445	2315	1923	0.8	2.7	6.5	76	50	6	Pakistan
7235	2750	5980	-0.4	11	18	71	0.864	2242	562	7.5	5.2	1.3	10	9	19	Panama
4976	1160	2420	2.1	26	38	36	0.525	2613	12754	2.8	...	1.3	37	19	88	Papua New Guinea
8158	1690	3650	1.1	24	22	54	0.706	2670	1231	4.3	2.9	1.4	9	7	30	Paraguay
55019	2310	3770	-1.6	7	38	55	0.717	1882	939	4.9	1.5	1.6	17	6	18	Peru
71865	1050	2850	1.5	22	32	46	0.672	2257	8273	2.4	2.4	1.6	6	5	109	Philippines
107829	2790	5400	-0.4	6	39	55	0.834	3301	451	4.6	5.5	2.5	2	1	40	Poland
96689	9740	12670	3.7	6	40	54	0.89	3634	353	7.6	5.4	2.9	13	13	*27	Portugal
27750	7500	7000	2.1	1	42	57	...	...	350	...	...	...	10	10	...	Puerto Rico
33488	1480	4360	-4	21	49	30	0.748	3051	538	3.3	3.1	3.1	5	1	3	Romania
331948	2240	4480	-5.1	7	38	55	0.792	...	222	4.8	4.4	7.4	3	0	12	Russia
1128	180	540	-5	37	17	46	0.187	1821	24967	1.9	3.8	4.4	48	30	92	Rwanda
133540	7040	9500	-1.9	6	51	43	0.774	2735	749	2.2	6.4	10.6	50	29	1	Saudi Arabia
5070	600	1780	-1.2	20	18	62	0.326	2262	18192	1.6	4.2	1.9	77	57	82	Senegal
762	180	580	-3.4	42	27	31	0.176	1694	11000	1.6	1.4	5.7	82	55	45	Sierra Leone
79831	26730	22770	6.2	0	36	64	0.9	...	714	3.5	3.3	5.9	14	4	6	Singapore
15848	2950	3610	-2.6	6	33	61	0.873	...	287	6.3	4.9	2.8	0	0	6	Slovak Rep.
16328	8200	10400	-1	5	39	56	0.886	...	500	7.9	6.2	1.5	0	0	...	Slovenia
4625	500	1000	-2.3	65	9	26	...	1499	13300	1.5	0.4	0.9	52	39	61	Somalia
130918	3160	5030	-1	5	31	64	0.716	2695	1500	7.9	7.1	2.9	18	18	10	South Africa
532347	13580	14520	2.6	3	31	66	0.934	3708	261	7.4	4.7	1.5	6	2	*31	Spain
12616	700	3250	2.7	23	25	52	0.711	2273	6843	1.9	3.2	4.9	13	7	31	Sri Lanka
20000	750	1050	0.6	36	18	46	0.333	2202	10000	0.3	...	4.3	65	42	8	Sudan

	Population									Land and Agriculture					Energy	Trade	
	Population Total 1997	Population Density 1997	Average Annual Change 1970-80	Average Annual Change 1990-97	Birth Rate 1997	Death Rate 1997	Fertility Rate 1995	Life Expectancy Average 1997	Urban Population 1995	Land Area	Arable and Permanent Crops	Permanent grassland	Forest	Agriculture Population 1995	Consumption per capita 1994	Imports per capita 1995	Exports per capita 1995
	millions	persons per km²	%	%	births per thousand population	deaths per thousand population	children	years	%	thousand km²	% of land area	% of land area	% of land area	% of economically active pop.	tonnes of coal	US $	US $
Surinam	0.5	3	-0.6	1.5	24	6	2.6	70	52	156	0	0	96	20	2.01	1565	873
Swaziland	1	55	3	3.1	43	10	4.6	58	29	17.2	11	62	7	34	...	1090	855
Sweden	8.9	22	0.3	0.7	11	11	1.7	78	84	412	7	1	68	4	6.79	7299	9051
Switzerland	7.1	180	0.2	1	11	10	1.5	78	61	39.6	11	29	32	5	4.5	10938	11088
Syria	15.3	83	3.5	2.9	39	6	4.8	67	52	184	30	45	3	33	1.28	325	280
Taiwan	21.7	603	2	0.9	15	6	1.8	76	76	36	26	11	52	19	2.5	4868	5238
Tajikistan	6	42	3	1.8	34	8	4.2	65	32	143	6	25	4	38	0.58	93	84
Tanzania	31.2	35	3.4	2.8	41	20	5.8	42	24	884	4	40	38	83	0.04	55	23
Thailand	60.8	119	2.7	0.9	17	7	1.8	69	19	511	41	2	26	60	1.07	1236	946
Togo	4.5	82	2.6	3.4	46	10	6.4	58	31	54.4	45	4	17	62	0.08	94	51
Trinidad & Tobago	1.3	253	1.1	0.2	16	7	2.1	70	70	5.13	24	2	46	9	7.53	1329	1904
Tunisia	9.2	59	2.2	1.9	24	5	2.9	73	57	155	32	20	4	24	0.75	886	614
Turkey	63.5	83	2.3	1.1	22	5	2.7	72	65	770	36	16	26	51	1.16	579	350
Turkmenistan	4.8	10	2.7	3.9	29	9	3.8	62	47	488	3	64	9	36	3.68	250	533
Uganda	20.8	104	3	2.4	45	21	6.7	40	12	200	34	9	32	83	0.03	50	22
Ukraine	51.5	85	0.6	-0.1	12	15	1.5	67	69	604	59	13	18	18	4.39	192	187
United Kingdom	58.6	243	0.1	0.3	13	11	1.7	77	90	242	25	46	10	2	5.33	4527	4130
United States	268	28	1.1	1	15	9	2.1	76	77	9573	20	25	30	3	11.39	2929	2222
Uruguay	3.3	19	0.4	0.7	17	9	2.2	75	90	175	7	77	5	14	0.78	899	660
Uzbekistan	23.8	56	2.9	2.1	29	8	3.7	65	42	425	11	50	3	34	2.94	111	138
Venezuela	22.5	26	3.5	1.9	24	5	3.1	72	92	882	4	20	34	11	3.75	553	854
Vietnam	77.1	237	2.3	2.1	22	7	3.1	67	20	325	21	1	30	69	0.16	30	30
Yemen	16.5	31	1.9	5.6	45	9	7.4	60	34	528	3	30	4	57	0.33	165	74
Yugoslavia	10.5	103	1	0.3	14	10	1.9	72	54	102	40	21	26	20	1.22	533	452
Zambia	9.5	13	3.2	2.4	44	24	5.7	45	45	743	7	40	43	74	0.19	12	94
Zimbabwe	12.1	31	3.1	3.7	32	19	3.8	60	32	387	7	44	23	67	0.7	231	183

	Land area thousand sq km	Population 1997 thousands
American Samoa	0.2	62
Andorra	0.45	75
Anguilla	0.1	10
Antigua & Barbuda	0.44	66
Aruba	0.19	70
Ascension I.	0.09	1.1
Bahrain	0.68	605
Belize	22.8	228
Bermuda	0.05	65
Bhutan	47	1790
British Virgin Is.	0.15	13
Brunei	5.27	300
Cape Verde Is.	4.03	410
Cayman Is.	0.26	35
Cocos Is.	0.01	1
Comoros	2.23	630
Cook Is.	0.23	20
Djibouti	23.2	650
Dominica	0.75	78
Equatorial Guinea	28.1	420
Eritrea	101	3500
Falkland Is.	12.2	2
Faroe Is.	1.4	45
Fiji	18.3	800
French Guiana	88.2	155

	Land area thousand sq km	Population 1997 thousands
French Polynesia	3.66	226
Gaza Strip	0.36	900
Gibraltar	0.01	28
Greenland	342	57
Grenada	0.34	99
Guadeloupe	1.69	440
Guam	0.55	161
Kiribati	0.73	85
Kuwait	17.8	2050
Liechtenstein	0.16	32
Macau	0.02	450
Maldives	0.3	275
Marshall Is.	0.18	60
Martinique	1.06	405
Mayotte	0.37	105
Micronesia	0.7	127
Monaco	0.002	33
Montserrat	0.1	12
Nauru	0.02	53
Netherlands Antilles	0.8	12
New Caledonia	18.3	210
Niue	0.26	192
Norfolk I.	0.04	2
Northern Marianas	0.48	2
Palau	0.49	17

	Land area thousand sq km	Population 1997 thousands
Pitcairn I.	0.05	0.05
Qatar	11	620
Réunion	2.5	680
St Kitts-Nevis	0.36	4
St Helena	0.3	6
St Lucia	0.61	150
St Pierre & Miquelon	0.23	7
St Vincent & the Grenadines	0.39	114
San Marino	0.06	26
Sâo Tomé & Principe	0.96	135
Seychelles	0.45	78
Solomon Is.	28	410
Svalbard	63	2.8
Tokelau	0.01	2
Tonga	0.72	105
Turks & Caicos Is.	0.43	15
Tuvalu	0.03	10
United Arab Emirates	83.6	2400
US Virgin Is.	0.34	110
Vanuatu	12.2	175
Vatican City	0.0004	1
Wallis & Futuna Is.	0.2	15
West Bank	5.9	1496
Western Sahara	267	280
Western Samoa	2.83	175

Wealth / Social Indicators / Aid

GNP 1995 (million US $)	GNP per capita 1995 (US $)	Real GDP per capita 1995 (US $)	Average Annual growth of Real GNP per capita 1985-95 (%)	GDP share Agriculture 1995 (%)	GDP share Industry 1995 (%)	GDP share services 1995 (%)	HDI Human Development Index 1994	Food Intake (calories per day)	Population per doctor 1993 (persons)	% of GNP spent on health 1990-95 (%)	% of GNP spent on education 1993-94 (%)	%o GNP spent on military 1995 (%)	Adult Illiteracy Female %	Adult Illiteracy Male %	given (*) and received per capita 1994 (US $)	
360	880	2250	0.7	22	23	55	0.792	2547	1200	2.9	3.6	3.9	9	5	183	Surinam
1051	1170	2880	0.6	10	25	65	0.582	2706	9250	7.2	6.8	...	24	22	59	Swaziland
209720	23750	18540	-0.1	2	32	66	0.936	2972	394	7.7	8.4	2.9	0	0	*189	Sweden
286014	40630	25860	0.2	3	32	65	0.93	3379	580	9.6	5.6	1.9	0	0	*135	Switzerland
15780	1120	5320	1	18	43	39	0.755	3175	1159	2.1	4.2	6.8	44	14	25	Syria
252000	12000	13000	7	3	42	55	...	3048	800	4.3		4.8	10	3	...	Taiwan
1976	340	920	-13	27	45	28	0.58	...	424	6.4	9.5	6.9	3	1	5	Tajikistan
3703	120	640	0.9	58	17	25	0.357	2018	22000	2.8	5	2.7	43	21	30	Tanzania
159630	2740	7540	8.4	11	40	49	0.833	2432	4416	5.3	3.8	2.5	8	4	15	Thailand
1266	310	1130	-2.8	38	21	41	0.365	2242	11385	1.7	6.1	2.5	63	33	47	Togo
4851	3770	8610	-1.6	3	42	55	0.88	2585	1520	3.9	4.5	1.3	3	1	20	Trinidad & Tobago
16369	1820	5000	1.8	12	29	59	0.748	3330	1549	5.9	6.3	2	45	21	8	Tunisia
169452	2780	5580	2.2	16	31	53	0.772	3429	976	4.2	3.3	3.6	28	8	5	Turkey
4125	920	3500	-9.6	31	31	38	0.723	...	306	2.8	7.9	1.9	3	1	3	Turkmenistan
4668	240	1470	2.8	50	14	36	0.328	2159	22399	3.9	1.9	2.6	50	26	43	Uganda
84084	1630	2400	-9.2	18	42	40	0.689	...	227	5.4	8.2	3	3	0	5	Ukraine
094734	18700	19260	1.4	2	32	66	0.931	3317	300	6.9	5.4	3.1	0	0	*53	United Kingdom
100007	26980	26980	1.4	2	26	72	0.942	3732	421	14.3	5.5	3.8	5	4	*33	United States
16458	5170	6630	3.3	9	26	65	0.883	2750	500	8.5	2.5	2.6	2	3	26	Uruguay
21979	970	2370	-3.9	33	34	33	0.662	...	282	3.5	11	3.6	4	1	1	Uzbekistan
65382	3020	7900	0.5	5	38	57	0.861	2618	633	7.1	5.1	1.1	10	8	4	Venezuela
17634	240	1200	4.2	28	30	42	0.557	2250	2279	5.2	...	4.3	9	4	8	Vietnam
4044	260	850	3.1	22	27	51	0.361	2203	4498	2.6	4.6	3.9	74	47	13	Yemen
14750	1400	4000	1.8	26	36	38	...	...	232	5.1	...	...	11	2	...	Yugoslavia
3605	400	930	-1	22	40	38	0.369	1931	10917	3.3	2.6	1.9	29	14	221	Zambia
5933	540	2030	-0.6	15	36	49	0.513	1985	7384	2.1	8.3	4.2	20	10	45	Zimbabwe

any figures for Luxembourg are included in those Belgium.

or energy, the figures for South Africa include those Botswana, Lesotho, Swaziland and Namibia.

e sign ... means that figures are not available.

opulation Total. This is an estimate for the mid-ar, 1997.

opulation Density. This is the total population vided by the land area, both quoted in the table.

opulation Change. This shows the average nual percentage change for the two periods, 70-80 and 1990-97.

irth and Death Rates and Life Expectancy. ese are estimates from the US Census Bureau. e Birth and Death rates are the number of those ccurrences per year, per thousand population. Life xpectancy is the number of years that a child born day can expect to live if the levels of mortality of day last throughout its life. The figure is the verage of that for men and women.

ertility Rate. This is the average number of ildren born to a woman in her lifetime.

rban Population. This is the percentage of the tal population living in urban areas. The definition urban is that of the individual nations and often cludes quite small towns.

Land Area. This is the total area of the country less the area covered by major lakes and rivers.

Arable Land and Permanent Crops. This excludes fallow land but includes temporary pasture.

Forest and Woodland. This includes natural and planted woodland and land recently cleared of timber which will be replanted.

Agricultural Population. This is the percentage of the economically active population working in agriculture. It includes those working in forestry, hunting and fishing.

Energy. All forms of energy have been expressed in an approximate equivalent of tonnes of coal per person.

Trade. The trade figures are for 1994 or 1995. In a few cases the figure is older than this but is the latest available. The total Import and Export figures have been divided by the population to give a figure in US $ per capita.

Gross National Product (GNP). This figure is an estimate of the value of a country's production and the average production per person for 1995, in US $. The GNP measures the value of goods and services produced in a country, plus the balance, positive or negative, of income from abroad, for example, from investments, interest on capital, money returned from workers abroad, etc. The Gross Domestic Product (GDP), is the GNP less the foreign balances. The adjoining three columns show the percentage contribution to the GDP made by the

agricultural, mining and manufacturing and service sectors of the economy. The average annual rate of change is for the GNP per capita in PPP $ during the period 1985-95

Real GDP per capita. Using official exchange rates to convert national currencies into US $ makes no attempt to reflect the varying domestic purchasing powers of the local currency. The UN has made these estimates of Real GDP taking into account these local purchasing values and they are called Purchasing Power Parity $.

Human Development Index. This is a calculation made by the UN Development Programme, using 1994 data and takes into account not only national income, but also life expectancy, adult literacy and the years in education. It is a measure of national human progress. The wealthy developed countries have an index approaching 1, and the figures range down to some of the poorer with an index of less than 0.1.

Food Intake. The figures are the average intake per person in calories per day. They are for 1992 and are the latest estimates that are available.

Adult Illiteracy. This is the percentage of the male and female population aged 15 and over who cannot read or write a simple sentence.

Aid. The bulk of the table is concerned with aid received but aid given is shown by an asterisk.

To convert square kilometres to square miles multiply by 0.39.

AZIMUTHAL OR ZENITHAL PROJECTIONS

These are constructed by the projection of part of the graticule from the globe onto a plane tangential to any single point on it. This plane may be tangential to the equator (equatorial case), the poles (polar case) or any other point (oblique case). Any straight line drawn from the point at which the plane touches the globe is the shortest distance from that point and is known as a great circle. In its Gnomonic construction any straight line on the map is a great circle, but there is great exaggeration towards the edges and this reduces its general uses. There are five different ways of transferring the graticule onto the plane and these are shown below. The diagrams below also show how the graticules vary, using the polar case as the example.

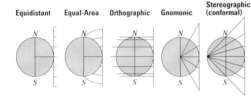

| Equidistant | Equal-Area | Orthographic | Gnomonic | Stereographic (conformal) |

Polar Case

The polar case is the simplest to construct and the diagram on the right shows the differing effects of all five methods of construction comparing their coverage, distortion etc., using North America as the example.

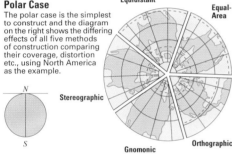

Oblique Case

The plane touches the globe at any point between the equator and poles. The oblique orthographic uses the distortion in azimuthal projections away from the centre to give a graphic depiction of the earth as seen from any desired point in space.

Equatorial Case

The example shown here is Lambert's Equivalent Azimuthal. It is the only projection which is both equal area and where bearing is true from the centre.

MAP PROJECTIONS

A map projection is the systematic depiction of the imaginary grid of lines of latitude and longitude from a globe onto a flat surface. The grid of lines is called the graticule and it can be constructed either by graphical means or by mathematical formulae to form the basis of a map. As a globe is three dimensional it is not possible to depict its surface on a flat map without some form of distortion. Preservation of one of the basic properties listed below can only be secured at the expense of the others and the choice of projection is often a compromise solution.

Correct Area
In these projections the areas from the globe are to scale on the map. This is particularly useful in the mapping of densities and distributions. Projections with this property are termed Equal Area, Equivalent or Homolographic.

Correct Distance
In these projections the scale is correct along the meridians, or in the case of the Azimuthal Equidistant scale is true along any line drawn from the centre of the projection. They are called Equidistant.

Correct Shape
This property can only be true within small areas as it is achieved only by having a uniform scale distortion along both x and y axes of the projection. The projections are called Conformal or Orthomorphic.

Map projections can be divided into three broad categories - azimuthal, conic and cylindrical. Cartographers use different projections from these categories depending on the map scale, the size of the area to be mapped, and what they want the map to show.

CONICAL PROJECTIONS

These use the projection of the graticule from the globe onto a cone which is tangential to a line of latitude (termed the standard parallel). This line is always an arc and scale is always true along it. Because of its method of construction it is used mainly for depicting the temperate latitudes around the standard parallel i.e. where there is least distortion. To reduce the distortion and include a larger range of latitudes, the projection may be constructed with the cone bisecting the surface of the globe so that there are two standard parallels each of which is true to scale. The distortion is thus spread more evenly between the two chosen parallels.

Simple Conical with one standard parallel

Bonne

This is a modification of the simple conic whereby the true scale along the meridians is sacrificed to enable the accurate representation of areas. However scale is true along each parallel but shapes are distorted at the edges.

Albers Conical Equal Area

This projection uses two standard parallels. The selection of these relative to the land area to be mapped is very important. It is equal area and is especially useful for large land masses oriented East-West, for example the U.S.A.

CYLINDRICAL AND OTHER WORLD PROJECTIONS

This group of projections are those which permit the whole of the Earth's surface to be depicted on one map. They are a very large group of projections and the following are only a few of them. Cylindrical projections are constructed by the projection of the graticule from the globe onto a cylinder tangential to the globe. Although cylindrical projections can depict all the main land masses, there is considerable distortion of shape and area towards the poles. One cylindrical projection, Mercator overcomes this shortcoming by possessing the unique navigational property that any straight line drawn on it is a line of constant bearing (loxodrome). It is used for maps and charts between 15° either side of the equator. Beyond this enlargement of area is a serious drawback, although it is used for navigational charts at all latitudes.

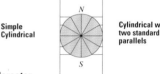

Simple Cylindrical

Cylindrical with two standard parallels

Mercator

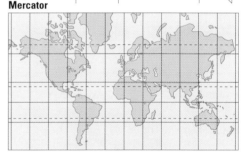

Eckert IV (pseudocylindrical equal area)

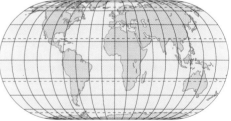

Hammer (polyconic equal area)

WORLD STUDY MAPS

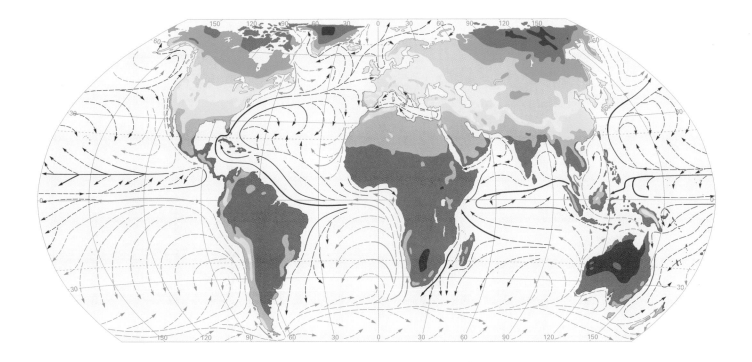

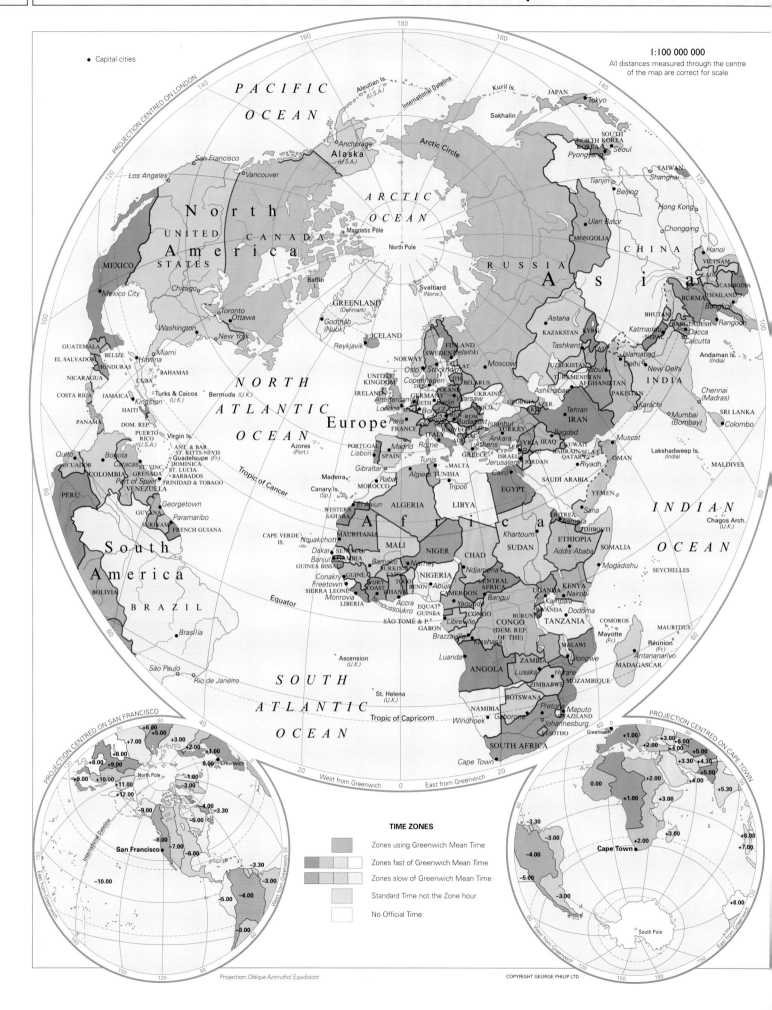

• Capital cities

1:100 000 000
All distances measured through the centre
of the map are correct for scale

PROJECTION CENTRED ON LONDON

**PACIFIC
OCEAN**

Aleutian Is.
(U.S.A.)

International Dateline

Kuril Is.

JAPAN

Tokyo

Sakhalin

Arctic Circle

**ARCTIC
OCEAN**

Anchorage

Alaska
(U.S.A.)

San Francisco

Vancouver

Magnetic Pole

North Pole

Svalbard
(Norw.)

NORTH
KOREA

SOUTH
KOREA
Seoul

Pyongyang

TAIWAN

Tianjin

Shanghai

Beijing

Hong Kong

Chongqing

Ulan Bator

MONGOLIA

CHINA

Hanoi

VIETNAM

LAOS

CAMBODIA

BURMA

Bangkok

THAILAND

Rangoon

Los Angeles

N o r t h

UNITED

CANADA

A m e r i c a

STATES

MEXICO

Chicago

Mexico City

Baffin

GREENLAND
(Denmark)

Godthåb
(Nuuk)

ICELAND

Reykjavik

A s i a

RUSSIA

Astana

KAZAKSTAN

KYRG

Tashkent

UZBEKISTAN

TURKMENISTAN

Ashkhabad

Kabul

AFGHANISTAN

PAKISTAN

Katmandu

NEPAL

BHUTAN

BANGLADESH

Dacca

Calcutta

Islamabad

Delhi

New Delhi

INDIA

Chennai
(Madras)

Andaman Is.
(India)

Toronto
Ottawa

Washington

New York

FINLAND

SWEDEN Helsinki

NORWAY

Oslo Stockholm

Copenhagen

Moscow

BELARUS

UKRAIN

GEORGIA AZER

ARM

Tehran

IRAN

Bagdad

Mumbai
(Bombay)

SRI LANKA

Colombo

GUATEMALA

EL SALVADOR BELIZE

HONDURAS

NICARAGUA

COSTA RICA

Miami

Havana

CUBA

BAHAMAS

JAMAICA

Kingston

HAITI

PANAMA

DOM. REP.

PUERTO
RICO
(U.S.A.)

Virgin Is.

Turks & Caicos
(U.K.)

Bermuda (U.K.)

**NORTH
ATLANTIC
OCEAN**

Azores
(Port.)

UNITED
KINGDOM

IRELAND

Amsterdam

London

GERMANY

NETH

Paris

FRANCE

Europe

PORTUGAL

Lisbon

Madrid

SPAIN

Gibraltar

Warsaw

POLAND

Berlin

Bonn

Budapest

ROM

ITALY

Rome

Athens

GREECE

Madeira

Canary Is.
(Sp.)

Rabat

MOROCCO

Algiers

TUNISIA

Tunis

Istanbul

TURKEY

Ankara

CYP

ISRAEL

Jerusalem

SYRIA IRAQ

Beirut

JORDAN

KUWAIT

BAHRAIN U.A.E.

QATAR

Riyadh

Muscat

OMAN

Lakshadweep Is.
(India)

MALDIVES

Chagos Arch.
(U.K.)

**INDIAN
OCEAN**

ANT. & BAR.
ST. KITTS-NEVIS
Guadeloupe (Fr.)
DOMINICA
ST. LUCIA
BARBADOS
TRINIDAD & TOBAGO

GRENADA
ST. VINC.

Quito

ECUADOR

Bogota

Caracas

COLOMBIA

VENEZUELA

PERU

GUYANA

Georgetown

SURINAM

Paramaribo

FRENCH GUIANA

**South
America**

BOLIVIA

BRAZIL

Brasília

São Paulo

Rio de Janeiro

Tropic of Cancer

WESTERN
SAHARA

El Aaiun

ALGERIA

LIBYA

Tripoli

EGYPT

Cairo

SAUDI ARABIA

YEMEN

Sana

ERITREA

Asmara

DJIBOUTI

CAPE VERDE
IS.

Nouakchott

MAURITANIA

Dakar

SENEGAL

GAMBIA

Banjul

GUINEA BISSAU

Conakry

GUINEA

Freetown

SIERRA LEONE

Monrovia

LIBERIA

A f r i c a

MALI

Bamako

BURKINA
FASO

Niamey

NIGER

CHAD

Ndjamena

SUDAN

Khartoum

ETHIOPIA

Addis Ababa

SOMALIA

Mogadishu

SEYCHELLES

IVORY
COAST

Yamoussoukro

Accra

GHANA

TOGO

BENIN

Abuja

NIGERIA

CAMEROON

CENTRAL
AFRICA

Bangui

Yaoundé

EQUAT.
GUINEA

SÃO TOMÉ & P.

GABON

Libreville

Brazzaville

CONGO

CONGO
(DEM. REP.
OF THE)

Kinshasa

UGANDA

Kampala

RWANDA

BURUNDI

KENYA

Nairobi

Dodoma

TANZANIA

COMOROS

Mayotte
(Fr.)

MAURITIUS

Réunion
(Fr.)

Antananarivo

MADAGASCAR

Equator

Ascension
(U.K.)

Luanda

ANGOLA

ZAMBIA

Lusaka

MALAWI

Lilongwe

Harare

ZIMBABWE

MOZAMBIQUE

St. Helena
(U.K.)

**SOUTH
ATLANTIC
OCEAN**

NAMIBIA

Windhoek

BOTSWANA

Gaborone

Pretoria

Maputo

SWAZILAND

Johannesburg

LESOTHO

SOUTH AFRICA

Cape Town

Tropic of Capricorn

West from Greenwich 0 East from Greenwich

PROJECTION CENTRED ON SAN FRANCISCO

+6.00
+7.00
+5.00
+3.00
+2.00
+1.00
+8.00
+8.00 +9.00
0.00 Greenwich
+9.00 +10.00 +11.00
-1.00
-3.00
North Pole
+12.00
-4.00
-3.30
-9.00
-5.00
-8.00
-6.00
San Francisco
-7.00
-3.30
-3.00
International Dateline
-10.00
-5.00 -4.00
-3.00

TIME ZONES

Zones using Greenwich Mean Time

Zones fast of Greenwich Mean Time

Zones slow of Greenwich Mean Time

Standard Time not the Zone hour

No Official Time

PROJECTION CENTRED ON CAPE TOWN

Greenwich
+1.00
+3.00
+2.00
+6.00
+4.00
+5.00
+3.30 +4.30
+5.00
0.00
+2.00
+4.00
+1.00
+5.30
+3.00
-3.30
-3.00
+2.00
+3.00
+8.00
-4.00
+7.00
-5.00
-3.00
+8.00
Cape Town
South Pole

Projection: *Oblique Azimuthal Equidistant*

COPYRIGHT GEORGE PHILIP LTD

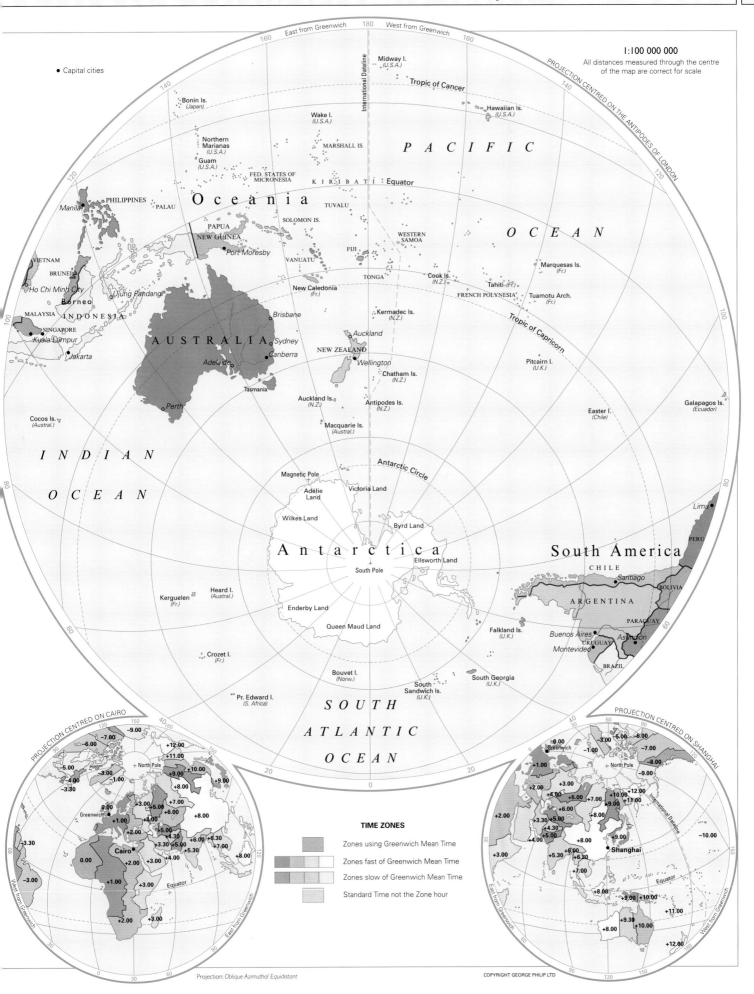

Projection: *Oblique Azimuthal Equidistant*

1:100 000 000
All distances measured through the centre
of the map are correct for scale

• Capital cities

TIME ZONES

Zones using Greenwich Mean Time

Zones fast of Greenwich Mean Time

Zones slow of Greenwich Mean Time

Standard Time not the Zone hour

COPYRIGHT GEORGE PHILIP LTD

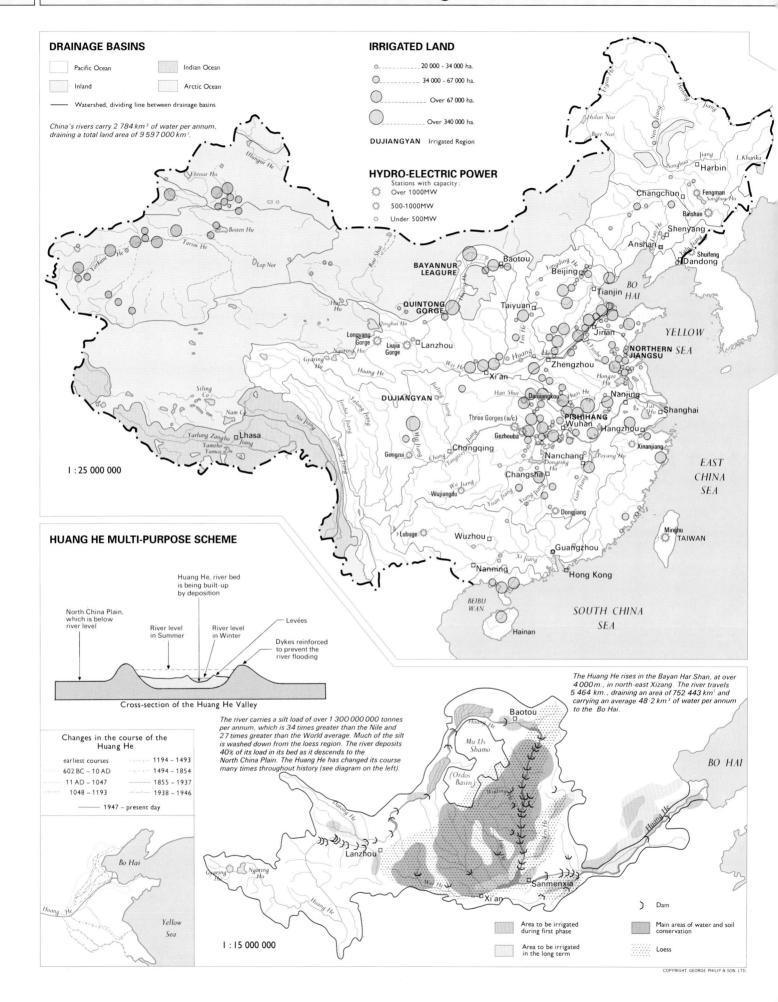

DRAINAGE BASINS

- Pacific Ocean
- Indian Ocean
- Inland
- Arctic Ocean

—— Watershed, dividing line between drainage basins

China's rivers carry 2 784 km³ of water per annum, draining a total land area of 9 597 000 km².

1 : 25 000 000

IRRIGATED LAND

- ○ — 20 000 - 34 000 ha.
- ● — 34 000 - 67 000 ha.
- ● — Over 67 000 ha.
- ● — Over 340 000 ha.

DUJIANGYAN Irrigated Region

HYDRO-ELECTRIC POWER

Stations with capacity:
- Over 1000MW
- 500-1000MW
- Under 500MW

HUANG HE MULTI-PURPOSE SCHEME

North China Plain, which is below river level

Huang He, river bed is being built-up by deposition

River level in Summer

River level in Winter

Levées

Dykes reinforced to prevent the river flooding

Cross-section of the Huang He Valley

Changes in the course of the Huang He

earliest courses
- 602 BC – 10 AD
- 1194 – 1493
- 11 AD – 1047
- 1494 – 1854
- 1048 – 1193
- 1855 – 1937
- 1938 – 1946

—— 1947 – present day

1 : 15 000 000

The Huang He rises in the Bayan Har Shan, at over 4 000 m., in north-east Xizang. The river travels 5 464 km., draining an area of 752 443 km² and carrying an average 48·2 km³ of water per annum to the Bo Hai.

The river carries a silt load of over 1 300 000 000 tonnes per annum, which is 34 times greater than the Nile and 27 times greater than the World average. Much of the silt is washed down from the loess region. The river deposits 40% of its load in its bed as it descends to the North China Plain. The Huang He has changed its course many times throughout history (see diagram on the left).

- Area to be irrigated during first phase
- Area to be irrigated in the long term
- Main areas of water and soil conservation
- Loess
-) Dam

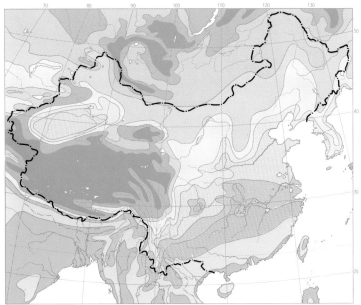

ANNUAL RAINFALL

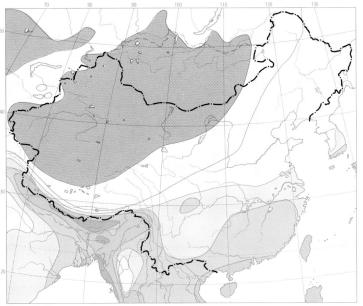

mm
3 000
2 000
1 500
1 000
500
250

In winter high pressure becomes established over Mongolia by November, leading to strong, dry and cold north-westerly, northerly and north-easterly winds over China. By April or May the high pressure gives way to a low centred over South Asia. Southern China begins to experience a southern warm and moist air stream, which is fully established by July or August. Typhoons affect China between July and September, bringing winds of hurricane force, high seas and heavy rain. Moving in from the east they do not usually penetrate far inland. South of the Yangtze all areas receive over 1250mm of rain per year. North of the Yangtze and in much of the west, under 500mm is experienced. Everywhere, but particularly in the north, a large percentage of the rainfall occurs in the summer. As annual rainfall decreases from the south-east to north-east, so the variability increases.

FROST-FREE PERIOD

Days per year
270
240
210
180
150
120
90
60

Frosts, but not every year

No frosts

Southern China and Sichuan have almost no frosts and plant growth goes on for the whole year. Further north the frost-free period decreases and much of Tibet, Sinkiang and Mongolia have only a third of the year free from frosts.

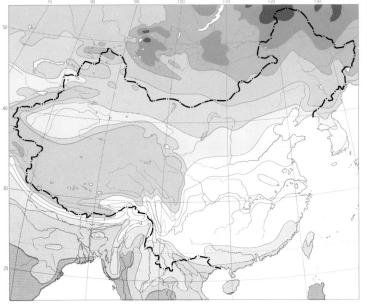

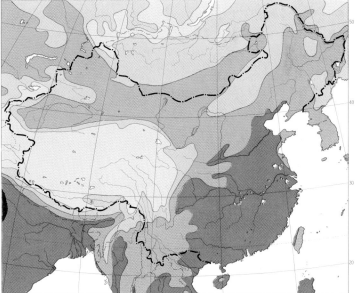

JANUARY TEMPERATURE

°C
20
15
10
5
0
-5
-10
-15
-20
-25
-30

In January in the extreme south of China the mean monthly temperature is 15°–20°C. In lowland China the temperature decreases northwards and Beijing is below freezing point. Ice forms on the Gulf of Bo Hai. Further north and in the high mountains and plateaux of the west the winter is very cold. The Sichuan basin, nearly 1600km inland but sheltered by the Daba Shan from the cold north-easterly winds, is warmer than the lower Yangtze at this season.

JULY TEMPERATURE

°C
30
25
20
15

In summer the temperature contrasts are not as great. The whole of China is affected by the warm humid flow of air from the south; Hong Kong, Chongqing, Beijing and Ürümqi have about the same mean monthly temperature for July. Some of the mountains in Tibet remain below freezing even in the summer.

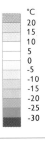

1:52 000 000

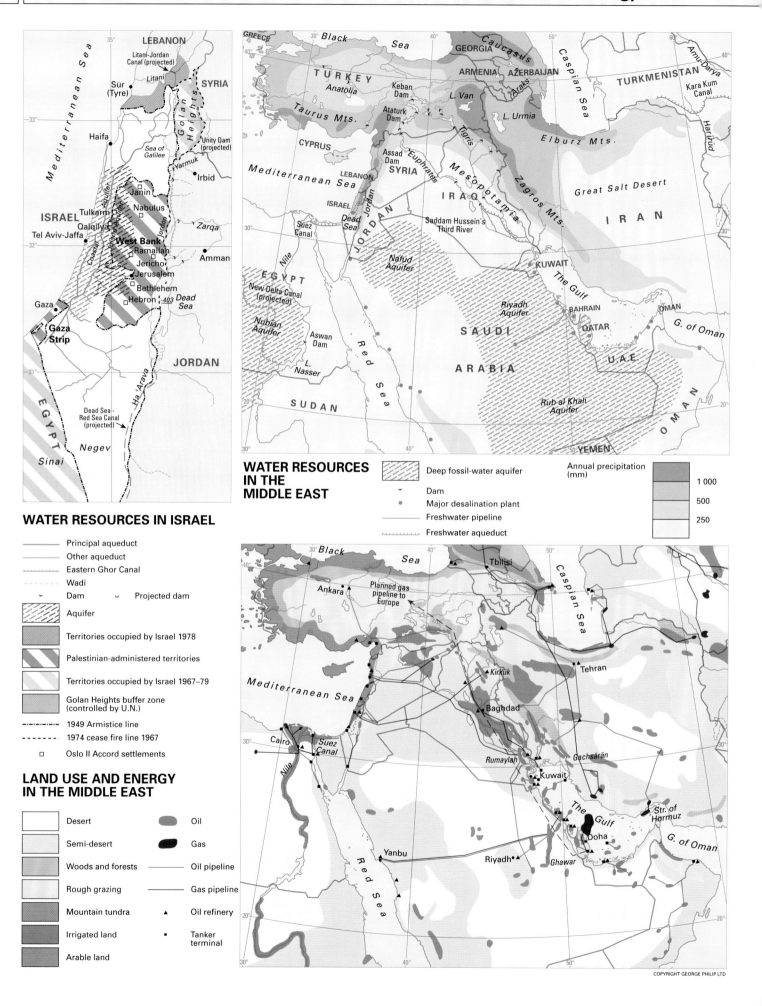

WATER RESOURCES IN ISRAEL

——————— Principal aqueduct

——————— Other aqueduct

·············· Eastern Ghor Canal

– – – – – Wadi

˅ Dam   ˇ Projected dam

▨ Aquifer

▨ Territories occupied by Israel 1978

▨ Palestinian-administered territories

▨ Territories occupied by Israel 1967–79

▨ Golan Heights buffer zone (controlled by U.N.)

–·–·–·– 1949 Armistice line

– – – – 1974 cease fire line 1967

▫ Oslo II Accord settlements

LAND USE AND ENERGY IN THE MIDDLE EAST

▢ Desert   ⬬ Oil

▢ Semi-desert   ⬬ Gas

▢ Woods and forests   —— Oil pipeline

▢ Rough grazing   —— Gas pipeline

▢ Mountain tundra   ▲ Oil refinery

▢ Irrigated land   ▪ Tanker terminal

▢ Arable land

WATER RESOURCES IN THE MIDDLE EAST

▨ Deep fossil-water aquifer

˅ Dam

• Major desalination plant

—— Freshwater pipeline

·············· Freshwater aqueduct

Annual precipitation (mm)

1 000

500

250

COPYRIGHT GEORGE PHILIP LTD

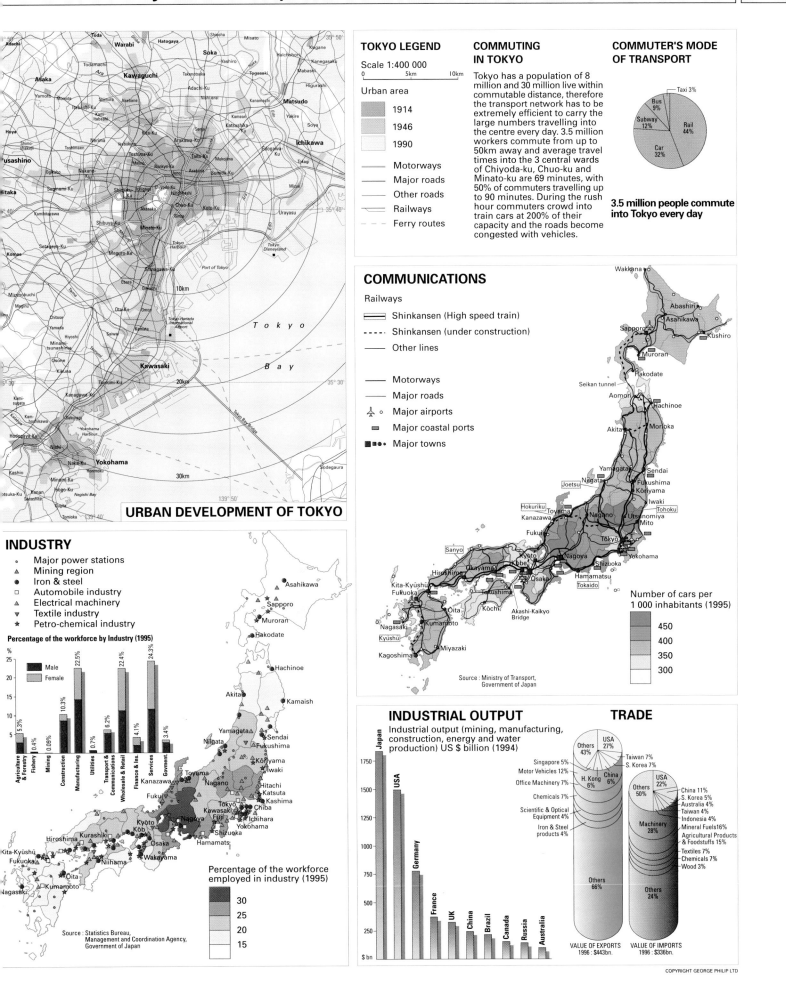

URBAN DEVELOPMENT OF TOKYO

TOKYO LEGEND

Scale 1:400 000

| 0 | 5km | 10km |

Urban area

- 1914
- 1946
- 1990

--- Motorways
--- Major roads
--- Other roads
--- Railways
--- Ferry routes

COMMUTING IN TOKYO

Tokyo has a population of 8 million and 30 million live within commutable distance, therefore the transport network has to be extremely efficient to carry the large numbers travelling into the centre every day. 3.5 million workers commute from up to 50km away and average travel times into the 3 central wards of Chiyoda-ku, Chuo-ku and Minato-ku are 69 minutes, with 50% of commuters travelling up to 90 minutes. During the rush hour commuters crowd into train cars at 200% of their capacity and the roads become congested with vehicles.

COMMUTER'S MODE OF TRANSPORT

- Taxi 3%
- Bus 9%
- Subway 12%
- Rail 44%
- Car 32%

3.5 million people commute into Tokyo every day

COMMUNICATIONS

Railways

- Shinkansen (High speed train)
- Shinkansen (under construction)
- Other lines

- Motorways
- Major roads
- Major airports
- Major coastal ports
- Major towns

Number of cars per 1 000 inhabitants (1995)

- 450
- 400
- 350
- 300

Source : Ministry of Transport, Government of Japan

INDUSTRY

- Major power stations
- Mining region
- Iron & steel
- Automobile industry
- Electrical machinery
- Textile industry
- Petro-chemical industry

Percentage of the workforce by Industry (1995)

■ Male
■ Female

Industry	%
Agriculture & Forestry	5.3%
Fishery	0.4%
Mining	0.09%
Construction	10.3%
Manufacturing	22.5%
Utilities	0.7%
Transport & Communications	6.2%
Wholesale & Retail	22.4%
Finance & Ins.	4.1%
Services	24.3%
Govnment.	3.4%

Percentage of the workforce employed in industry (1995)

- 30
- 25
- 20
- 15

Source : Statistics Bureau, Management and Coordination Agency, Government of Japan

INDUSTRIAL OUTPUT

Industrial output (mining, manufacturing, construction, energy and water production) US $ billion (1994)

Japan
USA
Germany
France
UK
China
Brazil
Canada
Russia
Australia

$ bn

TRADE

Others 43%
USA 27%
Taiwan 7%
S. Korea 7%
Singapore 5%
China 6%
H. Kong 6%
Motor Vehicles 12%
Office Machinery 7%
Chemicals 7%
Scientific & Optical Equipment 4%
Iron & Steel products 4%
Others 66%

VALUE OF EXPORTS 1996 : $443bn.

USA 22%
Others 50%
China 11%
S. Korea 5%
Australia 4%
Taiwan 4%
Indonesia 4%
Mineral Fuels 16%
Machinery 28%
Agricultural Products & Foodstuffs 15%
Textiles 7%
Chemicals 7%
Wood 3%
Others 24%

VALUE OF IMPORTS 1996 : $336bn.

The Southern African Development Co-ordination Conference (SADCC) was formed in 1980 and became the Southern African Development Community (SADC) in 1992. South Africa became a full member in 1994 and Mauritius joined in 1995. There are now 12 member countries.

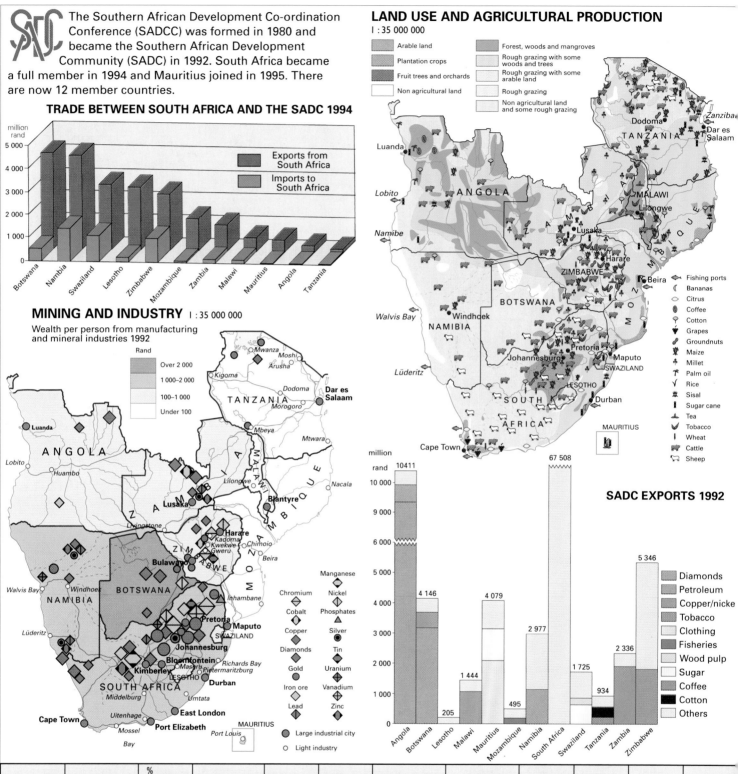

TRADE BETWEEN SOUTH AFRICA AND THE SADC 1994

million rand

5 000
4 000
3 000
2 000
1 000
0

Botswana, Namibia, Swaziland, Lesotho, Zimbabwe, Mozambique, Zambia, Malawi, Mauritius, Angola, Tanzania

Exports from South Africa
Imports to South Africa

MINING AND INDUSTRY   I : 35 000 000

Wealth per person from manufacturing and mineral industries 1992

Rand
Over 2 000
1 000–2 000
100–1 000
Under 100

Manganese, Chromium, Nickel, Cobalt, Phosphates, Copper, Silver, Diamonds, Tin, Gold, Uranium, Iron ore, Vanadium, Lead, Zinc

Large industrial city
Light industry

LAND USE AND AGRICULTURAL PRODUCTION
I : 35 000 000

Arable land
Plantation crops
Fruit trees and orchards
Non agricultural land
Forest, woods and mangroves
Rough grazing with some woods and trees
Rough grazing with some arable land
Rough grazing
Non agricultural land and some rough grazing

Fishing ports, Bananas, Citrus, Coffee, Cotton, Grapes, Groundnuts, Maize, Millet, Palm oil, Rice, Sisal, Sugar cane, Tea, Tobacco, Wheat, Cattle, Sheep

SADC EXPORTS 1992

million rand

10 000
9 000
6 000
5 000
4 000
3 000
2 000
1 000
0

Angola 10411, Botswana 4 146, Lesotho 205, Malawi 1 444, Mauritius 4 079, Mozambique 495, Namibia 2 977, South Africa 67 508, Swaziland 1 725, Tanzania 934, Zambia 2 336, Zimbabwe 5 346

Diamonds, Petroleum, Copper/nickel, Tobacco, Clothing, Fisheries, Wood pulp, Sugar, Coffee, Cotton, Others

	Population 1994 (thousands)	% Population growth 1990–1995	Human Development Index 1992	% Adult literacy 1992	% Urban population 1992	GNP 1993 (million US$)	GNP per capita 1992 (US$)	% employed in agriculture 1993	Agriculture as % of GDP 1993	% employed in industry 1993	Industry as % of GDP 1993
Angola	10 674	1.6	0.291	43	30	5 700	600	69	12	10	43
Botswana	1 392	2.6	0.763	67	25	3 630	2 590	61	6	11	47
Lesotho	1 836	3.4	0.473	69	27	1 254	660	23	10	33	47
Malawi	10 843	3.4	0.330	54	16	2 034	220	72	39	5	18
Mauritius	1 120	0.8	0.821	81	42	3 309	2 980	21	10	30	33
Mozambique	15 527	4.6	0.246	37	41	1 375	80	81	33	7	12
Namibia	1 635	2.3	0.611	40	43	2 594	1 660	33	10	22	27
South Africa	40 555	3.0	0.705	81	53	118 057	2 900	13	4	25	40
Swaziland	836	2.0	0.522	74	36	933	1 050	64	12	9	39
Tanzania	28 846	3.0	0.364	64	28	2 521	100	79	56	5	14
Zambia	9 196	3.3	0.425	75	45	3 152	370	68	34	8	36
Zimbabwe	11 002	4.1	0.539	83	36	5 756	540	67	15	8	36

Year	Urban %	Rural %	Homelands %	Total Population (millions)
1950	25.4	34.9	39.7	12.7
1960	29.6	31.3	39.1	16
1970	28.1	24.5	47.4	22
1980	26.7	20.6	52.7	29

In 1991 the total population of South Africa was estimated at 42 million. Since the breakdown of apartheid, the population of the major cities has grown very rapidly. Thousands of people, unable to make a living off the land, are moving to the cities creating a huge demand for employment and housing in the urban areas.

POPULATION GROWTH AND DISTRIBUTION

This table shows how population growth, forced removals and controls on black urbanisation have affected population distribution since 1950.

The column marked Rural reflects people who own or are employed on commercial farms. Most of the former Homeland population are to some extent dependent on income from urban or commercial farm employment.

POPULATION DENSITY

Number of people per km² 1991

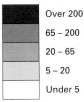

Over 200	
65 – 200	
20 – 65	
5 – 20	
Under 5	

HUMAN DEVELOPMENT

The Human Development Index (HDI) is calculated using social and economic indicators, including income, life expectancy, adult literacy and education.

Wealthy developed areas measure highest on the index.

This map shows clearly that South Africa's least developed areas are the former Homelands and where most people are poorly paid farm workers.

Human Development Index 1991

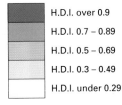

H.D.I. over 0.9	
H.D.I. 0.7 – 0.89	
H.D.I. 0.5 – 0.69	
H.D.I. 0.3 – 0.49	
H.D.I. under 0.29	

South Africa average : 0.7
Sub - Saharan Africa average : 0.34
World average : 0.76

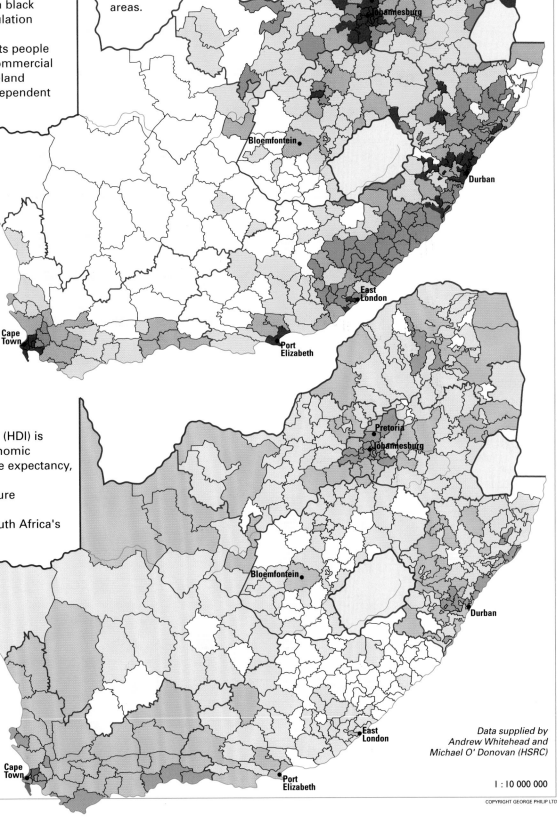

Data supplied by Andrew Whitehead and Michael O' Donovan (HSRC)

1 : 10 000 000

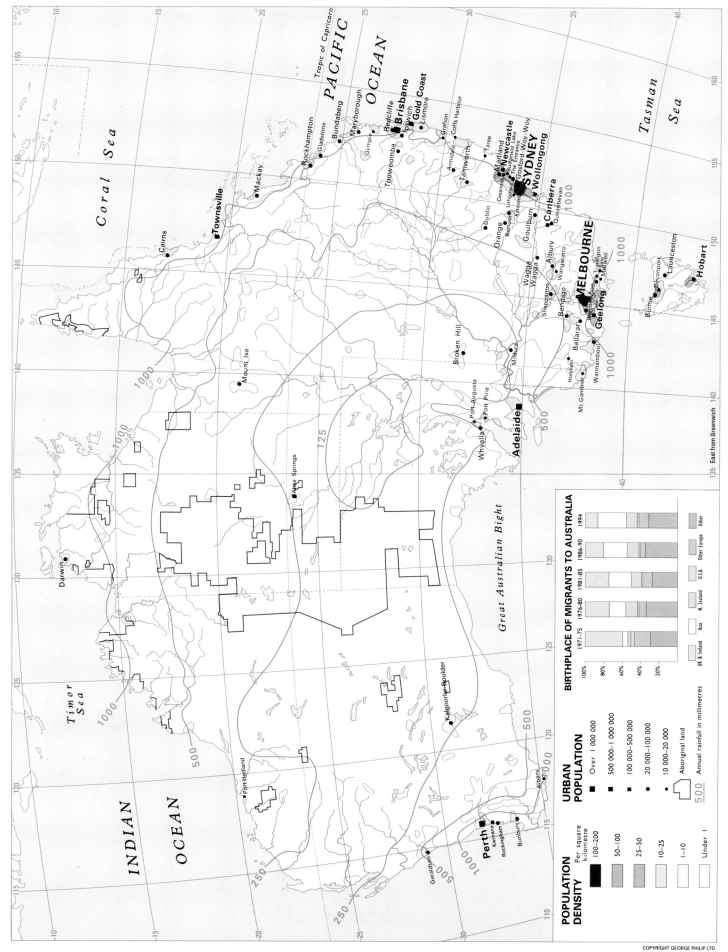

POPULATION DENSITY
Per square kilometre
- 100–200
- 50–100
- 25–50
- 10–25
- 1–10
- Under 1

URBAN POPULATION
- ■ Over 1 000 000
- ■ 500 000–1 000 000
- ■ 100 000–500 000
- ● 20 000–100 000
- • 10 000–20 000
- Aboriginal land
- 500 Annual rainfall in millimetres

BIRTHPLACE OF MIGRANTS TO AUSTRALIA
1971-75 1976-80 1981-85 1986-90 1994

- UK & Ireland
- Asia
- N. Zealand
- U.S.A.
- Other Europe
- Other

COPYRIGHT GEORGE PHILIP LTD

1 : 20 000 000

1 : 30 000 000

MINING AND INDUSTRY

Chromium Tin Zinc Gold

Bauxite Copper Iron ore Manganese

Coal Oil

EXPORTS

Brazil Total Exports 1995 $46 505.4 million

Others

Food & live animals 21.4%
(of which coffee 5.3%)

Machinery 19.0%
(of which motor
vehicles 6.3%)

Crude materials
13.1% (of which
iron ore 6.0%)

Fuel 0.9%

Chemicals 6.5%

Manufactured Goods 25.2%
(of which iron and steel 9.3%)

IMPORTS

Brazil Total Imports 1995 $53 736.7 million

Others

Food & live animals 8.9%

Crude materials 4.7%

Fuel 12.1%

Machinery 39.1%
(of which motor
vehicles 10.8%)

Chemicals 15%

Manufactured Goods 11.5%
(of which textiles 2.6%)

CROPS AND LIVESTOCK

Fishing ports Cotton Tea

Bananas Groundnuts Tobacco

Cacao Maize Cattle

Citrus fruit Potatoes Pigs

Coconuts Rice

Coffee Sugar cane

AGRICULTURE

Industrial

Arable land

Plantation crops

Pasture

Forest, woods and mangroves

Rough grazing

Fortaleza

Recife

Salvador

Brasilia

Belo Horizonte

São Paulo

Rio de Janeiro

Pôrto Alegre

DEFORESTATION

False colours have been chosen to highlight the destruction of the rainforest. The dark green of the natural forest contrasts with the pinks of levelled forest, within a typical linear, branching pattern of destruction. ▶

Thousands of hectares of forest cleared annually, tropical countries surveyed 1981–85, 1987–90 and 1990–95. Loss as a percentage of remaining stocks is shown in figures on each column.

1990–95

1987–90

1981–85

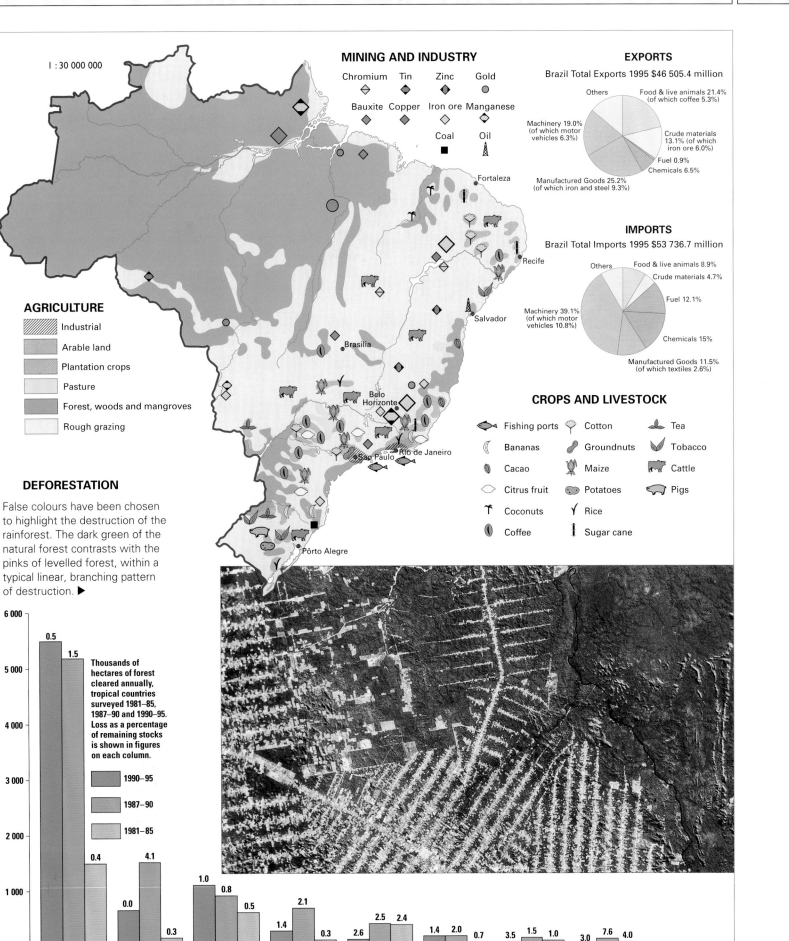

	Brazil	India	Indonesia	Burma	Thailand	Vietnam	Philippines	Costa Rica
1990–95	0.5	0.0	1.0	1.4	2.6	1.4	3.5	3.0
1987–90	1.5	4.1	0.8	2.1	2.5	2.0	1.5	7.6
1981–85	0.4	0.3	0.5	0.3	2.4	0.7	1.0	4.0

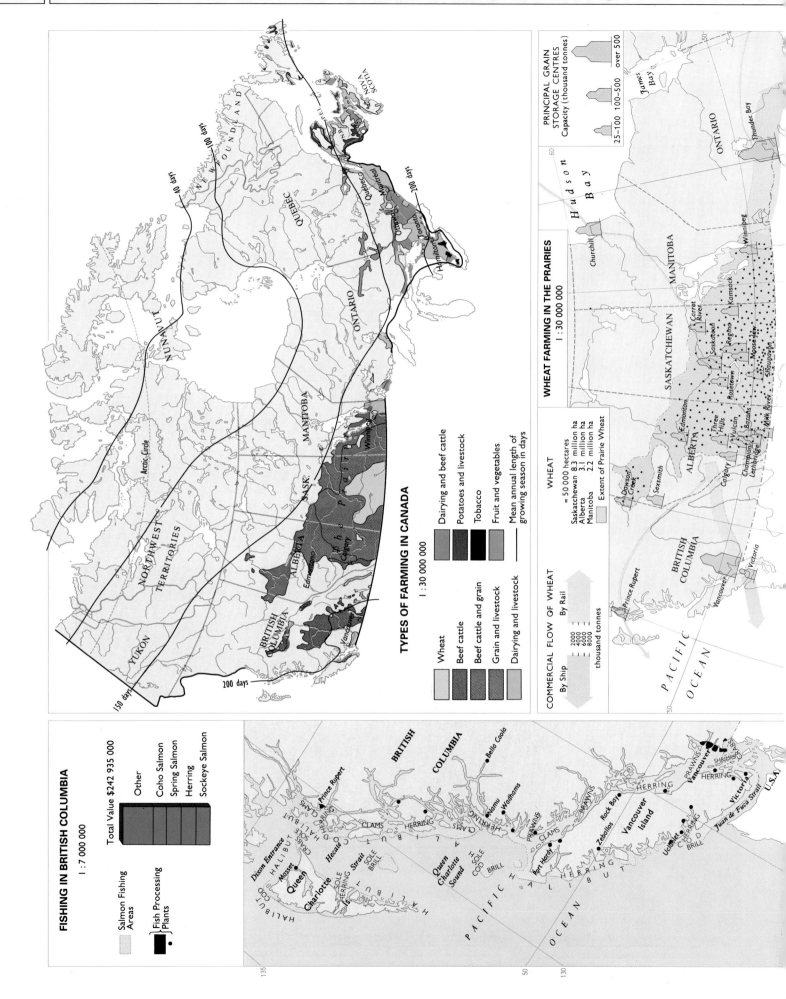

TYPES OF FARMING IN CANADA

1 : 30 000 000

- Wheat
- Beef cattle
- Beef cattle and grain
- Grain and livestock
- Dairying and livestock
- Dairying and beef cattle
- Potatoes and livestock
- Tobacco
- Fruit and vegetables
- Mean annual length of growing season in days

PRINCIPAL GRAIN STORAGE CENTRES Capacity (thousand tonnes)

- 25–100
- 100–500
- over 500

WHEAT FARMING IN THE PRAIRIES

1 : 30 000 000

WHEAT

= 50 000 hectares

Saskatchewan	8.3 million ha
Alberta	3.1 million ha
Manitoba	2.2 million ha

Extent of Prairie Wheat

COMMERCIAL FLOW OF WHEAT

By Ship   By Rail

2000
4000
6000
8000

thousand tonnes

FISHING IN BRITISH COLUMBIA

1 : 7 000 000

Total Value $242 935 000

- Other
- Coho Salmon
- Spring Salmon
- Herring
- Sockeye Salmon

- Salmon Fishing Areas
- Fish Processing Plants

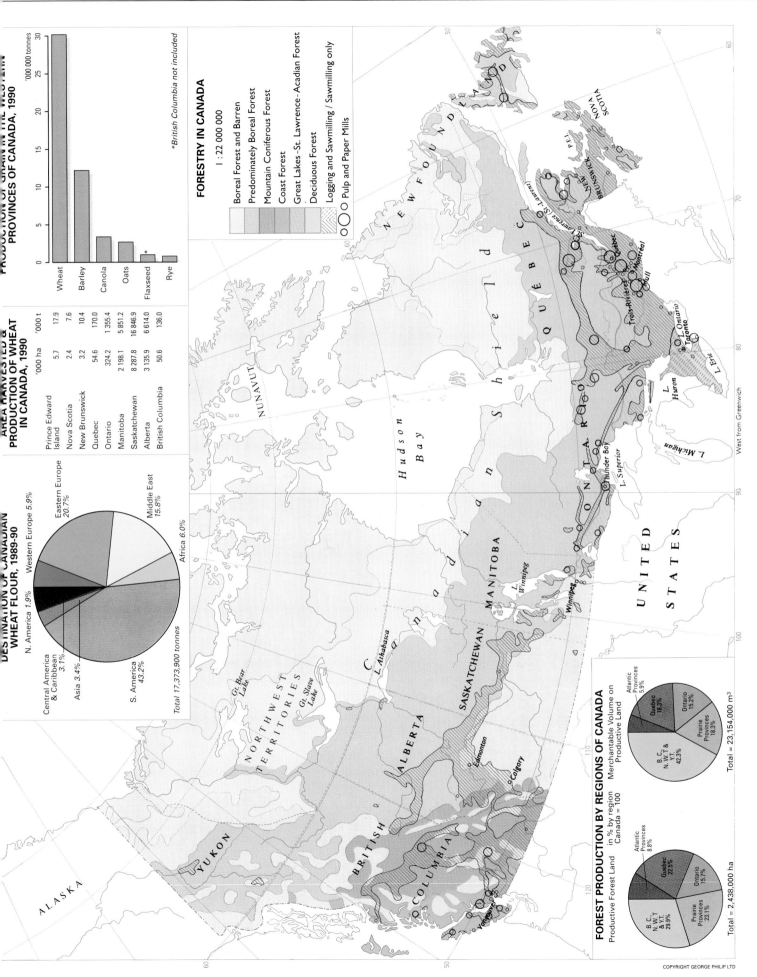

PRODUCTION OF GRAIN IN THE WESTERN PROVINCES OF CANADA, 1990

'000 000 tonnes

*British Columbia not included

(Bar chart values for: Wheat, Barley, Canola, Oats, Flaxseed*, Rye)

AREA HARVESTED & PRODUCTION OF WHEAT IN CANADA, 1990

	'000 ha	'000 t
Prince Edward Island	5.7	17.9
Nova Scotia	2.4	7.6
New Brunswick	3.2	10.4
Quebec	54.6	170.0
Ontario	324.2	1 355.4
Manitoba	2 198.1	5 851.2
Saskatchewan	8 287.8	16 846.9
Alberta	3 135.9	6 614.0
British Columbia	50.6	136.0

DESTINATION OF CANADIAN WHEAT FLOUR, 1989-90

- Eastern Europe 20.7%
- Western Europe 5.9%
- Middle East 15.8%
- Africa 6.0%
- S. America 43.2%
- N. America 1.9%
- Central America & Caribbean 3.1%
- Asia 3.4%

Total 17,373,900 tonnes

FORESTRY IN CANADA

1 : 22 000 000

- Boreal Forest and Barren
- Predominately Boreal Forest
- Mountain Coniferous Forest
- Coast Forest
- Great Lakes - St. Lawrence - Acadian Forest
- Deciduous Forest
- Logging and Sawmilling / Sawmilling only
- Pulp and Paper Mills

FOREST PRODUCTION BY REGIONS OF CANADA

Merchantable Volume on Productive Land — in % by region Canada = 100

- Atlantic Provinces 5.9%
- Quebec 18.3%
- Ontario 15.2%
- Prairie Provinces 18.3%
- B.C., N.W.T & Y.T. 42.3%

Total = 23,154,000 m³

Productive Forest Land

- Atlantic Provinces 8.8%
- Quebec 22.5%
- Ontario 15.7%
- Prairie Provinces 23.1%
- B.C., N.W.T & Y.T. 29.9%

Total = 2,438,000 ha

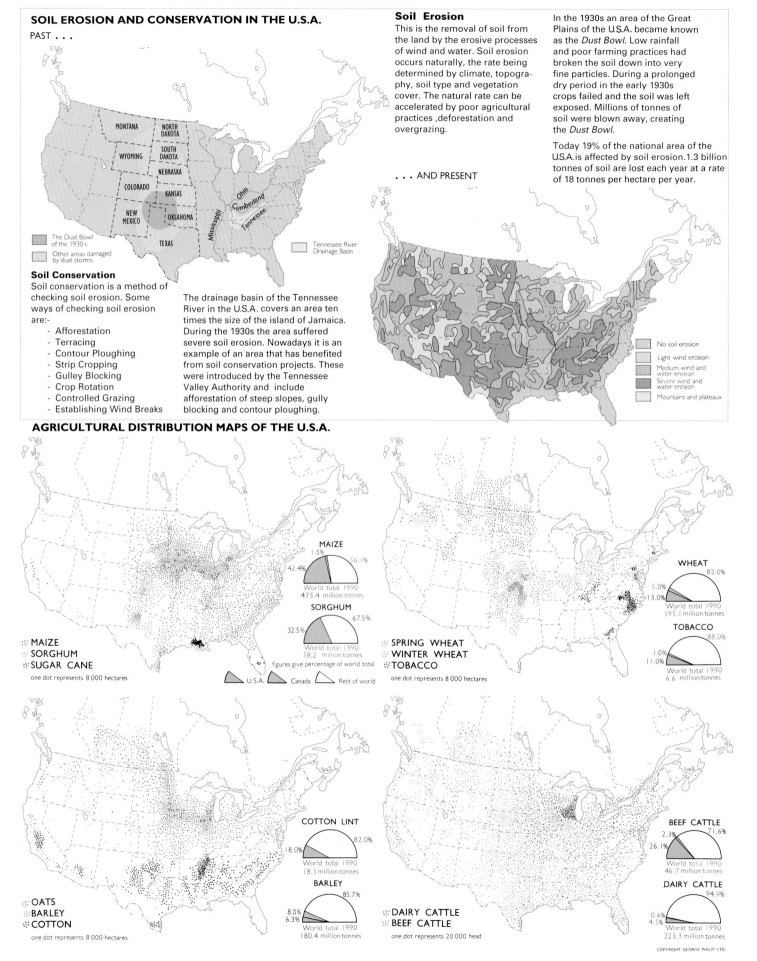

SOIL EROSION AND CONSERVATION IN THE U.S.A.

PAST . . .

The Dust Bowl of the 1930s

Other areas damaged by dust storms

Tennessee River Drainage Basin

Soil Conservation

Soil conservation is a method of checking soil erosion. Some ways of checking soil erosion are:-
- Afforestation
- Terracing
- Contour Ploughing
- Strip Cropping
- Gulley Blocking
- Crop Rotation
- Controlled Grazing
- Establishing Wind Breaks

The drainage basin of the Tennessee River in the U.S.A. covers an area ten times the size of the island of Jamaica. During the 1930s the area suffered severe soil erosion. Nowadays it is an example of an area that has benefited from soil conservation projects. These were introduced by the Tennessee Valley Authority and include afforestation of steep slopes, gully blocking and contour ploughing.

Soil Erosion
This is the removal of soil from the land by the erosive processes of wind and water. Soil erosion occurs naturally, the rate being determined by climate, topography, soil type and vegetation cover. The natural rate can be accelerated by poor agricultural practices ,deforestation and overgrazing.

. . . AND PRESENT

In the 1930s an area of the Great Plains of the U.S.A. became known as the *Dust Bowl*. Low rainfall and poor farming practices had broken the soil down into very fine particles. During a prolonged dry period in the early 1930s crops failed and the soil was left exposed. Millions of tonnes of soil were blown away, creating the *Dust Bowl*.

Today 19% of the national area of the U.S.A. is affected by soil erosion. 1.3 billion tonnes of soil are lost each year at a rate of 18 tonnes per hectare per year.

No soil erosion

Light wind erosion

Medium wind and water erosion

Severe wind and water erosion

Mountains and plateaux

AGRICULTURAL DISTRIBUTION MAPS OF THE U.S.A.

:: MAIZE
:: SORGHUM
:: SUGAR CANE

one dot represents 8 000 hectares

MAIZE
1.5% 56.1%
42.4%
World total 1990
475.4 million tonnes

SORGHUM
67.5%
32.5%
World total 1990
58.2 million tonnes

figures give percentage of world total

U.S.A.   Canada   Rest of world

:: SPRING WHEAT
:: WINTER WHEAT
:: TOBACCO

one dot represents 8 000 hectares

WHEAT
82.0%
5.0%
13.0%
World total 1990
595.1 million tonnes

TOBACCO
88.0%
1.0%
11.0%
World total 1990
6.6 million tonnes

:: OATS
:: BARLEY
:: COTTON

one dot represents 8 000 hectares

COTTON LINT
82.0%
18.0%
World total 1990
18.5 million tonnes

BARLEY
85.7%
8.0%
6.3%
World total 1990
180.4 million tonnes

:: DAIRY CATTLE
:: BEEF CATTLE

one dot represents 20 000 head

BEEF CATTLE
2.3% 71.6%
26.1%
World total 1990
46.7 million tonnes

DAIRY CATTLE
94.9%
0.6%
4.5%
World total 1990
223.3 million tonnes

1:60 000 000

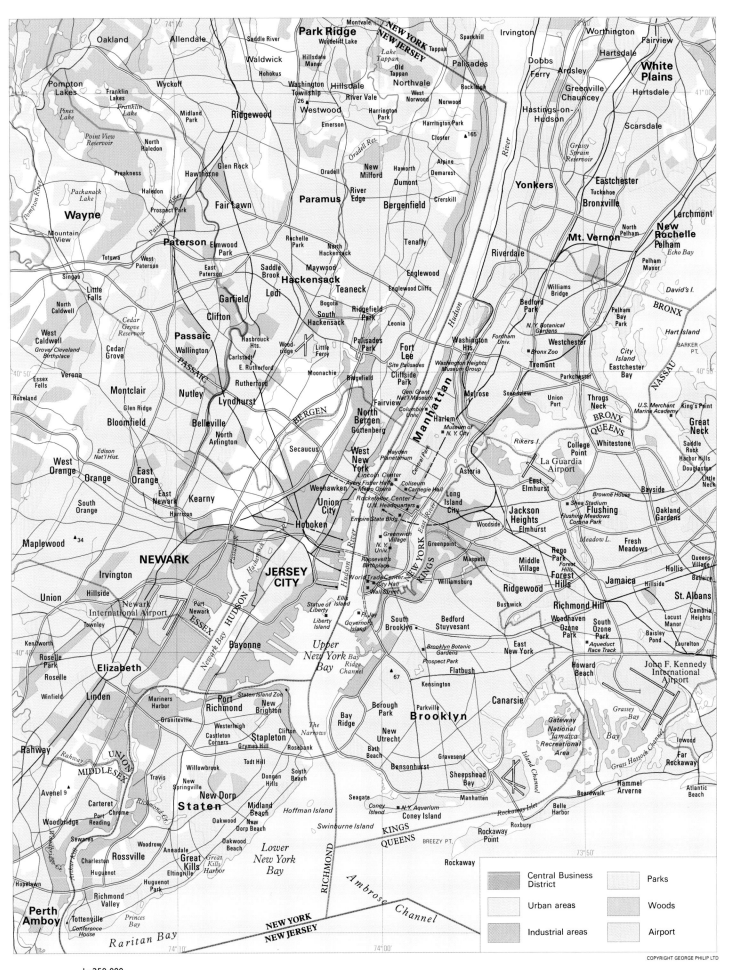

Oakland · Allendale · Saddle River · **Park Ridge** · Montvale · **NEW YORK** · Sparkhill · Irvington · Worthington · Fairview

Woodcliff Lake · **NEW JERSEY** · Tappan · Hartsdale

Waldwick · Hillsdale Manor · *Lake Tappan* · Palisades · Dobbs · Ardsley · **White Plains**

Pompton Lakes · Franklin Lakes · Wyckoff · Hohokus · Old Tappan · Northvale · Ferry · Greenville · Hartsdale

Pines Lake · Midland Park · Washington Township · Hillsdale · River Vale · West Norwood · Rockleigh · Hastings-on-Hudson · Chauncey

Point View Reservoir · North Haledon · Ridgewood · 26 · Westwood · Emerson · Harrington Park · Norwood · Scarsdale

Preakness · Glen Rock · Hawthorne · Oradell · New Milford · Haworth · Closter · ▲165 · Grassy Sprain Reservoir

Packanack Lake · **Wayne** · Paterson · Elmwood Park · Fair Lawn · Rochelle Park · North Hackensack · Dumont · Demarest · Alpine · **Yonkers** · **Eastchester** · Bronxville

Mountain View · Totowa · West Paterson · East Paterson · Saddle Brook · Maywood · Englewood · River Edge · Bergenfield · Cresskill · Tenafly · **Mt. Vernon** · North Pelham · **New Rochelle** · Larchmont

Singac · Little Falls · Garfield · Lodi · Bogota · Ridgefield Park · Englewood Cliffs · Riverdale · Williams Bridge · Pelham · Echo Bay

North Caldwell · Cedar Grove Reservoir · Clifton · South Hackensack · Teaneck · Leonia · Bedford Park · N.Y. Botanical Gardens · Westchester · **BRONX** · David's I. · Pelham Manor

West Caldwell · Grover Cleveland Birthplace · **Passaic** · Wallington · Hasbrouck Hts. · Wood-ridge · Little Ferry · **Palisades Park** · **Fort Lee** · Washington Hts. · Fordham Univ. · Bronx Zoo · Tremont · Hart Island · BARKER PT.

Cedar Grove · Verona · Carlstadt · E. Rutherford · Moonachie · Site Palisades · Cliffside Park · Washington Heights Museum Group · Parkchester · City Island · Eastchester Bay · **NASSAU**

Essex Fells · Roseland · Montclair · Nutley · Rutherford · Ridgefield · Gen. Grant Nat'l Mem. · Manhattan · Melrose · Soundview · Union Port · Throgs Neck · U.S. Merchant Marine Academy · King's Point

Glen Ridge · Lyndhurst · Fairview · North Bergen · Guttenberg · Columbia Univ. · Harlem · Museum of N.Y. City · Rikers I. · College Point · **BRONX** · **QUEENS** · Whitestone · Great Neck · Saddle Rock · Harbor Hills

West Orange · Bloomfield · Belleville · North Arlington · **West New York** · Hayden Planetarium · Central Park · Astoria · La Guardia Airport · East Elmhurst · Bayside · Douglaston · Little Neck

Orange · **East Orange** · East Newark · Secaucus · Lincoln Center · Ayery Fisher Hall · Metro Opera · Coliseum · Carnegie Hall · Long Island City · Woodside · Flushing · Shea Stadium · Browne House · Oakland Gardens

South Orange · Kearny · Weehawken · **Union City** · Rockefeller Center · U.N. Headquarters · Flushing Meadows Corona Park · Jackson Heights · Elmhurst · Meadow L. · Fresh Meadows

Maplewood · ▲34 · Harrison · Hoboken · Empire State Bldg. · Greenwich Village · N.Y. Univ. · Greenpoint · Woodside · Rego Park · Middle Village · Forest Hills · Hollis · Queens Village

NEWARK · Irvington · **JERSEY CITY** · World Trade Center · City Hall · Wall Street · Williamsburg · Maspeth · Forest Park · **Ridgewood** · **Forest Hills** · **Jamaica** · Hillside · Bellaire

Union · Hillside · Port Newark · Statue of Liberty · Ellis Island · Roosevelt's Birthplace · Bedford Stuyvesant · Bushwick · **Richmond Hill** · Woodhaven · Locust Manor · St. Albans · Cambria Heights

Newark International Airport · Liberty Island · Governors Island · Ft. Jay · South Brooklyn · East New York · Ozone Park · South Ozone Park · Baisley Pond · Laurelton

Kenilworth · Townley · Bayonne · **Upper New York Bay** · Brooklyn Botanic Gardens · Aqueduct Race Track · Howard Beach · **John F. Kennedy International Airport**

Roselle Park · Roselle · **Elizabeth** · Bay Ridge Channel · Prospect Park · Flatbush · Grassey Bay

Winfield · Linden · Mariners Harbor · Port Richmond · New Brighton · Borough Park · Parkville · 67 · Kensington · **Canarsie** · Gateway National Jamaica Recreational Area · Inwood

Rahway · Graniteville · Westerleigh · Clifton · The Narrows · Bay Ridge · New Utrecht · **Brooklyn** · Island Channel · Grass Hassock Channel · Far Rockaway

UNION · **MIDDLESEX** · Castleton Corners · Stapleton · Rosebank · Bath Beach · Bensonhurst · Gravesend · Sheepshead Bay · Boardwalk · Hammel · Arverne · Atlantic Beach

Avenel · 9 · Travis · Willowbrook · Todt Hill · Dongan Hills · South Beach · Seagate · Manhatten · Belle Harbor

Carteret · Chrome · **New Springville** · **New Dorp** · Hoffman Island · N.Y. Aquarium · Coney Island · Rockaway Inlet · Roxbury

Port Reading · Woodbridge · **Staten** · Midland Beach · New Dorp Beach · Swinburne Island · **KINGS** · **QUEENS** · BREEZY PT. · Rockaway Point

Sewaren · Oakwood · Oakwood Beach · **Lower New York Bay** · **RICHMOND** · Rockaway

Perth Amboy · Rossville · **Great Kills** · Great Kills Harbor · Eltingville · Huguenot · Huguenot Park · *Princes Bay* · **NEW YORK** · **NEW JERSEY** · *Ambrose Channel*

Hopelawn · Tottenville · Conference House · *Raritan Bay*

1 : 250 000

0 1 2 3 4 5 6 7 8 9 10 km

Central Business District		Parks	
Urban areas		Woods	
Industrial areas		Airport	

COPYRIGHT GEORGE PHILIP LTD

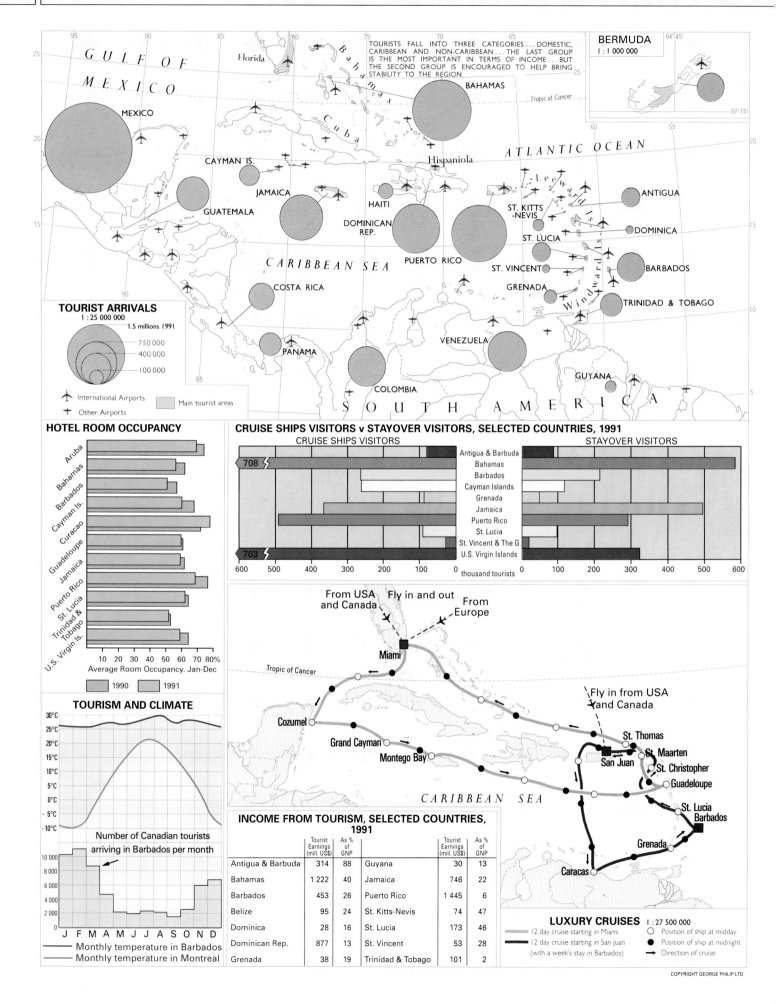

TOURISTS FALL INTO THREE CATEGORIES...DOMESTIC, CARIBBEAN AND NON-CARIBBEAN...THE LAST GROUP IS THE MOST IMPORTANT IN TERMS OF INCOME...BUT THE SECOND GROUP IS ENCOURAGED TO HELP BRING STABILITY TO THE REGION.

BERMUDA
1 : 1 000 000

GULF OF MEXICO

Florida

MEXICO

BAHAMAS

Cuba

Tropic of Cancer

ATLANTIC OCEAN

CAYMAN IS.

JAMAICA

GUATEMALA

Hispaniola

HAITI

DOMINICAN REP.

PUERTO RICO

Leeward Is.

ST. KITTS -NEVIS

ST. LUCIA

ST. VINCENT

ANTIGUA

DOMINICA

BARBADOS

GRENADA

TRINIDAD & TOBAGO

Windward Is.

CARIBBEAN SEA

COSTA RICA

PANAMA

VENEZUELA

GUYANA

COLOMBIA

SOUTH AMERICA

TOURIST ARRIVALS
1 : 25 000 000

1.5 millions 1991
750 000
400 000
100 000

✈ International Airports
✈ Other Airports
Main tourist areas

HOTEL ROOM OCCUPANCY

Aruba
Bahamas
Barbados
Cayman Is.
Curacao
Guadeloupe
Jamaica
Puerto Rico
St. Lucia
Trinidad & Tobago
U.S. Virgin Is.

10 20 30 40 50 60 70 80%
Average Room Occupancy. Jan-Dec

☐ 1990 ☐ 1991

CRUISE SHIPS VISITORS v STAYOVER VISITORS, SELECTED COUNTRIES, 1991

CRUISE SHIPS VISITORS | | STAYOVER VISITORS

Antigua & Barbuda
Bahamas 708
Barbados
Cayman Islands
Grenada
Jamaica
Puerto Rico
St. Lucia
St. Vincent & The G.
U.S. Virgin Islands 703

600 500 400 300 200 100 0 | 0 100 200 300 400 500 600
thousand tourists

TOURISM AND CLIMATE

30°C
25°C
20°C
15°C
10°C
5°C
0°C
-5°C
-10°C

Number of Canadian tourists arriving in Barbados per month

10 000
8 000
6 000
4 000
2 000
0

J F M A M J J A S O N D

— Monthly temperature in Barbados
— Monthly temperature in Montreal

From USA and Canada — Fly in and out
From Europe

Miami
Tropic of Cancer

Cozumel

Grand Cayman

Montego Bay

Fly in from USA and Canada

St. Thomas
St. Maarten
San Juan
St. Christopher
Guadeloupe
St. Lucia
Barbados
Grenada

Caracas

CARIBBEAN SEA

INCOME FROM TOURISM, SELECTED COUNTRIES, 1991

	Tourist Earnings (mill. US$)	As % of GNP		Tourist Earnings (mill. US$)	As % of GNP
Antigua & Barbuda	314	88	Guyana	30	13
Bahamas	1 222	40	Jamaica	746	22
Barbados	453	26	Puerto Rico	1 445	6
Belize	95	24	St. Kitts-Nevis	74	47
Dominica	28	16	St. Lucia	173	46
Dominican Rep.	877	13	St. Vincent	53	28
Grenada	38	19	Trinidad & Tobago	101	2

LUXURY CRUISES
1 : 27 500 000

— 12 day cruise starting in Miami
— 12 day cruise starting in San Juan (with a week's stay in Barbados)

○ Position of ship at midday
● Position of ship at midnight
→ Direction of cruise

INDEX TO
WORLD MAPS

The index contains the names of all the principal places and features shown on the World Maps. Each name is followed by an additional entry in italics giving the country or region within which it is located. The alphabetical order of names composed of two or more words is governed primarily by the first word and then by the second. This is an example of the rule:

New South Wales □, *Australia*.. **34 G8**   33 0S   146 0E
New York □, *U.S.A.* **43 D10**   42 40N   76 0W
New York City, *U.S.A.* **43 E11**   40 45N   74 0W
New Zealand ■, *Oceania*............ **35 J13**   40 0S   176 0E
Newark, *U.S.A.* **43 F10**   39 42N   75 45W

Physical features composed of a proper name (Erie) and a description (Lake) are positioned alphabetically by the proper name. The description is positioned after the proper name and is usually abbreviated:

Erie, L., *N. Amer.* **42 D7**   42 15N   81 0W

Where a description forms part of a settlement or administrative name, however, it is always written in full and put in its true alphabetical position:

Mount Isa, *Australia*...................... **34 E6**   20 42S   139 26E

Names beginning with M' and Mc are indexed as if they were spelt Mac. Names beginning St. are alphabetized under Saint, but Santa and San are all spelt in full and are alphabetized accordingly. If the same placename occurs two or more times in the index and all are in the same country, each is followed by the name of the administrative subdivision in which it is located. The names are placed in the alphabetical order of the subdivision. For example:

Columbus, Ga., *U.S.A.* **41 D10**   32 30N   84 58W
Columbus, Ind., *U.S.A.* **42 F5**   39 14N   85 55W
Columbus, Ohio, *U.S.A.* **42 F6**   39 57N   83 1W

The number in bold type which follows each name in the index refers to the number of the map page where that feature or place will be found. This is usually the largest scale at which the place or feature appears.

The letter and figure which are in bold type immediately after the page number give the grid square on the map page, within which the feature is situated. The letter represents the latitude and the figure the longitude. In some cases the feature itself may fall within the specified square, while the name is outside.

For a more precise location, the geographical co-ordinates which follow the letter-figure references give the latitude and the longitude of each place. The first set of figures represent the latitude, which is the distance north or south of the Equator measured as an angle at the centre of the Earth. The Equator is latitude 0°, the North Pole is 90°N, and the South Pole 90°S.

The second set of figures represent the longitude, which is the distance east or west of the prime meridian, which runs through Greenwich, England. Longitude is also measured as an angle at the centre of the Earth and is given east or west of the prime meridian, from 0° to 180° in either direction.

The unit of measurement for latitude and longitude is the degree, which is subdivided into 60 minutes. Each index entry states the position of a place in degrees and minutes, a space being left between the degrees and the minutes. The latitude is followed by N(orth) or S(outh) and the longitude by E(ast) or W(est).

Rivers are indexed to their mouths or confluences, and carry the symbol ⤳ after their names. A solid square ■ follows the name of a country, while an open square □ refers to a first order administrative area.

ABBREVIATIONS USED IN THE INDEX

Afghan. – Afghanistan
Ala. – Alabama
Alta. – Alberta
Amer. – America(n)
Arch. – Archipelago
Ariz. – Arizona
Ark. – Arkansas
Atl. Oc. – Atlantic Ocean
B. – Baie, Bahia, Bay, Bucht, Bugt
B.C. – British Columbia
Bangla. – Bangladesh
C. – Cabo, Cap, Cape, Coast
C.A.R. – Central African Republic
C. Prov. – Cape Province
Calif. – California
Cent. – Central
Chan. – Channel
Colo. – Colorado

Conn. – Connecticut
Cord. – Cordillera
Cr. – Creek
D.C. – District of Columbia
Del. – Delaware
Domin. – Dominica
Dom. Rep. – Dominican Republic
E. – East
El Salv. – El Salvador
Eq. Guin. – Equatorial Guinea
Fla. – Florida
Falk. Is. – Falkland Is.
G. – Golfe, Golfo, Gulf
Ga. – Georgia
Guinea–Biss. – Guinea–Bissau
Hd. – Head
Hts. – Heights
I.(s). – Ile, Ilha, Insel,

Isla, Island, Isle(s)
Ill. – Illinois
Ind. – Indiana
Ind. Oc. – Indian Ocean
Ivory C. – Ivory Coast
Kans. – Kansas
Ky. – Kentucky
L. – Lac, Lacul, Lago, Lagoa, Lake, Limni, Loch, Lough
La. – Louisiana
Lux. – Luxembourg
Madag. – Madagascar
Man. – Manitoba
Mass. – Massachusetts
Md. – Maryland
Me. – Maine
Medit. S. – Mediterranean Sea
Mich. – Michigan
Minn. – Minnesota
Miss. – Mississippi

Mo. – Missouri
Mont. – Montana
Mozam.– Mozambique
Mt.(s).– Mont, Monte, Monti, Montaña, Mountain
N. – Nord, Norte, North, Northern
N.B. – New Brunswick
N.C. – North Carolina
N. Cal. – New Caledonia
N. Dak. – North Dakota
N.H. – New Hampshire
N.J. – New Jersey
N. Mex. – New Mexico
N.S. – Nova Scotia
N.S.W. – New South Wales
N.W.T. – North West Territory
N.Y. – New York
N.Z. – New Zealand

Nebr. – Nebraska
Neths. – Netherlands
Nev. – Nevada
Nfld. – Newfoundland
Nic. – Nicaragua

Okla. – Oklahoma
Ont. – Ontario
Oreg. – Oregon
P.E.I. – Prince Edward Island
Pa. – Pennsylvania
Pac. Oc. – Pacific Ocean
Papua N.G. – Papua New Guinea
Pen. – Peninsula, Peninsule
Phil. – Philippines
Pk. – Park, Peak
Plat. – Plateau
Prov. – Province,

Provincial
Pt. – Point
Pta. – Ponta, Punta
Pte. – Pointe
Qué. – Québec
Queens. – Queensland
R. – Rio, River
R.I. – Rhode Island
Ra.(s). – Range(s)
Reg. – Region
Rep. – Republic
Res. – Reserve, Reservoir
S. – San, South
Si. Arabia – Saudi Arabia
S.C. – South Carolina
S. Dak. – South Dakota
S. Leone – Sierra Leone
Sa. – Serra, Sierra
Sask. – Saskatchewan
Scot. – Scotland
Sd. – Sound

Sib. – Siberia
St. – Saint, Sankt, Sint
Str. – Strait, Stretto
Switz. – Switzerland
Tas. – Tasmania
Tenn. – Tennessee
Tex. – Texas
Trin. & Tob. – Trinidad & Tobago
U.A.E. – United Arab Emirates
U.K. – United Kingdom
U.S.A. – United States of America
Va. – Virginia
Vic. – Victoria
Vol. – Volcano
Vt. – Vermont
W. – West
W. Va. – West Virginia
Wash. – Washington
Wis. – Wisconsin

INDEX TO WORLD MAPS

Aachen — Banda Aceh

A

Aachen, *Germany* 10 C4 50 45N 6 6 E
Aalborg, *Denmark* 6 G9 57 2N 9 54 E
Aarau, *Switz.* 10 E5 47 23N 8 4 E
Aare →, *Switz.* 10 E5 47 33N 8 14 E
Aarhus, *Denmark* 6 G10 56 8N 10 11 E
Abadan, *Iran* 24 B3 30 22N 48 20 E
Abbeville, *France* 8 A4 50 6N 1 49 E
Abéché, *Chad* 29 F9 13 50N 20 35 E
Abeokuta, *Nigeria* 30 C2 7 3N 3 19 E
Aberdeen, *U.K.* 7 C5 57 9N 2 5W
Abidjan, *Ivory C.* 28 G4 5 26N 3 58W
Abitibi L., *Canada* 42 A8 48 40N 79 40W
Abkhazia □, *Georgia* 15 F7 43 12N 41 5 E
Abohar, *India* 23 D5 30 10N 74 10 E
Abu Dhabi, *U.A.E.* 24 C4 24 28N 54 22 E
Abuja, *Nigeria* 30 C3 9 16N 7 2 E
Acapulco, *Mexico* 44 D5 16 51N 99 56W
Accomac, *U.S.A.* 43 G10 37 43N 75 40W
Accra, *Ghana* 30 C1 5 35N 0 6W
Acklins I., *Bahamas* 45 C10 22 30N 74 0W
Aconcagua, *Argentina* 47 F3 32 39S 70 0W
Acre □, *Brazil* 46 C2 9 1S 71 0W
Adamawa Highlands, *Cameroon* 29 G7 7 20N 12 20 E
Adana, *Turkey* 15 G6 37 0N 35 16 E
Adapazarı, *Turkey* 15 F5 40 48N 30 25 E
Addis Ababa, *Ethiopia* 29 G12 9 2N 38 42 E
Adelaide, *Australia* 34 G6 34 52S 138 30 E
Adelaide, *S. Africa* 31 C4 32 42S 26 20 E
Aden, *Yemen* 24 D3 12 45N 45 0 E
Aden, G. of, *Asia* 24 D3 12 30N 47 30 E
Adirondack Mts., *U.S.A.* 43 D10 44 0N 74 0W
Admiralty Is., *Papua N. G.* 36 H6 2 0S 147 0 E
Ado-Ekiti, *Nigeria* 30 C3 7 38N 5 12 E
Adoni, *India* 25 D6 15 33N 77 18 E
Adour →, *France* 8 E3 43 32N 1 32W
Adrar, *Algeria* 28 C4 27 51N 0 11W
Adrian, *U.S.A.* 42 E5 41 54N 84 2W
Adriatic Sea, *Medit. S.* 12 C6 43 0N 16 0 E
Ægean Sea, *Medit. S.* 13 E11 38 30N 25 0 E
Afghanistan ■, *Asia* 24 B5 33 0N 65 0 E
'Afif, *Si. Arabia* 24 C3 23 53N 42 56 E
Agadès, *Niger* 30 A3 16 58N 7 59 E
Agadir, *Morocco* 28 B3 30 28N 9 55W
Agartala, *India* 23 H13 23 50N 91 23 E
Agen, *France* 8 D4 44 12N 0 38 E
Agra, *India* 23 F6 27 17N 77 58 E
Agrigento, *Italy* 12 F5 37 19N 13 34 E
Aguascalientes, *Mexico* 44 C4 21 53N 102 12W
Agulhas, C., *S. Africa* 31 C3 34 52S 20 0 E
Ahmadabad, *India* 23 H4 23 0N 72 40 E
Ahmadnagar, *India* 25 D6 19 7N 74 46 E
Ahmadpur, *Pakistan* 23 E3 29 12N 71 10 E
Ahvaz, *Iran* 24 B3 31 20N 48 40 E
Ahvenanmaa Is., *Finland* 6 F11 60 15N 20 0 E
Aïr, *Niger* 28 E6 18 30N 8 0 E
Aisne →, *France* 8 B5 49 26N 2 50 E
Aix-en-Provence, *France* 8 E6 43 32N 5 27 E
Aix-les-Bains, *France* 8 D6 45 41N 5 53 E
Ajaccio, *France* 8 F8 41 55N 8 40 E
Ajanta Ra., *India* 23 J5 20 28N 75 50 E
Ajaria □, *Georgia* 15 F7 41 30N 42 0 E
Ajmer, *India* 23 F5 26 28N 74 37 E
Akashi, *Japan* 19 B4 34 45N 134 58 E
Akita, *Japan* 19 A7 39 45N 140 7 E
Akola, *India* 23 J6 20 42N 77 2 E
Akranes, *Iceland* 6 B2 64 19N 22 5W
Akron, *U.S.A.* 42 E7 41 5N 81 31W
Aktyubinsk, *Kazakstan* 15 D10 50 17N 57 10 E
Akure, *Nigeria* 30 C3 7 15N 5 5 E
Akureyri, *Iceland* 6 B4 65 40N 18 6W
Al Ḥudaydah, *Yemen* 24 D3 14 50N 43 0 E
Al Hufūf, *Si. Arabia* 24 C3 25 25N 49 45 E
Al Jawf, *Si. Arabia* 24 C2 29 55N 39 40 E
Al Kut, *Iraq* 24 B3 32 30N 46 0 E
Al Qatif, *Si. Arabia* 24 C3 26 35N 50 0 E
Al 'Ula, *Si. Arabia* 24 C2 26 35N 38 0 E
Alabama □, *U.S.A.* 41 D9 33 0N 87 0W
Aland Is. = Ahvenanmaa Is., *Finland* 6 F11 60 15N 20 0 E
Alaska □, *U.S.A.* 38 B5 64 0N 154 0W
Alaska, G. of, *Pac. Oc.* 38 C5 58 0N 145 0W
Alaska Peninsula, *U.S.A.* 38 C4 56 0N 159 0W
Alaska Range, *U.S.A.* 38 B4 62 50N 151 0W
Alba-Iulia, *Romania* 11 E12 46 8N 23 39 E
Albacete, *Spain* 9 C5 39 0N 1 50W
Albania ■, *Europe* 13 D9 41 0N 20 0 E
Albany, *Australia* 34 H2 35 1S 117 58 E
Albany, *Ga., U.S.A.* 41 D10 31 35N 84 10W
Albany, *N.Y., U.S.A.* 43 D11 42 39N 73 45W
Albany →, *Canada* 39 C11 52 17N 81 31W
Albert L., *Africa* 32 D6 1 30N 31 0 E
Alberta □, *Canada* 38 C8 54 40N 115 0W
Albertville, *France* 8 D7 45 40N 6 22 E
Albi, *France* 8 E5 43 56N 2 9 E
Albion, *U.S.A.* 42 D5 42 15N 84 45W
Albuquerque, *U.S.A.* 40 C5 35 5N 106 39W
Albury, *Australia* 34 H8 36 3S 146 56 E
Alcalá de Henares, *Spain* 9 B4 40 28N 3 22W
Aldabra Is., *Seychelles* 27 G8 9 22S 46 28 E
Aldan →, *Russia* 18 C14 63 28N 129 35 E
Aleksandrovsk-Sakhalinskiy, *Russia* 18 D16 50 50N 142 20 E
Alençon, *France* 8 B4 48 27N 0 4 E
Alès, *France* 8 D6 44 9N 4 5 E
Alessándria, *Italy* 12 B3 44 54N 8 37 E
Ålesund, *Norway* 6 F9 62 28N 6 12 E
Aleutian Is., *Pac. Oc.* 36 B10 52 0N 175 0W
Alexander Arch., *U.S.A.* 38 C6 56 0N 136 0W
Alexandria, *Egypt* 29 B10 31 13N 29 58 E
Alexandria, *La., U.S.A.* 41 D8 31 18N 92 27W
Alexandria, *Va., U.S.A.* 42 F9 38 48N 77 3W
Algarve, *Portugal* 9 D1 36 58N 8 20W
Algeciras, *Spain* 9 D3 36 9N 5 28W
Algeria ■, *Africa* 28 C5 28 30N 2 0 E
Algiers, *Algeria* 28 A5 36 42N 3 8 E
Alicante, *Spain* 9 C5 38 23N 0 30W
Alice Springs, *Australia* 34 E5 23 40S 133 50 E
Aligarh, *India* 23 F7 27 55N 78 10 E
Alipur Duar, *India* 23 F12 26 30N 89 35 E
Aliquippa, *U.S.A.* 42 E7 40 37N 80 15W
Aliwal North, *S. Africa* 31 C4 30 45S 26 45 E
Alkmaar, *Neths.* 10 B3 52 37N 4 45 E
Allahabad, *India* 23 G8 25 25N 81 58 E
Allegan, *U.S.A.* 42 D5 42 32N 85 51W
Allegheny →, *U.S.A.* 42 E8 40 27N 80 1W
Allegheny Plateau, *U.S.A.* 42 G7 38 0N 80 0W
Allentown, *U.S.A.* 43 E10 40 37N 75 29W
Alleppey, *India* 25 E6 9 30N 76 28 E
Allier →, *France* 8 C5 46 57N 3 4 E
Alma, *U.S.A.* 42 D5 43 23N 84 39W
Almaty, *Kazakstan* 18 E9 43 15N 76 57 E
Almelo, *Neths.* 10 B4 52 22N 6 42 E
Almería, *Spain* 9 D4 36 52N 2 27W
Alor, *Indonesia* 22 D4 8 15S 124 30 E
Alpena, *U.S.A.* 42 C6 45 4N 83 27W
Alps, *Europe* 10 E5 46 30N 9 30 E
Alsace, *France* 8 B7 48 15N 7 25 E
Altai, *Mongolia* 20 B4 46 40N 92 45 E
Altay, *China* 20 B3 47 48N 88 10 E
Altoona, *U.S.A.* 42 E8 40 31N 78 24W
Altun Shan, *China* 20 C3 38 30N 88 0 E
Alwar, *India* 23 F6 27 38N 76 34 E
Amadjuak L., *Canada* 39 B12 65 0N 71 8W
Amagasaki, *Japan* 19 B4 34 42N 135 20 E
Amarillo, *U.S.A.* 40 C6 35 13N 101 50W
Amazon →, *S. Amer.* 46 C4 0 5S 50 0W
Ambala, *India* 23 D6 30 23N 76 56 E
Ambikapur, *India* 23 H9 23 15N 83 15 E
Ambon, *Indonesia* 22 D4 3 35S 128 20 E
American Samoa □, *Pac. Oc.* 35 C17 14 20S 170 40W
Amiens, *France* 8 B5 49 54N 2 16 E
Amman, *Jordan* 24 B2 31 57N 35 52 E
Amos, *Canada* 42 A8 48 35N 78 5W
Amravati, *India* 23 J6 20 55N 77 45 E
Amreli, *India* 23 J3 21 35N 71 17 E
Amritsar, *India* 23 D5 31 35N 74 57 E
Amroha, *India* 23 E7 28 53N 78 30 E
Amsterdam, *Neths.* 10 B3 52 23N 4 54 E
Amsterdam, *U.S.A.* 43 D10 42 56N 74 11W
Amudarya →, *Uzbekistan* 18 E7 43 58N 59 34 E
Amundsen Gulf, *Canada* 38 A7 71 0N 124 0W
Amundsen Sea, *Antarctica* 48 E1 72 0S 115 0W
Amur →, *Russia* 18 D16 52 56N 141 10 E
An Najaf, *Iraq* 24 B3 32 3N 44 15 E
An Nasiriyah, *Iraq* 24 B3 31 0N 46 15 E
An Nhon, *Vietnam* 22 B2 13 55N 109 7 E
Anadyr, *Russia* 18 C19 64 35N 177 20 E
Anadyr, G. of, *Russia* 18 C20 64 0N 180 0 E
Anaheim, *U.S.A.* 40 D3 33 50N 117 55W
Anambas Is., *Indonesia* 22 C2 3 20N 106 30 E
Anantnag, *India* 23 C5 33 45N 75 10 E
Anar, *Iran* 24 B4 30 55N 55 13 E
Anatolia, *Turkey* 15 G5 39 0N 30 0 E
Anchorage, *U.S.A.* 38 B5 61 13N 149 54W
Ancona, *Italy* 12 C5 43 38N 13 30 E
Anda, *China* 21 B7 46 24N 125 19 E
Andalucía □, *Spain* 9 D3 37 35N 5 0W
Andaman Is., *Ind. Oc.* 25 D8 12 30N 92 30 E
Anderson, *U.S.A.* 42 E5 40 10N 85 41W
Andes, *S. Amer.* 46 E3 20 0S 68 0W
Andhra Pradesh □, *India* 25 D6 18 0N 79 0 E
Andorra ■, *Europe* 9 A6 42 30N 1 30 E
Andreanof Is., *U.S.A.* 38 C2 52 0N 178 0W
Ándria, *Italy* 12 D7 41 13N 16 17 E
Andros I., *Bahamas* 45 C9 24 30N 78 0W
Angara →, *Russia* 18 D11 58 5N 94 20 E
Ånge, *Sweden* 6 F11 62 31N 15 35 E
Angel Falls, *Venezuela* 46 B3 5 57N 62 30W
Angerman →, *Sweden* 6 F11 62 40N 18 0 E
Angers, *France* 8 C3 47 30N 0 35W
Anglesey, *U.K.* 7 E4 53 17N 4 20W
Angola ■, *Africa* 33 G3 12 0S 18 0 E
Angoulême, *France* 8 D4 45 39N 0 10 E
Angoumois, *France* 8 D4 45 50N 0 25 E
Anguilla ■, *W. Indies* 44 J18 18 14N 63 5W
Anhui □, *China* 21 C6 32 0N 117 0 E
Anjou, *France* 8 C3 47 20N 0 15W
Ankara, *Turkey* 15 G5 39 57N 32 54 E
Ann, C., *U.S.A.* 43 D12 42 38N 70 35W
Ann Arbor, *U.S.A.* 42 D6 42 17N 83 45W
Annaba, *Algeria* 28 A6 36 50N 7 46 E
Annapolis, *U.S.A.* 42 F9 38 59N 76 30W
Annecy, *France* 8 D7 45 55N 6 8 E
Annobón, *Atl. Oc.* 27 G4 1 25S 5 36 E
Anshun, *China* 20 D5 26 18N 105 57 E
Antalya, *Turkey* 15 G5 36 52N 30 45 E
Antananarivo, *Madag.* 33 H9 18 55S 47 31 E
Antarctic Pen., *Antarctica* 48 D4 67 0S 60 0W
Antibes, *France* 8 E7 43 34N 7 6 E
Anticosti I., *Canada* 43 A16 49 30N 63 0W
Antigua & Barbuda ■, *W. Indies* 44 K20 17 20N 61 48W
Antofagasta, *Chile* 47 E2 23 50S 70 30W
Antsiranana, *Madag.* 33 G9 12 25S 49 20 E
Antwerp, *Belgium* 10 C3 51 13N 4 25 E
Anyang, *China* 21 C6 36 5N 114 21 E
Aomori, *Japan* 19 F12 40 45N 140 45 E
Aparri, *Phil.* 22 B4 18 22N 121 38 E
Apeldoorn, *Neths.* 10 B3 52 13N 5 57 E
Apennines, *Italy* 12 B4 44 0N 10 0 E
Apia, *W. Samoa* 35 C16 13 50S 171 50W
Appalachian Mts., *U.S.A.* 42 G7 38 0N 80 0W
Appleton, *U.S.A.* 42 C3 44 16N 88 25W
Aqmola, *Kazakstan* 18 D9 51 10N 71 30 E
Ar Ramadi, *Iraq* 24 B3 33 25N 43 20 E
Arabian Desert, *Egypt* 29 C11 27 30N 32 30 E
Arabian Gulf = Gulf, The, *Asia* 24 C4 27 0N 50 0 E
Arabian Sea, *Ind. Oc.* 24 D5 16 0N 65 0 E
Aracaju, *Brazil* 46 D6 10 55S 37 4W
Arad, *Romania* 11 E11 46 10N 21 20 E
Arafura Sea, *E. Indies* 22 D5 9 0S 135 0 E
Aragón □, *Spain* 9 B5 41 25N 0 40W
Araguaia →, *Brazil* 46 C5 5 21S 48 41W
Arak, *Iran* 24 B3 34 0N 49 40 E
Arakan Yoma, *Burma* 25 C8 20 0N 94 40 E
Aral, *Kazakstan* 18 E8 46 41N 61 45 E
Aral Sea, *Asia* 18 E8 44 30N 60 0 E
Arcachon, *France* 8 D3 44 40N 1 10W
Arctic Ocean, *Arctic* 48 B17 78 0N 160 0W
Arctic Red River, *Canada* 38 B6 67 15N 134 0W
Ardabil, *Iran* 24 B3 38 15N 48 18 E
Ardennes, *Belgium* 10 D3 49 50N 5 5 E
Arendal, *Norway* 6 G9 58 28N 8 46 E
Arequipa, *Peru* 46 D2 16 20S 71 30W
Argentan, *France* 8 B3 48 45N 0 1W
Argentina ■, *S. Amer.* 47 F3 35 0S 66 0W
Arima, *Trin. & Tob.* 44 S20 10 38N 61 17W
Arizona □, *U.S.A.* 40 D4 34 0N 112 0W
Arkansas □, *U.S.A.* 41 D8 35 0N 92 30W
Arkansas →, *U.S.A.* 41 D8 33 47N 91 4W
Arkhangelsk, *Russia* 14 B7 64 38N 40 36 E
Arles, *France* 8 E6 43 41N 4 40 E
Arlington, *U.S.A.* 42 F9 38 53N 77 7W
Arlon, *Belgium* 10 D3 49 42N 5 49 E
Armenia ■, *Asia* 15 F7 40 20N 45 0 E
Arnhem, *Neths.* 10 C3 51 58N 5 55 E
Arnhem Land, *Australia* 34 C5 13 10S 134 30 E
Arnprior, *Canada* 42 C9 45 26N 76 21W
Arrah, *India* 23 G10 25 35N 84 32 E
Arran, *U.K.* 7 D4 55 34N 5 12W
Arras, *France* 8 A5 50 17N 2 46 E
Artois, *France* 8 A5 50 20N 2 30 E
Aru Is., *Indonesia* 22 D5 6 0S 134 30 E
Arunachal Pradesh □, *India* 25 C8 28 0N 95 0 E
Arusha, *Tanzania* 32 E7 3 20S 36 40 E
Arviat, *Canada* 38 B10 61 10N 94 15W
Asab, *Namibia* 31 B2 25 30S 18 0 E
Asahigawa, *Japan* 19 F12 43 46N 142 22 E
Asansol, *India* 23 H11 23 40N 87 1 E
Asbestos, *Canada* 43 C12 45 47N 71 58W
Asbury Park, *U.S.A.* 43 E10 40 13N 74 1W
Ascension I., *Atl. Oc.* 27 G2 8 0S 14 15W
Ashkhabad, *Turkmenistan* 18 F7 38 0N 57 50 E
Ashland, *Ky., U.S.A.* 42 F6 38 28N 82 38W
Ashland, *Ohio, U.S.A.* 42 E6 40 52N 82 19W
Ashtabula, *U.S.A.* 42 E7 41 52N 80 47W
Asifabad, *India* 23 K7 19 20N 79 24 E
Asir □, *Si. Arabia* 24 D3 18 40N 42 30 E
Asmara, *Eritrea* 29 E12 15 19N 38 55 E
Assam □, *India* 23 F13 26 0N 93 0 E
Assen, *Neths.* 10 B4 53 0N 6 35 E
Assisi, *Italy* 12 C5 43 4N 12 37 E
Asti, *Italy* 12 B3 44 54N 8 12 E
Astrakhan, *Russia* 15 E8 46 25N 48 5 E
Asturias □, *Spain* 9 A3 43 15N 6 0W
Asunción, *Paraguay* 47 E4 25 10S 57 30W
Aswân, *Egypt* 29 D11 24 4N 32 57 E
Atacama Desert, *Chile* 47 E3 24 0S 69 20W
Atbara, *Sudan* 29 E11 17 42N 33 59 E
Atbara →, *Sudan* 29 E11 17 40N 33 56 E
Athabasca →, *Canada* 38 C8 58 40N 110 50W
Athabasca, L., *Canada* 38 C9 59 15N 109 15W
Athens, *Greece* 13 F10 37 58N 23 46 E
Athens, *U.S.A.* 42 F6 39 20N 82 6W
Atikokan, *Canada* 42 A2 48 45N 91 37W
Atlanta, *U.S.A.* 41 D10 33 45N 84 23W
Atlantic City, *U.S.A.* 43 F10 39 21N 74 27W
Atlantic Ocean 2 E9 0 0 20 0W
Atyraū, *Kazakstan* 18 E7 47 5N 52 0 E
Au Sable →, *U.S.A.* 42 C6 44 25N 83 20W
Aube →, *France* 8 B5 48 34N 3 43 E
Auburn, *Ind., U.S.A.* 42 E5 41 22N 85 4W
Auburn, *N.Y., U.S.A.* 42 D9 42 56N 76 34W
Aubusson, *France* 8 D5 45 57N 2 11 E
Auch, *France* 8 E4 43 39N 0 36 E
Auckland, *N.Z.* 35 H13 36 52S 174 46 E
Aude →, *France* 8 E5 43 13N 3 14 E
Augrabies Falls, *S. Africa* 31 B3 28 35S 20 20 E
Augsburg, *Germany* 10 D6 48 25N 10 52 E
Augusta, *Ga., U.S.A.* 41 D10 33 28N 81 58W
Augusta, *Maine, U.S.A.* 43 C13 44 19N 69 47W
Aunis, *France* 8 C3 46 5N 0 50W
Aurangabad, *Bihar, India* 23 G10 24 45N 84 18 E
Aurangabad, *Maharashtra, India* 23 K5 19 50N 75 23 E
Aurillac, *France* 8 D5 44 55N 2 26 E
Aurora, *U.S.A.* 42 E3 41 45N 88 19W
Austin, *U.S.A.* 40 D7 30 17N 97 45W
Australia ■, *Oceania* 34 E5 23 0S 135 0 E
Australian Alps, *Australia* 34 H8 36 30S 148 30 E
Australian Capital Territory □, *Australia* 34 H8 35 30S 149 0 E
Austria ■, *Europe* 10 E8 47 0N 14 0 E
Autun, *France* 8 C6 46 58N 4 17 E
Auvergne, *France* 8 D5 45 20N 3 15 E
Auxerre, *France* 8 C5 47 48N 3 32 E
Avallon, *France* 8 C5 47 30N 3 53 E
Avellino, *Italy* 12 D6 40 54N 14 47 E
Avignon, *France* 8 E6 43 57N 4 50 E
Ávila, *Spain* 9 B3 40 39N 4 43W
Avranches, *France* 8 B3 48 40N 1 20W
Axiós →, *Greece* 13 D10 40 57N 22 35 E
Ayers Rock, *Australia* 34 F5 25 23S 131 5 E
Ayr, *U.K.* 7 D4 55 28N 4 38W
Azamgarh, *India* 23 F9 26 5N 83 13 E
Azerbaijan ■, *Asia* 15 F8 40 20N 48 0 E
Azores, *Atl. Oc.* 2 C8 38 44N 29 0W
Azov, Sea of, *Europe* 15 E6 46 0N 36 30 E
Azuero Pen., *Panama* 45 F8 7 30N 80 30W

B

Babol, *Iran* 24 B4 36 40N 52 50 E
Babuyan Chan., *Phil.* 22 B4 18 40N 121 30 E
Bacău, *Romania* 11 E14 46 35N 26 55 E
Bacolod, *Phil.* 22 B4 10 40N 122 57 E
Bad Axe, *U.S.A.* 42 D6 43 48N 83 0W
Badajoz, *Spain* 9 C2 38 50N 6 59W
Badalona, *Spain* 9 B7 41 26N 2 15 E
Baden-Württemberg □, *Germany* 10 D5 48 20N 8 40 E
Baffin I., *Canada* 39 B12 68 0N 75 0W
Baghdad, *Iraq* 24 B3 33 20N 44 30 E
Baguio, *Phil.* 22 B4 16 26N 120 34 E
Bahamas ■, *N. Amer.* 45 C10 24 0N 75 0W
Baharampur, *India* 23 G12 24 2N 88 27 E
Bahawalpur, *Pakistan* 23 E3 29 24N 71 40 E
Bahía = Salvador, *Brazil* 46 D6 13 0S 38 30W
Bahía □, *Brazil* 46 D5 12 0S 42 0W
Bahía Blanca, *Argentina* 47 F3 38 35S 62 13W
Bahraich, *India* 23 F8 27 38N 81 37 E
Bahrain ■, *Asia* 24 C4 26 0N 50 35 E
Baia Mare, *Romania* 11 E12 47 40N 23 35 E
Baie-St-Paul, *Canada* 43 B12 47 28N 70 32W
Baikal, L., *Russia* 18 D12 53 0N 108 0 E
Baja California, *Mexico* 44 B2 31 10N 115 12W
Bakersfield, *U.S.A.* 40 C3 35 23N 119 1W
Bakhtaran, *Iran* 24 B3 34 23N 47 0 E
Baku, *Azerbaijan* 15 F8 40 29N 49 56 E
Balabac Str., *E. Indies* 22 C3 7 53N 117 5 E
Balaghat, *India* 23 J8 21 49N 80 12 E
Balaton, *Hungary* 11 E9 46 50N 17 40 E
Balboa, *Panama* 44 H14 8 57N 79 34W
Baldwin, *U.S.A.* 42 D5 43 54N 85 51W
Balearic Is., *Spain* 9 C7 39 30N 3 0 E
Baleshwar, *India* 23 J11 21 35N 87 3 E
Bali, *Indonesia* 22 D3 8 20S 115 0 E
Balıkeşir, *Turkey* 13 E12 39 35N 27 58 E
Balikpapan, *Indonesia* 22 D3 1 10S 116 55 E
Balkan Mts., *Bulgaria* 13 C10 43 15N 23 0 E
Balkhash, L., *Kazakstan* 18 E9 46 0N 74 50 E
Ballarat, *Australia* 34 H7 37 33S 143 50 E
Balqash, *Kazakstan* 18 E9 46 50N 74 50 E
Balrampur, *India* 23 F9 27 30N 82 20 E
Balsas →, *Mexico* 44 D4 17 55N 102 10W
Baltic Sea, *Europe* 6 G11 57 0N 19 0 E
Baltimore, *U.S.A.* 42 F9 39 17N 76 37W
Bam, *Iran* 24 C4 29 7N 58 14 E
Bamako, *Mali* 28 F3 12 34N 7 55W
Bamberg, *Germany* 10 D6 49 54N 10 54 E
Bamenda, *Cameroon* 30 C4 5 57N 10 11 E
Bancroft, *Canada* 42 C9 45 3N 77 51W
Banda, *India* 23 G8 25 30N 80 26 E
Banda Aceh, *Indonesia* 22 C1 5 35N 95 20 E

INDEX TO WORLD MAPS

Banda Is. **Brussels**

Banda Is., *Indonesia* **22 D4** 4 37S 129 50 E
Banda Sea, *Indonesia* **22 D4** 6 0S 130 0 E
Bandar Abbas, *Iran* **24 C4** 27 15N 56 15 E
Bandar Khomeyni, *Iran* **24 B3** 30 30N 49 5 E
Bandar Seri Begawan, *Brunei* **22 C3** 4 52N 115 0 E
Bandundu, *Congo (Zaïre)* **32 E3** 3 15S 17 22 E
Bandung, *Indonesia* **22 D2** 6 54S 107 36 E
Bangalore, *India* **25 D6** 12 59N 77 40 E
Banggai Arch., *Indonesia* **22 D4** 1 40S 123 30 E
Bangka, *Indonesia* **22 D2** 2 0S 105 50 E
Bangka Str., *Indonesia* **22 D2** 2 30S 105 30 E
Bangkok, *Thailand* **22 B2** 13 45N 100 35 E
Bangladesh ■, *Asia* **23 H13** 24 0N 90 0 E
Bangor, *U.S.A.* **43 C13** 44 48N 68 46W
Bangui, *C.A.R.* **32 D3** 4 23N 18 35 E
Bangweulu, L., *Zambia* **32 G6** 11 0S 30 0 E
Banja Luka, *Bos.-H.* **12 B7** 44 49N 17 11 E
Banjarmasin, *Indonesia* **22 D3** 3 20S 114 35 E
Banjul, *Gambia* **28 F1** 13 28N 16 40W
Banks I., *Canada* **38 A7** 73 15N 121 30W
Bankura, *India* **23 H11** 23 11N 87 18 E
Bannu, *Pakistan* **23 C3** 33 0N 70 18 E
Banská Bystrica, *Slovak Rep.* **11 D10** 48 46N 19 14 E
Banyak Is., *Indonesia* **22 C1** 2 10N 97 10 E
Baoding, *China* **21 C6** 38 50N 115 28 E
Baoji, *China* **20 C5** 34 20N 107 5 E
Baotou, *China* **21 B6** 40 32N 110 2 E
Bar Harbor, *U.S.A.* **43 C13** 44 23N 68 13W
Bar-le-Duc, *France* **8 B6** 48 47N 5 10 E
Baracaldo, *Spain* **9 A4** 43 18N 2 59W
Baramula, *India* **23 B5** 34 15N 74 20 E
Baran, *India* **23 G6** 25 9N 76 40 E
Baranovichi, *Belarus* **11 B14** 53 10N 26 0 E
Barbados ■, *W. Indies* **44 P22** 13 10N 59 30W
Barberton, *S. Africa* **31 B5** 25 42S 31 2 E
Barberton, *U.S.A.* **42 E7** 41 0N 81 39W
Barcelona, *Spain* **9 B7** 41 21N 2 10 E
Barddhaman, *India* **23 H11** 23 14N 87 39 E
Bardstown, *U.S.A.* **42 G5** 37 49N 85 28W
Bareilly, *India* **23 E7** 28 22N 79 27 E
Barents Sea, *Arctic* **48 B8** 73 0N 39 0 E
Barhi, *India* **23 G10** 24 15N 85 25 E
Bari, *Italy* **12 D7** 41 8N 16 51 E
Bari Doab, *Pakistan* **23 D4** 30 20N 73 0 E
Barisal, *Bangla.* **23 H13** 22 45N 90 20 E
Barito →, *Indonesia* **22 D3** 4 0S 114 50 E
Barkly Tableland, *Australia* **34 D6** 17 50S 136 40 E
Barkly West, *S. Africa* **31 B3** 28 5S 24 31 E
Barletta, *Italy* **12 D7** 41 19N 16 17 E
Barmer, *India* **23 G3** 25 45N 71 20 E
Barnaul, *Russia* **18 D10** 53 20N 83 40 E
Barques, Pt. Aux, *U.S.A.* **42 C6** 44 4N 82 58W
Barquísimeto, *Venezuela* **46 A3** 10 4N 69 19W
Barrancabermeja, *Colombia* **46 B2** 7 0N 73 50W
Barranquilla, *Colombia* **46 A2** 11 0N 74 50W
Barre, *U.S.A.* **43 C11** 44 12N 72 30W
Barrie, *Canada* **42 C8** 44 24N 79 40W
Barry's Bay, *Canada* **42 C9** 45 29N 77 41W
Bashkortostan □, *Russia* **14 D10** 54 0N 57 0 E
Basilan, *Phil.* **22 C4** 6 35N 122 0 E
Baskatong, Rés., *Canada* **43 B10** 46 46N 75 50W
Basle, *Switz.* **10 E4** 47 35N 7 35 E
Basque Provinces = País Vasco □, *Spain* **9 A4** 42 50N 2 45W
Basra, *Iraq* **24 B3** 30 30N 47 50 E
Bass Str., *Australia* **34 H8** 39 15S 146 30 E
Basse-Terre, *Guadeloupe* **44 M20** 16 0N 61 44W
Bassein, *Burma* **25 D8** 16 45N 94 30 E
Basseterre, *St. Kitts & Nevis* **44 K19** 17 17N 62 43W
Basti, *India* **23 F9** 26 52N 82 55 E
Bastia, *France* **8 E8** 42 40N 9 30 E
Bata, *Eq. Guin.* **32 D1** 1 57N 9 50 E
Batangas, *Phil.* **22 B4** 13 35N 121 10 E
Batavia, *U.S.A.* **42 D8** 43 0N 78 11W
Bath, *U.K.* **7 F5** 51 23N 2 22W
Bath, *Maine, U.S.A.* **43 D13** 43 55N 69 49W
Bath, *N.Y., U.S.A.* **42 D9** 42 20N 77 19W
Bathurst, *Australia* **34 G8** 33 25S 149 31 E
Bathurst, *Canada* **43 B15** 47 37N 65 43W
Batna, *Algeria* **28 A6** 35 34N 6 15 E
Baton Rouge, *U.S.A.* **41 D8** 30 27N 91 11W
Battambang, *Cambodia* **22 B2** 13 7N 103 12 E
Batticaloa, *Sri Lanka* **25 E7** 7 43N 81 45 E
Battle Creek, *U.S.A.* **42 D5** 42 19N 85 11W
Batu Is., *Indonesia* **22 D1** 0 30S 98 25 E
Batu Pahat, *Malaysia* **22 C2** 1 50N 102 56 E
Batumi, *Georgia* **15 F7** 41 39N 41 44 E
Bavaria = Bayern □, *Germany* **10 D6** 48 50N 12 0 E
Bawean, *Indonesia* **22 D3** 5 46S 112 35 E
Bay City, *U.S.A.* **42 D6** 43 36N 83 54W
Bayamo, *Cuba* **45 C9** 20 20N 76 40W
Bayan Har Shan, *China* **20 C4** 34 0N 98 0 E
Bayern □, *Germany* **10 D6** 48 50N 12 0 E
Bayeux, *France* **8 B3** 49 17N 0 42W
Bayonne, *France* **8 E3** 43 30N 1 28W
Bayrūt, *Lebanon* **24 B2** 33 53N 35 31 E
Beacon, *U.S.A.* **43 E11** 41 30N 73 58W
Beagle, Canal, *S. Amer.* **47 H3** 55 0S 68 30W
Béarn, *France* **8 E3** 43 20N 0 30W
Beauce, Plaine de la, *France* **8 B4** 48 10N 1 45 E
Beaufort Sea, *Arctic* **48 B18** 72 0N 140 0W
Beaufort West, *S. Africa* **31 C3** 32 18S 22 36 E
Beauharnois, *Canada* **43 C11** 45 20N 73 52W
Beaumont, *U.S.A.* **41 D8** 30 5N 94 6W
Beaune, *France* **8 C6** 47 2N 4 50 E
Beauvais, *France* **8 B5** 49 25N 2 8 E
Beaver Falls, *U.S.A.* **42 E7** 40 46N 80 20W
Beaver I., *U.S.A.* **42 C5** 45 40N 85 33W
Beawar, *India* **23 F5** 26 3N 74 18 E
Béchar, *Algeria* **28 B4** 31 38N 2 18W
Beckley, *U.S.A.* **42 G7** 37 47N 81 11W
Bedford, *Ind., U.S.A.* **42 F4** 38 52N 86 29W
Bedford, *Va., U.S.A.* **42 G8** 37 20N 79 31W
Bei'an, *China* **21 B7** 48 10N 126 20 E
Beijing, *China* **21 C6** 39 55N 116 20 E
Beira, *Mozam.* **33 H6** 19 50S 34 52 E
Békéscsaba, *Hungary* **11 E11** 46 40N 21 5 E
Bela, *Pakistan* **23 F1** 26 12N 66 20 E
Belarus ■, *Europe* **11 B14** 53 30N 27 0 E
Belau = Palau ■, *Pac. Oc.* **36 G5** 7 30N 134 30 E
Belaya Tserkov, *Ukraine* **11 D16** 49 45N 30 10 E
Belcher Is., *Canada* **39 C12** 56 15N 78 45W
Belém, *Brazil* **46 C5** 1 20S 48 30W
Belfast, *S. Africa* **31 B5** 25 42S 30 2 E
Belfast, *U.K.* **7 D4** 54 37N 5 56W
Belfast, *U.S.A.* **43 C13** 44 26N 69 1W
Belfort, *France* **8 C7** 47 38N 6 50 E
Belgaum, *India* **25 D6** 15 55N 74 35 E
Belgium ■, *Europe* **10 C3** 50 30N 5 0 E
Belgorod, *Russia* **15 D6** 50 35N 36 35 E
Belgrade, *Serbia, Yug.* **13 B9** 44 50N 20 37 E
Beliton Is., *Indonesia* **22 D2** 3 10S 107 50 E
Belize ■, *Cent. Amer.* **44 D7** 17 0N 88 30W
Belize City, *Belize* **44 D7** 17 25N 88 0W
Bellaire, *U.S.A.* **42 E7** 40 1N 80 45W
Bellary, *India* **25 D6** 15 10N 76 56 E
Belle-Ile, *France* **8 C2** 47 20N 3 10W
Belle Isle, Str. of, *Canada* **39 C14** 51 30N 56 30W
Bellefontaine, *U.S.A.* **42 E6** 40 22N 83 46W
Belleville, *Canada* **42 C9** 44 10N 77 23W
Bellingshausen Sea, *Antarctica* **48 D3** 66 0S 80 0W
Bellinzona, *Switz.* **10 E5** 46 11N 9 1 E
Belmopan, *Belize* **44 D7** 17 18N 88 30W
Belo Horizonte, *Brazil* **46 D5** 19 55S 43 56W
Belonia, *India* **23 H13** 23 15N 91 30 E
Belorussia = Belarus ■, *Europe* **11 B14** 53 30N 27 0 E
Beltsy, *Moldova* **11 E14** 47 48N 28 0 E
Belukha, *Russia* **18 E10** 49 50N 86 50 E
Ben Nevis, *U.K.* **7 C4** 56 48N 5 1W
Benares = Varanasi, *India* **23 G9** 25 22N 83 0 E
Bendigo, *Australia* **34 H7** 36 40S 144 15 E
Benevento, *Italy* **12 D6** 41 8N 14 45 E
Bengal, Bay of, *Ind. Oc.* **23 K12** 15 0N 90 0 E
Bengbu, *China* **21 C6** 32 58N 117 20 E
Benghazi, *Libya* **29 B9** 32 11N 20 3 E
Bengkulu, *Indonesia* **22 D2** 3 50S 102 12 E
Beni Suef, *Egypt* **29 C11** 29 5N 31 6 E
Benidorm, *Spain* **9 C5** 38 33N 0 9W
Benin ■, *Africa* **30 C2** 10 0N 2 0 E
Benin, Bight of, *W. Afr.* **30 C2** 5 0N 3 0 E
Benin City, *Nigeria* **30 C3** 6 20N 5 31 E
Benoni, *S. Africa* **31 B4** 26 11S 28 18 E
Benton Harbor, *U.S.A.* **42 D4** 42 6N 86 27W
Benue →, *Nigeria* **30 C3** 7 48N 6 46 E
Benxi, *China* **21 B7** 41 20N 123 48 E
Berbérati, *C.A.R.* **32 D3** 4 15N 15 40 E
Berea, *U.S.A.* **42 G5** 37 34N 84 17W
Bérgamo, *Italy* **12 B3** 45 41N 9 43 E
Bergen, *Norway* **6 F9** 60 20N 5 20 E
Bergerac, *France* **8 D4** 44 51N 0 30 E
Berhala Str., *Indonesia* **22 D2** 1 0S 104 15 E
Berhampur = Brahamapur, *India* **23 K10** 19 15N 84 54 E
Bering Sea, *Pac. Oc.* **36 B9** 58 0N 171 0 E
Bering Strait, *U.S.A.* **38 B3** 65 30N 169 0W
Berlin, *Germany* **10 B7** 52 30N 13 25 E
Berlin, *U.S.A.* **43 C12** 44 28N 71 11W
Bermuda ■, *Atl. Oc.* **45 A12** 32 45N 65 0W
Berne, *Switz.* **10 E4** 46 57N 7 28 E
Berry, *France* **8 C5** 46 50N 2 0 E
Berwick, *U.S.A.* **42 E9** 41 3N 76 14W
Berwick-upon-Tweed, *U.K.* **7 D5** 55 46N 2 0W
Besançon, *France* **8 C7** 47 15N 6 2 E
Bethal, *S. Africa* **31 B4** 26 27S 29 28 E
Bethlehem, *S. Africa* **31 B4** 28 14S 28 18 E
Bethlehem, *U.S.A.* **43 E10** 40 37N 75 23W
Béthune, *France* **8 A5** 50 30N 2 38 E
Bettiah, *India* **23 F10** 26 48N 84 33 E
Betul, *India* **23 J6** 21 58N 77 59 E
Béziers, *France* **8 E5** 43 20N 3 12 E
Bhagalpur, *India* **23 G11** 25 10N 87 0 E
Bhandara, *India* **23 J7** 21 5N 79 42 E
Bhanrer Ra., *India* **23 H7** 23 40N 79 45 E
Bharatpur, *India* **23 F6** 27 15N 77 30 E
Bhatinda, *India* **23 D5** 30 15N 74 57 E
Bhatpara, *India* **23 H12** 22 50N 88 25 E
Bhavnagar, *India* **23 J4** 21 45N 72 10 E
Bhilwara, *India* **23 G5** 25 25N 74 38 E
Bhima →, *India* **25 D6** 16 25N 77 17 E
Bhiwani, *India* **23 E6** 28 50N 76 9 E
Bhopal, *India* **23 H6** 23 20N 77 30 E
Bhubaneshwar, *India* **23 J10** 20 15N 85 50 E
Bhuj, *India* **23 H2** 23 15N 69 49 E
Bhusaval, *India* **23 J5** 21 3N 75 46 E
Bhutan ■, *Asia* **23 F13** 27 25N 90 30 E
Biafra, B. of, *Africa* **26 F4** 3 30N 9 20 E
Biała Podlaska, *Poland* **11 B12** 52 4N 23 6 E
Białystok, *Poland* **11 B12** 53 10N 23 10 E
Biarritz, *France* **8 E3** 43 29N 1 33W
Biddeford, *U.S.A.* **43 D12** 43 30N 70 28W
Bié Plateau, *Angola* **33 G3** 12 0S 16 0 E
Biel, *Switz.* **10 E4** 47 8N 7 14 E
Bielefeld, *Germany* **10 B5** 52 1N 8 33 E
Bielsko-Biała, *Poland* **11 D10** 49 50N 19 2 E
Bien Hoa, *Vietnam* **22 B2** 10 57N 106 49 E
Big Rapids, *U.S.A.* **42 D5** 43 42N 85 29W
Bighorn Mts., *U.S.A.* **40 B5** 44 30N 107 30W
Bihar, *India* **23 G10** 25 5N 85 40 E
Bihar □, *India* **23 G10** 25 0N 86 0 E
Bikaner, *India* **23 E4** 28 2N 73 18 E
Bikini Atoll, *Pac. Oc.* **36 F8** 12 0N 167 30 E
Bilaspur, *India* **23 H9** 22 2N 82 15 E
Bilbao, *Spain* **9 A4** 43 16N 2 56W
Billings, *U.S.A.* **40 A5** 45 47N 108 30W
Bina-Etawah, *India* **23 G7** 24 13N 78 14 E
Binghamton, *U.S.A.* **43 D10** 42 6N 75 55W
Binjai, *Indonesia* **22 C1** 3 20N 98 30 E
Bioko, *Eq. Guin.* **30 D3** 3 30N 8 40 E
Birmingham, *U.K.* **7 E6** 52 29N 1 52W
Birmingham, *U.S.A.* **41 D9** 33 31N 86 48W
Biscay, B. of, *Atl. Oc.* **8 D1** 45 0N 2 0W
Bishkek, *Kyrgyzstan* **18 E9** 42 54N 74 46 E
Bisho, *S. Africa* **31 C4** 32 50S 27 23 E
Biskra, *Algeria* **28 B6** 34 50N 5 44 E
Bismarck Arch., *Papua N. G.* **34 A9** 2 30S 150 0 E
Bissau, *Guinea-Biss.* **28 F1** 11 45N 15 45W
Bitolj, *Macedonia* **13 D9** 41 5N 21 10 E
Bitterfontein, *S. Africa* **31 C2** 31 1S 18 32 E
Biwa-Ko, *Japan* **19 B5** 35 15N 136 10 E
Biysk, *Russia* **18 D10** 52 40N 85 0 E
Black Forest = Schwarzwald, *Germany* **10 D5** 48 30N 8 20 E
Black Sea, *Eurasia* **15 F6** 43 30N 35 0 E
Black Volta →, *Africa* **30 C1** 8 41N 1 33W
Blackburn, *U.K.* **7 E5** 53 45N 2 29W
Blackpool, *U.K.* **7 E5** 53 49N 3 3W
Blacksburg, *U.S.A.* **42 G7** 37 14N 80 25W
Blagoveshchensk, *Russia* **18 D14** 50 20N 127 30 E
Blanc, Mont, *Alps* **8 D7** 45 48N 6 50 E
Blantyre, *Malawi* **33 H6** 15 45S 35 0 E
Blenheim, *N.Z.* **35 J13** 41 38S 173 57 E
Blitar, *Indonesia* **22 D3** 8 5S 112 11 E
Bloemfontein, *S. Africa* **31 B4** 29 6S 26 7 E
Bloemhof, *S. Africa* **31 B4** 27 38S 25 32 E
Blois, *France* **8 C4** 47 35N 1 20 E
Bloomington, *U.S.A.* **42 F4** 39 10N 86 32W
Bloomsburg, *U.S.A.* **42 E9** 41 0N 76 27W
Blue Mts., *Oreg., U.S.A.* **40 A3** 45 15N 119 0W
Blue Mts., *Pa., U.S.A.* **42 E9** 40 30N 76 30W
Blue Nile →, *Sudan* **29 E11** 15 38N 32 31 E
Blue Ridge Mts., *U.S.A.* **41 C10** 36 30N 80 15W
Bluefield, *U.S.A.* **42 G7** 37 15N 81 17W
Bobcaygeon, *Canada* **42 C8** 44 33N 78 33W
Bobo-Dioulasso, *Burkina Faso* **28 F4** 11 8N 4 13W
Bóbr →, *Poland* **10 B8** 52 4N 15 4 E
Bobruysk, *Belarus* **11 B15** 53 10N 29 15 E
Bochum, *Germany* **10 C4** 51 28N 7 13 E
Boden, *Sweden* **6 E12** 65 50N 21 42 E
Bodø, *Norway* **6 E10** 67 17N 14 24 E
Bodrog →, *Hungary* **11 D11** 48 11N 21 22 E
Bogor, *Indonesia* **22 D2** 6 36S 106 48 E
Bogotá, *Colombia* **46 B2** 4 34N 74 0W
Bogra, *Bangla.* **23 G12** 24 51N 89 22 E
Bohemian Forest = Böhmerwald, *Germany* **10 D7** 49 8N 13 14 E
Böhmerwald, *Germany* **10 D7** 49 8N 13 14 E
Bohol, *Phil.* **22 C4** 9 50N 124 10 E
Bohol Sea, *Phil.* **22 C4** 9 0N 124 0 E
Boise, *U.S.A.* **40 B3** 43 37N 116 13W
Bolgatanga, *Ghana* **30 B1** 10 44N 0 53W
Bolivia ■, *S. Amer.* **46 D3** 17 6S 64 0W
Bolivian Plateau, *S. Amer.* **46 D3** 20 0S 67 30W
Bologna, *Italy* **12 B4** 44 29N 11 20 E
Bolshevik I., *Russia* **18 B12** 78 30N 102 0 E
Bolton, *U.K.* **7 E5** 53 35N 2 26W
Bolzano, *Italy* **12 A4** 46 30N 11 20 E
Boma, *Congo (Zaïre)* **32 F2** 5 50S 13 4 E
Bombay = Mumbai, *India* **25 D6** 18 55N 72 50 E
Bonifacio, *France* **8 F8** 41 24N 9 10 E
Bonn, *Germany* **10 C4** 50 46N 7 6 E
Boonville, *U.S.A.* **42 F4** 38 3N 87 16W
Boothia, Gulf of, *Canada* **39 A11** 71 0N 90 0W
Boothia Pen., *Canada* **38 A10** 71 0N 94 0W
Borås, *Sweden* **6 G10** 57 43N 12 56 E
Bordeaux, *France* **8 D3** 44 50N 0 36W
Borisov, *Belarus* **11 A15** 54 17N 28 28 E
Borneo, *E. Indies* **22 C3** 1 0N 115 0 E
Bornholm, *Denmark* **6 G11** 55 10N 15 0 E
Bosnia-Herzegovina ■, *Europe* **12 B7** 44 0N 17 0 E
Bosporus, *Turkey* **13 D13** 41 10N 29 10 E
Boston, *U.S.A.* **43 D12** 42 22N 71 4W
Bothnia, G. of, *Europe* **6 F12** 63 0N 20 15 E
Botletle →, *Botswana* **31 A3** 20 10S 23 15 E
Botoşani, *Romania* **11 E14** 47 42N 26 41 E
Botswana ■, *Africa* **31 A3** 22 0S 24 0 E
Bouaké, *Ivory C.* **28 G3** 7 40N 5 2W
Bouar, *C.A.R.* **32 C3** 6 0N 15 40 E
Boulogne-sur-Mer, *France* **8 A4** 50 42N 1 36 E
Bourbonnais, *France* **8 C5** 46 28N 3 0 E
Bourg-en-Bresse, *France* **8 C6** 46 13N 5 12 E
Bourges, *France* **8 C5** 47 9N 2 25 E
Bourgogne, *France* **8 C6** 47 0N 4 50 E
Bourke, *Australia* **34 G8** 30 8S 145 55 E
Bournemouth, *U.K.* **7 F6** 50 43N 1 52W
Bowling Green, *Ky., U.S.A.* **42 G4** 36 59N 86 27W
Bowling Green, *Ohio, U.S.A.* **42 E6** 41 23N 83 39W
Bracebridge, *Canada* **42 C8** 45 2N 79 19W
Bräcke, *Sweden* **6 F11** 62 45N 15 26 E
Bradford, *U.K.* **7 E6** 53 47N 1 45W
Bradford, *U.S.A.* **42 E8** 41 58N 78 38W
Braga, *Portugal* **9 B1** 41 35N 8 25W
Brahamapur, *India* **23 K10** 19 15N 84 54 E
Brahmanbaria, *Bangla.* **23 H13** 23 58N 91 15 E
Brahmani →, *India* **23 J11** 20 39N 86 46 E
Brahmaputra →, *India* **23 H12** 23 58N 89 50 E
Brăila, *Romania* **11 F14** 45 19N 27 59 E
Brampton, *Canada* **42 D8** 43 45N 79 45W
Brandenburg, *Germany* **10 B7** 52 25N 12 33 E
Brandenburg □, *Germany* **10 B6** 52 50N 13 0 E
Brandon, *Canada* **38 D10** 49 50N 99 57W
Brandvlei, *S. Africa* **31 C3** 30 25S 20 30 E
Brantford, *Canada* **42 D7** 43 10N 80 15W
Bras d'Or, L., *Canada* **43 C17** 45 50N 60 50W
Brasília, *Brazil* **46 D5** 15 47S 47 55W
Braşov, *Romania* **11 F13** 45 38N 25 35 E
Brassey Ra., *Malaysia* **22 C3** 5 0N 117 15 E
Bratislava, *Slovak Rep.* **11 D9** 48 10N 17 7 E
Brattleboro, *U.S.A.* **43 D11** 42 51N 72 34W
Brazil, *U.S.A.* **42 F4** 39 32N 87 8W
Brazil ■, *S. Amer.* **46 D5** 12 0S 50 0W
Brazzaville, *Congo* **32 E3** 4 9S 15 12 E
Breda, *Neths.* **10 C3** 51 35N 4 45 E
Bredasdorp, *S. Africa* **31 C3** 34 33S 20 2 E
Bregenz, *Austria* **10 E5** 47 30N 9 45 E
Breiðafjörður, *Iceland* **6 B2** 65 15N 23 15W
Bremen, *Germany* **10 B5** 53 4N 8 47 E
Bremerhaven, *Germany* **10 B5** 53 33N 8 36 E
Brenner P., *Austria* **10 E6** 47 2N 11 30 E
Bréscia, *Italy* **12 B4** 45 33N 10 15 E
Brest, *Belarus* **11 B12** 52 10N 23 40 E
Brest, *France* **8 B1** 48 24N 4 31W
Bretagne, *France* **8 B2** 48 10N 3 0W
Brewer, *U.S.A.* **43 C13** 44 48N 68 46W
Breyten, *S. Africa* **31 B4** 26 16S 30 0 E
Briançon, *France* **8 D7** 44 54N 6 39 E
Bridgeport, *U.S.A.* **43 E11** 41 11N 73 12W
Bridgeton, *U.S.A.* **43 F10** 39 26N 75 14W
Bridgetown, *Barbados* **44 P22** 13 5N 59 30W
Bridgewater, *Canada* **43 C15** 44 25N 64 31W
Brighton, *U.K.* **7 F6** 50 49N 0 7W
Bríndisi, *Italy* **13 D7** 40 39N 17 55 E
Brisbane, *Australia* **34 F9** 27 25S 153 2 E
Bristol, *U.K.* **7 F5** 51 26N 2 35W
Bristol Channel, *U.K.* **7 F4** 51 18N 4 30W
British Columbia □, *Canada* **38 C7** 55 0N 125 15W
British Isles, *Europe* **4 E5** 54 0N 4 0W
Brits, *S. Africa* **31 B4** 25 37S 27 48 E
Britstown, *S. Africa* **31 C3** 30 37S 23 30 E
Brittany = Bretagne, *France* **8 B2** 48 10N 3 0W
Brive-la-Gaillarde, *France* **8 D4** 45 10N 1 32 E
Brno, *Czech Rep.* **11 D9** 49 10N 16 35 E
Brocken, *Germany* **10 C6** 51 47N 10 37 E
Brockville, *Canada* **43 C10** 44 35N 75 41W
Broken Hill, *Australia* **34 G7** 31 58S 141 29 E
Brooks Ra., *U.S.A.* **38 B5** 68 40N 147 0W
Bruay-en-Artois, *France* **8 A5** 50 29N 2 33 E
Bruce, Mt., *Australia* **34 E2** 22 37S 118 8 E
Brugge, *Belgium* **10 C2** 51 13N 3 13 E
Brunei ■, *Asia* **22 C3** 4 50N 115 0 E
Brunswick, *Germany* **10 B6** 52 15N 10 31 E
Brunswick, *U.S.A.* **43 D13** 43 55N 69 58W
Brussels, *Belgium* **10 C3** 50 51N 4 21 E

INDEX TO WORLD MAPS

INDEX TO WORLD MAPS

INDEX TO WORLD MAPS

Groot Vis James B.

Groot Vis →, *S. Africa* **31 C4** 33 28S 27 5 E
Gross Glockner, *Austria* **10 E7** 47 5N 12 40 E
Groundhog →, *Canada* **42 A6** 48 45N 82 58W
Groznyy, *Russia* **15 F8** 43 20N 45 45 E
Grudziądz, *Poland* **11 B10** 53 30N 18 47 E
Guadalajara, *Mexico* **44 C4** 20 40N 103 20W
Guadalajara, *Spain* **9 B4** 40 37N 3 12W
Guadalete →, *Spain* **9 D2** 36 35N 6 13W
Guadalquivir →, *Spain* **9 D2** 36 47N 6 22W
Guadarrama, Sierra de, *Spain* **9 B4** 41 0N 4 0W
Guadeloupe □, *W. Indies* **44 L20** 16 20N 61 40W
Guadiana →, *Portugal* **9 D2** 37 14N 7 22W
Guadix, *Spain* **9 D4** 37 18N 3 11W
Guam ■, *Pac. Oc.* **36 F6** 13 27N 144 45 E
Guangdong □, *China* **21 D6** 23 0N 113 0 E
Guangxi Zhuangzu Zizhiqu □, *China* **21 D5** 24 0N 109 0 E
Guangzhou, *China* **21 D6** 23 5N 113 10 E
Guantánamo, *Cuba* **45 C9** 20 10N 75 14W
Guaporé →, *Brazil* **46 D3** 11 55S 65 4W
Guatemala, *Guatemala* **44 E6** 14 40N 90 22W
Guatemala ■, *Cent. Amer.* **44 D6** 15 40N 90 30W
Guayaquil, *Ecuador* **46 C2** 2 15S 79 52W
Guaymas, *Mexico* **44 B2** 27 59N 110 54W
Guelph, *Canada* **42 D7** 43 35N 80 20W
Guéret, *France* **8 C4** 46 11N 1 51 E
Guilin, *China* **21 D6** 25 18N 110 15 E
Guinea ■, *W. Afr.* **28 F2** 10 20N 11 30W
Guinea, Gulf of, *Atl. Oc.* **26 F3** 3 0N 2 30 E
Guinea-Bissau ■, *Africa* **28 F2** 12 0N 15 0W
Guingamp, *France* **8 B2** 48 34N 3 10W
Guiyang, *China* **20 D5** 26 32N 106 40 E
Guizhou □, *China* **20 D5** 27 0N 107 0 E
Gujarat □, *India* **23 H3** 23 20N 71 0 E
Gujranwala, *Pakistan* **23 C5** 32 10N 74 12 E
Gujrat, *Pakistan* **23 C5** 32 40N 74 2 E
Gulbarga, *India* **25 D6** 17 20N 76 50 E
Gulf, The, *Asia* **24 C4** 27 0N 50 0 E
Guna, *India* **23 G6** 24 40N 77 19 E
Guntur, *India* **25 D7** 16 23N 80 30 E
Gurgaon, *India* **23 E6** 28 27N 77 1 E
Gurkha, *Nepal* **23 E10** 28 5N 84 40 E
Guyana ■, *S. Amer.* **46 B4** 5 0N 59 0W
Guyenne, *France* **8 D4** 44 30N 0 40 E
Gwadar, *Pakistan* **24 C5** 25 10N 62 18 E
Gwalior, *India* **23 F7** 26 12N 78 10 E
Gweru, *Zimbabwe* **33 H5** 19 28S 29 45 E
Gyandzha, *Azerbaijan* **15 F8** 40 45N 46 20 E
Gympie, *Australia* **34 F9** 26 11S 152 38 E
Györ, *Hungary* **11 E9** 47 41N 17 40 E
Gyumri, *Armenia* **15 F7** 40 47N 43 50 E

H

Haarlem, *Neths.* **10 B3** 52 23N 4 39 E
Hachinohe, *Japan* **19 F12** 40 30N 141 29 E
Hadd, Ras al, *Oman* **24 C4** 22 35N 59 50 E
Haeju, *N. Korea* **21 C7** 38 3N 125 45 E
Hafizabad, *Pakistan* **23 C4** 32 5N 73 40 E
Hafnarfjörður, *Iceland* **6 B3** 64 4N 21 57W
Hagen, *Germany* **10 C4** 51 21N 7 27 E
Hagerstown, *U.S.A.* **42 F9** 39 39N 77 43W
Hague, C. de la, *France* **8 B3** 49 44N 1 56W
Haguenau, *France* **8 B7** 48 49N 7 47 E
Haifa, *Israel* **24 B2** 32 46N 35 0 E
Haikou, *China* **21 D6** 20 1N 110 16 E
Hail, *Si. Arabia* **24 C3** 27 28N 41 45 E
Hailar, *China* **21 B6** 49 10N 119 38 E
Haileybury, *Canada* **42 B8** 47 30N 79 38W
Hainan □, *China* **21 E5** 19 0N 109 30 E
Haiphong, *Vietnam* **20 D5** 20 47N 106 41 E
Haiti ■, *W. Indies* **45 D10** 19 0N 72 30W
Hakodate, *Japan* **19 F12** 41 45N 140 44 E
Ḥalab, *Syria* **24 B2** 36 10N 37 15 E
Halberstadt, *Germany* **10 C6** 51 54N 11 3 E
Halden, *Norway* **6 G10** 59 9N 11 23 E
Haldwani, *India* **23 E7** 29 31N 79 30 E
Halifax, *Canada* **43 C16** 44 38N 63 35W
Halle, *Germany* **10 C6** 51 30N 11 56 E
Halmahera, *Indonesia* **22 C4** 0 40N 128 0 E
Halmstad, *Sweden* **6 G10** 56 41N 12 52 E
Hama, *Syria* **24 B2** 35 5N 36 40 E
Hamadan, *Iran* **24 B3** 34 52N 48 32 E
Hamamatsu, *Japan* **19 B5** 34 45N 137 45 E
Hamar, *Norway* **6 F10** 60 48N 11 7 E
Hamburg, *Germany* **10 B5** 53 33N 9 59 E
Hämeenlinna, *Finland* **6 F12** 61 0N 24 28 E
Hameln, *Germany* **10 B5** 52 6N 9 21 E
Hamersley Ra., *Australia* **34 E2** 22 0S 117 45 E
Hamilton, *Bermuda* **45 A12** 32 15N 64 45W
Hamilton, *Canada* **42 D8** 43 15N 79 50W
Hamilton, *N.Z.* **35 H14** 37 47S 175 19 E
Hamilton, *U.S.A.* **42 F5** 39 24N 84 34W
Hamm, *Germany* **10 C4** 51 40N 7 50 E
Hammerfest, *Norway* **6 D12** 70 39N 23 41 E
Hammond, *U.S.A.* **42 E4** 41 38N 87 30W
Hammonton, *U.S.A.* **43 F10** 39 39N 74 48W
Hancock, *U.S.A.* **42 B3** 47 8N 88 35W
Hangzhou, *China* **21 C7** 30 18N 120 11 E
Hannover, *Germany* **10 B5** 52 22N 9 46 E
Hanoi, *Vietnam* **20 D5** 21 5N 105 55 E
Hanover, *U.S.A.* **42 F9** 39 48N 76 59W
Haora, *India* **23 H12** 22 37N 88 20 E
Haparanda, *Sweden* **6 E12** 65 52N 24 8 E
Happy Valley-Goose Bay, *Canada* **39 C13** 53 15N 60 20W
Hapur, *India* **23 E6** 28 45N 77 45 E
Harare, *Zimbabwe* **33 H6** 17 43S 31 2 E
Harbin, *China* **21 B7** 45 48N 126 40 E
Harbor Beach, *U.S.A.* **42 D6** 43 51N 82 39W
Hardanger Fjord, *Norway* **6 F9** 60 5N 6 0 E
Harding, *S. Africa* **31 C4** 30 35S 29 55 E
Hari →, *Indonesia* **22 D2** 1 16S 104 5 E
Haridwar, *India* **23 E7** 29 58N 78 9 E
Haringhata →, *Bangla.* **23 J12** 22 0N 89 58 E
Härnösand, *Sweden* **6 F11** 62 38N 17 55 E
Harrisburg, *U.S.A.* **42 E9** 40 16N 76 53W
Harrismith, *S. Africa* **31 B4** 28 15S 29 8 E
Harrisonburg, *U.S.A.* **42 F8** 38 27N 78 52W
Harrisville, *U.S.A.* **42 C6** 44 39N 83 17W
Hart, *U.S.A.* **42 D4** 43 42N 86 22W
Hartford, Conn., *U.S.A.* **43 E11** 41 46N 72 41W
Hartford, Ky., *U.S.A.* **42 G4** 37 27N 86 55W
Harts →, *S. Africa* **31 B3** 28 24S 24 17 E
Harvey, *U.S.A.* **42 E4** 41 36N 87 50W
Haryana □, *India* **23 E6** 29 0N 76 10 E
Harz, *Germany* **10 C6** 51 38N 10 44 E
Hasa, *Si. Arabia* **24 C3** 26 0N 49 0 E
Hastings, *U.S.A.* **42 D5** 42 39N 85 17W
Hathras, *India* **23 F7** 27 36N 78 6 E
Hatteras, C., *U.S.A.* **41 C11** 35 14N 75 32W
Haugesund, *Norway* **6 G9** 59 23N 5 13 E
Havana, *Cuba* **45 C8** 23 8N 82 22W
Havel →, *Germany* **10 B7** 52 50N 12 3 E
Haverhill, *U.S.A.* **43 D12** 42 47N 71 5W
Hawaiian Is., *Pac. Oc.* **40 H17** 20 30N 156 0W
Hawkesbury, *Canada* **43 C10** 45 37N 74 37W
Hay River, *Canada* **38 B8** 60 51N 115 44W
Hazard, *U.S.A.* **42 G6** 37 15N 83 12W
Hazaribag, *India* **23 H10** 23 58N 85 26 E
Hazleton, *U.S.A.* **42 E10** 40 57N 75 59W
Hearst, *Canada* **42 A6** 49 40N 83 41W
Heath Pt., *Canada* **43 A17** 49 8N 61 40W
Hebei □, *China* **21 C6** 39 0N 116 0 E
Hechuan, *China* **20 C5** 30 2N 106 12 E
Heerlen, *Neths.* **10 C3** 50 55N 5 58 E
Hefei, *China* **21 C6** 31 52N 117 18 E
Hegang, *China* **21 B8** 47 20N 130 19 E
Heidelberg, *Germany* **10 D5** 49 24N 8 42 E
Heilbron, *S. Africa* **31 B4** 27 16S 27 59 E
Heilbronn, *Germany* **10 D5** 49 9N 9 13 E
Heilongjiang □, *China* **21 B7** 48 0N 126 0 E
Hejaz, *Si. Arabia* **24 C2** 26 0N 37 30 E
Helgoland, *Germany* **10 A4** 54 10N 7 53 E
Helmand →, *Afghan.* **24 B5** 31 12N 61 34 E
Helsingborg, *Sweden* **6 G10** 56 3N 12 42 E
Helsinki, *Finland* **6 F13** 60 15N 25 3 E
Henan □, *China* **21 C6** 34 0N 114 0 E
Henderson, *U.S.A.* **42 G4** 37 50N 87 35W
Hengyang, *China* **21 D6** 26 52N 112 33 E
Henlopen, C., *U.S.A.* **43 F10** 38 48N 75 6W
Herat, *Afghan.* **24 B5** 34 20N 62 7 E
Herford, *Germany* **10 B5** 52 7N 8 39 E
Hermanus, *S. Africa* **31 C2** 34 27S 19 12 E
Hermosillo, *Mexico* **44 B2** 29 10N 111 0W
Hernád →, *Hungary* **11 D11** 47 56N 21 8 E
's-Hertogenbosch, *Neths.* **10 C3** 51 42N 5 17 E
Hessen □, *Germany* **10 C5** 50 30N 9 0 E
High Atlas, *Morocco* **28 B3** 32 30N 5 0W
Hildesheim, *Germany* **10 B5** 52 9N 9 56 E
Hillsdale, *U.S.A.* **42 E5** 41 56N 84 38W
Hilo, *U.S.A.* **40 J17** 19 44N 155 5W
Hilversum, *Neths.* **10 B3** 52 14N 5 10 E
Himachal Pradesh □, *India* **23 D6** 31 30N 77 0 E
Himalaya, *Asia* **23 E10** 29 0N 84 0 E
Himeji, *Japan* **19 B4** 34 50N 134 40 E
Hindu Kush, *Asia* **23 B2** 36 0N 71 0 E
Hingoli, *India* **23 K6** 19 41N 77 15 E
Hinton, *U.S.A.* **42 G7** 37 40N 80 54W
Hiroshima, *Japan* **19 B3** 34 24N 132 30 E
Hisar, *India* **23 E5** 29 12N 75 45 E
Hispaniola, *W. Indies* **45 D10** 19 0N 71 0W
Hjälmaren, *Sweden* **6 G11** 59 18N 15 40 E
Ho Chi Minh City, *Vietnam* **22 B2** 10 58N 106 40 E
Hobart, *Australia* **34 J8** 42 50S 147 21 E
Hódmezövásárhely, *Hungary* **11 E11** 46 28N 20 22 E
Hoggar, *Algeria* **28 D6** 23 0N 6 30 E
Hohhot, *China* **21 B6** 40 52N 111 40 E
Hokkaidō □, *Japan* **19 F12** 43 30N 143 0 E
Holguín, *Cuba* **45 C9** 20 50N 76 20W
Hollams Bird I., *Namibia* **31 A1** 24 40S 14 30 E
Holland, *U.S.A.* **42 D4** 42 47N 86 7W
Homs, *Syria* **24 B2** 34 40N 36 45 E
Honduras ■, *Cent. Amer.* **44 E7** 14 40N 86 30W
Honduras, G. de, *Caribbean* **44 D7** 16 50N 87 0W
Hong Kong, *China* **21 D6** 22 11N 114 14 E
Hongha →, *Vietnam* **20 D5** 22 0N 104 0 E
Honiara, *Solomon Is.* **35 B10** 9 27S 159 57 E
Honolulu, *U.S.A.* **40 H16** 21 19N 157 52W
Honshū, *Japan* **19 B6** 36 0N 138 0 E
Hooghly →, *India* **23 J12** 21 56N 88 4 E
Hoopeston, *U.S.A.* **42 E4** 40 28N 87 40W
Hoorn, *Neths.* **10 B3** 52 38N 5 4 E
Hopetown, *S. Africa* **31 B3** 29 34S 24 3 E
Hopkinsville, *U.S.A.* **42 G4** 36 52N 87 29W
Hormuz, Str. of, *The Gulf* **24 C4** 26 30N 56 30 E
Horn, C., *Chile* **47 H3** 55 50S 67 30W
Hornavan, *Sweden* **6 E11** 66 15N 17 30 E
Hornell, *U.S.A.* **42 D9** 42 20N 77 40W
Hornepayne, *Canada* **42 A5** 49 14N 84 48W
Horsham, *Australia* **34 H7** 36 44S 142 13 E
Hospitalet de Llobregat, *Spain* **9 B7** 41 21N 2 6 E
Hotan, *China* **20 C2** 37 25N 79 55 E
Houghton, *U.S.A.* **42 B3** 47 7N 88 34W
Houghton L., *U.S.A.* **42 C5** 44 21N 84 44W
Houlton, *U.S.A.* **43 B14** 46 8N 67 51W
Houston, *U.S.A.* **41 E7** 29 46N 95 22W
Hovd, *Mongolia* **20 B4** 48 2N 91 37 E
Hövsgöl Nuur, *Mongolia* **20 A5** 51 0N 100 30 E
Howell, *U.S.A.* **42 D6** 42 36N 83 56W
Howick, *S. Africa* **31 B5** 29 28S 30 14 E
Howrah = Haora, *India* **23 H12** 22 37N 88 20 E
Høyanger, *Norway* **6 F9** 61 13N 6 4 E
Hradec Králové, *Czech Rep.* **10 C8** 50 15N 15 50 E
Hron →, *Slovak Rep.* **11 E10** 47 49N 18 45 E
Huainan, *China* **21 C6** 32 38N 116 58 E
Huambo, *Angola* **33 G3** 12 42S 15 54 E
Huancayo, *Peru* **46 D2** 12 5S 75 12W
Huangshi, *China* **21 C6** 30 10N 115 3 E
Hubei □, *China* **21 C6** 31 0N 112 0 E
Hudiksvall, *Sweden* **6 F11** 61 43N 17 10 E
Hudson →, *U.S.A.* **43 E10** 40 42N 74 2W
Hudson Bay, *Canada* **39 C11** 60 0N 86 0W
Hudson Falls, *U.S.A.* **43 D11** 43 18N 73 35W
Hudson Str., *Canada* **39 B13** 62 0N 70 0W
Hue, *Vietnam* **22 B2** 16 30N 107 35 E
Huelva, *Spain* **9 D2** 37 18N 6 57W
Huesca, *Spain* **9 A5** 42 8N 0 25W
Hughenden, *Australia* **34 E7** 20 52S 144 10 E
Hull = Kingston upon Hull, *U.K.* **7 E6** 53 45N 0 21W
Hull, *Canada* **43 C10** 45 25N 75 44W
Humboldt →, *U.S.A.* **40 B3** 39 59N 118 36W
Húnaflói, *Iceland* **6 B3** 65 50N 20 50W
Hunan □, *China* **21 D6** 27 30N 112 0 E
Hungary ■, *Europe* **11 E10** 47 20N 19 20 E
Hungnam, *N. Korea* **21 C7** 39 49N 127 45 E
Hunsrück, *Germany* **10 D4** 49 56N 7 27 E
Huntington, Ind., *U.S.A.* **42 E5** 40 53N 85 30W
Huntington, W. Va., *U.S.A.* **42 F6** 38 25N 82 27W
Huntsville, *Canada* **42 C8** 45 20N 79 14W
Huntsville, *U.S.A.* **41 D9** 34 44N 86 35W
Huron, L., *U.S.A.* **42 C6** 44 30N 82 40W
Húsavík, *Iceland* **6 A5** 66 3N 17 21W
Hwang-ho →, *China* **21 C6** 37 55N 118 50 E
Hyderabad, *India* **25 D6** 17 22N 78 29 E
Hyderabad, *Pakistan* **23 G2** 25 23N 68 24 E
Hyères, *France* **8 E7** 43 8N 6 9 E
Hyères, Is. d', *France* **8 E7** 43 0N 6 20 E

I

Ialomiţa →, *Romania* **11 F14** 44 42N 27 51 E
Iaşi, *Romania* **11 E14** 47 10N 27 40 E
Ibadan, *Nigeria* **30 C2** 7 22N 3 58 E
Ibagué, *Colombia* **46 B2** 4 20N 75 20W
Iberian Peninsula, *Europe* **4 H5** 40 0N 5 0W
Ibiza, *Spain* **9 C6** 38 54N 1 26 E
Iceland ■, *Europe* **6 B4** 64 45N 19 0W
Ichinomiya, *Japan* **19 B5** 35 18N 136 48 E
Idaho □, *U.S.A.* **40 B4** 45 0N 115 0W
Idar-Oberstein, *Germany* **10 D4** 49 43N 7 16 E
Ife, *Nigeria* **30 C2** 7 30N 4 31 E
Iglésias, *Italy* **12 E3** 39 19N 8 32 E
Igluligaarjuk, *Canada* **38 B10** 63 30N 90 45W
Ignace, *Canada* **42 A2** 49 30N 91 40W
Iguaçu Falls, *Brazil* **47 E4** 25 41S 54 26W
Iisalmi, *Finland* **6 F13** 63 32N 27 10 E
IJsselmeer, *Neths.* **10 B3** 52 45N 5 20 E
Ikaluktutiak, *Canada* **38 B9** 69 10N 105 0W
Ikerre-Ekiti, *Nigeria* **30 C3** 7 25N 5 19 E
Ila, *Nigeria* **30 C2** 8 0N 4 39 E
Île-de-France, *France* **8 B5** 49 0N 2 20 E
Ilesha, *Nigeria* **30 C2** 7 37N 4 40 E
Ilhéus, *Brazil* **46 D6** 14 49S 39 2W
Ili →, *Kazakstan* **18 E9** 45 53N 77 10 E
Iller →, *Germany* **10 D6** 48 23N 9 58 E
Illinois □, *U.S.A.* **41 C9** 40 15N 89 30W
Iloilo, *Phil.* **22 B4** 10 45N 122 33 E
Ilorin, *Nigeria* **30 C2** 8 30N 4 35 E
Imperatriz, *Brazil* **46 C5** 5 30S 47 29W
Imphal, *India* **25 C8** 24 48N 93 56 E
Inari, L., *Finland* **6 E13** 69 0N 28 0 E
Inchon, *S. Korea* **21 C7** 37 27N 126 40 E
Incomáti →, *Mozam.* **31 B5** 25 46S 32 43 E
Indals →, *Sweden* **6 F11** 62 36N 17 30 E
India ■, *Asia* **23 K7** 20 0N 78 0 E
Indiana, *U.S.A.* **42 E8** 40 37N 79 9W
Indiana □, *U.S.A.* **42 E4** 40 0N 86 0W
Indianapolis, *U.S.A.* **42 F4** 39 46N 86 9W
Indigirka →, *Russia* **18 B16** 70 48N 148 54 E
Indonesia ■, *Asia* **22 D3** 5 0S 115 0 E
Indore, *India* **23 H5** 22 42N 75 53 E
Indre →, *France* **8 C4** 47 16N 0 11 E
Indus →, *Pakistan* **23 G1** 24 20N 67 47 E
Ingolstadt, *Germany* **10 D6** 48 46N 11 26 E
Inn →, *Austria* **10 D7** 48 35N 13 28 E
Inner Mongolia □, *China* **21 B6** 42 0N 112 0 E
Innsbruck, *Austria* **10 E6** 47 16N 11 23 E
Inowrocław, *Poland* **11 B10** 52 50N 18 12 E
Insein, *Burma* **25 D8** 16 50N 96 5 E
Interlaken, *Switz.* **10 E4** 46 41N 7 50 E
Inuvik, *Canada* **38 B6** 68 16N 133 40W
Invercargill, *N.Z.* **35 K12** 46 24S 168 24 E
Inverness, *U.K.* **7 C4** 57 29N 4 13W
Ionia, *U.S.A.* **42 D5** 42 59N 85 4W
Ionian Is., *Greece* **13 E9** 38 40N 20 0 E
Ionian Sea, *Medit. S.* **13 E7** 37 30N 17 30 E
Iowa □, *U.S.A.* **41 B8** 42 18N 93 30W
Iowa City, *U.S.A.* **41 B8** 41 40N 91 32W
Ipoh, *Malaysia* **22 C2** 4 35N 101 5 E
Ipswich, *U.K.* **7 E7** 52 4N 1 10 E
Iquique, *Chile* **46 E2** 20 19S 70 5W
Iquitos, *Peru* **46 C2** 3 45S 73 10W
Iráklion, *Greece* **13 G11** 35 20N 25 12 E
Iran ■, *Asia* **24 B4** 33 0N 53 0 E
Iran Ra., *Malaysia* **22 C3** 2 20N 114 50 E
Irapuato, *Mexico* **44 C4** 20 40N 101 30W
Iraq ■, *Asia* **24 B3** 33 0N 44 0 E
Ireland ■, *Europe* **7 E2** 53 50N 7 52W
Irian Jaya □, *Indonesia* **22 D5** 4 0S 137 0 E
Iringa, *Tanzania* **32 F7** 7 48S 35 43 E
Irish Sea, *U.K.* **7 E4** 53 38N 4 48W
Irkutsk, *Russia* **18 D12** 52 18N 104 20 E
Iron Gate, *Europe* **11 F12** 44 42N 22 30 E
Iron Mountain, *U.S.A.* **42 C3** 45 49N 88 4W
Ironton, *U.S.A.* **42 F6** 38 32N 82 41W
Irrawaddy →, *Burma* **25 D8** 15 50N 95 6 E
Irtysh →, *Russia* **18 C8** 61 4N 68 52 E
Ísafjörður, *Iceland* **6 A2** 66 5N 23 9W
Isar →, *Germany* **10 D7** 48 48N 12 57 E
Isère →, *France* **8 D6** 44 59N 4 51 E
Iseyin, *Nigeria* **30 C2** 8 0N 3 36 E
Ishpeming, *U.S.A.* **42 B4** 46 29N 87 40W
İskenderun, *Turkey* **15 G6** 36 32N 36 10 E
Islamabad, *Pakistan* **23 C4** 33 40N 73 10 E
Island Pond, *U.S.A.* **43 C12** 44 49N 71 53W
Ismâ'ilîya, *Egypt* **29 B11** 30 37N 32 18 E
Israel ■, *Asia* **24 B2** 32 0N 34 50 E
Issoire, *France* **8 D5** 45 32N 3 15 E
İstanbul, *Turkey* **13 D13** 41 0N 29 0 E
Istres, *France* **8 E6** 43 31N 4 59 E
Istria, *Croatia* **10 F7** 45 10N 14 0 E
Itaipu Dam, *Brazil* **47 E4** 25 30S 54 30W
Italy ■, *Europe* **12 C5** 42 0N 13 0 E
Ithaca, *U.S.A.* **42 D9** 42 27N 76 30W
Ivanava, *Belarus* **11 B13** 52 7N 25 29 E
Ivano-Frankovsk, *Ukraine* **11 D13** 48 40N 24 40 E
Ivanovo, *Russia* **14 C7** 57 5N 41 0 E
Ivory Coast ■, *Africa* **28 G3** 7 30N 5 0W
Ivujivik, *Canada* **39 B12** 62 24N 77 55W
Iwaki, *Japan* **19 A7** 37 3N 140 55 E
Iwo, *Nigeria* **30 C2** 7 39N 4 9 E
Ixopo, *S. Africa* **31 C5** 30 11S 30 5 E
Izhevsk, *Russia* **14 C9** 56 51N 53 14 E
İzmir, *Turkey* **13 E12** 38 25N 27 8 E

J

Jabalpur, *India* **23 H7** 23 9N 79 58 E
Jackson, Ky., *U.S.A.* **42 G6** 37 33N 83 23W
Jackson, Mich., *U.S.A.* **42 D5** 42 15N 84 24W
Jackson, Miss., *U.S.A.* **41 D8** 32 18N 90 12W
Jacksonville, *U.S.A.* **41 D10** 30 20N 81 39W
Jacobabad, *Pakistan* **23 E2** 28 20N 68 29 E
Jaén, *Spain* **9 D4** 37 44N 3 43W
Jaffna, *Sri Lanka* **25 E7** 9 45N 80 2 E
Jagersfontein, *S. Africa* **31 B4** 29 44S 25 27 E
Jahrom, *Iran* **24 C4** 28 30N 53 31 E
Jaipur, *India* **23 F5** 27 0N 75 50 E
Jakarta, *Indonesia* **22 D2** 6 9S 106 49 E
Jalalabad, *Afghan.* **23 B3** 34 30N 70 29 E
Jalgaon, *India* **23 J5** 21 0N 75 42 E
Jalna, *India* **23 K5** 19 48N 75 38 E
Jalpaiguri, *India* **23 F12** 26 32N 88 46 E
Jamaica ■, *W. Indies* **44 J16** 18 10N 77 30W
Jamalpur, *Bangla.* **23 G12** 24 52N 89 56 E
Jamalpur, *India* **23 G11** 25 18N 86 28 E
Jambi, *Indonesia* **22 D2** 1 38S 103 30 E
James B., *Canada* **39 C11** 51 30N 80 0W

INDEX TO WORLD MAPS

Jamestown Kushtia

Jamestown, Ky., U.S.A. 42 G5 36 59N 85 4W
Jamestown, N.Y., U.S.A. 42 D8 42 6N 79 14W
Jammu, India 23 C5 32 43N 74 54 E
Jammu & Kashmir □, India 23 B6 34 25N 77 0 E
Jamnagar, India 23 H3 22 30N 70 6 E
Jamshedpur, India 23 H11 22 44N 86 12 E
Jaora, India 23 H5 23 40N 75 10 E
Japan ■, Asia 19 G11 36 0N 136 0 E
Japan, Sea of, Asia 19 G11 40 0N 135 0 E
Japurá →, Brazil 46 C3 3 8S 65 46W
Jask, Iran 24 C4 25 38N 57 45 E
Jaunpur, India 23 G9 25 46N 82 44 E
Java, Indonesia 22 D3 7 0S 110 0 E
Java Sea, Indonesia 22 D2 4 35S 107 15 E
Jedda, Si. Arabia 24 C2 21 29N 39 10 E
Jeffersonville, U.S.A. 42 F5 38 17N 85 44W
Jelenia Góra, Poland 10 C8 50 50N 15 45 E
Jena, Germany 10 C6 50 54N 11 35 E
Jerez de la Frontera, Spain 9 D2 36 41N 6 7W
Jersey City, U.S.A. 43 E10 40 44N 74 4W
Jerusalem, Israel 24 B2 31 47N 35 10 E
Jessore, Bangla. 23 H12 23 10N 89 10 E
Jhang Maghiana, Pakistan 23 D4 31 15N 72 22 E
Jhansi, India 23 G7 25 30N 78 36 E
Jhelum, Pakistan 23 C4 33 0N 73 45 E
Jhelum →, Pakistan 23 D4 31 20N 72 10 E
Jiamusi, China 21 B8 46 40N 130 26 E
Jian, China 21 D6 27 6N 114 59 E
Jiangsu □, China 21 C7 33 0N 120 0 E
Jiangxi □, China 21 D6 27 30N 116 0 E
Jihlava →, Czech Rep. 11 D9 48 55N 16 36 E
Jilin, China 21 B7 43 44N 126 30 E
Jilin □, China 21 B7 44 0N 127 0 E
Jima, Ethiopia 29 G12 7 40N 36 47 E
Jinan, China 21 C6 36 38N 117 1 E
Jinja, Uganda 32 D6 0 25N 33 12 E
Jinzhou, China 21 B7 41 5N 121 3 E
Jixi, China 21 B8 45 20N 130 50 E
João Pessoa, Brazil 46 C6 7 10S 34 52W
Jodhpur, India 23 F4 26 23N 73 8 E
Johannesburg, S. Africa 31 B4 26 10S 28 2 E
Johnson City, U.S.A. 43 D10 42 7N 75 58W
Johnstown, U.S.A. 42 E8 40 20N 78 55W
Johor Baharu, Malaysia 22 C2 1 28N 103 46 E
Joliet, U.S.A. 42 E3 41 32N 88 5W
Joliette, Canada 43 B11 46 3N 73 24W
Jolo, Phil. 22 C4 6 0N 121 0 E
Jönköping, Sweden 6 G10 57 45N 14 10 E
Jonquière, Canada 43 A12 48 27N 71 14W
Jordan ■, Asia 24 B2 31 0N 36 0 E
Jos, Nigeria 30 C3 9 53N 8 51 E
Juan de Fuca Str., Canada 40 A2 48 15N 124 0W
Juiz de Fora, Brazil 46 E5 21 43S 43 19W
Jullundur, India 23 D5 31 20N 75 40 E
Junagadh, India 23 J3 21 30N 70 30 E
Juneau, U.S.A. 38 C6 58 18N 134 25W
Junggar Pendi, China 20 B3 44 30N 86 0 E
Jupiter →, Canada 43 A16 49 29N 63 37W
Jura, Europe 8 C7 46 40N 6 5 E
Jutland, Denmark 6 G9 56 25N 9 30 E
Jyväskylä, Finland 6 F13 62 14N 25 50 E

K

K2, Pakistan 23 B6 35 58N 76 32 E
Kabardino Balkaria □, Russia 15 F7 43 30N 43 30 E
Kābul, Afghan. 23 B2 34 28N 69 11 E
Kabwe, Zambia 33 G5 14 30S 28 29 E
Kachin □, Burma 25 C8 26 0N 97 30 E
Kaduna, Nigeria 30 B3 10 30N 7 21 E
Kaesong, N. Korea 21 C7 37 58N 126 35 E
Kagoshima, Japan 19 D2 31 35N 130 33 E
Kai Is., Indonesia 22 D5 5 55S 132 45 E
Kaifeng, China 21 C6 34 48N 114 21 E
Kaiserslautern, Germany 10 D4 49 26N 7 45 E
Kaitaia, N.Z. 35 H13 35 8S 173 17 E
Kajaani, Finland 6 F13 64 17N 27 46 E
Kakinada, India 25 D7 16 57N 82 11 E
Kalaallit Nunaat = Greenland □, N. Amer. 48 C4 66 0N 45 0W
Kalahari, Africa 31 A3 24 0S 21 30 E
Kalamazoo, U.S.A. 42 D5 42 17N 85 35W
Kalamazoo →, U.S.A. 42 D4 42 40N 86 10W
Kalemie, Congo (Zaïre) 32 F5 5 55S 29 9 E
Kalgoorlie-Boulder, Australia 34 G3 30 40S 121 22 E
Kalimantan, Indonesia 22 D3 0 0 114 0 E
Kaliningrad, Russia 14 D3 54 42N 20 32 E
Kalisz, Poland 11 C10 51 45N 18 8 E
Kalkaska, U.S.A. 42 C5 44 44N 85 11W
Kalmar, Sweden 6 G11 56 40N 16 20 E
Kalmykia □, Russia 15 E8 46 5N 46 1 E
Kaluga, Russia 14 D6 54 35N 36 10 E
Kama →, Russia 14 C9 55 45N 52 0 E
Kamchatka, Russia 18 D18 57 0N 160 0 E
Kamina, Congo (Zaïre) 32 F5 8 45S 25 0 E
Kamloops, Canada 38 C7 50 40N 120 20W
Kampala, Uganda 32 D6 0 20N 32 30 E
Kampuchea = Cambodia ■, Asia 22 B2 12 15N 105 0 E
Kamyanets-Podilskyy, Ukraine 11 D14 48 45N 26 40 E
Kananga, Congo (Zaïre) 32 F4 5 55S 22 18 E
Kanawha →, U.S.A. 42 F6 38 50N 82 9W
Kanazawa, Japan 19 A5 36 30N 136 38 E
Kanchenjunga, Nepal 23 F12 27 50N 88 10 E
Kanchipuram, India 25 D6 12 52N 79 45 E
Kandy, Sri Lanka 25 E7 7 18N 80 43 E
Kane, U.S.A. 42 E8 41 40N 78 49W
Kangean Is., Indonesia 22 D3 6 55S 115 23 E
Kanin Pen., Russia 14 A8 68 0N 45 0 E
Kankakee, U.S.A. 42 E4 41 7N 87 52W
Kankakee →, U.S.A. 42 E3 41 23N 88 15W
Kankan, Guinea 28 F3 10 23N 9 15W
Kano, Nigeria 30 B3 12 2N 8 30 E
Kanpur, India 23 F8 26 28N 80 20 E
Kansas □, U.S.A. 40 C7 38 30N 99 0W
Kansas City, Kans., U.S.A. 41 C8 39 7N 94 38W
Kansas City, Mo., U.S.A. 41 C8 39 6N 94 35W
Kanye, Botswana 31 A4 24 55S 25 28 E
Kaohsiung, Taiwan 21 D7 22 35N 120 16 E
Kaolack, Senegal 28 F1 14 5N 16 8W
Kaposvár, Hungary 11 E9 46 25N 17 47 E
Kapuas →, Indonesia 22 D2 0 25S 109 20 E
Kapuas Hulu Ra., Malaysia 22 C3 1 30N 113 30 E
Kapuskasing, Canada 42 A6 49 25N 82 30W
Kara Bogaz Gol, Turkmenistan 15 F9 41 0N 53 30 E
Kara Kum, Turkmenistan 18 F8 39 30N 60 0 E
Kara Sea, Russia 18 B8 75 0N 70 0 E
Karachi, Pakistan 23 G1 24 53N 67 0 E
Karaganda, Kazakstan 18 E9 49 50N 73 10 E
Karakoram Ra., Pakistan 23 B6 35 30N 77 0 E
Karasburg, Namibia 31 B2 28 0S 18 44 E
Karbala, Iraq 24 B3 32 36N 44 3 E
Karelia □, Russia 14 A5 65 30N 32 30 E
Karimata Is., Indonesia 22 D2 1 25S 109 0 E
Karimunjawa Is., Indonesia 22 D3 5 50S 110 30 E
Karlskrona, Sweden 6 G11 56 10N 15 35 E
Karlsruhe, Germany 10 D5 49 0N 8 23 E
Karlstad, Sweden 6 G10 59 23N 13 30 E
Karnal, India 23 E6 29 42N 77 2 E
Karnataka □, India 25 D6 13 15N 77 0 E
Kärnten □, Austria 10 E8 46 52N 13 30 E
Karsakpay, Kazakstan 18 E8 47 55N 66 40 E
Kasai →, Congo (Zaïre) 32 E3 3 30S 16 10 E
Kashan, Iran 24 B4 34 5N 51 30 E
Kashi, China 20 C2 39 30N 76 2 E
Kassalâ, Sudan 29 E12 15 30N 36 0 E
Kassel, Germany 10 C5 51 18N 9 26 E
Kasur, Pakistan 23 D5 31 5N 74 25 E
Katha, Burma 25 C8 24 10N 96 30 E
Katihar, India 23 G11 25 34N 87 36 E
Katmandu, Nepal 23 F10 27 45N 85 20 E
Katowice, Poland 11 C10 50 17N 19 5 E
Katsina, Nigeria 30 B3 13 0N 7 32 E
Kattegat, Denmark 6 G10 57 0N 11 20 E
Kauai, U.S.A. 40 H15 22 3N 159 30W
Kaukauna, U.S.A. 42 C3 44 17N 88 17W
Kaunas, Lithuania 14 D3 54 54N 23 54 E
Kavála, Greece 13 D11 40 57N 24 28 E
Kawagoe, Japan 19 B6 35 55N 139 29 E
Kawardha, India 23 J8 22 0N 81 17 E
Kawasaki, Japan 19 B6 35 35N 139 42 E
Kayes, Mali 28 F2 14 25N 11 30W
Kayseri, Turkey 15 G6 38 45N 35 30 E
Kazakstan ■, Asia 18 E9 50 0N 70 0 E
Kazan, Russia 14 C8 55 50N 49 10 E
Kazerun, Iran 24 C4 29 38N 51 40 E
Kebnekaise, Sweden 6 E11 67 53N 18 33 E
Kecskemét, Hungary 11 E10 46 57N 19 42 E
Kediri, Indonesia 22 D3 7 51S 112 1 E
Keene, U.S.A. 43 D11 42 56N 72 17W
Keetmanshoop, Namibia 31 B2 26 35S 18 8 E
Kefallinía, Greece 13 E9 38 20N 20 30 E
Keflavík, Iceland 6 B2 64 2N 22 35W
Kelang, Malaysia 22 C2 3 2N 101 26 E
Kelowna, Canada 38 D8 49 50N 119 25W
Kemerovo, Russia 18 D10 55 20N 86 5 E
Kemi, Finland 6 E12 65 44N 24 34 E
Kemi →, Finland 6 E12 65 47N 24 32 E
Kendari, Indonesia 22 D4 3 50S 122 30 E
Kenhardt, S. Africa 31 B3 29 19S 21 12 E
Kenitra, Morocco 28 B3 34 15N 6 40W
Kenosha, U.S.A. 42 D4 42 35N 87 49W
Kent, U.S.A. 42 E7 41 9N 81 22W
Kenton, U.S.A. 42 E6 40 39N 83 37W
Kentucky □, U.S.A. 42 G5 37 0N 84 0W
Kentucky →, U.S.A. 42 F5 38 41N 85 11W
Kentville, Canada 43 C15 45 6N 64 29W
Kenya ■, Africa 32 D7 1 0N 38 0 E
Kenya, Mt., Kenya 32 E7 0 10S 37 18 E
Kerala □, India 25 D6 11 0N 76 15 E
Kerch, Ukraine 15 E6 45 20N 36 20 E
Kerinci, Indonesia 22 D2 1 40S 101 15 E
Kermadec Trench, Pac. Oc. 35 G15 30 30S 176 0W
Kerman, Iran 24 B4 30 15N 57 1 E
Kestell, S. Africa 31 B4 28 17S 28 42 E
Ketchikan, U.S.A. 38 C6 55 21N 131 39W
Kewaunee, U.S.A. 42 C4 44 27N 87 31W
Keweenaw B., U.S.A. 42 B3 47 0N 88 15W
Keweenaw Pen., U.S.A. 42 B3 47 30N 88 0W
Keweenaw Pt., U.S.A. 42 B4 47 25N 87 43W
Key West, U.S.A. 41 F10 24 33N 81 48W
Keyser, U.S.A. 42 F8 39 26N 78 59W
Khabarovsk, Russia 18 E15 48 30N 135 5 E
Khairpur, Pakistan 23 F2 27 32N 68 49 E
Khamas Country, Botswana 31 A4 21 45S 26 30 E
Khandwa, India 23 J6 21 49N 76 22 E
Khanewal, Pakistan 23 D3 30 20N 71 55 E
Khaniá, Greece 13 G11 35 30N 24 4 E
Kharagpur, India 23 H11 22 20N 87 25 E
Khargon, India 23 J5 21 45N 75 40 E
Kharkov, Ukraine 15 E6 49 58N 36 20 E
Khartoum, Sudan 29 E11 15 31N 32 35 E
Khaskovo, Bulgaria 13 D11 41 56N 25 30 E
Khatanga, Russia 18 B12 72 0N 102 20 E
Kherson, Ukraine 15 E5 46 35N 32 35 E
Khmelnitskiy, Ukraine 11 D14 49 23N 27 0 E
Khorixas, Namibia 31 A1 20 16S 14 59 E
Khorramshahr, Iran 24 B3 30 29N 48 15 E
Khouribga, Morocco 28 B3 32 58N 6 57W
Khulna, Bangla. 23 H12 22 45N 89 34 E
Khulna □, Bangla. 23 H12 22 25N 89 35 E
Khumago, Botswana 31 A3 20 26S 24 32 E
Khushab, Pakistan 23 C4 32 20N 72 20 E
Khuzdar, Pakistan 23 F1 27 52N 66 30 E
Kicking Horse Pass, Canada 38 C8 51 28N 116 16W
Kiel, Germany 10 A6 54 19N 10 8 E
Kiel Canal = Nord-Ostsee-Kanal →, Germany 10 A5 54 12N 9 32 E
Kielce, Poland 11 C11 50 52N 20 42 E
Kieler Bucht, Germany 10 A6 54 35N 10 25 E
Kiev, Ukraine 11 C16 50 30N 30 28 E
Kigali, Rwanda 32 E6 1 59S 30 4 E
Kigoma-Ujiji, Tanzania 32 E5 4 55S 29 36 E
Kikwit, Congo (Zaïre) 32 E3 5 0S 18 45 E
Kilimanjaro, Tanzania 32 E7 3 7S 37 20 E
Kimberley, S. Africa 31 B3 28 43S 24 46 E
Kimberley Plateau, Australia 34 D4 16 20S 127 0 E
Kincardine, Canada 42 C7 44 10N 81 40W
Kindu, Congo (Zaïre) 32 E5 2 55S 25 50 E
King William's Town, S. Africa 31 C4 32 51S 27 22 E
Kingston, Canada 42 C9 44 14N 76 30W
Kingston, Jamaica 44 K17 18 0N 76 50W
Kingston, N.Y., U.S.A. 43 E10 41 56N 73 59W
Kingston, Pa., U.S.A. 43 E10 41 16N 75 54W
Kingston upon Hull, U.K. 7 E6 53 45N 0 21W
Kingstown, St. Vincent 44 P20 13 10N 61 10W
Kinshasa, Congo (Zaïre) 32 E3 4 20S 15 15 E
Kirensk, Russia 18 D12 57 50N 107 55 E
Kirgiz Steppe, Eurasia 15 D10 50 0N 55 0 E
Kiribati ■, Pac. Oc. 36 H10 5 0S 180 0 E
Kirkenes, Norway 6 E14 69 40N 30 5 E
Kirkland Lake, Canada 42 A7 48 9N 80 2W
Kirkuk, Iraq 24 B3 35 30N 44 21 E
Kirkwood, S. Africa 31 C4 33 22S 25 15 E
Kirov, Russia 14 C8 58 35N 49 40 E
Kirovograd, Ukraine 15 E5 48 35N 32 20 E
Kirthar Range, Pakistan 23 F1 27 0N 67 0 E
Kiruna, Sweden 6 E12 67 52N 20 15 E
Kisangani, Congo (Zaïre) 32 D5 0 35N 25 15 E
Kishanganj, India 23 F12 26 3N 88 14 E
Kishinev, Moldova 11 E15 47 0N 28 50 E
Kisumu, Kenya 32 E6 0 3S 34 45 E
Kitakyūshū, Japan 19 C2 33 50N 130 50 E
Kitchener, Canada 42 D7 43 27N 80 29W
Kíthira, Greece 13 F10 36 8N 23 0 E
Kitimat, Canada 38 C7 54 3N 128 38W
Kittanning, U.S.A. 42 E8 40 49N 79 31W
Kitwe, Zambia 33 G5 12 54S 28 13 E
Kivu, L., Congo (Zaïre) 32 E5 1 48S 29 0 E
Kladno, Czech Rep. 10 C8 50 10N 14 7 E
Klagenfurt, Austria 10 E8 46 38N 14 20 E
Klar →, Sweden 6 G10 59 23N 13 32 E
Klawer, S. Africa 31 C2 31 44S 18 36 E
Klerksdorp, S. Africa 31 B4 26 53S 26 38 E
Klipplaat, S. Africa 31 C3 33 1S 24 22 E
Klondike, Canada 38 B6 64 0N 139 26W
Klyuchevsk Vol., Russia 18 D18 55 50N 160 30 E
Knossós, Greece 13 G11 35 16N 25 10 E
Knoxville, U.S.A. 41 C10 35 58N 83 55W
Knysna, S. Africa 31 C3 34 2S 23 2 E
Kōbe, Japan 19 B4 34 45N 135 10 E
Koblenz, Germany 10 C4 50 21N 7 36 E
Kobroor, Indonesia 22 D5 6 10S 134 30 E
Koch Bihar, India 23 F12 26 22N 89 29 E
Kodiak I., U.S.A. 38 C4 57 30N 152 45W
Koffiefontein, S. Africa 31 B4 29 30S 25 0 E
Koforidua, Ghana 30 C1 6 3N 0 17W
Koh-i-Bābā, Afghan. 23 B1 34 30N 67 0 E
Kohat, Pakistan 23 C3 33 40N 71 29 E
Kokchetav, Kazakstan 18 D8 53 20N 69 25 E
Kokomo, U.S.A. 42 E4 40 29N 86 8W
Kokstad, S. Africa 31 C4 30 32S 29 29 E
Kola Pen., Russia 14 A6 67 30N 38 0 E
Kolar, India 25 D6 13 12N 78 15 E
Kolguyev I., Russia 14 A8 69 20N 48 30 E
Kolhapur, India 25 D6 16 43N 74 15 E
Kolomna, Russia 14 C6 55 8N 38 45 E
Kolwezi, Congo (Zaïre) 32 G5 10 40S 25 25 E
Kolyma →, Russia 18 C18 69 30N 161 0 E
Kolyma Ra., Russia 18 C17 63 0N 157 0 E
Komandorskiye Is., Russia 18 D18 55 0N 167 0 E
Komatipoort, S. Africa 31 B5 25 25S 31 55 E
Komi □, Russia 14 B10 64 0N 55 0 E
Kompong Cham, Cambodia 22 B2 12 0N 105 30 E
Kompong Chhnang, Cambodia 22 B2 12 20N 104 35 E
Kompong Som, Cambodia 22 B2 10 38N 103 30 E
Komsomolets I., Russia 18 A11 80 30N 95 0 E
Komsomolsk, Russia 18 D15 50 30N 137 0 E
Konin, Poland 11 B10 52 12N 18 15 E
Konya, Turkey 15 G5 37 52N 32 35 E
Korce, Albania 13 D9 40 37N 20 50 E
Korea, North ■, Asia 21 C7 40 0N 127 0 E
Korea, South ■, Asia 21 C7 36 0N 128 0 E
Korea Strait, Asia 21 C7 34 0N 129 30 E
Kōriyama, Japan 19 A7 37 24N 140 23 E
Korla, China 20 B3 41 45N 86 4 E
Körös →, Hungary 11 E11 46 43N 20 12 E
Kortrijk, Belgium 10 C2 50 50N 3 17 E
Kos, Greece 13 F12 36 50N 27 15 E
Košice, Slovak Rep. 11 D11 48 42N 21 15 E
Kosovo □, Serbia, Yug. 13 C9 42 30N 21 0 E
Kosti, Sudan 29 F11 13 8N 32 43 E
Kostroma, Russia 14 C7 57 50N 40 58 E
Koszalin, Poland 10 A9 54 11N 16 8 E
Kota, India 23 G5 25 14N 75 49 E
Kota Baharu, Malaysia 22 C2 6 7N 102 14 E
Kota Kinabalu, Malaysia 22 C3 6 0N 116 4 E
Kotka, Finland 6 F13 60 28N 26 58 E
Kotri, Pakistan 23 G2 25 22N 68 22 E
Kotuy →, Russia 18 B12 71 54N 102 6 E
Kounradskiy, Kazakstan 18 E9 46 59N 75 0 E
Kra, Isthmus of, Thailand 22 B1 10 15N 99 30 E
Kragujevac, Serbia, Yug. 13 B9 44 2N 20 56 E
Krajina, Bos.-H. 12 B7 44 45N 16 35 E
Kraków, Poland 11 C10 50 4N 19 57 E
Krasnodar, Russia 15 E6 45 5N 39 0 E
Krasnoturinsk, Russia 14 C11 59 46N 60 12 E
Krasnovodsk, Turkmenistan 15 F9 40 5N 53 5 E
Krasnoyarsk, Russia 18 D11 56 8N 93 0 E
Kratie, Cambodia 22 B2 12 32N 106 10 E
Krefeld, Germany 10 C4 51 20N 6 33 E
Kremenchug, Ukraine 15 E5 49 5N 33 25 E
Krishna →, India 25 D7 15 57N 80 59 E
Krishnanagar, India 23 H12 23 24N 88 33 E
Kristiansand, Norway 6 G9 58 8N 8 1 E
Kristiansund, Norway 6 F9 63 7N 7 45 E
Krivoy Rog, Ukraine 15 E5 47 51N 33 20 E
Kroonstad, S. Africa 31 B4 27 43S 27 19 E
Krosno, Poland 11 D11 49 42N 21 46 E
Kruger Nat. Park, S. Africa 31 A5 23 30S 31 40 E
Krugersdorp, S. Africa 31 B4 26 5S 27 46 E
Kruisfontein, S. Africa 31 C3 33 59S 24 43 E
Kruševac, Serbia, Yug. 13 C9 43 35N 21 28 E
Kuala Lumpur, Malaysia 22 C2 3 9N 101 41 E
Kuala Terengganu, Malaysia 22 C2 5 20N 103 8 E
Kualakapuas, Indonesia 22 D3 2 55S 114 20 E
Kucing, Malaysia 22 C3 1 33N 110 25 E
Kudat, Malaysia 22 C3 6 55N 116 55 E
Kugluktuk, Canada 38 B8 67 50N 115 5W
Kumanovo, Macedonia 13 C9 42 9N 21 42 E
Kumasi, Ghana 30 C1 6 41N 1 38W
Kumayri = Gyumri, Armenia 15 F7 40 47N 43 50 E
Kumbakonam, India 25 D6 10 58N 79 25 E
Kunlun Shan, Asia 20 C3 36 0N 86 30 E
Kunming, China 20 D5 25 1N 102 41 E
Kuopio, Finland 6 F13 62 53N 27 35 E
Kupang, Indonesia 22 E4 10 19S 123 39 E
Kür →, Azerbaijan 15 G8 39 29N 49 15 E
Kurashiki, Japan 19 B3 34 40N 133 50 E
Kurdistan, Asia 24 B3 37 20N 43 30 E
Kure, Japan 19 B3 34 14N 132 32 E
Kurgan, Russia 18 D8 55 26N 65 18 E
Kuril Is., Russia 18 E17 45 0N 150 0 E
Kurnool, India 25 D6 15 45N 78 0 E
Kursk, Russia 14 D6 51 42N 36 11 E
Kuruman, S. Africa 31 B3 27 28S 23 28 E
Kuruman →, S. Africa 31 B3 26 56S 20 39 E
Kurume, Japan 19 C2 33 15N 130 30 E
Kushiro, Japan 19 F12 43 0N 144 25 E
Kushtia, Bangla. 23 H12 23 55N 89 5 E

INDEX TO WORLD MAPS